A Hardware Interfacing And Control Protocol

Using RobotBASIC And The Propeller Chip

John Blankenship & Samuel Mishal

Contents At A Glance

Table Of Contents

Foreword

Robot. That word is at the beginning of RobotBASIC for a good reason. RobotBASIC (RB) is a programming language based on BASIC (Beginners All-purpose Symbolic Instruction Code) with a built-in Integrated Development Environment (IDE). It is **RobotBASIC** because one of the powerful features of this language centers around a simulated environment for a virtual robot.

You can run RB on a PC and use the language for robot simulation. A little more specifically you can open up a window from RB, put a little round graphical robot into that window and programmatically drive that robot around on screen. You can add walls or objects for the robot to bump into. The program that you write in RB can use the virtual sensors of this robot to detect collision with objects, which you can draw on screen. There is a lot of learning that you can do about robots by using this little virtual robot within the simulated environment.

RB has more than just this simulation capability, though. You can move from controlling the robot in your simulation to controlling a real robot very easily. All of the commands that move the graphic robot around in the simulation can be piped out the serial port of a PC. That port can be connected via a hardwired tether (or via wireless) to a robot perhaps of your own design. The robot can be equipped with sensors such as collision detection that then signal back to the RB program running on the PC. That is a powerful thing. You have a robot consisting of motors and sensors with low-level functions controlled by a microcontroller on that robot, but the higher brain functions are realized using the power of a PC: a multi-core, multi-gigahertz, multi-gigabyte machine.

That is quite a nice setup for robotics. You have robot hardware with an array of sensors and motors controlled by a microcontroller. The microcontroller may be an Atmel AVR on an Arduino board, for example, or may be the Parallax multicore Propeller, as this book uses. Microcontrollers are fine chips - I make my living designing with them - but they don't have the relatively vast storage capability and graphic display ability that is on the common PC. This connection to a PC running RobotBASIC provides a significant boost to the brainpower of the robot.

Here is where I feel like a TV commercial salesman saying "But wait! We'll sell you TWO Slicermatics at that price and include a free...."

The reason for that? It is because RB doesn't have to have anything to do with robots. You get a lot more than a useful tool for robotics. Despite being called RobotBASIC, RB is a powerful language even if you don't turn on the robot simulation aspects. RobotBASIC is derived from the BASIC of the good old days when a PC didn't have much more power than what today would be a microcontroller. It is derived from BASIC, though. It has its history with BASIC, but RB is a modern implementation of BASIC that well exceeds the "30 GOTO 10" idiom now nearly obsolete. It is similar to BASIC and has the comfortable feel of BASIC. Heck it will even run old BASIC programs that have line numbers with very few modifications. RB is a very capable, very modern BASIC.

John Blankenship and Samuel Mishal are the authors of "Enhancing the Pololu 3pi with RobotBASIC". That book follows the paradigm I illustrated of using RB on a PC to control a robot. This book, though, takes things farther by showing that a PC running RB can be the front end for a wide variety of embedded devices, not just robots. The PC can act as the queen bee to a bunch of worker bees. RobotBASIC provides the power well beyond 'old' BASIC to interface to many devices other than robots. John and Sam have rejected my suggestion to rename RobotBASIC to '**More-than-Robot-better-than-BASIC**'.

Robert Severson
USBmicro
CircuitGizmos

Preface

The objective of this book is to provide an attainable solution for effecting communications between a PC and electronic hardware. You might wish to have an electronic device do some tasks like switching relays or actuating some motors and reading some transducers, while the PC does the Artificial Intelligence (AI). You might have a system that carries out some complicated tasks and you wish to use the PC to display data and control instrumentation using an effective and ergonomic GUI. Perhaps you have distributed nodes of sensors collecting data over a wide area and you want to use the PC as the central controller for data collection, storage and analysis (see Chapter 10) with the nodes communicating with the PC over wireless links or even across a LAN, WAN or the Internet (see Chapter 9).

Until now, anyone creating a control application had to make a choice; use the microcontroller or the PC for their projects. As a student, hobbyist, or engineer you most likely have wished to utilize the PC's capabilities in your projects - keyboard, data storage, Internet connectivity, arrays, floating point math, graphical user interface (GUI), 2D and 3D graphics and more. While some of the more powerful microcontrollers (e.g. the Parallax multi-core Propeller Chip) can actually do many of these things, it can be complex to implement any one of them, let alone several at the same time. In contrast, these features are already available and readily usable on a PC.

In the past, using a PC in electronic control projects was common practice and quite easy to do. The PC used to have I/O ports that were easily usable to interface with electronics projects and it was easily programmable to do deterministic timing without being unpredictably preempted by a complex multitasking operating system performing a myriad of other jobs. The PC grew progressively more complex, powerful and sophisticated with GUI, multitasking, 3D graphics, virtual memory management, and much more. But it also became extremely convoluted to program while also prohibiting any access to low-level I/O systems; as a result most are nowadays only using the PC as a cross compiler to upload programs to a microcontroller.

In the meantime, microcontrollers (µCs) have been steadily advancing in capabilities and becoming more powerful, easier to program and much less costly. Naturally, engineers and hobbyists are opting to use them for their projects instead of the PC. However, most µCs lack the data storage and processing power as well as the user interfacing facilities of the PC and many engineers and hobbyists find themselves wishing to combine the two. Even though µCs are preferred for controlling electronics hardware and for robotics projects, it is evident that microcontroller-based applications can benefit greatly from the PC's capabilities.

This book will detail a new conceptual model as a design strategy for incorporating the PC with µCs in your projects so that you no longer have to choose between the two (see Chapter 1). We aim to show *techniques and strategies* that can be implemented with many µC and most PC programming languages to create a *protocol* for interfacing and combining the PC and µC (or multiple microcontrollers) where the shortcomings of each are overcome by the capabilities of the other. We will expound *methodologies* for implementing a *firmware layer* on top of any amalgamation of hardware to act as a conduit for a *software layer* to carry out *real time control* of the overall integrated system. The details and particulars of the hardware and software are incidental. Rather, what is of primary significance is how the combination implements a *communications protocol* (Chapter 6).

Although we utilize a specific microcontroller (Parallax multi-core Propeller Chip[1]) and a specific PC programming language (RobotBASIC[2]), you should be able to utilize the strategy and methodology developed here as a ***template*** to create your ***own*** system of any combination of hardware controlled by a PC software of your design through a protocol of your devising implemented by a firmware layer applicable to your system.

The Propeller Chip – a multi-cored processor in a single chip with eight 32-bit processors running in parallel and sharing a common RAM – with its powerful programming language (Spin) facilitates implementing ***multitasking and parallel processing,*** which are the crux of the book's outlined techniques (see Chapter 5).

RobotBASIC is used as the PC programming language (interpreter/compiler) for its powerful readily usable tools that enable a programmer of any expertise to create GUI programs and to effect hardware communications that would need a high level of programming proficiency in other languages. Another advantage of RB is its suite of commands and functions that can be used with great ease to carry out communications over a LAN, WAN or the Internet. As we will see in Chapter 9, the ease with which we accomplish control over the network of the complex system developed here would have required a book on its own to explain had it been implemented in another language.

To illustrate the strategy with concrete examples we use a variety of hardware modules that are typical of most devices you are likely to require in a electronics projects (see Chapters 7 and 8). Despite the fact that the hardware is most often used for robotic projects, it is sufficiently general to be of utility in numerous systems because the devices typify most of what may be utilized with a microcontroller.

> (i) We hope this book will give you a running start on the way to achieving your own system using a PC and microcontrollers to create complex electronics control projects. Whether you want to build a Robot (Chapter 10) or an RUV (Remote Underwater Vehicle) using parallel processing (Chapter 5), with GUI Instruments such as a Compass and Accelerometer and SONAR (Chapters 7 and 8), or you wish to collect data from distributed loggers over the Internet (Chapter 9) and want to store the data on a central PC to graph and analyze the collected information (Chapter 10), we hope you will find the techniques and projects in this book helpful in accomplishing your own projects.

Acknowledgements

We are greatly indebted to Dr. Don J. Latham for his erudite and meticulous attention to detail on all levels while editing and reviewing this book. His wide and deep knowledge of engineering (all of them), piloting, programming and English contributed to this book and raised its quality tremendously. Thanks Don for all the corrections, improvements and great suggestions.

We are grateful to John Gallichotte and Jim Salvino for creating and maintaining the RobotBASIC forum and for all their support over the years on many levels. John's support for and promotion of RB in education and engineering circles is tireless. John and Jim, you are great uncles to RB.

We thank Robert Severson for a most delightful, gracious and witty foreword and for his support for RobotBASIC. His immensely useful U4x1 devices are a great addition to RB.

Parallax is the embodiment of excellence in all aspects from product innovation and dedication to education to customer service and support. Thanks Parallax for all the fun we had using your products and the edification we acquired reading your material and for the unparalleled customer support and service. Many thanks for the technical support team Dave Andreae and Kevin Cook and also the engineering team David Carrier and Daniel Harris. Their technical expertise and suggestions contributed to this book. Extra special thanks for Stephanie Lindsay for her support over the years. We owe her much gratitude.

Many thanks to Ted Lewis for being a friend indeed and for all his suggestions.

We are also very grateful to all the members on the RobotBASIC Forum for all their suggestions and requests for improvements of RB, because of them RB is better than ever.

Many thanks to the members of the Propeller Forum. Their willingness to help and to elucidate what they have learned, enhance the experience of using the wonderful Propeller Chip. Thanks Chip Gracey for creating the Propeller.

To Sharon, May and Rany.

Chapter 1

Introduction

A while back, the PC, with its parallel port, ISA and PCI buses, and serial port provided a viable and powerful as well as moderately easy to program controller for electronic hardware projects. The PC had easily expandable I/O buses and with the microprocessors of the time it was easy to implement Assembly or higher level programs that utilized the *interrupts* ability of the processor to achieve multitasking and ***deterministic real time control***, where you could create accurate and repeatable signals. With the support of the Operating System (OS), resources such as File I/O, Graphics, Mouse, Speaker, and so forth were easily accessible and of major utility to an electronics hardware control project.

With the ever-increasing tighter control by the OS over the facilities of PC and its processor, programming hardware I/O on the PC became progressively more convoluted with each new version of the Windows OS. Furthermore, the fact that the operating systems these days are continuously performing tasks in the background makes it extremely hard to implement deterministic real time control. To aggravate the situation even further, the operating system now prohibits and denies the use of the PC's hardware through programming languages without the use of special SDKs (Software Development Kits). And to add further difficulties, PC's no longer have any readily usable serial ports or parallel ports, and the bus is almost impossible to use.

All this means that engineers desiring to use a PC to control electronics systems have to resort to using specialized hardware and software designed by companies that have the inside knowledge of how to bypass the OS obstacles. For example, LabVIEW™ provides hardware products that can be used on the PC's I/O bus along with a proprietary specialized programming interface to utilize these devices. Such systems lack the versatility and flexibility desired by many engineers, and are usually overly costly. You, of course, can still use the PC to do hardware interfacing if you have the appropriate SDKs and are versed with Visual C++ and the COM model and know how to use DLLs and .NET programming and have a degree in computer science with many years of experience and so on and so forth.

Due to the tremendous difficulty in bypassing the OS obstacles surrounding the PC's hardware, many hobbyists find it exceedingly prohibitive in time and cost to program a PC for interfacing with external electronics. With the availability of powerful and easy-to-use microcontrollers, many hobbyists find it a lot easier and cheaper to use them for their projects and nowadays are mostly using the PC only as a cross-compiler to program the μCs through IDEs (Integrated Development Environments) provided by μC manufacturers. This is a very regrettable situation because the PC can be an extremely important and utilitarian component in a hardware control project for numerous compelling reasons.

1.1 Why Do We Need the PC?

Consider the following program and its resulting output shown in Figure 1.1.

```
Inlineinputmode
Input "Enter your name:",Name
Input "Enter the year you were born:",BYear
Age = round(year(now())-ToNumber(BYear,0))
Print "hello ",Name," you are ",Age," years old"
```

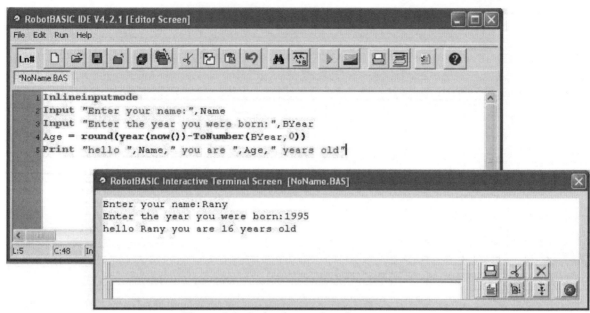

Figure 1.1: A simple user interface program

Despite the fact that this program is only 5 lines of code, and despite its simple actions, you would be extremely hard pressed to produce an equivalent process using a microcontroller alone. What most people take for granted about using a PC system with an appropriate program such as the above, are the numerous support systems that underlie the resulting overall interaction. The program may seem simple at face value but in fact it is an extremely complex one. As a user of the programming language (e.g. RobotBASIC) you did not have to concern yourself with a plethora of details. These details are neither trivial nor simple. If in reality you had to implement all the processes that enable the above program to work you might have to spend months and you would have to be a software engineer of the highest caliber.

Let's examine what the 5 lines of code accomplish. The first line is not important for now. The second and third lines each carry out two actions. They display a message on the screen and then wait for an input from the user. In order to do these two deceptively simple actions, numerous calls to underlying OS facilities have to be performed. The program has to request from the OS permission to output to the screen. It has to also tell the OS which window it is outputting to and what coordinates. It has to tell the OS what font and what color to output to the screen. All this on top of what the content of the output string is. This content itself had to be retrieved from its location in the RAM of the PC. This action of acquiring the text from some memory area in itself requires numerous calls to OS facilities. Waiting for a user input, again, necessitates countless calls to the OS to be able to interact with the keyboard and interpret its input. More memory actions have to be performed in order to store the user key presses and collate them into a string.

The code in the fourth line performs a staggering amount of work. It may not seem so when you look at it. At the logical level the code converts the user's birth year, inputted in text, to a numerical value and defaults to 0 if it is an invalid value. It then obtains the current year and subtracts the given year and stores the result in a memory variable.

On the hardware level it is prohibitive to list here what actions are needed. However, consider the facilities made available in this line. We had to determine the current date. We had to figure out the year from that date. We also had to perform the action of converting the user's input from a text representation of the year to a numerical value. This is a very involved algorithm in and of itself. You would need a program bigger than the original one just to perform this action. To be able to do the mathematical calculations, again, the program has to make many calls to the OS. This fourth line of code alone requires a program of thousands of lines if you were to implement all the necessary low-level functions it performs. The code in the fifth line is similar to the second and third in that it outputs to the screen and it also needs a lot of background processing to be able to concatenate all the required output strings and number.

The above description does not even scratch the surface of what the RobotBASIC language is in fact performing for you when you type and run the simple 5 lines of code above. This is precisely the power and utility of the PC when used with an appropriately simple to use yet powerful language. If you had to program the above on a microcontroller, you as the programmer would have to take care of *all* the necessary sub-systems to be able to accomplish the transaction with the user, the keyboard, the screen, the real time clock and the math processor.

Notwithstanding all the complexity, the above program can still be achieved on a capable microcontroller. This is because the input and output mechanisms are relatively simple. Imagine now if the program's action was similar to that shown in Figure 1.2 (also see Figures 8.11, 8.15 or 10.2). The GUI (Graphical User Interface) alone would be impossible to achieve on almost all the microcontrollers available nowadays. Even if you did achieve a modicum of what can be accomplished on the PC, the amount of work would be prohibitive and then there will be hardly any memory or I/O lines left over to do anything else. And the final outcome will not even begin to approach the quality attainable on a PC.

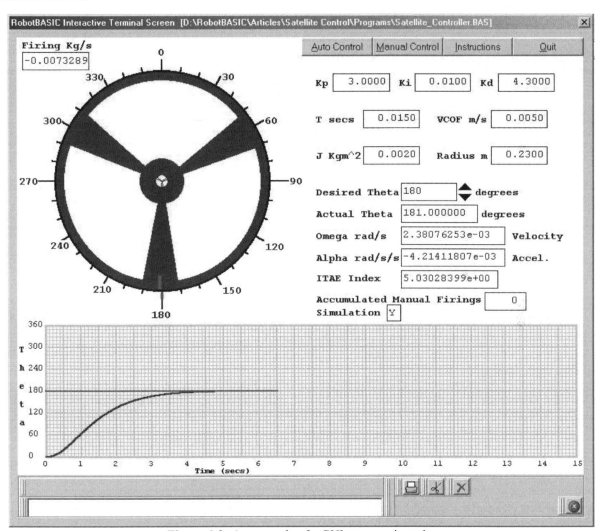

Figure 1.2: An example of a GUI program in action

⚠Many of the limitations of microcontrollers discussed below do not apply to the Propeller multi-core Chip, as you will see throughout this book. You can do things with the Propeller never thought possible with a microcontroller. It has eight processors (cogs) in one chip that can operate simultaneously, either independently or cooperatively, sharing common resources through a central hub. In fact the PPDB (Figure 2.2) used in later chapters can be made into a PC more powerful than some of the PCs of not too long ago.

⚠️Many modern microcontrollers are also very powerful and all the work we do in this book with the Propeller is very much applicable to these microcontrollers. The techniques we will elaborate in the next ten chapters are just as achievable with these capable microcontrollers as they are with the Propeller.

1.1.1 Advantages of Using a PC

What is not widely appreciated is that even though microcontrollers (µCs) are easy to program and are seemingly able to do just about anything, in fact they are very limited when compared to microprocessors (µPs). Most hobbyists will not usually be hindered by the limitations since their projects are often not overly complicated and often a single µC is sufficient for most projects.

Effective Operator Interfacing

A µC is just that – a *controller*. It is designed with the express purpose of controlling hardware. A µC is superb for controlling digital I/O and even in certain cases some analog I/O as well. If a project requires hardware control without much user interaction then a µC is the best possible choice. However, if the project requires more extensive *operator interfacing and data processing* then you need to use a µP, which is a lot more suited to doing just that – *processing*.

Using a PC with its graphics capabilities in a control project you can create an *ergonomic operator interface*. You can use GUI components and 2D and 3D graphics to provide the user with *intuitive* and effective **feedback** and *control* over the system (see Figures 1.2, 8.11 and 8.15).

Processing Power

A µC is limited in the amount of RAM and ROM available to it. Unlike a µP which is designed to process data, a µC does not make available its *memory buses* and has a fixed memory. This means that there is no way to expand the memory available to it except by using some of its I/O lines. Indeed, you can, with ingenuity and sufficient finagling, make a microcontroller achieve some impressive acts. Even so, that is not what a µC was designed for. The aphorism *"Horses For Courses"* comes to mind here. Of course you can use a screwdriver as a hammer, but think how much better it would be to use an actual hammer.

Algorithmic and Data Processing Power

Most µCs are limited in their ability to manipulate *arrays* and perform *floating-point* as well as other high-level math operations. Even simple *multiplication* and *division* are limited or in some cases hard to implement. Simple projects may not require many mathematical calculations, but more complex projects will usually require the processing power of a PC.

To accomplish most *Artificial Intelligence (AI) algorithms*, structures such as *Multi-Dimensional Arrays, Files, Databases, Queues, Lists, Binary trees, Graphs, Stacks, Searching, Sorting, Fast Fourier Transforms* and much more are necessary. There are not many µCs that can be programmed to handle such constructs at the level required by even simple AI projects. Consider for instance the case of controlling a robotic arm. Most µCs would not even approach adequacy for some of the number crunching required to calculate the forward and reverse kinematics of a 5-degrees of freedom arm. Calculating the Jacobian alone would task the majority µCs to the extreme.

Utilizing Simulations

An effective and powerful design methodology in engineering is to use *simulations.* Simulations provide an extremely effective method for testing a system before spending much time and money building the real hardware. A simulated system allows engineers to try out various algorithms and ideas, to examine what-if situations and to hone the control algorithms. All this can be accomplished with safety and minimal expenditure.

Once a simulation is perfected it can be used to train operators while the physical system is being built. A simulation enables catastrophic training scenarios to be thrown at the operator with none of the obvious ramifications. Think of a flight simulator where a pilot can fail and crash and still go back home that evening to his family unscathed.

Once the hardware system is available the very same programs that controlled the simulations can be used to control the real hardware instead of the software simulation algorithms that emulated the hardware. The time spent developing the simulation would have been efficiently used and becomes an integral part of the overall design process. Operators do not need to be retrained and there is no need to translate the control algorithms to the native language of the hardware microcontroller. Moreover, the control algorithms can be as complex as needed without being hindered by limitations in the processing ability of the microcontroller. No new equipment is required to effect the user-interface since the same PC systems used for the simulation are used with the real hardware.

An example of such a system is shown in Figure 1.2 above; also see Chapter 10 for more examples. Figure 1.3 below is a schematic layout of how this can be conceptually achieved. If you look at Figure 1.2 on the middle right hand part of the image, just above the graph area, you would see a box labeled *Simulation*. If this box is set to N (no) then a user interacting with the system would be in fact interacting with the real hardware being driven by the program. If the box is set to Y (yes) then the interaction would be with the algorithms that simulate the hardware. Notice that the very same user interface is used for both the real and simulated interaction.

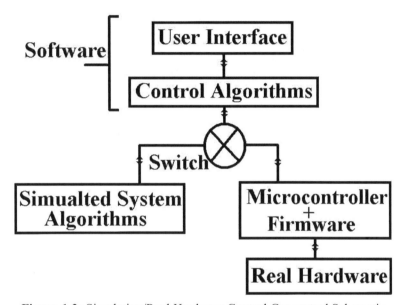

Figure 1.3: Simulation/Real Hardware Control Conceptual Schematic

Access to the Internet or LAN

Most μCs do not have the capacity to provide a TCP or UDP stack. To enable a microcontroller to communicate over the Internet one has to use a specialized module. This adds extra expense to the project and may not be a versatile option. If we use a PC in the project then the PC can also act as the conduit for achieving Internet communications using a wired or wireless link (Wi-Fi). Additionally if the link between the PC and the hardware is also wireless (XBee), then the hardware would be able to communicate through the Internet or LAN completely wirelessly. See Chapter 9 for how to implement such a system and see Figure 9.7 for various layouts.

1.1.2 Versatility and Reusability

What makes the PC such a versatile device? A PC is a Rolodex, a diary, a personal planner, a book, a typewriter, a CD player, a DVR – the list is endless. However, when you first start the machine it is none of that. What makes it become all these things is its ability to run programs that make it accomplish the tasks necessary for acting as the appropriate analogue.

What is a PC? It is a set of ***hardware*** with a capable μP appropriately programmed with the right Operating System (***firmware***). When you want to make the PC perform a particular task you give it a series of instructions (***software***) that it can understand. This software tells the PC what hardware to use as well as how and when in order to be able to emulate the analogous tasks. See Figure 1.4.

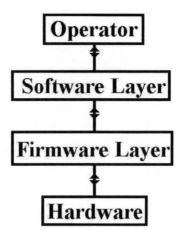

Figure 1.4: Conceptual model of a PC system

This conceptual model is the secret of the power and *versatility* of a PC system. Imagine if every time you wanted to make the PC perform a different task to what it is currently doing you had to:

❑   Fire up another machine.
❑   Load a program on the machine.
❑   Connect the PC to the machine.
❑   Write a program in the machine that has *all* the firmware as well the software required.
❑   Compile them.
❑   Upload the compiled result to the PC.
❑   Unplug the PC.
❑   Run the PC.
❑   Test if the new software is working.
❑   If it is not repeat the above steps after having first used the other machine to fix the problem.
❑   If you need to do a new action on the PC, repeat the above steps having first devised the necessary new software for the action.

You can imagine that not many people would be using computers. The above process would soon get to be too irksome to say the least. Yet, if you have not noticed, that is exactly what we do every time we want to run a new program on a μC. Notice too, that it is not just the software that we upload to the μC, rather it is the firmware as well as the software. We don't normally think of it that way. We think of the uploaded program as one program. However if you are using things like LCDs, Key Pads, Serial Ports and so forth, then every program you do has a common set of basic underlying subroutines that make these devices function. Most often you just cut and paste or #include these routines into your program. But these subroutines in fact constitute a firmware. Your new code would be the software.

We also tend to think of the μC as being independent of the PC. But in reality it is not. The μC would not be versatile if we did not have the PC. We would not be able to quickly and easily change its action (load it with new software). So in fact, *the PC is a crucial and integral part of the life cycle of a μC system*. Read the previous statement again. Mull over it for a few minutes. What makes the μC versatile and useful is the PC. Without the PC, using a μC would be quite aggravating and perhaps impossible.

If what you need is to make a μC based system be a versatile one, you will need the PC. However, with the traditional method of using a PC just as a cross-compiler and IDE platform to program the μC, the PC constitutes only an *implicit function* of the final resulting system once the μC is carrying out the designed task.

> ⓘ Don't think of the PC as just a μP. The PC is a ***complex combination of systems*** that are the culmination of over 60 years of engineering expertise by thousands of innovators. Every time you use a PC you are "riding on the shoulders of giants". By opting to incorporate a PC in your design you are starting from an advanced position instead of from scratch.

1.2 A Paradigm Shift

What we are proposing in this book is a new ***paradigm***. What we want is to ***make the microcontroller an explicitly integral component of an overall PC system***.

On a PC when we want to load new software we do not need another machine to do so. We even can use a programming language on the PC itself, to write a new software if a commercial one is not available. However on a μC system in the traditional way we use it, this would not be possible. Nevertheless, if we expand our ***conceptual perception*** of what a μC system is and regard the PC as an integral component in the system then in fact we can write software and run it on the μC without relying on an external device, since now the PC is actually part of the system.

This new paradigm is not as simple as just ***thinking*** of the PC as important. Rather, it is a concrete and decisive action that has to be taken to realize the benefits of such a new concept. We need to setup the μC to be a sub-system of the PC as an overall unit. Just like the PC has a hard disk or a sound card or an LCD screen, so will the μC be yet another hardware sub-system in the PC's repertoire of peripheral devices, much like a printer or a scanner and so forth,

What you may not have actually realized about devices that constitute a PC system is that in fact many of them have their own μCs onboard. Hard Disks these days are almost standalone devices. In actuality, PC peripheral devices communicate with the μP using a μC (or even a μP) of their own, utilizing the ***SATA bus lines***. ***USB ports*** are nothing more than another kind of ***bus line*** to the PC's μP.

In concrete terms, the μC + firmware become a substitution for the old parallel ports and serial ports. All you need is the right programming language and you can successfully make the PC an electronics hardware control and experimentations platform just like in the old days, but with even more power and versatility as well as functional utility. See Figure 1.5.

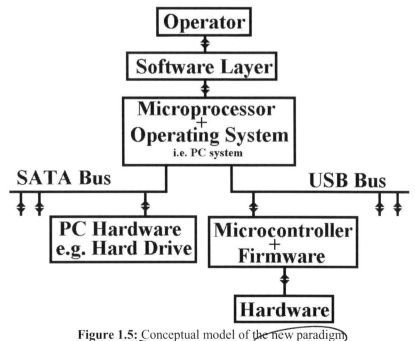

Figure 1.5: Conceptual model of the new paradigm

> The PC alone is no longer a viable hardware controller. The μC alone is a poor user interfacing and data processing platform. However, with our *new paradigm* and using RobotBASIC to be able to communicate through the USB ports with the appropriate software and firmware we can convert the PC and μC *together* into a very powerful, efficient, and versatile hardware control and experimentation platform with ergonomic and effective user interfaces. The next ten chapters of this book will show you how to program a μC with the right firmware to make it an integral subsystem of the PC. This way you can carry out control of electronic hardware as easily as using a PC.

1.2.1 The RobotBASIC Advantage

As you saw above, all you need to implement the new paradigm is a programming language that makes it easy to communicate with the microcontroller. There are a plethora of languages out there that can *eventually* achieve this. Many of them however are complex and have very steep learning curves. Many of them also require a lot of resources on the PC and cannot be used on the fly. They need installation and cannot be used from such devices as a flash drive or a CD. All of them are quite powerful; however, you would need lots of experience to be able to use them at a functional level.

What is desirable is a language that can be used at any level of expertise and yet produces programs at a level a professional in other languages would produce. RobotBASIC (RB) is one such language. There are numerous advantages to using RB listed on its web site. The ones of immediate import to our paradigm shift are the ability to:

> ➤ Communicate with devices on the USB ports such as a microcontroller or XBee transceiver.
> ➤ Communicate with Bluetooth devices.
> ➤ Communicate over the Internet or LAN using TCP or UDP.
> ➤ Fully Control the U4x1 family of devices from USBmicro[3] (see later).

With RB's 2D and 3D graphics engines and its extensive GUI components, combined with its numerous commands and functions for math and matrices and File I/O (low and high level) as well as the tremendously easy syntax, RB enables even the most novice programmer to create programs for controlling hardware with ergonomic and professional looking interfaces (see Figure 1.2 or 8.15).

Another major advantage of RB is its integrated *robot simulator* as well as its associated *robotic hardware communications protocol.* See Chapter 10 for more details on both these systems. As we saw in the previous section, a simulation should be an indispensable part of the design cycle carried out by a prudent engineer.

> One very effective and convenient method to implement the new paradigm explained above is through the U4x1 USB I/O family of devices from USBmicro[3]. RobotBASIC has an extensive set of functions that enable easy use of the U4x1's port I/O, SPI and 1-Wire communications, control of two Stepper Motors and control of High-Voltage-High-Current built in Relays. This family of devices is an excellent and powerful substitute for a μC in certain classes of projects (or to use in conjunction with a μC) that you may want to consider. In addition to the information resources available at the USBmicro web site, we have an in-depth tutorial[66] teaching how to use these devices on our web site.

> The RobotBASIC IDE and compiled RB programs can run under any Windows OS version from 95 to W7 from a CD or Flash drive with no installation required. Also RB makes it easy to interact with the parallel port and ISA/PCI buses on older PCs. This makes RB ideal for making use of old PC's and giving them a new life as electronics hardware experimentation platforms, instead of a reason for spouses to complain about them taking too much storage space.

1.2.2 Various Arrangements

There are various alternatives for how to incorporate a μC as an extension of the PC's hardware:

1. Laptop, Notebook or Desktop directly wired through a USB to an appropriate USB to TTL Serial converter which then is wired to two of the μC's I/O lines as Rx and Tx lines.

    This option is not very mobile if you use a Desktop, but even with a Notebook it may be too bulky for some situations (e.g. a small robot). The U4x1 devices would be an excellent option here as well.

2. A PC Motherboard + SD card or USB flash memory to hold the OS and software, directly wired to the μC as in option one above.

    This option is mobile but not very convenient if you require user interfacing and active real-time system monitoring. However, this option is great for mobile applications that require the computational augmentation the PC motherboard provides. You can also combine it with option 3. Again, the U4x1 devices would be an excellent option here too.

3. The PC is connected to a wireless transceiver (see Chapter 9) through its USB port. The μC is also connected to a compatible transceiver through two of its I/O lines. The transceivers act as a wire replacement between the PC and the μC.

    This is the most versatile alternative and it has the power of being mobile and at the same time providing user interfacing and real time systems monitoring. This would be the option of choice for a distributed or a mobile system (e.g. robots or monitoring stations).

1.3 Distributed Parallel Processing

Complex engineering systems comprise numerous subsystems that can be thought of as a collection of subtasks. You should divide a complex system into simpler subsystems (just like you do for a complex programming project). Each subtask can be controlled by a dedicated μC along with some additional circuitry. The overall project is coordinated by the PC as a master controller which communicates with the various subordinate μCs. The ***distributed processing*** provided with this ***divide-and-conquer*** strategy, allows the PC to require less I/O conduits than would have been needed if it had to control all the sub-processes directly. Also due to the ***parallel processing*** provided by the various μCs, ***multitasking*** is readily achievable (see Chapter 5).

On the PC you can have an overall controller software program or even multiple programs running in parallel, with each program controlling one USB port that carries throughput to the μC. These software programs can also communicate with each other using hard disk files or the UDP protocol (despite being on the same PC) to transfer data between each other if the need arises.

The PC provides the ***AI Brain***. The microcontrollers only deal with reading ***transducers*** and activating ***actuators*** but not with why they need to do so. The PC decides ***what*** and ***why*** and ***delegates the how*** to the microcontrollers. The μC is programmed with the appropriate firmware to be able to communicate with the PC software and to be able to control the various hardware components it is dedicated to. The firmware is therefore quite simple with only sufficient complexity to independently control its subtask according to parameters transmitted to it by the PC software.

1.3.1 A Remote Computational Platform (RCP)

A PC used in the manner described above can be easily converted into a ***Remote Computational Platform (RCP)*** by using wireless or Wi-Fi connections to all the subordinate μCs. This provides levels of functionality and diversity that facilitate many interesting possibilities.

The RCP also acts as an ***operator interface*** node that provides operators with information about and control over the system and with the ability to ***reconfigure the system dynamically*** (i.e. while it is working) and/or to ***override*** the system's automatic actions when required. This remote control can also take place across the Internet (see Chapter 9).

There are numerous advantages in having an RCP. Think of Planetary exploration. If you have an orbiting RCP that controls multiple surface Rovers, you can simultaneously explore multiple regions, rather than being limited by one explorer. Also each individual explorer is simple and expendable. The RCP stays "safe" up in orbit and does not incur the possibility of damage during landing. Since there are numerous explorers, there would be no problem if one or more are damaged during the landing. You will still be able to achieve the mission or reassign another rover to take over the task of its defunct "sibling". With this option a robotic platform can be kept small. Only the sensory and actuations systems are needed onboard and perhaps some gyros and accelerometers – in the case of airborne or seagoing platforms – for doing attitude control or an INS (inertial navigation).

> ⚠Also with the RCP option, once the robot is configured and its onboard microcontrollers programmed, it never needs to be tampered with again. *All the work can now be done through the PC to make the robot do different tasks and actions* depending on the projects. You can even *reconfigure* the robot in *real time* while it is *in the field* still doing its work. You can convey to it imperatives to make it alter its previously assigned behavior remotely while it is still in the field.

Some *lateral thinking* and a *paradigm shift in conceptualization* are necessary to appreciate this kind of robot. Most people think that an autonomous robot has to be human like. We humans do not have an RCP – or do we; food for thought. An autonomous robot is still autonomous even though it is using *additional not onboard brains*.

Another advantage of this idea is that you can have multiple robots sharing the same RCP to act as a *hive* or *matrix* of robots. They can then intercommunicate and be orchestrated all at the same time through the RCP. Moreover, the RCP can provide information to the hive that is otherwise not possible to obtain by the individual robots. Imagine having a robot able to access the Internet to collect some data it requires (e.g. GPS augmentation, weather data, satellite imagery). Think of a hive that is distributed over remote places but yet can communicate and orchestrate actions by using the Internet as a communications link. Researchers call hive members "Agents". Currently this kind of structure is under intense research. RESISTANCE IS FUTILE.

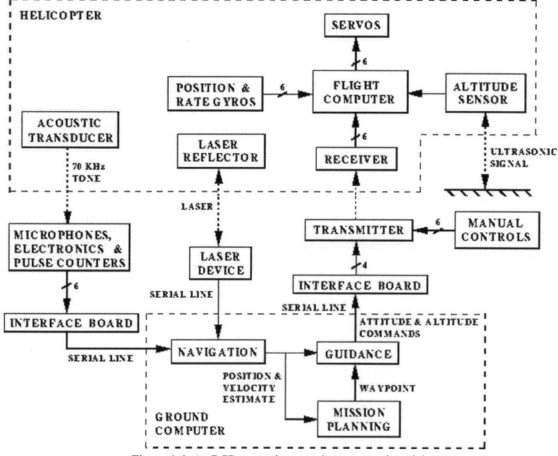

Figure 1.6: An RCP research system's conceptual model.

See Figure 1.6 for the conceptual model of an RCP used by a researcher at MIT[4] to implement a helicopter control system. The controller onboard the helicopter is able to autonomously maintain the vehicle's attitude. But to go places or to change altitude the decisions come from the ground controller (PC). The RCP communicates through three serial links with three μC-based devices. One uses RF transceivers. Another uses a LASER link (similar to Infrared). The third uses Ultrasound. Notice how the RCP provides the *mission planning* aspect – in other words the AI.

1.4 What Will You Learn?

The goal of this book is to show a *strategic methodology* for implementing the new paradigm expounded in Section 1.2. We will gradually evolve a series of programs into a capable and functional *firmware layer* that can be used to carry out the *communications protocol* between the μC and the *software system* running on the PC.

Along the way we will use an amalgamation of hardware (such as an accelerometer, ultrasound ranger, infrared line sensors, compass, servomotors, potentiometers and more) to demonstrate the utility of the *overall concept* by controlling the hardware through software programs to carry out *real time control* of the *integrated system*. Even though we are using specific hardware and a specific μC and PC programming language, the aim is not to teach these particular systems or even the particular protocol. Rather the aim is that you would be able to *utilize the methodology as a template to achieve your own requirements*.

The *multitasking and parallel processing* concept is of paramount importance and you will need to use it regardless of the particulars of your system. This book will utilize the concept almost right from the start.

There are four levels at which a person can acquire a new skill:
> **Rote:** where a skill can be repeated only by emulation, with no understanding for why it is performed so.
> **Understanding:** where one still can only repeat the skill but now with an understanding for why it is applied within the particular application with which one is familiar.
> **Application:** where the skill can be applied in different situations and with understanding. However, there is no additional innovation of technique.
> **Correlation:** where one can adapt the skill to apply it to new applications in an innovative manner.

> (i) We hope this book will induce you all the way to the correlation level where no matter what new situation you face you would find the information acquired here an inspiration for you in creating your own unique and innovative solutions.

1.5 What Do You Need To Know?

This is not a book about learning how to program RobotBASIC or Spin. Nor is it about how to use particular devices. All these are skills best acquired from the resources mentioned in Appendix A. However, this book is about how to create a system to allow a PC to control electronics hardware in an efficient and useful way.

You are not expected to be an expert in any of the systems used in the book. In most cases we do show enough detail to be useful even to a novice. However, you are expected to be at a level of knowledge where you can read code and discern the algorithms in it. If you are not familiar with certain syntax, you are expected to read the manuals and learn about the particulars you are not sure about.

We will use RobotBASIC (www.RobotBASIC.com) and Spin (www.Parallax.Com/Propeller) at an intermediate to advanced level and there will be a few programming techniques and tricks to achieve efficient results. Some of these may be explained in some detail. However, you are expected to be sufficiently versed in both languages to be able to follow along with the explanations since not *every* detail might be expounded. You should be familiar with these languages, at the very least, beyond the beginner level. You can find tutorials for both at their respective web sites (see items 1, 2, 62, 63, 65 in Appendix A).

In RobotBASIC we will use techniques for serial communications and for communication across the Internet. Detailed Tutorials for both these can be found at our website (see items 18-20, 57 in Appendix A). Additionally there are numerous YouTube video tutorials about the RobotBASIC language (see item 63 in Appendix A).

There are also five other books that teach RobotBASIC at an advanced as well as a beginner and intermediate levels. There are many links on the RB web site but also see item 62 in Appendix A. The book *Hardware Interfacing With RobotBASIC, the Fundamentals* is designed to be a precursor to this book for beginners(search for it on www.Amazon.com or see the link www.RobotBASIC.com).

Similarly, for the Spin language as well as most of the hardware used here, there are tutorials, specification sheets, example code and much more on the Parallax web site (see Appendix A). Also see www.parallax.com/propeller/qna and www.parallax.com/propeller.

You are expected to be able to read schematics and translate them into physical wiring arrangements. We assume that you are versed with electronics hardware and are able to determine what you need from specification sheets and other information resources that would augment whatever detail we give in this book.

1.6 An Overview of the Chapters

In **Chapter 2** we list the required hardware and software, so you can collect the necessary equipment before you start building the projects and prepare it to be ready for later chapters.

In **Chapter 3** we develop programs to test the initially simple hardware setup. This verifies the hardware and software systems and provides a working starting point. Also it provides base line programs for carrying out serial communications that can be evolved as we progress through the book. We also learn certain important facts about serial communications buffers.

In **Chapter 4** we develop further sophistication in the software establishing some GUI programming techniques. We further develop the serial communications techniques required to achieve effective interaction between the PC and the Propeller. We also learn about some pitfalls in serial communications and how to avoid them using software handshaking and how to use software to complement and enhance the hardware and to work around certain limitations that may arise.

In **Chapter 5** we delve into the all-important concepts of Multitasking and Parallel Processing. We look at the three different techniques of Polling, Interrupts and Parallel Processing. We learn about timing and timers in RB and Spin. We learn about memory sharing using pointers in Spin. We also learn about semaphores and flagging. For examples of parallel processing we utilize frequency generation and use that to create musical tones and tunes on a speaker. Additionally, we learn about avoiding some elusive traps while utilizing parallel programming in general and the Propeller Chip in particular.

In chapters prior to **Chapter 6**, we utilize *ad hoc protocols* to effect the communications as required by the systems being developed at the time; every program had a different technique and a different standard. This would be sufficient for small one-off projects but not adequate for complex more general ones. In Chapter 6 we develop a *standard protocol* to effect the communications on a more versatile and robust level. We then demonstrate how the protocol provides fault adaptability and tolerance as well as versatility while using it in complex GUI software programs that provide professional looking instrumentation applications on the PC.

Before **Chapter 7** only simple hardware was utilized to experiment with the techniques being learned. This aided in keeping the complexity at a minimum while concentrating on the algorithmic content rather than being mired in the details and intricacies of hardware. In Chapter 7, armed with the sophistication of parallel processing and a versatile communications protocol, we start imparting more complexity to the hardware. We add an ultrasound ranger, two continuous motion servomotors and two potentiometers. Initially we develop each system on its own and develop simple test programs in firmware and software to establish a base line mechanism for using them. We then integrate them into one overall system. We gradually evolve the firmware developed in Chapter 6 to allow the software to control and interact with the hardware by means of the established protocol with everything functioning in parallel in a smooth and controlled manner. We then go on to impart more abilities to the firmware and also develop another complex GUI software program to utilize the improved firmware and hardware.

In **Chapter 8** we add further hardware and outline a general and methodical strategy for incorporating *any* hardware into the firmware and protocol. Additionally, we learn more sophisticated programming techniques in both Spin and RobotBASIC. We add a compass, an accelerometer, a standard servomotor to be a turret for the ranger, infrared line sensors, ability to save system parameters to an EEPROM, and a better way to use a speaker. We also learn about RB's 3D graphics engine and see how to develop professional looking instrumentation.

In **Chapter 9** we see how to make the hardware system remote from the controlling PC using wireless communication with systems such as the XBee and Bluetooth. Another method for achieving *remote control* is over a Local Area Network with Wi-Fi or across the globe using the Internet. We do this using RB's simple to use yet powerful suite of TCP commands and functions.

In **Chapter 10** we look at the RobotBASIC simulated robot and see how to use RB's inbuilt protocol to effect control over the hardware developed in previous chapters using it as a *robot emulator*. In fact, the protocol developed in chapter 6 and implemented in Chapters 7 and 8 is followed by RB's inbuilt protocol exactly. In this chapter we see how to use the simulator to develop a program to make the simulated robot move in the simulated environment on the screen. But then we see how the very same program with the change of a single number can be made to drive the hardware. All this is possible due to RB's intrinsic protocol that follows the same standards we develop throughout the book. We then go on to use the simulator protocol to develop a simplistic INS (inertial navigation system) to prove how versatile the protocol can be.

In **Chapter 11** we examine some of the limitations of the firmware and we discuss and suggest possible improvements. As an example for how some of these improvements can be implemented we go ahead and create an extended firmware that applies some of those suggestions. We also talk about the soon to be developed RROS (RobotBASIC Robotic Operating System) which is a more sophisticated and general version of the strategies and techniques elucidated in this book.

1.7 Icons Used In This Book

The icon ⓘ denotes a point of interest of which you should be aware. The icon ⚠ denotes a warning about something that could lead to problems if you are not fully aware of the pertinent facts. The icon ☺ is to prompt you to laugh whenever *we think* we made a joke. You might think otherwise but you *should* laugh regardless; it is good for the mind.

In code listings we will sometimes draw attention to some lines of code in particular from among the other lines in the listing. There are three levels (other than normal code):

```
Normal code
First level is Bolded text in the listing.
        Called Bold code or lines.
Second level is in white text on a dark gray background.
        Called Highlighted code or lines.
Third level is white text on black background.
        Called Reverse code or lines.
```

> ⚠️ We often refer to RB or the Propeller or Spin by saying something to the effect: "you will send to RB…" or "RB will expect…." meaning a program created in RB running on the PC either within the RB IDE or as a compiled executable (exe) running as a standalone program in the OS. Likewise for the Propeller or Spin when we say "the Propeller will …." or "Spin wants to…" we mean a program written in Spin (or PASM or both) then compiled and uploaded to the Propeller and is currently running on the Propeller.

1.8 Webpage Reference Links in This Book

We use many devices and refer to many items that can be viewed on the Web. In the book's text such items are underlined and numbered with a superscripted number. You need to use the superscript number adjacent to the reference and index in the list given in appendix A to find the full URL address of the relevant link. You will also find Appendix A included in a PDF file in the downloadable Zip file that contains all the source code of the book (see Section 1.9). This will be useful since you can click on the link in the PDF file to visit the site instead of having to type the URL by hand in the browser.

1.9 Downloading the Source Code of the Book

You can download from www.RobotBASIC.com a Zip file containing all the code (Spin and RB) organized in folders for each chapter. Additionally there is a file called System_References.PDF, which has in it all the appendices at the end of this book and a selection of some of the figures but in color. There will also be an additional download file containing corrections for any critical errors in the book. There will be no need to download this file since it will remain empty, of course ☺.

Hardware & Software Setup

The projects we will carry out require hardware and software that have to be configured in a specific way to assure a common reference point from which to proceed. This chapter will describe how to arrange the systems and what will be required for later chapters.

2.1 Hardware Setup

We will develop many of the projects on the <u>Propeller Demo Board (Part#32100)</u> [5] (PDB Figure 2.1). This board is very convenient and is the most ubiquitous. It also has LEDs built in that will be very useful for the initial work. Furthermore, there are 7 free pins that can be used for input as we will see later.

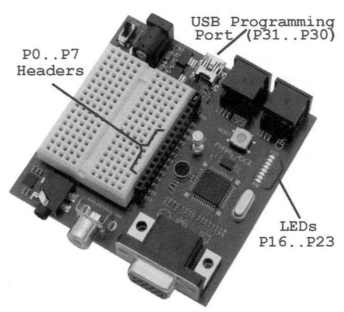

USB Programming
Port (P31..P30)

P0..P7
Headers

LEDs
P16..P23

Figure 2.1: The Propeller Demo Board (PDB)

The PDB is adequate for the initial stages, however due to its amble bread-boarding space and availability of free I/O pins we will use the Propeller Professional Development (Part#32111) [6] (PPDB Figure 2.2) for the later more hardware oriented projects. This board has useful and convenient already wired hardware and is most suitable for projects using hardware like servomotors and potentiometers. You can use the PPDB from the start instead of the PDB.

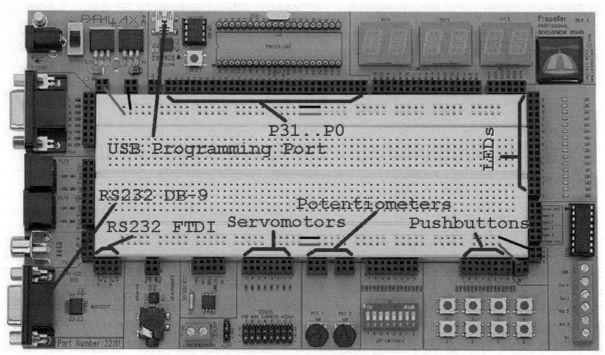

Figure 2.2: The Propeller Professional Development Board (PPDB)

Figure 2.3: The PropPlug (PP)

We also need to use the Propeller Plug (part#32201)[7] (PP Figure 2.3) or you can use the Parallax USB2Ser Development Tool (Part#28024)[8]. If you prefer to use standard RS232 ports, the PPDB is good for that because it provides a DB-9 RS232 level port that we can use (bottom left in Figure 2.2). For connecting the USB programming port (top left in Figure 2.2) to a normal RS232 port on the PC, you can use the Parallax USB to Serial (RS-232) Adapter (Part#28031)[9]

As shown in Figures 2.4 and 2.5, we will not connect the RES pin of the PP. The VSS pin must be connect to the ground on the board (black). The TX pin is the pin that brings the data in from the outside and **transmits** it to the Propeller and we will connect this to P0 on the propeller (yellow). The RX pin is the pin that **receives** data from the Propeller and sends it to the outside we will connect this to P1 on the Propeller (blue).

In the Spin programs we will call P0 the RB_Rx pin and P1 the RB_Tx pin. This is because from the point of view of the Propeller, P0 will be used to **receive** data from the RobotBASIC programs and P1 is used to **transmit** data to RB.

(i) If you use the USB2SER, the pins are in a different order from that on the PP but the connection is to the TX and RX as above. Also connect a 1KΩ resistor between the TX pin and P0 since the USB2SER uses 5V.

If you have neither the PDB nor the PPDB you can still carryout most of the projects on almost any other Propeller board that makes available P0..P7 and P16..P23 as free pins. However, for the more hardware oriented projects in Chapters 7 and 8 you will need more I/O pins (See Figure B.2 in Appendix B). For most of the projects you will need to connect LEDs to P16..P23 and Active-Low Pushbuttons to P7..P5.

⚠ Before wiring your board and powering it up, you must erase the EEPROM and RAM to ensure the Propeller Chip is blank. After you have read Section 2.2 carry out the procedure in Section 2.2.1

On the PDB there are already LEDs connected to P16..P23. On the PPDB all the pins are free but it has LEDs already appropriately wired and all you have to do is connect a wire from the header of the pin to the header of the LED as shown in Figure 2.4.

On the PPDB there are 8 Pushbuttons wired as Active-Low buttons. We will use three of them to connect to P7..P5 as shown in Figure 2.4. For The PDB we need to wire up the three pushbuttons to be active low as shown in Figure 2.5 using the schematic shown in Figure 2.6.

For other boards you may have to provide your own LEDs with a resistor connected as shown in Figure 2.7 and also connect pushbuttons as we did for the PDB.

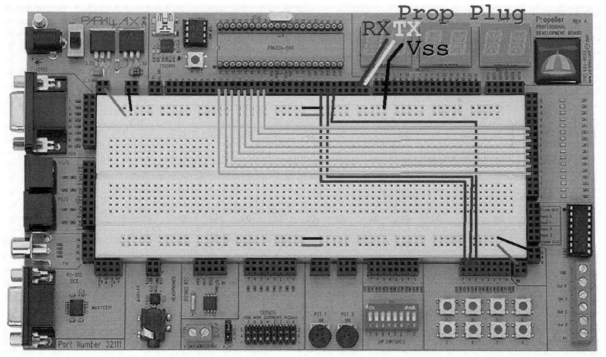

Figure 2.4: How to setup the PPDB for the initial work.

Figure 2.5: How to setup the PDB.

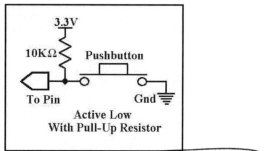

Figure 2.6: Schematic for an Active-Low Pushbutton Circuit.

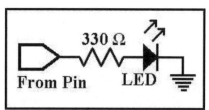

Figure 2.7: Schematic for an Active-High LED circuit.

All the projects up to Chapter 6 can be completed on the PDB but projects in Chapters 7 and 8 are best on the PPDB. If you have both the PDB and the PPDB you may want to use the PDB initially for convenience and then switch over to the PPDB later. On the other hand it might be best to do all the projects on the PPDB from the start.

If you only have the PDB and do not wish to invest in a PPDB then you can still carry out the projects up to Chapter 7.7. However, instead of real servomotors you will see the signal on the P16 and P17 LEDs. You won't be able to add a compass and accelerometer or the QTIs (line sensors) since the PDB does not make the required pins available or the required breadboard space. Remember that with this option you won't be able to see any servomotors actually moving. Instead you will just observe the LEDs being slightly brighter or dimmer depending on the servomotor's signal.

In Chapter 7 we will use the <u>Ping))) Ultrasonic Sensor (Part#28015)</u> [10] (Figure 2.8). For motors we will use two <u>Parallax Continuous Rotation Servomotors (Part#900-00008)</u> [11] . Also we will use two Potentiometers (Pots). The pots will be used in an R-C setup to enable reading the variable resistor's analog value using R-C charge-discharge time method for doing an Analog-To-Digital conversion (ADC) using the Propeller. On the PPDB the pots are already available and we will have to add the other components as show in Figure 7.6. For other boards you will have to provide two pots as shown in the schematic in Figure 7.6.

In Chapter 8 we will use the <u>Honeywell HMC6352 Compass Module (Part#29323)</u> [12] (Figure 2.9) and an <u>H48C Tri-Axis Accelerometer module (Part#28026)</u> [13](Figure 2.10) and the <u>QTI Infrared Line Sensor (Part#555-27401)</u> [14] (Figure 2.11)

Figure 2.8: The Parallax Ultrasonic Ranger, Ping)))   **Figure 2.9:** The HMC6352 Compass Module

Figure 2.10: H48C Tri-Axis Accelerometer   **Figure 2.11:** QTI Infrared Line Sensor

In Appendix B, see Figure B.3 for schematics for all hardware connections. Also see Figure B.2 for the utilization of the pins on the Propeller Chip. For a conceptual schematic of the final system see Figure B.1. For a screen shot of one of the final software systems we will develop see Figure 8.15. Also see Figure B.4 for how the system will look when all hardware is added.

2.2 Software Setup

To program the Propeller we will use Spin and the Propeller Tool (**PT**), which is Spin's Integrated Development Environment (IDE). To aid in debugging programs we will also use the Propeller Serial Terminal (**PST**) connected to the Propeller via the USB port which the PT uses to program the propeller.

> (i) Press the function key F7 while in the PT IDE to determine the number of the port connected to the Propeller and set the PST to use that port (Figure 2.12).

> ⚠ If the PST is active it will be using the port, so the PT won't be able to use it and will fail upon trying to program the Propeller. If you ever see the message in Figure 2.13, make sure the PST is deactivated.

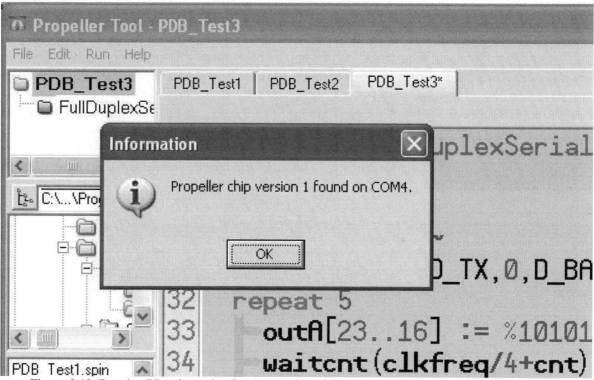

Figure 2.12: Pressing F7 to determine the port number of the USB port for programming the Propeller.

The PST can be made to always release the port whenever it loses focus. That is if you switch focus over to another window (e.g. the PT) then the PST will automatically be disabled and will release the port. This is useful and nice. However, in certain situation you may want to disable this feature because you may want to keep the PST active while interacting with other programs. In those situations, **remember** to always disable the PST again before you try to program the Propeller. If you ever see the message in Figure 2.13 it means that the PST is still enabled and is holding the port. For now make sure that the PST is configured to be automatically disabled when its window loses focus (Figure 2.14).

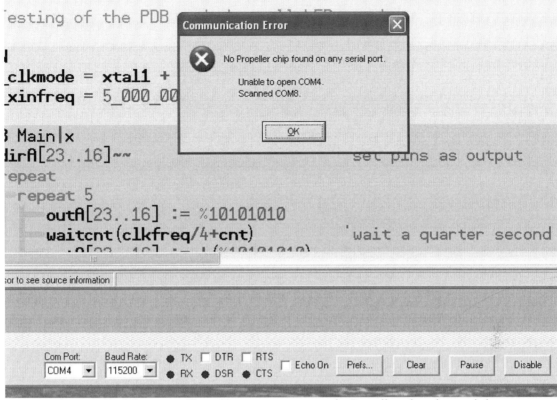

Figure 2.13: What you will see if you try to program the Propeller when the port is busy.

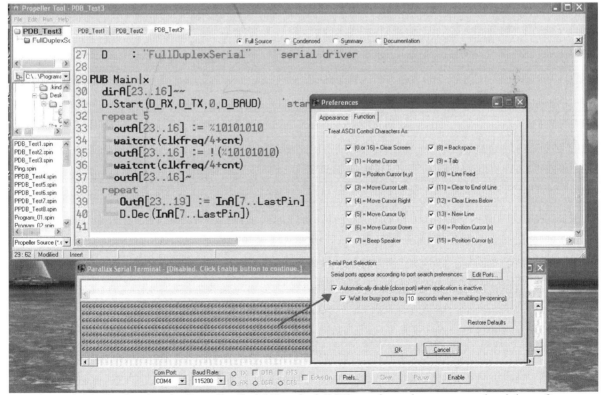

Figure 2.14: Configuring the Propeller Serial Terminal (PST) to release the com port when it loses focus.

Figure 2.15: Setup with two ports connected simultaneously

We will use <u>RobotBASIC</u> [2] with all the projects. Initially we will have RB communicating with the Propeller through the same USB port as the one used to program it. This is to demonstrate that communicating RB and the Propeller can be effected with just one port. *Also, with this option we do not need another device (the PP) to communicate with the Propeller and we save on the use of two I/O pins*.

> ⚠ Whenever we say RB or RobotBASIC or PC, we mean a *software program* that has been developed in the RobotBASIC programming language and has either been compiled and is running on the PC as a standalone executable, or is running within the RB IDE. Similarly, when we say the Propeller, or Spin we mean a *firmware program* running on the Propeller Chip after having been compiled and uploaded to the Propeller to either its RAM (F10) or EEPROM (F11).

> ⓘ RobotBASIC is an *interpreter* and a *compiler*. You can develop and run programs within an IDE session where you need a copy of RB itself. When done with debugging you can compile the program into a standalone executable that runs under any version of the Windows OS from 95 upwards without any need for RB itself to be running.

Many of the programs will need to communicate with RB while also being debugged. For debugging we need to display information from the Propeller on the PST terminal. Therefore we will need to communicate RB with the Propeller using the Propeller Plug (Figures 2.3, 2.4 and 2.5) while also communicating with the PST on the programming port. We will have the setup shown in Figure 2.15.

We will also use the PST as another *process* in the projects to simulate actions going on inside the Propeller and to illustrate how the Propeller can be displaying information of its actions on a display port. Due to the power of the Propeller, this port could be a TV screen or an LCD monitor or a VGA display. Most of these are easily useable with the Propeller, but they will add unnecessary clutter to the projects and since we are already using a PC to program the Propeller, why not use it as the display device. This is readily achievable through the PST and is another illustration of how the PC is useful in our projects

Our objective is to control *real physical hardware* (such as a robot) with the Propeller as the I/O controller. An LCD display on the hardware side might be useful on certain projects especially if the hardware is wirelessly controlled and is remote from the PC. Since many LCDs are driven using a serial protocol, then the programs we develop to display messages on the PST can be effortlessly made to work on an LCD. Using a TV or VGA is an altogether different process. Additionally, the TV and VGA drivers require more COGs than might be affordable since we need to dedicate most cogs to the processes required to run the hardware and its systems.

> ⚠ There is a problem with using the programming port (P31..P30) to also communicate with the Propeller. This will be explained in more details in Chapter 3.5. It is due to the Propeller resetting whenever a program takes hold of the serial port and drives the DTR line low. If you want to use the programming port to also communicate to another program (e.g. RB), you must always program the Propeller with the *F11 option (not F10)* to assure that the program is in EEPROM not just RAM. This way, when the Propeller resets, the program is not lost and can be restarted normally.

2.2.1 Ensuring the Propeller Chip is Blank

Whichever board you use you need to make sure that the Propeller is de-programmed before using it in the setups explained in Chapter 2.1. This is to ensure that there is no program in the EEPROM that will start running when you power up. Since we will connect hardware to the Propeller's pins, a preexisting program may cause I/O clashing which can cause a short.

Remove any preexisting projects from the breadboard and make sure there are no components and no connections to any pins on the Propeller.

In the Propeller Tool IDE write the following one line program

```
Pub Main
```

Then press F11 to compile and upload the program to the EEPROM. This will clear the EEPROM and will make the Propeller revert to a state with all pins configured as input and will then go to sleep with no running cogs. The entire chip will be dormant.

> ⚠ Beware when wiring hardware to any microcontroller. Any already loaded program in its memory might cause electrical shorts on the I/O pins when the program is run. A pin set to be output high wired directly to ground would immediately damage the pin if not the entire chip when it is powered up.

2.3 Summary

This chapter showed:
- ❑ What hardware and software would be used to accomplish the projects for the coming chapters.
- ❑ How to prepare the boards.
- ❑ How to clear any preexisting firmware.

Testing the Hardware and Serial Communications

In Chapter 2 we setup a Propeller board with three active-low pushbuttons connected to P7..P5 and eight LEDs connected to P23..P16. We also connected the board to the PC via *two* USB links. One through the programming port connect to P31..P30 and the second one through a Propeller Plug (PP) connected to P0..P1. We will now develop programs to test:

> ➤ The LEDs.
> ➤ The Pushbuttons.
> ➤ Communicating with the PST through the programming port.
> ➤ Communicating with RobotBASIC through the programming port.
> ➤ Communicating with RB through the PP.
> ➤ Communicating with RB and the PST simultaneously.

If at any stage you find that there is a problem and some LEDs are not lighting when they should or a pushbutton is not giving the right result make sure to check all the wiring and that the hardware is as it is supposed to be. Then check that the programming is as it is supposed to be according to the listings. You may want to type some of the programs to acquire a better understanding for the details but it is easier to download all the programs contained in a zip file available from our web site. The file contains all the source code in this book as well as third party *objects* that will be needed (e.g. FullDuplexSerial). It also contains other resources.

3.1 Testing the LEDs

Compile the program Test_01.Spin below and upload it to the Propeller using F10 or F11. The program will continuously exercise the LEDs in varying patterns. Notice the use of the **WaitCnt()** function to delay a certain amount of time. In this case it is a quarter of a second. The code should not present any difficulty. The program repeats a sequence of blinking the LEDs 5 times, then turns them off then turns the LEDs on one at a time but keeping the previous one on. It then turns them on one at a time in reverse order but turning each one off before going on to the next one. The whole sequence is repeated indefinitely. Notice the use of the << operator to shift a one to the right position. The ~~ operator is used to set all the bits 23..16 in the direction register to 1 which causes the pins to become output pins. The ~ operator is used to set the bits 23..16 in the output register to 0. The ! operator is used to invert the bits of the pattern.

When you run the program make sure all the 8 LEDs are switching on and that there are no dud ones.

Test_01.Spin

```
'No companion RB program
'Use F10 to upload to RAM
CON
  _clkmode = xtal1 + pll16x
  _xinfreq = 5_000_000

PUB Main|x
  dirA[23..16]~~                     'set pins as output  ✓
  repeat
    repeat 5
      outA[23..16] := %10101010
      waitcnt(clkfreq/4+cnt)         'wait a quarter second
      outA[23..16] := (!)(%10101010)   invert
      waitcnt(clkfreq/4+cnt)
    outA[23..16]~                    'clear the pins  ✓
    repeat x from 0 to 7
      outA[23..16] += 1 << x
      waitcnt(clkfreq/4+cnt)
    repeat x from 7 to 0
      outA[23..16] := 1 << x
      waitcnt(clkfreq/4+cnt)
```

3.2 Testing the Pushbuttons

Compile Test_02.Spin and upload the program. It will blink the LEDs and then will turn them all off after which it will continuously read the status of the three pushbuttons and set three LEDs to reflect their state.

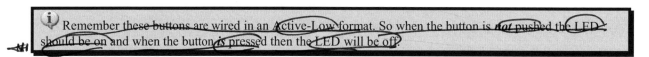

Remember these buttons are wired in an Active-Low format. So when the button is *not* pushed the LED should be on and when the button *is* pressed then the LED will be off.

There is no need to use **dirA[7..5]~** to set the pins to input because the Propeller's pins are all configured as input pins by default upon startup, but you can do so if you wish. Now try the program again but with the line:

```
outA[21..23] := inA[7..5]
```

instead of the last line. What happens? Why? This is a useful feature and can also be a source of error if you are not careful. We will discuss this later in more detail.

Test_02.Spin

```
'No companion RB program
'Use F10 to upload to RAM
'Use Program_03.BAS as the RB program
'Use F11 to upload to EEPROM
CON
  _clkmode = xtal1 + pll16x
  _xinfreq = 5_000_000

PUB Main
  dirA[23..16]~~                     'output pins
  repeat 5
    outA[23..16] := %10101010
    waitcnt(clkfreq/4+cnt)
    outA[23..16] := !(%10101010)
```

```
    waitcnt(clkfreq/4+cnt)
    outA[23..16]~
  repeat
    outA[23..21] := inA[7..5]          'output = input
```

3.3 Asynchronous Serial Communication

In the following programs we will use serial communications to send data out from the Propeller to RB and the PST. This will be achieved by using a Full Duplex Asynchronous Serial communications **Driver**.

Parallax Inc has a web resource called Propeller Object Exchange Library (ObEx) [15]. This is an indispensable resource you should utilize often. It is a library of utility programs and low-level drivers for all sorts of services like Serial, I^{2}C, 1-Wire, LCDs, sensors and much more. There you will find two drivers for serial communications, SerialMirror.Spin (SM) [16] and FullDuplexSerial.Spin (FDS) [17]. We will use these drivers throughout this book to perform the necessary low-level serial bit banging to send out asynchronous serial bytes of data from the Propeller to the outside and also to receive bytes from the outside into the propeller. Remember that all the programs in this document are available in a zip file on our web site[2]. In the file we also make available a copy of the FDS and SM files. This will make it more convenient for you to program all the projects.

Both the FDS and SM perform the same actions. The difference between them is a subtle low-level detail that is not important for now. We will see what it is later when it would be more relevant and can be appreciated. For now, just note that we will use the SM to drive the communications with the PST and FDS to drive the communications with RB.

Both drivers are Full Duplex, which means that we can be send and receive simultaneously, and Buffered, meaning that when bytes are received/sent they are stored in a memory area until they can be used. Serial buffers are limited in size and can become full, at which point data will be lost. So you have to make sure that incoming data is extracted and acted upon before the buffer becomes full.

RobotBASIC has its own **built in** serial com driver that is also full duplex and buffered. The PST is a program designed by Parallax to be able to receive and send data through a serial port using full duplex and buffered serial communications.

The outcome of this is that we can easily communicate between RB (or PST) and the Propeller and can send and receive data bytes without losing any if the receiving program is busy doing other tasks. The PST is a specialized program that waits for data to come in or, if you type characters in its text box, they will be sent to the Propeller. There is no need to do anything to make it work other than enable it and make sure that it is connected to the right com port.

RobotBASIC, however, is a programming language and you have to write a program to make it send or receive data through the serial port. If you are not familiar with serial communications you should review the following three documents that explain how to carry out serial communication with RobotBASIC in a lot more detail:

      RobotBASIC_Serial_IO.pdf [18]
      RobotBASIC_To_PropellerChip_Comms.pdf[19]
      RobotBASIC_To_BS2_Comms.pdf [20]

In Spin, sending and receiving are achieved using methods in the FDS (or SM) objects. These methods are:

Start()	starts the driver working with the required baud rate and using the right pins
Tx()	sends a byte; waits if the buffer is full
Rx	reads a byte from the buffer; waits forever until one is available
RxCheck	reads a byte from the buffer; does not wait if one is not available (returns -1 if no byte is read)
Str()	sends a zero terminated string of bytes
Dec()	sends a text representation of a number (as opposed to the number itself)

In RobotBASIC we will use the following commands:

SetCommPort	starts the com port with the required baud rate and port number
SerPorts	obtains a list of valid serial ports
SerialOut	sends bytes out depending on the parameters of the command
SerIn	receives bytes but with no waiting if there are none available
SerBytesIn	waits with a timeout for a certain number of bytes to arrive
CheckSerBuffer	checks if there are any bytes in the receive buffer
ClearSerBuffer	empties the send and/or receive buffers
GetStrByte()	extracts a particular byte from the received buffer

One thing to keep in mind is if the send rate is faster than a receiver can process the incoming bytes, the receive buffer will overflow and data will be lost. You should always make sure that your programs will always attended to the receive buffer before it overflows. You may need to move the data to a bigger buffer where the program can process the data at its own rate. In RB the send and receive buffers are 4096 bytes long each. In FDS and SM the buffers are 16 bytes only.

3.4 Testing Communication with the PST

Test_03.Spin is very similar to Test_02 but adds the code in bold. In addition to setting the LEDs to reflect the status of the pushbuttons, the program now also sends the value formed from the pushbuttons as a text number to the PST. After compiling and uploading the program (using F10 or F11) switch over to the PST window and make sure that it is setup to use the same com port as the one used to program the Propeller and then click the *Enable* button. You should now see a continuous stream of a number that will change as you push the buttons (Figure 3.1).

Test_03.Spin

```
'No companion RB program but uses the PST
'Use F10 to upload to RAM
CON
  _clkmode = xtal1 + pll16x
  _xinfreq = 5_000_000
  D_TX    = 30
  D_RX    = 31
  D_BAUD  = 115200
  LastPin = 5   'change this to 4 to observe floating Input effect

OBJ
  D    : "SerialMirror"     'serial driver

PUB Main
  dirA[23..16]~~
  D.Start(D_RX,D_TX,0,D_BAUD)    'start the serial driver
  repeat 5
    outA[23..16] := %10101010
    waitcnt(clkfreq/4+cnt)
    outA[23..16] := !(%10101010)
    waitcnt(clkfreq/4+cnt)
    outA[23..16]~
  repeat
    outA[23..20] := inA[7..LastPin]   'output = input ...notice extra bit
    D.Dec(inA[7..LastPin])            'transmit the value to PST
```

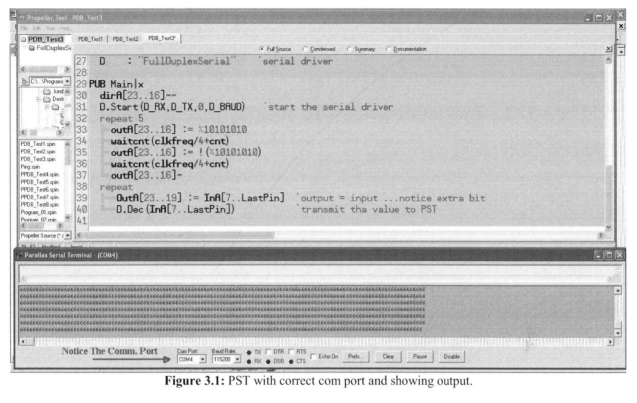

Figure 3.1: PST with correct com port and showing output.

Notice the way we instantiate (see Chapter 5.4.1) the SM object and how we use the **D.Start()** method to start it working. Also notice how the statement **D.Dec(inA[7..LastPin]** is used to send the bits of the pushbuttons' status to the PST. We use constants to define the pins to be used for the communications to make it a lot easier to change things, as we will see later. We will see later why we have **LastPin** as a constant rather than just using the number 5 as we did in Test_02.Spin.

> ⓘ Whenever we give a new listing similar to a previous one, the additional code or changed code will be in bold text. In some cases where we need to discuss certain lines in more detail these lines will be highlighted or reversed (see Chapter 1.7).

3.4.1 Floating Input Pins

Before we move on to the next program, there is an important point to be aware of. The Propeller does not have internal Pull-Up resistors for the I/O pins. This means that when a pin is setup as an input pin and we wish to read its status, we must make sure it is *always* connected to a valid High or Low. If this is not the case the pin may read a false high or low in an oscillating and unpredictable manner. To illustrate this, change the highlighted line at the top of Test_03.Spin to say:

```
LastPin = 4
```

Changing the 5 to a 4 will make the program use P4 as well as P7..P5. Since we have no connection to this pin it is a *floating* input pin. Connect a wire to the pin's header but do not connect it to anything. Run the program. Now observe the LED that corresponds to the pin. It should be off, but it may turn on occasionally. This is more likely to happen when you touch the wire, which introduces capacitance that causes the pin to read a false high or may even oscillate.

⚠ If you observe a weird behavior make sure that input pins are correctly wired and can never become floating. Also make sure you check the battery condition if you are running the board from a battery. A low battery charge can cause the Propeller to RESET unpredictably. This can make your programs appear to be faulty and you may spend hours trying to figure out the reason. One way to test for reset conditions is to use Test_01.Spin and observe the pattern sequence. If a reset is occurring the pattern sequence will become interrupted and will repeat from the beginning all over again.

⚠Using motors powered with the same power supply as the one used to power the Propeller may cause power drops that can reset the Propeller. One way to avoid this is to use a separate power supply but if the motors are not drawing too much current you can add a large capacitor (1000 µF) across the Vdd and Vss lines as we will see later.

ⓘ An effective method for detecting a reset situation is to have your programs perform an easily observable and distinctive sequence of blinking an LED or more upon startup. This way if you observe the pattern you can conclude that a reset situation has occurred and not waste time trying to figure out what is going awry with your programming when in fact it is due to the power supply. If you are in the process of developing a program you will usually use F10 to upload it to RAM. If you upload a program (e.g. Test_01.Spin) to the EEPROM, and a reset occurs you can easily realize the fact from the distinctive patterns. *However, make sure that I/O pin levels are not going to clash with your current experiment and hardware setup.*

3.5 Communicating RB Through the Programming Port

Test_04 is very similar to Test_03 and is to test the communication with RB through the programming port. Just like the PST test, when you compile and upload the program (**using F11**) switch over to RB and run Test_04.BAS below. As with the PST you will see a number repeatedly printed on the screen. Press the buttons on the board and observe how the number changes.

The program uses the FDS, which has the same methods as the SM object. In this program we use the **TX()** method not the **Dec()** method. The reason for this is that in the PST we want to display the *text number* that represents the byte so we convert the byte using the **Dec()** method to a text number. However, since RB is a programming language we can do the conversion *if needed* in RB and all we need to do is send the actual byte value, so we use the **TX()** method.

In the RB program we use the command **CheckSerBuffer** to check if there are any bytes in the serial buffer before we actually read it using the **SerIn** command. The **SerIn** command will read *all* the bytes that are in the buffer; there might be more than one. So when we read the buffer we may want to check how many bytes have actually been read. This is done with the **Length()** function. The function **GetStrByte()** is used to extract a particular byte from the buffer. Therefore the statement **GetStrByte(s,Length(s))** in fact extracts the value of the *last* byte in the buffer we just obtained with the **SerIn s** command.

Why do we not care about the other bytes and only print out the last byte? This will be explained more in Chapter 4.2. But for now run Test_03 with the PST again and observe that when you push the pushbuttons the value is not immediately reflected on the PST screen; there are numerous printouts of the previous state before the new state is reflected. With the Test_04 and RB there is a lot less printing of numbers and the number changes quickly to reflect the new state of the buttons. This is why we ignore all the other bytes in the buffer and only print the last one. Since the last one is the one that best reflects the *current* state of the buttons, all the others may be the value of old states.

Test_04.Spin

```
'Use Test_04.BAS as the companion RB program
'Use F11 to upload to EEPROM
CON
  _clkmode = xtal1 + pll16x
  _xinfreq = 5_000_000
  RB_TX        = 30          'use RB through the
  RB_RX        = 31          'programming port
  RB_BAUD      = 115200


OBJ
  RB    : "FullDuplexSerial"    'serial driver


PUB Main
  dirA[23..16]~~
  RB.Start(RB_RX,RB_TX,0,RB_BAUD)    'start the serial driver
  repeat 5
    outA[23..16] := %10101010
    waitcnt(clkfreq/4+cnt)
    outA[23..16] := !(%10101010)
    waitcnt(clkfreq/4+cnt)
    outA[23..16]~
  repeat
    outA[23..21] := inA[7..5]   'output = input
    RB.Tx(inA[7..5])                'transmit the value to RB
```

Test_04.BAS

```
//RB program to work with the Test_04.Spin
Port = 4  'change this as per your system
setCommport Port,br115200
while true
   CheckSerBuffer x
   if x
     SerIn s
     print getStrByte(s,Length(s));
   endif
wend
```

3.5.1 A Note About String and Byte Buffers

In RobotBASIC strings function in a double capacity. They are strings just like a sentence with characters in them and you can print out the characters on the screen by printing the string. So when you say

```
s = "Test"
```

you are assigning the characters T, e, s and t to the 1st, 2nd etc. bytes in the string. If you later say

```
print substring(s,2,1)
```

it will print the letter **e** on the screen because the second character in the string is **e**. On the other hand if you say

```
print substring(s,2)
```

you will see **est** printed on the screen. By not specifying how many characters you want to extract as we did earlier you will get all the remaining characters starting with the 2nd character as specified.

In its alternative capacity a string in RB is a storage space for bytes – a *byte buffer*. In this capacity we do not regard the bytes as necessarily characters of the alphabet. Rather they are numbers that can range from 0 to 255 (i.e. bytes). A byte value of 15 for instance is not a valid alphabetical character and if you try to print the string with that byte in it you will see garbage printed on the screen. However 15 could be a valid state of some pins (0%1111 in binary).

When we receive bytes from the Propeller we will put them in a byte buffer. So when we say
```
SerIn s
```
We are actually extracting all the bytes from the serial receive buffer and putting them in the variable **s** which now will be a string or a byte buffer.

If we know that the data coming from the Propeller is in fact going to be a proper string with text we can then say
```
print s
```
to see the text. However, if the buffer contains numbers that are values of some process that the Propeller is sending to RB then we cannot just print **s**. If we do we may get some garbage looking characters which are the characters whose ASCII codes are the numbers in the bytes.

Instead we have to use the function **GetStrByte()** to extract the nth byte from the buffer as a number. As an example we will use the same variable as before filled with "Test". So now if we say
```
print getstrbyte(s,2)
```
we will see the number 101 printed on the screen since that is the numerical value of the 2nd byte, which is the ASCII code of the character **e**. The function **GetStrByte()** will treat the variable as a byte buffer and give you the numerical value of the byte in the position you extract.

> (i) In RobotBASIC there are many functions to deal with strings and many to deal with byte buffers. You can use them interchangeably but always keep in mind that a string function will give you the character while the byte-buffer function will give you the number. In fact **GetStrByte()** as its name indicates is a hybrid function since it gives us the number value of the byte but it will deal with the variable as a string. With strings the character count starts with 1. So the 1st character is character 1. Byte-buffers are basically a ***one-dimensional array of bytes*** and the first character is character number 0. It is up to you what you use. An array of bytes is a string and a string is an array of bytes. They are the exact same thing. RB will treat the string as an array if you use byte-buffer functions and commands and will use it as a string if you use string functions. Just keep in mind that the ***value of a byte*** is a number that you can use in calculations while a ***character byte*** is a string just like any other except it is a string of one character. For a more detailed tutorial about this subject see Section 3 in the document RobotBASIC_Networking.Pdf[57] on the RobotBASIC web site.

To illustrate the differences and the similarities between the various functions run this program:
```
s = "Test" \ ss = BuffWrite("",0,"Test")
print s;ss
print SubString(s,2,1);Buffread(s,1,1)
print SubString(s,2);Buffread(s,1,-1)
print Ascii(SubString(s,2,1));GetStrByte(s,2);BuffReadB(s,1)
print char(101);BuffwriteB("",0,101)
```

The output is
```
Test     Test
e        e
est      est
101      101      101
e        e
```

Notice how in **BuffRead()** and **BuffReadB()** we use 1 not 2 as we did in **SubString()**. This is, as explained above, because the character count in buffer functions starts with 0 not 1 as in string functions. Note how the functions can be used to return the same values.

3.5.2 Problem with Resetting the Propeller (use F11 not F10)

There is one thing you must be aware of when using the programming port (P30..31) to communicate RB with the Propeller. The programming port on the Propeller also has a line in the serial port called DTR. This line is electrically connected also to the Propeller's RESET (active low) pin. Many programs may momentarily reset the DTR line on the serial port when they acquire or release the serial port which will in turn cause the Propeller to reboot.

This can be useful or annoying depending on the situation. The Propeller Tool (PT) uses this to control resetting the Propeller during the programming process. RB can also make use of this feature to reset the Propeller when needed using the following lines

```
SetSerDTR 1
SetSerDTR 0
SetSerDTR 1
```

This can be useful to make sure that the program is restarted to guarantee a determinable sequence of communications and to synchronize the RB program with the Propeller program. However, this also can be annoying in that the moment the RB program is started or halted it will acquire or release the serial port. This will also reset the DTR line which resets the Propeller.

This is not a problem if the program is stored in the EEPROM (F11). However, if the program is stored in RAM (F10) it will be lost when the Propeller resets. This means that every time you want to modify the RB program and then execute it you will have to reprogram the Propeller before you run the program again. The problem is eliminated by using the function key F11 while in the PT IDE to program the Propeller instead of F10. That is, upload the program to the EEPROM not the RAM.

Another possible headache is if you are using the programming port and RB is running and using that port then you cannot program the Propeller since the programming port is being used and you will see the same message as in Figure 2.13. So if you are testing and forget an RB program running and try to reprogram the Propeller, an error will occur. Of course, this is easily fixed and is not much of a problem; all you have to do is stop the RB program. But it can be annoying.

The way we can avoid the above two minor problems is by using a different port to communicate RB with the Propeller. This also leaves the programming port to be used by the PST for debugging. There are other advantages to using a different port that will be explained in the next section.

3.6 Communicating RB Through the Propeller Plug (PP)

With the arrangement shown in Figure 2.4 we can program the Propeller while an RB program is still running. We can also terminate and rerun RB with programs that are in the RAM of the Propeller instead of the EEPROM. This is advantageous because EEPROMs have a limited (but large) number of times you can reprogram them. So uploading test programs to the RAM saves EEPROM cycles.

Another advantage is that now we can use the PST and RB *simultaneously* and we can display data and debugging information or other messages using both programs; this provides many possibilities. We will do this with many programs later. A third advantage is that it will facilitate moving over to a wireless setup (Chapter 9). In fact there would be no program changes to accommodate a wireless setup if we are already using a separate port.

The program Test_05.Spin will exercise this option using the Propeller Plug connected as shown in Figures 2.4 and 2.5. It is exactly the same action as in Test_04 but with the pins P0 and P1 as the Rx and Tx pins (respectively) instead of P31 and P30 which are the programming port pins.

Connect the PP as in Chapter 2 (see Figure 2.4 or 2.5, also see Figure B.3 in Appendix B) and compile and upload the Spin program *(F10 no need for F11 any longer)*. We will use Test_04.BAS to run with Test_05.Spin, however, we do need to change the value of the variable **Port** (2nd line) to be the correct port. You can use RB to ascertain this but you will need to write a small program to do so. On the other hand, the PST will give that information a lot quicker since it is already running. At the bottom of the PST window is a drop down list box (see Figure 3.2) that has a list of all the valid serial ports. Since we have two (programming port and the PP port) so there will be two numbers. One is the programming port, which we have been using so far, the other is the port connected to the PP and that is the number to which we should set the variable **Port**.

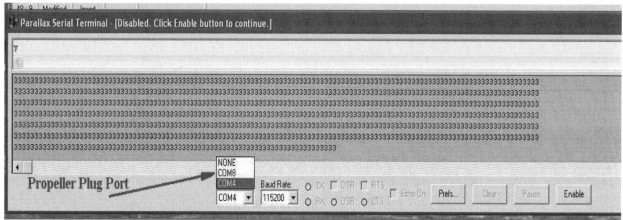

Figure 3.2: PST showing a list of available com ports.

If you prefer to use RB to determine the list of available ports use the following program:

AvailablePorts.Bas

```
//AvailablePorts.Bas
//using RB to determine available ports
SerPorts P
if P != ""
   print "Available ports are"+crlf()+P
else
   print "There are no valid serial ports"
endif
```

The only differences in Test_05.Spin from Test_04.Spin are the lines that define the constants **RB_TX** and **RB_RX** in the **Con** section of the program. Also we need to compile it with F10 instead of F11 since now we do not need to upload it to the EEPROM. We will list only the section of the program that has changes.

Test_05.Spin (only changes)

```
'Use Test_04.BAS as the companion RB program
'Use F10 to upload to RAM
CON
   _clkmode = xtal1 + pll16x
   _xinfreq = 5_000_000
   RB_TX       = 1              'use RB through the
   RB_RX       = 0              'propeller plug
   RB_BAUD     = 115200
```

3.7 Communicating With the PST and RB Simultaneously

To illustrate how both RB and the PST can communicate with the Propeller *simultaneously* we will use Test_06.Spin below. For the RB program use Test_04.Bas again. The PST will use the programming port and RB will use the PP port.

The lines in bold are what is different from Test_05.Spin. After pressing F10 in the PT IDE switch over to RB and run the program then switch over to the PST and enable it. You should now observe both the PST and RB windows scrolling the value of the pushbuttons. Press the buttons on the Propeller board and observe how the number changes on both the PST and RB.

> ⚠ You must run RB before going over to the PST because the PST will be disabled automatically if you enable it then go over to RB. This is why we may on some occasions wish to have the PST not be disabled when it loses focus; but then it will cause a problem if you forget to disable it before you try to program the Propeller. You may even sometimes forget that the PST is still holding the com port and then when you try to program the Propeller you will see the error shown in Figure 2.13 and you will think there is a big problem. Be aware of this and always check that the PST (or RB if it is using the programming port) is not still holding the port when you try to program the Propeller.

Test_06.Spin

```
'Use Test_04.BAS as the companion RB program
'Also uses the PST
'Use F10 to upload to RAM
CON
  _clkmode = xtal1 + pll16x
  _xinfreq = 5_000_000
  RB_TX    = 1              'use RB through the
  RB_RX    = 0              'propeller plug
  RB_BAUD  = 115200
  D_TX     = 30             'the PST to use the programming
  D_RX     = 31             'port
  D_BAUD   = 115200

OBJ
  RB   : "FullDuplexSerial"     'RB serial driver
  D    : "SerialMirror"         'PST serial driver

PUB Main
  dirA[23..16]~~
  RB.Start(RB_RX,RB_TX,0,RB_BAUD)     'start the serial driver for RB
  D.Start(D_RX,D_TX,0,D_BAUD)         'start the serial driver for the PST
  repeat 5
    outA[23..16] := %10101010
    waitcnt(clkfreq/4+cnt)
    outA[23..16] := !(%10101010)
    waitcnt(clkfreq/4+cnt)
    outA[23..16]~
  repeat
    outA[23..21] := inA[7..5]   'output = input
    RB.Tx(inA[7..5])            'transmit the value to RB
    D.Dec(inA[7..5])            'transmit the value to the PST
```

3.8 Summary

In this chapter we have:
- Tested the LEDs and Pushbuttons.
- Tested the serial communications between the Propeller and RB.
- Tested the serial communications between the Propeller and the PST.
- Communicated the Propeller and RB through the programming port as well as through a secondary port.
- Communicated the Propeller with RB and the PST simultaneously.
- Examined the distinctions and similarities between byte buffers and strings.
- Learnt how to avoid the problem of the Propeller resetting when using the programming port as a communication port with RB.

Basic Communications and I/O

In Chapter 3 we verified that everything is working properly and ready. We also gained some experience in programming RB to communicate with the Propeller Chip and in using the PST to display information from the Propeller simultaneously while communicating with RB. Eventually we will be creating a complex and interesting system with useful hardware and real functionality. When building complex systems the modularization principle should be followed. Whether in software or hardware it is prudent that a complex system be divided into smaller sections and each section designed and tested as a standalone system. Later when all the subsystems have been verified we can *gradually integrate* all of them together and if at any stage there is a problem we can conclude that it is most likely the *interfacing* of the subsystems which is causing the problem rather than the subsystems themselves since they have already been verified. At the design stage the various subsystems should be designed with the aim of integration always in mind. Additionally, before doing the real design, it may be necessary to *experiment* with new ideas and new methods to see how they work and gain experience in how to design them.

In keeping with this methodology, this chapter will build up a few programs with a gradually increasing complexity. The programs will serve two purposes:
  - Gain experience in creating RB and Spin programs that do some work in unison.
  - Create tools to be used for the final goal of creating a complex multifaceted system controlled by RB.

All the programs from this point onwards will always be paired-up in two languages:
  - Spin to run on the Propeller chip.
  - RobotBASIC (RB) to run on the PC.

The programs are designed to work in unison. The Spin programs *in this chapter* must be uploaded to the Propeller using F11 since we are using the programming port as the communication port too. The programs in this chapter are not complicated and therefore we will not need to use the PST for debugging. When it is time to run the system, use F11 to program the Propeller then switch to the RB IDE and run the RB program.

> (i) Before re-programming the Propeller make sure to stop any running RB program in order to release the com port.

4.1 Sending Data From RB to the Propeller

In Chapter 3 we programmed RB to receive a byte from the Propeller much like we did with the PST. However, RB is a programming language and we can do a lot more than just receive and display some numbers. We will see the full power provided by RB in later programs, but first we need to build up experience. In this section we will create an RB program to *send* data to the Propeller. We will use a GUI interface (checkboxes) to emulate 8 dipswitches. RB will read the state of the dipswitches and form a byte value and send it to the Propeller. The propeller will receive the byte and set 8 LEDs to represent the status of the 8 dipswitches on the RB GUI screen.

In the RB program, notice the use of checkboxes and how the byte to be sent is formed from the 8-bits. Also notice the use of the **SerialOut** command to send the byte. When creating the byte to be sent to the Propeller from the status of the checkboxes (lines in bold), the order of the bits is reversed to allow for the fact that the checkboxes are numbered 0 to 7 from left to right while a byte has bits 0 to 7 from right to left. This is the kind of operation best suited for programming languages. In a programming language you can do *remapping* of bits and order of incoming data and so forth using code. We will see in later programs how this concept can be useful in many situations.

Program_01.Spin

```
'Use Program_01.BAS as the companion RB program
'Use F11 to upload to EEPROM
CON
  _clkmode = xtal1 + pll16x
  _xinfreq = 5_000_000
  RB_TX    = 30
  RB_RX    = 31
  RB_BAUD  = 115200
OBJ
  RB      : "FullDuplexSerial"
PUB Main
  RB.Start(RB_RX,RB_TX,0,RB_BAUD)   'start the serial driver
  dirA[16..23]~~                    'set pins as output
  repeat                            'endless loop
    outA[23..16] := RB.RX           'assign the pins the value received from RB
```

Program_01.BAS

```
//works with Program_01.Spin
Port = 4  //change this as per your system
Main:
    setcommport Port,br115200   //set serial comms
    xystring 10,10,"Click on the Checkbox to light up the corresponding LED"
    for i=0 to 7
      AddCheckBox "DS"+i,60+20*i,40," "   //add checkboxes as bits to form the
    next                                  //number to send
    while true
       x =0
       for i=0 to 7            //form the byte from the individual bits
          if GetCheckBox("DS"+i) then x += 1<<(7-i)
              //notice the (7-i) to reverse the order
       next
       serialout x                        //send it
       xystring 240,40,"=",x,spaces(20) //also display the decimal value
    wend
end
```

4.1.1 Sending Characters, Bytes, Words, Longs and Floats with RB

In RobotBASIC there are two commands to send data through the serial port:
- **SerOut**
- **SerialOut**

The difference between the two is when sending numbers. When sending text they are the same. Each will accept a comma separated list of a combination of numbers and strings or expressions that result in numbers or a strings.

A string can either be a normal string variable or an expression that results in a string or can be a byte buffer that you have previously filled with bytes using string functions and commands or byte buffer functions and commands.

The numbers can be any numerical expression. The difference between **SerOut** and **SerialOut** is that when you send a number using **SerOut** it will be converted to its character equivalent.

So when you say
```
N = 1241
SerOut 123+6, 8, N
```

What is sent out through the serial port are the following *eight characters*:
```
"1" "2" "9" "8" "1" "2" "4" "1"
```

Notice they are characters. So in fact what is sent out are the eight bytes that have the numerical values:
```
49  50  57  56  49  50  52  49
```
since the ASCII codes for the digit "1" is 49 and "2" is 50 and so forth. **SerOut** converts numbers to their character equivalent before sending them out.

In contrast **SerialOut** sends numbers as numerical bytes without converting to text first. So if we say
```
N = 1241
SerialOut 123+6, 8, N
```

What is in fact sent out through the serial port are *three bytes*. The first one has the value 129 and the second has the value 8, as expected, but the third has the value 217.

Why 217 and not 1241? Well, 1241 is not a byte number. Bytes go from 0 to 255. Since the number 1241 (0x04D9 in hex) is two bytes (04 and D9) then the Least Significant Byte (LSB) D9 (217 in decimal) will be the one sent.

So **SerialOut** will send numbers as bytes not as text and any number bigger than 255 will be truncated to a byte value by ignoring any bytes other than the LSB.

> In RobotBASIC we use the prefix **0x** to designate a hexadecimal number, and **0%** to designate a binary number. In Spin the prefix **$** (no 0 before) is used to designate a hex and **%** (no 0 before) to designate binary numbers. In RB 0xA5 = 0%10100101 = 165. In Spin $A5 = %1010_0101 = 165.

So how do we send a number bigger than a byte? You can either send it as a text number (**SerOut**) or you can send it out as individual bytes. For example if you know it is only two bytes (Word) then we decide to send the Least Significant Byte First (LSBF)
```
N=1241
Serialout N, N >> 8
```

Or we can send it the Most Significant Byte First (MSBF)
```
N=1241
SerialOut N >> 8, N
```

If it is a Long (4 bytes) then we can send it as above (LSBF)

```
N=1241
For I=0 to 3
   SerialOut GetByte(N,I)
Next
```

Or MSBF

```
N=1241
For I=3 to 0
   SerialOut GetByte(N,I)
Next
```

Or as a 32-bit Integer

```
N=1241
SerialOut BuffWrite("",0,N)
```

Notice the functions **GetByte()** and **BuffWrite()**. The **BuffWrite()** statement above created a 4 byte buffer and that is what was sent. In the case of **N** being 1241 the buffer bytes take on the values as follows

```
D9   04   00   00
```

The 1st byte is D9 which is the LSByte in the number. The number 1241 when taken as a 32-bit number (4 bytes) is 0x000004D9. Notice how the LSByte is the first byte in the buffer. We will see an example of this later and we will see how the Propeller can receive these 4 bytes and recreate the number as needed.

> The format where the 1st byte in the buffer is the LSB of the number is called the Little-Endian format and is what is used in RB as well as the Propeller to store Long Integer numbers. For a more detailed tutorial about this subject see Section 3 in the document RobotBASIC_Networking.Pdf[57] on the RobotBASIC web site.

What do we do if the number is a floating point value? This issue is not of much importance as far as the Propeller is concerned since the Propeller is an integer microcontroller and has no floating point format as its native format. Nevertheless the Propeller is able to perform floating point math if needed with the addition of some PASM code.

RobotBASIC uses 64-bit (8 bytes) floating point numbers. The Propeller however uses 32-bit floating point numbers. RB can send a floating point out as a 32-bit or as a 64-bit IEEE Little-Endian format using the appropriate function:

```
N=34.678
SerialOut BuffWrite("",0,N)      //send as a 64-bit
SerialOut BuffWriteF32("",0,N)   //send as a 32-bit
```

Also see the functions and commands: **BuffPrintB**, **BuffPrintT** and **PutStrByte()**.

4.1.2 Extracting Numbers from a Received Buffer

In Section 4.1.1 we saw how to insert numbers in a buffer and send it. When we receive data from the Propeller we have to know what we received. If the data received is all characters (text) then we use the buffer just as a string value. If the data is a combination of text and numbers we will need to know two things:
  ➢ The order of the data.
  ➢ The type of the data.

So we need to know where text starts and ends in the buffer and also where the numbers are and what type (byte, word, long, float etc.). Some buffer functions you can use to extract numbers are: **BuffRead()**, **BuffReadB()**, **BuffReadI()**, **BuffReadF()**, **BuffReadF32()**. Also See **GetStrByte()**. We can use buffer functions or we can use string functions. For extracting numbers it is best to use buffer functions and for extracting characters you can use either.

⚠️With buffer functions the byte counts starts with 0, so the first byte is byte 0. With string functions the character count starts with 1, so the first character is character 1. For a more detailed tutorial about this subject see Section 3 in the document RobotBASIC_Networking.Pdf[57] on the RobotBASIC web site.

4.2 Receiving Data with a GUI Display

In this project the RB program will again **receive** a byte with the first three bits representing the status of the pushbuttons on the Propeller side. The program will then set three checkboxes to display the status of those buttons. So we have a system where the status of buttons pushed on the Propeller side is represented **visually** on the screen of the RB program. Remember the pushbuttons are Active-Low.

Program_02.Spin

```
'Use Program_02.BAS as the companion RB program
'Use F11 to upload to EEPROM
CON
  _clkmode = xtal1 + pll16x
  _xinfreq = 5_000_000
  RB_TX    = 30
  RB_RX    = 31
  RB_BAUD  = 115200
OBJ
  RB     : "FullDuplexSerial"
PUB Main
  RB.Start(RB_RX,RB_TX,0,RB_BAUD)
  repeat
    RB.TX(inA[7..5])            'send the byte to RB
```

Program_02.Bas

```
//works with Program_02.Spin
Port = 4  //change this as per your system
Main:
    setcommport Port,br115200   //set serial comms
    xystring 10,10,"Press the buttons on the Propeller and see the "+\
                "corresponding Checkbox change"
    for i=0 to 2
      AddCheckBox "LED"+i,60+20*i,40," "   //add checkboxes as bits
    next
    while true
      CheckSerBuffer x \ if !x then continue //if no byte loop
      serin s                      //get bytes
      x = GetStrByte(s,Length(s))  //get the value of the last byte
      for i=0 to 2
        SetCheckBox "LED"+i,GetBit(x,i)
      next
    wend
end
```

4.2.1 Serial Streaming Speeds and Buffering

Let's examine an important issue with Program_02.Bas. The Propeller program is sending bytes out at a very high rate. This may be a very large amount of bytes representing a current state of the pushbuttons. Now if RB is reading these bytes while you push the buttons it will be a while before the new state is reflected on the RB screen since all the previous state bytes are still being processed. That is why the line in bold is used. This will get the value of the **last** byte in the buffer after reading the whole buffer content using **SerIn**. This means that rather than read the bytes one by one as they arrive, we read the entire buffer and ignore all bytes other than the last one, so the status will be updated quicker.

Now try the RB program below with the same Spin program above (Program_02.Spin)

Program_02_B.BAS

```
//works with Program_02.Spin
Port = 4  //change this as per your system
Main:
    setcommport Port,br115200   //set serial comms
    xystring 10,10,"Press the buttons on the Propeller and see the "+\
                   "corresponding checkbox change"
    for i=0 to 2
       AddCheckBox "LED"+i,60+20*i,40," "   //add checkboxes as bits
    next
    clearserbuffer //clear any previous data
    while true
       serin s \if !length(s) then continue  //get bytes
       for i=1 to length(s)
          x = GetStrByte(s,i)  //get the value of the byte
          for i=0 to 2
             SetCheckBox "LED"+i,GetBit(x,i)
          next
       next
    wend
end
```

It fails; the pushbutton status is not updated correctly. This is because the buffer is inundated due to the very large amounts of data being sent and the program is not processing them in time.

One way to resolve this is to insert a delay in the Spin program to slow down the data sending. In the Spin code add this line right after the line in bold and run it again with Program_02_B.BAS

```
WaitCnt(ClkFreq/100+cnt)  'delay 10 milliseconds
```

Now the program works and the states of the pushbuttons are updated on the RB screen correctly. You can see that with a slight change of the receiving program you may not obtain the desired results. You have to take into account situations such as these where data transfer occurs *asynchronously* and the rates of transmission and reception are different.

4.2.2 Hand Shaking

A much better solution than to arbitrarily slow down the transfer rate (as we did above) is to use a handshaking mechanism. Rather than leaving the Propeller to screech out bytes without consideration for the receiver, we should let the Propeller send the status of the pushbuttons *only when requested*. How do we do this? The method we will use in the following programs is called *Hand Shaking*. There are many ways to implement a hand shaking protocol. We will develop an effective one in later chapters. In Section 4.3 we will use a simple method of *orchestrating* the data exchange between the Propeller and RB by having the Propeller wait for a byte to come in from RB and only when the byte arrives does the Propeller send the status of the pushbuttons.

As you will see, this method allows the transfer rate to be as fast as possible without an arbitrary delay that might be too long or too short. If it is too long then we do not have an optimal rate. If it is too short then, as you have seen above, the system will eventually fail due to buffer overflow. This method does have a limitation, however, that we will discuss later.

4.2.3 Data Remapping

Another issue of importance is the fact that as wired on the PDB (or PPDB) the pushbuttons are Active-Low. This means that if the button is **not** pushed its pin will be high and its corresponding LED on the RB screen will be on and vice versa. If you prefer an Active-High button there are three ways to achieve one:

1. Change the hardware
   Changing the wiring of the pushbuttons to a pull-down format will change the button to be active-high (or you can use normally closed pushbuttons). However, this is not usually an option (e.g. in the PPDB).

2. Change the Spin program
   This is simply achieved by inverting the bits before sending the byte value to RB by changing the bold line in the spin code to: (notice the bold **!**):

   ```
   RB.TX(!inA[7..5])
   ```

   The ! operator is called the Bit Invert operator. It inverts bits in a number so that any bits that are 1 will become a 0 and vice versa. So this will then make the bit corresponding to the button become 1 when it is pushed and 0 when not.

   In situations where you are communicating with a firmware which you cannot or do not know how to change, this option becomes as unwieldy as the one above.

3. Change the RB program
   The easiest and most attainable method is to use RB to invert the bits before displaying them by changing the bold line in the RB program to (notice the bold ~):

   ```
   x = ~GetStrByte(s,Length(s))   //get the value of the last one
   ```

   The ~ operator is the RB equivalent of the ! in Spin. It is the operator that inverts the bits of a number.

Options 2 and 3 highlight a very important point. With this kind of project, **software** makes it possible to overcome certain hardware or firmware limitations by adding some **data remapping** in code. We will see how this can be useful in even more difficult situations later.

For now note that by remapping, you can manipulate the data received from hardware in any way that is necessary. Hardware limitations or constraints can be overcome using **software-data-remapping** of bits and bytes or using mathematical formulas to convert values (see Chapter 7.3); for example when the hardware sends a temperature value in Fahrenheit and you need to display it in Celsius.

4.2.4 An Example of Data Remapping

We are currently using the PDB to test the programs. As we have wired the pushbuttons (Figure 2.5) and viewing the PDB from the left side as shown in the picture, we have them from right to left, wired to P7..P5. So the rightmost button is P7. If you look at Program_02.Spin you will notice that the **inA[7.. 5]** is reading the pushbuttons with the right button (again viewing the board from the left side of the picture) as bit 2 (third bit) in the formed byte. When RB receives the byte and sets the checkboxes it sets them in the reverse order. That is the left most checkbox is now corresponding to P5's (bit 0) pushbutton and so on. The final outcome is – if you are viewing the PDB from the left side of the picture in Figure 2.5 – the checkboxes on the RB screen will also be the correct orientation and a true representation of the buttons as viewed on the PDB.

All this is confusing at first glance, but if you just consider the issue for a few seconds you can gain appreciation for how **data remapping** of the bits' order can make it easy to rectify some problems. Now consider this (just for a bit more confusion), the PPDB as wired in Figure 2.4, P7 is the leftmost button (opposite to the PDB). So if you are using the PPDB to run the Program_02 pair, the display on RB's screen will be in reverse order and the button on the right is paired with the checkbox on the left. This is also the case if you were to view the PDB from the right side of the picture as displayed in Figure 2.5.

Now think what can we do to rectify this? Before reading on, take a moment and think about what you can do. Do not peak. Which option do you prefer from among the following three options?

1. Rewire the PPDB

2. Change the bold line in the Spin code
    ```
    RB.TX(inA[7..5])            'send the byte to RB
    ```
    to
    ```
    RB.TX(inA[5..7])            'send the byte to RB
    ```

3. Change the bold line in the RB code
    ```
    SetCheckBox "LED"+i,GetBit(x,i)
    ```
    to
    ```
    SetCheckBox "LED"+i,GetBit(x,2-i)
    ```

Can you see how easy it is to change things in *code* as opposed to hardware? Option 1 is obviously prohibitive. Options 2 and 3 are equally easy and in this particular situation they are equally possible to do. However, option 2 may not be possible in certain cases where it is *difficult* or *cumbersome* (e.g. inside a robot). In some cases it may even be impossible to *reprogram* the Propeller. In these situations the easiest and most attainable option is number 3.

ℹ️ If you are interfacing RB to a system of hardware and firmware, RB makes it very feasible to *remap* data to be suitable for the end user. You can do this in both directions. You can remap data coming from a user interface to make it suitable for the hardware before you send it out. You can remap data coming from the hardware before you present it to the end user (See Chapter 7).

This remapping is a powerful concept and is one of the major reasons for using a PC system as an interface between the user and hardware-firmware systems. We will explore this concept further when it is time to do more useful things later on. For now keep in mind that it is a lot easier to make changes on the RB side of things and that making the hardware perform in a different way is a lot easier using an RB program than it is to do so by modifying the hardware or reprogramming the firmware (often neither of these is an available option).

4.3 Sending and Receiving Data with a GUI Display

Program_03.Bas is a combination of both the previous programs with a slight change. Rather than using checkboxes to represent the status of the pushbuttons from the PDB we use red circles to *simulate* LEDs. So when a pushbutton on the PDB is pressed/released it will turn on/off an LED on the RB screen. Remember the buttons are Active-Low, so we will use bit inversion within the RB program to make it act is if it were Active-high (i.e. using option 3 in Section 4.2.2).

The program will read the status of the checkboxes on the RB interface and send that to the PDB which will set its LEDs accordingly and then send the status of its pushbuttons to RB. When RB receives the byte it will represent the status with simulated LEDs on its screen but after inverting the bits to make the pushbuttons appear to be active-high.

This sequence of interaction is a way of handshaking and will overcome the buffer swamping effect seen in Section 4.2.1. The Propeller receives the byte to set the LEDs as soon as RB is ready to send it and RB will wait for the byte representing the pushbuttons to arrive before it sends the next byte. This way the data sending and receiving is *synchronized* and is optimal.

Notice the Spin program uses the **Rx** method for receiving the byte. This method will wait forever for a byte to come in. This is exactly what we need *at this stage* since we want the Propeller to not send its byte until it has received a byte from RB. We shall see later why this might not be a good method, but for now it is sufficient for our current project.

Program_03.Spin

```
'Use Program_03.BAS as the companion RB program
'Use F11 to upload to EEPROM
CON
  _clkmode = xtal1 + pll16x
  _xinfreq = 5_000_000
  RB_TX    = 30
  RB_RX    = 31
  RB_BAUD  = 115200
OBJ
  RB     : "FullDuplexSerial"
PUB Main
  RB.Start(RB_RX,RB_TX,0,RB_BAUD)
  dirA[16..23]~~
  repeat
     outA[23..16] := RB.RX     ' receive the byte and set the LEDs
     RB.TX(inA[7..5])          ' read the buttons and send the states
```

Program_03.Bas

```
//works with Program_03.Spin
Port = 4  //change this as per your system
Main:
    setcommport Port,br115200   //set serial comms
    xystring 10,10,"Click on the checkbox to light up the corresponding LED"
    xystring 10,70,"Press the buttons on the Propeller and see the "+\
                "corresponding checkbox change"
    for i=0 to 7
       AddCheckBox "DS"+i,60+20*i,40," "    //add checkboxes as bits to form the
    next                                     //number to send
    delay 2000  //wait for the Propeller to be ready
    while true
       x =0
       for i=0 to 7    //form the byte from the individual bits
          if GetCheckBox("DS"+i) then x += 1<<(7-i)
       next
       serialout x  \ xystring 240,40,"=",x,spaces(20)
       repeat
          CheckSerBuffer x //wait for data in the buffer
       until x
       serin s
       x = ~GetStrByte(s,Length(s)) //value of the last byte and invert it
       for i=0 to 2
          if GetBit(x,i)
             circlewh 60+i*40,100,30,30,red,red   //simulate LED on
          else
             circlewh 60+i*40,100,30,30,red       //Simulate LED off
          endif
       next
    wend
end
```

4.3.1 An Exercise

If you are currently using the PPDB instead of the PDB then do you know how to change the RB program to make the simulated LEDs on the RB screen correspond in orientation to the order of the pushbuttons on the PPDB (as viewed in Figure 2.4)? Do you know how to do it in the Spin program? (See Section 4.2.3).

Also, notice how the LEDs on the PPDB (as viewed from the right side of Figure 2.4) are also in reverse order to the orientation of the checkboxes on the RB screen. Can you rectify this in either the RB or Spin programs?

The Solution

Change the bold line in the listing of the RB program to

```
if GetBit(x,2-i)
```

or change the bold line in the Spin listing to

```
RB.TX(inA[5..7])         ' read the buttons and send the states
```

Change the highlighted line in the listing of the RB program to

```
if GetCheckBox("DS"+i) then x += 1<<(i)
```

or change the highlighted line in the Spin listing to

```
outA[16..23] := RB.RX    ' receive the byte and set the LEDs
```

4.3.2 An Exercise in Troubleshooting Weird Problems

Program_03_B.Bas below is a modified version of Program_03.BAS (bold and highlighted lines). Run it with Program_02.Spin. Now try to click on the checkboxes. Observe the LEDs on the Propeller. They are responding normally. Now try to press the pushbuttons on the Propeller board. What is going on? Why is the status not being reflected on the RB screen?

Now do this:

Press a pushbutton on the PDB and keep it pressed. While it is pressed observe that the RB LED has *not* changed accordingly. Now while the PDB button is still pressed, click any of the checkboxes on the RB side. The LED on the PDB side should respond to the checkbox change, *but* now the LED on the RB screen has also changed to reflect the pushbutton status. Why is it working now? Try again, push another button on the PDB; still, no change. Now again click on a checkbox. The LED representing the pushed button lights up. Again it worked only after you clicked on a checkbox but not before. Why?

What is different about the program? Study Program_03_B.BAS and try to figure out why this version of the program is not updating the PDB buttons' state except after you change the state of the checkboxes.

Do not look at the solution below until you have tried to figure out the problem. This is a good exercise. Sometimes the best way to learn is by making mistakes.

Program_03_B.Bas

```
//Program_03_B.Bas
//works with Program_03.Spin
//faulty program as an exercise in problem solving
Port = 4  //change this as per your system
Main:
    setcommport Port,br115200    //set serial comms
    xystring 10,10,"Click on the checkbox to light up the corresponding LED"
    xystring 10,70,"Press the buttons on the Propeller and see the "+\
               "corresponding checkbox change"
    for i=0 to 7
       AddCheckBox "DS"+i,60+20*i,40," "    //add checkboxes as bits to form the
    next                                    //number to send
    delay 2000 //wait for the Propeller to be ready
    n= 0
    while true
       x =0
       for i=0 to 7   //form the byte from the individual bits
          if GetCheckBox("DS"+i) then x += 1<<(7-i)
```

```
         next
         if x != n  //if current states are changed then send the new state
            serialout x  \ xystring 240,40,"=",x,spaces(20)
            n = x  //store current state
         endif
         CheckSerBuffer x //wait for data in the buffer
         if !x then continue
         serin s
         x = ~GetStrByte(s,Length(s))  //value of the last byte and invert it
         for i=0 to 2
            if GetBit(x,i)
               circlewh 60+i*40,100,30,30,red,red  //simulate LED on
            else
               circlewh 60+i*40,100,30,30,red      //Simulate LED off
            endif
         next
      wend
end
```

Comment out the lines in bold (only the bold not the highlighted ones) and run the program again. It should work now. So the problem is definitely with the change we made. What do these changes achieve? The changes make it such that the status of the checkboxes is only sent to the Propeller when there is a change. At first glance, this sounds like a good idea. It is efficient. Only send data if there is a need. Nevertheless, this causes a problem. Remember that we have made it so that the PDB only sends the status of the pushbuttons *after* it has received the status of the checkboxes. So if there is no change in the checkboxes, RB never sends it and thus never receives the status of the pushbuttons even when they have changed.

For the sake of our *handshaking protocol* where the Propeller is controlled by RB and RB has to send a byte to the Propeller, before it sends its byte we must always ensure that RB sends a byte to let the Propeller send its. This way whenever the pushbuttons' status changes it will still be sent even though the status of the checkboxes is not changed.

> (i) This is another instance of how a small seemingly minor change or difference in design can cause perplexing oddities. Debugging hardware and its firmware is a difficult process. This is why it should be the aim to make all changes in software not in firmware or hardware. Once the combination of hardware is fixed and the firmware is working properly, all changes to make the system work in different ways should ideally be made in software where it is easy to effect changes and to debug problems.

4.4 Summary

In this chapter we have:
- ❑ Seen how to send data from an RB program to the propeller.
- ❑ Seen how to send strings, characters, bytes, words, longs and floats.
- ❑ Seen Commands and functions for extracting data from and inserting data into a byte buffer.
- ❑ Played with some simple GUI components and graphics animation.
- ❑ Seen how handshaking eliminates buffer swamping and helps make the sending/receiving process optimally synchronized.
- ❑ Seen how data remapping is a powerful way to manipulate data to correct for both the hardware and firmware shortcomings.
- ❑ Seen how small changes can cause weird problems.

Multitasking & Parallel Processing

In Chapter 4 we gained experience in communicating RB and the Propeller and we developed a system for controlling the process by having RB initiate the interaction. The Spin program repeatedly waits for RB to send information. Once the data from the PC is received, the Propeller responds by using the received information to set or interrogate certain hardware and then sends its information. The RB program uses that information and goes on to send the next information. The process repeats ad infinitum. This is an excellent procedure in that we have an orderly system with no swamping and buffer overflow due to disparate and asynchronous transfer rates and processing speeds.

However, we do have a slight glitch with this methodology. The system is fine if the Spin program does not need to do anything else other than wait for RB to send its data. Consider these lines of code from Program_03.Spin:

```
repeat
    outA[23..16] := RB.RX     ' receive the byte and set the LEDS
    RB.TX(inA[7..5])          ' read the buttons and send the states
```

RB.RX is the method used to receive a byte of data from RB. This method will continue trying to receive the byte *forever*. The Spin program will not proceed to the next statement until the byte is received. This, of course is exactly what we want since the next statement sends data and we did not want this to take place until RB is ready to receive it. But, this becomes a problem if we want the Spin program to do other things in the background while it is waiting for the byte from RB to arrive. Unfortunately, with this strategy we cannot do this.

The concept of doing things in the background while waiting for other things to happen is called *Multitasking*. Another related concept is called *Parallel Processing* which is another way to do multiple tasks at the same time or what *appears to be* at the same time. Consider if we wanted Program_03.Spin to also blink an LED at the same time it is waiting to receive the byte from RB. With the current program this is not possible, since the **RB.RX** method will wait for the byte and there is no way to go off to do something else occasionally.

In this chapter we will examine how we can achieve this multitasking action. There are three ways we can achieve multitasking in a program:
  ➢ Interrupts
  ➢ Polling
  ➢ Parallel Processing

5.1 Multitasking Using Interrupts

This option is not available for us using the Propeller and Spin. The Propeller is a parallel processing microcontroller, which, as we will see later, is a much better option than interrupts. So interrupts will not be much use in projects using the Propeller (and a good thing too). Nonetheless, this is an option that is widely used with other microcontrollers and may be something you would like to use in other projects. RobotBASIC is able to perform ***Interrupt-Driven*** processing, and we will use it to learn briefly about this option using RB programs. Even so, despite the fact that RB makes it easy to learn about interrupt-driven programming, it is a complex issue and is hard to achieve ***real*** multitasking with it. You are much better off using the Propeller, which is an amazing technology that makes it painless to achieve ***real*** multitasking without having to acquire a PhD in computer science before you do so.

What exactly is an interrupt? Well, as the name implies, it is a signal that occurs while a program is performing a task that forces the program to branch to a particular place in code memory and execute some action, then go back to where it was when it was interrupted to proceed where it left off. The interrupt can be any one of a variety of things. It can be the press of a button, or the arrival of data on a serial port, or the tick of a clock. In microcontrollers, for example, it can be the change of state (e.g. high to low) on an I/O pin, or the overflow of a register, or a transition on an encoder, and the like.

This is actually the way all microprocessors and microcontrollers have been achieving multitasking up until the advent of multi-cored processors not too long ago. We will not delve into this now antiquated, yet ubiquitous, methodology other than to see it in action because RB makes it very simple to do so.

In fact, interrupt operation is not ***really*** multitasking. It just appears to be so due to the speed of processing achievable with microcontrollers and processors. In reality the processor is only doing one task at a time, since while off attending to the interruption the main task it was executing is halted. Nevertheless, if attending to the interruption takes only a few lines of code, the main task will appear to have never been halted. But since the action carried out in response to the interruption has been accomplished along with the actions in the main process then both appear to us mere humans as if they were executed simultaneously.

Compare this to the human brain. The human brain is capable of true multitasking in that it can attend to the eyes and the muscles in your arm and hand while also still making your heart beat and receive information from your ears and nose.

5.1.1 RobotBASIC Simulation of a Microcontroller

Before going on to examine how RB interrupts work, let's have a look at an RB program that simulates something you can do with a microcontroller. Let's say we have a microcontroller that blinks an LED at a particular on/off duration:

Blinker_01.Bas

```
i=0 \ duration = 500 \ data clr;white,red
t = timer()
while true
    circlewh 10,10,30,30,red,clr[i]
    delay duration \ i = !i
    //if timer()-t > duration then i = !i \ t=timer()
wend
```

This program works as desired and blinks an LED on for 500 ms and off for 500. Try changing the duration. For now ignore the commented bold line.

In fact the program is faulty:
1. It does not account for the time it takes to execute code. So it is not really at the desired rate. To verify this run Blinker_01_B.Bas (see below). After about a minute or so the ***perceived*** count of seconds as counted by the number of blinks will start to lag behind the ***actual*** lapsed time in seconds. The reason is that the perceived

time as counted by the number of blinks does not take into account the time it took to execute the code for the loop and for the counting and so forth. This takes very little time of course and if the duration was larger you may not even see any discrepancy for a long time. The shorter the duration the quicker you will see a lag. Try changing the 200 to 100 (in Blinker_01_B.Bas) and see what happens, also change it to 700 and see what happens. In summary, this method of counting time is faulty but works for slow rates and for a low count.

2. The real problem however, is that while the program, hence the processor, is executing the delay statement it cannot do anything else. The delay duration is just wasted time.

Blinker_01_B.Bas
```
i=0 \ duration = 200 \ data clr;white,red
t = timer() \ n=0
while true
    circlewh 10,10,30,30,red,clr[i]
    delay duration \ i = !i
    n++ \ xystring 10,300,n*duration/1000;(timer()-t)/1000
wend
```

We can solve both problems in Blinker_01.Bas by commenting out the highlighted line and un-commenting the bold line. With this change we are using a timer so that the LED is blinked at the right rate which is not affected by the time it took to execute other lines of code. Also since the program does not sit in a ***delay***, which does nothing else other than count time, we can now do other things inside the loop. For example with this method we can now blink other LEDs at different rates (see Blinker_02.Bas), while with the previous version we would not have been able to do so.

Blinker_02.Bas
```
Main:
  data clrs;white,red,white,green,white,yellow
  data rates;200,500,1000
  data states;0,0,0
  data timers;timer(),timer(),timer()
  while true
     for i=0 to 2
        circlewh 10+100*i,10,30,30,clrs[i*2+1],clrs[states[i]+i*2]
        if timer()-timers[i] > rates[i]
            states[i] = !states[i]
            timers[i]=timer()
        endif
     next
  wend
End
```

5.1.2 Using Interrupts in RobotBASIC

Now let's see how an interrupt may be used. Say there is a pushbutton that when pushed the program Blinker_02.Bas should toggle the color of the LED between blue and red. The bold and highlighted lines in Blinker_03.Bas (see below) are the new lines added to implement the action.

Notice that the bold lines constitute what is called the ***interrupt handler***; code that will be executed whenever the interrupt occurs. The handler has to do certain ***initialization*** tasks, then the ***work*** it needs to do, and before returning it must do certain ***finalization*** tasks. In a microcontroller the initialization tasks are to, for instance, disable further interrupts, clear certain flags, save the current program counters, and stack pointers and so forth. The finalization tasks are to update registers and re-enable interrupts reinstate the program counter and pop the stacks and such. With RB, initialization and finalization tasks (but nowhere as complicated) are also necessary as explained in the RobotBASIC help file. Also, it is necessary that an interrupt handler be brief and to only have a small amount of code to be executed. Otherwise the interruption will be too long and the multitasking ***illusion*** would be lost.

Blinker_03.Bas

```
Main:
    addbutton "Blue",10,60
    onButton bHandler
    data clrs;white,red,white,green,white,yellow
    data rates;200,500,1000
    data states;0,0,0
    data timers;timer(),timer(),timer()
    while true
        for i=0 to 2
            circlewh 10+100*i,10,30,30,clrs[i*2+1],clrs[states[i]+i*2]
            if timer()-timers[i] > rates[i]
                states[i] = !states[i]
                timers[i]=timer()
            endif
        next
    wend
End
bHandler:
    lb = LastButton()    //initialization
    if lb == "Blue"
        renamebutton lb,"Red"   \ clrs[1] = blue
    elseif lb == "Red"
        renamebutton lb,"Blue"  \ clrs[1] = red
    endif
    onButton bHandler    //finalization
return
```

It is important to note that the above seems all too easy. This is because RobotBASIC is an excellent language that enables doing such things easily. However, with microprocessors and microcontrollers achieving interrupt handling is not an easy or trivial task. There are numerous considerations and obstacles that can make interrupts fail if not designed and coded correctly. Additionally, in the programs above, RB did scads of housekeeping for you in the background, alleviating the need for you the programmer to have to do all those intricate and confusing details. On the other hand with a microcontroller you have to attend to all these details yourself.

In any case, we will not use this method with the Propeller chip since there is no need for interrupts due to its ability to do *real* multitasking without having to resort to the illusion of one. If you opt to use another microcontroller, then you will need to learn about its interrupt capabilities and how to program for them. If your processor does not support interrupts, then you need to consider using another one. It will not be easy to achieve viable multitasking without an effective interrupt mechanism.

5.2 Multitasking Using Polling

The second method for achieving multitasking is yet another illusion. Polling is the action of occasionally glancing over to see if something else other than the task at hand needs attending to. Think of *polling as a self-imposed interrupt*. Imagine you are working on your computer and are typing something. Your work requires that you answer emails when they arrive. If you have setup your email program to sound a bell whenever an email arrives, you have an interrupt. However if you do not have that ability then you can elect to, either regularly or whenever you feel like it, stop your typing and go over to the email program to check if there is an email.

The polling mechanism can be fine if every time you go to check for an email there happens to be one and moreover, it has not been sitting there for too long. If you frequently go to check and there is no email then you are wasting too much time. If you go there too seldom and emails pile up or you lose certain ones because you did not attend to them on time or they sit there for too long, then again you are not functioning correctly.

Interrupts are in fact the optimal method for this kind of multitasking in that you only abandon the task at hand when emails arrives and do not waste time checking when there are none. Also with interrupts you will never miss an email due to not going there in time to check if one has arrived. Polling is not an efficient mechanism for handling time-critical and frequent interruptions. However, it is an option that you can use and in many situations it is an adequate strategy and is easy to implement.

5.2.1 Polling in RobotBASIC

In fact, in Blinker_03.Bas in Section 5.1.2 we used polling. Whenever we executed these lines

```
if timer()-timers[i] > rates[i]
    states[i] = !states[i]
    timers[i]=timer()
endif
```

We *polled the time*. We stopped the normal flow of the main program and checked to see if the stopwatch timers have become more than the allotted period and if they were, we entered into the body of the if-block and executed the desired work. If the timer was not yet elapsed the if-block was skipped.

This is exactly what polling is; in this case we are polling the timer. Another thing we did in the program was to use interrupts to handle the button pushes. Blinker_04.Bas below shows how to implement polling instead of interrupts to handle the button push.

Blinker_04.Bas

```
Main:
  addbutton "Blue",10,60
  data clrs;white,red,white,green,white,yellow
  data rates;200,500,1000
  data states;0,0,0
  data timers;timer(),timer(),timer()
  while true
    for i=0 to 2
       circlewh 10+100*i,10,30,30,clrs[i*2+1],clrs[states[i]+i*2]
       if timer()-timers[i] > rates[i]
           states[i] = !states[i]
           timers[i]=timer()
       endif
       lb = LastButton()
       if lb == "Blue"
           renamebutton lb,"Red" \ clrs[1] = blue
       elseif lb == "Red"
           renamebutton lb,"Blue" \ clrs[1] = red
       endif
    next
  wend
End
```

5.2.2 Polling on the Propeller Chip

Let's now see how we can implement polling with Spin on the Propeller Chip. Just as in Blinker_04.Bas, we will make Blinker_04.SPIN blink three LEDs on P23..P21 at different rates, we will also use the pushbutton on P5. However, we cannot change the colors of the LEDs on the Propeller. Instead, if the button is pressed the P23 LED will stop blinking and the P18 LED will blink in its place at the same rate until the button is released.

Blinker_04.Spin

```
'No companion RB program
'Use F10 to upload to RAM
CON
  _clkmode = xtal1 + pll16x
  _xinfreq = 5_000_000

Dat
  ratesV long 200,500,1000  'blinking rates in milliseconds
  Pins   byte 23,22,21      'pin used for LEDs

Var
  long rates[3],timers[3]

PUB Main|i
  dirA[16..23]~~           'set pins as output
  repeat i from 0 to 2
    rates[i] := ratesV[i] * (clkfreq/1000) 'establish the delay interval in ms
    timers[i] := cnt                       'initialize the timer

  repeat
    if inA[5]              'if NOT button pushed
      Pins[0] := 23        'blink LED on P23
      outA[18]~
    else
      Pins[0] := 18        'if pushed then blink LED on P18
      outA[23]~
    repeat i from 0 to 2   'check time out for the blinking
      if cnt-timers[i] > rates[i]
        !outA[Pins[i]]
        Timers[i] := cnt 'reset the timer
```

5.2.3 Counting Time in Spin

The algorithmic logic of Blinker_04.Spin is very similar to Blinker_04.Bas except for the code in bold. Notice how we obtain the timer in Spin. In RB we used the function **Timer()** which returns the current timer status in *milliseconds*. In Spin the register **cnt** accomplishes a *similar* thing except that it returns the current timer status in *ticks of the clock of the Propeller*.

Every time the Propeller's clock ticks the register **cnt** is incremented by 1. We never really need to know what the value in it is. However, at a particular time we can save the value currently in it (**t := cnt**). Later we can subtract the saved value from the current value of **cnt** and compare it to another value (**if cnt-t > x**) to check if a certain period of time has elapsed.

The snag is what should this compare value **x** be. Since **cnt** is incremented by one every time the clock ticks then if we know how many times the clock ticks per second or millisecond or microsecond we can use that rate and multiply it by the required interval.

If the clock ticks, say, at the rate of **n** ticks per second then if we want a delay of 1 second then we use **n** instead of **x**. If we want 200 milliseconds we would use **200*(n/1000)**. Why **n/1000**? Well, since if it ticks at **n** ticks a second then in 1/1000 of a second it will obviously tick n/1000 times. So if we want 200 milliseconds then we will need **200*(n/1000)** ticks. If we want 33 microseconds then we use **33*(n/1000000)** ticks instead of **x**.

Integer Multiplication Overflow

There is one problem to consider. The Propeller performs 32-bit integer math. So if you say 500*n/1000 you may not get the same value as when you say **500*(n/1000)**.

In normal math the two expressions are the same and you *should* get the same answer. However when you are limited to integer math with limited resolution then there is always the problem with *multiplication overflow*. Therefore, if **n** is large enough to cause a multiplication overflow then **500*n/1000** is not the same as **500*(n/1000)**. The first expression will do the multiplication first then the division. However the multiplication will cause an overflow and when the division occurs it takes place on a wrong number that is the result of the overflowed multiplication. In the second format we only do the multiplication on the result of the division which was forced to take place first by the parenthesis. Division cannot result in an overflow (only underflow which results in 0). So if **n** is not smaller than the number you divide it by then the second format will always result in the right answer while the first format *can* result in the wrong answer.

Determining the Clock Frequency

How do we know what is **n**? There are three ways:
1. You know the frequency of the clock. Normally for the Propeller this is 80_000_000 ticks per second (80 MHz). So use this number. For Z milliseconds use **if (cnt-t) > Z*80_000**, for Z microseconds use **if (cnt-t) > Z*80**.
2. If you use a different clock frequency you do not want to have to change the value you used all over your program. Instead, declare some constants in your program. For instance **MilliSecs = 80_000** and **MicroSecs = 80**. If we need a period of Z milliseconds we use **if (cnt-t) > Z*MilliSecs** and for Z microseconds we use **if (cnt-t) > Z*MicroSecs.**
3. If the Propeller is running at a different rate which you do not know a priori then you cannot use the above two options. However, Spin provides a constant that is always set to the correct clock frequency. It is called **ClkFreq**. So for Z milliseconds we would use **if (cnt-t) > Z*(ClkFreq/1000)** and for Z microseconds **if (cnt-t) > Z*(ClkFreq/1000_000)**. Notice we have to do the division first as discussed above.

> (i) Polling is a useful option and as you see, it works fine for situations like the above. Nonetheless, you have to be careful with timing and you have to insure that time critical operations are not missed before they are polled.

5.3 True Multitasking with Parallel Processing

Interrupts and Polling are functional methods and are what has been traditionally used in numerous viable systems; they work well. Polling is simple but not easy to make optimal. Interrupts is the better of the two methods but is hard and complex to program.

The third alternative, Parallel Processing, is in fact the most effective alternative. With parallel processing we can achieve *real* multitasking instead of the *illusion* of it. In the past this option has been expensive and complicated and only available to few systems. With the advent of the most innovative microcontroller, the Propeller Chip, all this has changed. It is now possible to implement parallel processing cheaply, easily and effectively. It is truly an innovation and a revolution on many levels.

What is parallel processing? There was a movie a while back called Multiplicity that starred Michael Keaton. In it Michael was overtaxed by the number of things he had to juggle in his life. As one person he could not be in two places at the same time. He could not pick up the children from school while attending a meeting at work and painting the fence. If only he could have multiple versions of himself. He could then do all those tasks *simultaneously*. You cannot really be picking up the children from school in one part of town and then occasionally jump over to the other side of town to attend to a meeting when it is time for you to speak. So the option of polling or interrupting is not possible in this situation. The only way for Michael to multitask these life obligations is to either, allocate them non-overlapping time slots and allow for travel from one to the other, or he can clone himself and assign each clone the various tasks. Being clones of course they are just as capable as Michael. Michael and his clones can all be doing disparate tasks ***independently and simultaneously***.

There is one limitation however. If a task requires that two or more Michaels have to be using the car to travel in different directions then only one Michael can use the car and the other Michaels will have to wait until the car becomes free. Also, it is not advisable that any other Michaels should have "access" to Michael's wife other than the original Michael. But Michael's wife and the other Michaels may have different opinions on that.

Well, enough with Michael and his clones, let's look at the Propeller. One of the amazing things about the Propeller chip is that it is in fact 8 microcontrollers in one chip (with a surprisingly reasonable price tag). Another remarkable thing about it is the Spin language. This high-level language is easy to learn and easy to use but more importantly it has all the tools you need to create ***real parallel processing*** with exceptional ease and elegance.

As an example, consider what a non-trivial robot system has to accomplish:
1. Control motors with PWM which require constant updating.
2. If wheel encoders are used then constant attention has to be given to the quadrature signals to calculate and keep fresh the current count.
3. Attend to various sensors like Bumpers and Infrared or maybe line sensors.
4. Other systems such as compasses or GPS etc. will also have to be interacted with.
5. If the robot is doing any communications to a central command then this too will have to be performed.

A single processor will be extremely tasked to accomplish the above and even interrupts and polling would not be adequate due to too many interruptions. For instance a wheel quadrature counter can never really be made to function in a system that has to do all the above and at the same time give proper interrupt or polling time slots to be able to not miss quadrature states.

5.3.1 Using Helper Modules

One solution is to use ***helper modules***. For instance a motor controller module[21] allows a microcontroller to employ ***set-it-and-leave-it*** approach to controlling a robot's wheels. This in effect is parallel processing. Since the module allows the controller to specify the direction and speed of the motor and then go off to do whatever it needs to do without having to worry about maintaining the PWM signals required to keep the motors running.

There are numerous helper modules like these that free up the microcontroller and allow it to manage other tasks. In fact with this methodology the microcontroller is nothing more than an overall manager of various other controllers. Most of these modules are in themselves microcontrollers dedicated to doing nothing but the task they are supposed to do (e.g. pulse the motors). If there are no available or affordable modules that can do a task you require and wish to accomplish in parallel then you can easily design your own helper module utilizing a microcontroller to do the task.

Frequently the control of these modules is achieved with a communication between the main controller and the controller onboard the module. Often this control boils down to the main controller sending a byte or two of data (settings and parameters). The module's controller then uses this data to set up its parameters then continues accordingly doing what it needs to do independently and in parallel with the other actions of the main controller.

This strategy is in reality what makes it possible today to design effective robots that can be controlled with controllers of modest capabilities. Many projects on today's robots would be quite impossible if it were not for the employment of helper modules such as are available at www.Parallax.com and many other similar web sites.

5.3.2 Using Multiple Microcontrollers

Some disadvantages of the helper-modules strategy of achieving parallel processing and true multitasking is that the modules are not cheap and the variety of interfacing protocols required is bewildering and cumbersome.

Imagine if you had the ability to utilize many microcontrollers with minimal wiring and cheaply and where all of them can communicate with each other via a shared memory rather than through a bit-banging serial protocol (slow). This would be ideal. We won't be limited to available modules, we won't incur prohibitive expenses, and we would have no bottleneck in communications.

Well, that is exactly what the Propeller Chip is. It is 8 microcontrollers in one package that share 32KB of RAM. Moreover, the Propeller makes it possible to achieve parallelism with effectiveness that would be hard to achieve otherwise.

5.4 Parallel Processing with the Propeller Chip

We will now convert Program_03.Spin into a parallel processing program. In fact, you have been using the Propeller's parallel processing ability ever since Chapter 3.4. You may not have realized that the FDS and SM serial drivers each use one of the 8 sub-microcontrollers in the Propeller Chip. Whenever we used these drivers we were in effect already utilizing parallel processing. The FDS (or SM) object runs in its own COG (the sub-microcontroller is called COG in the Propeller Chip's parlance).

If you think about what the FDS and the SM modules do you will realize the power of these objects. They, independently of your program, sit in the background listening to the RX Pin (receiver pin) to see if any data is coming and then if data comes in they do the Bit-Banging required to achieve the Asynchronous Serial Communications; they then store that data in a memory area in the shared RAM (receive buffer). Your module can then call methods to extract the data. Also when you use the **Tx()** or **Dec()** or **Str()** methods in the modules you are in fact sending the data to the shared RAM (send buffer) which the object will then send out on the TX pin while also checking if it is allowed to send and so on.

All this is happening in parallel to other tasks you are doing in the main cog. Our programs so far have only utilized one cog (the start up one) and have not utilized any parallel processing save for the FDS and SM objects. So how do we do our own multiprocessing using our own parallel processes? Well, that is exactly what we are going to do from this point onwards. We will progressively build up to a complex and intricate (yet easy to understand and achieve) system that will be a major step towards creating a powerful hardware control system (e.g. a robot) using the Propeller and RobotBASIC as partners.

We will start by gradually converting Program_03.Spin to be a parallel processing system and then add to it some more functionality. All this will serve the purpose of comparing how the program can be made infinitely more versatile and capable than its *linear-flow* counterpart. Armed with the knowledge and experience that the next few sections will provide, we will have the tools required to create the complex system needed to achieve our final overall objective of interfacing and controlling a complex hardware system using the PC.

5.4.1 Modularization in Preparation

The first step is to convert Program_03.Spin into a modular system (but not object-based quite yet). To help us in organizing this task we need to analyze what the separate functions in the program are.

> (i) In fact the FDS and SM modules are Objects. Therefore, we are using object-based programming already. However, our own program is not modularized into objects *yet*. We will do this in Section 5.5.

The program performs the following *logically separate* actions:
1. Communicates with RB to receive the LEDs status byte and to send the pushbuttons status.
2. Reads the pushbuttons status and makes it available for the communications process to send to RB.
3. Sets the LEDs from the byte received from RB by the communications process.

With the aim of eventually making these three tasks independent and run in parallel, we should separate Program_03.Spin into its *logical parts*.

Since Program_04.Spin below and the next few improvements on it are the same as Program_03.Spin from Chapter 4.3, we will continue to use Program_03.BAS from Chapter 4.3 as the companion RB program to run with them.

Program_04.Spin

```
'Use Program_03.BAS as the companion RB program
'Use F11 to upload to EEPROM
CON
  _clkmode = xtal1 + pll16x
  _xinfreq = 5_000_000
  RB_TX    = 30
  RB_RX    = 31
  RB_BAUD  = 115200


Var
  byte ReceivedByte, ByteToSend
OBJ
  RB      : "FullDuplexSerial"

PUB Main|x
  RB.Start(RB_RX,RB_TX,0,RB_BAUD)
  dirA[16..23]~~
  repeat
    repeat
        x := RB.RXcheck
    until x <> -1
    ReceivedByte := x
    SetLEDs(@ReceivedByte)
    ReadPins(@ByteToSend)
    RB.TX(ByteToSend)

Pri SetLEDs(ReceivedByteAddr)
  outA[23..16] := Byte[ReceivedByteAddr]

Pri ReadPins(ByteToSendAddr)
  Byte[ByteToSendAddr] := inA[7..5]
```

Notice the way we have created the subroutines (methods) **SetLEDs()** and **ReadPins()**. As their names indicate they do just that. Compare them to what we had in Program_03.Spin.

A Variable's Address in Memory (Pointer)

The **Main**, **SetLEDs()** and **ReadPins()** methods need to use the same variables to do their work and need access to these variables. There is a nuance in this program that may be considered a bit of an advanced concept. It is the usage of the **address** of a variable rather than the variable itself.

The methods **SetLEDs()** and **ReadPins()** at this particular stage do not in reality need to be passed the address of the variable to be set/read as a parameter. However, in the next few evolutions of the program we will need to do so; might as well do it right at this stage. The reason that they do not really need to be passed the address is that the methods reside in the same module (**object**), so any memory variables defined in the **Var** or **Dat** (see later) sections are automatically available and visible to the methods. However, when we (as we will eventually do) run the methods in their own separate objects we will have to pass the addresses of the variables to be used since methods in an object have no access to variables declared in other objects except through a **pointer** to the variable.

Therefore when the method is called we pass it the address of the variable it needs to use. This is achieved with the **@** operator. When the method needs to use the variable it uses its address to access its value. This is achieved with the **Byte[address]** construct. If the variable is a **Long** or a **Word** then we would use that instead of **Byte[]**.

A Brief Note About Objects and Methods

We shall discuss objects in Section 5.5.1 where we will be creating objects. However, some background information is needed here. Spin is *object-based*. If you are not familiar with the OOP concept of programming don't worry much about it. All it really boils down to in the end is that you can divide your program into *files (objects)*. Each file has the following sections: Con, Var, Obj and Dat. Also it can have as many Pub and Pri *methods (subroutines)* as it needs.

A program then would be a *main file* (called *top-level-object*) and various other sub-files. All the files have the same structure as above. In the Obj section you can define the sub-files you need (*instantiating*). These sub-files are given an *alias (an instance name)*. This is what we did when we used the FDS and the SM objects. We called one RB and the other D (for debug). Sub-files may use sub-files of their own.

Whenever you need to use a method (a *subroutine*) from a sub-file (a sub-object) you use the alias of the object and a dot and then the name of the method you want to use form the object. This is what we did when we used the **TX()** or **Dec()** methods. We used **RB.TX()** or **D.Dec()**. Only Pub methods in an object can be called this way from outside the object. If you look inside the FDS file, for example, and search for the **Dec()** subroutine (method) you would see that it had a Pub before it.

All objects also can have their own constants (Con), variables (Var) and data (Dat) sections. The data and variables in an object cannot be used by methods other than the ones in the object. All the methods in an object (file) can use the variables or data declared in the Var or Dat sections and of course the constants in Con.

To use variables in another object you can do either of the following:
- ❑ Use a pointer to the variable (addresses of the variable in the RAM). You can then use it as mentioned in the preceding section.
- ❑ Use Pub methods (called *getters* and *setters*). You pass the value to set the variable to as a parameter to the setter method which will then set the variable to that value. To read the value of the variable the getter method returns its value as the method's (*function*) return value.

Hiding of variables and private methods is a useful way of managing the utilization of an object so that others can use it like a black box without having to worry about its innards (*encapsulation*). We will create our own objects soon and all this will be put to practice.

5.4.2 Initial Multitasking With Polling

Another improvement to the program in preparation for later work is the use of the **RxCheck** method instead of the **Rx** method to receive the byte from RB. The **RxCheck** method does not wait until there is a byte. If there is a byte it returns its value, and if there is no byte it will return -1. The construct in the bold code lines in fact achieves the same thing as **RX** because in the final outcome the code will wait for a byte until one comes in. However, within the loop we now can do other things while waiting for a byte to arrive instead of just sitting idle.

Since now we are using *polling* we can do other things inside the repeat-until loop. In Program_04_B.Spin the bold and highlighted lines achieve a multitasking of blinking an LED on P23 with durations of 2 seconds on and 2 seconds off. It uses the same technique we used in Blinker_04.Spin. We are still using Program_03.Bas on the RB side, but, the left most checkbox is ineffective now since the 8th LED is used for the Blinking action. Also notice that P23 is not set by the byte that comes from RB.

There is a problem with this program; when you first run it the LED on P23 will blink correctly. However, when you run RB it will stop doing so. Try it again. Reload the Spin program but do not run RB. Notice how the LED is in actuality blinking as it is supposed to. But, when you run RB, the blinking stops. Can you figure out why this is so? Think about it for a moment before reading on.

Program_04_B.Spin

```
'Use Program_03.BAS as the companion RB program
'Use F11 to upload to EEPROM
CON
  _clkmode = xtal1 + pll16x
  _xinfreq = 5_000_000
  RB_TX     = 30
  RB_RX     = 31
  RB_BAUD   = 115200
  Blink_Time = 160_000_000   '2 secs


Var
  byte ReceivedByte, ByteToSend
OBJ
  RB      : "FullDuplexSerial"

PUB Main|x,t
  RB.Start(RB_RX,RB_TX,0,RB_BAUD)
  dirA[16..23]~~
  repeat
    t := cnt                  'init timer
    repeat
      x := RB.RXcheck
      if (cnt-t)> Blink_Time 'if timeout
        !outA[23]             'toggle LED
        t := cnt             'reset timer
    until x <> -1
    ReceivedByte := x
    SetLEDs(@ReceivedByte)
    ReadPins(@ByteToSend)
    RB.TX(ByteToSend)

Pri SetLEDs(ReceivedByteAddr)
  outA[22..16] := Byte[ReceivedByteAddr]

Pri ReadPins(ByteToSendAddr)
  Byte[ByteToSendAddr] := inA[7..5]
```

Remove the highlighted line and place it *above* the 1st **Repeat** statement and try the program again. The LED should be blinking and after you run RB it will continue to do so. Can you now see what was wrong?

What does the highlighted line achieve? It reinitializes the stopwatch timer. So if it is inside the first repeat-loop it will be reinitialized every time through the loop and if the loop is executed many times over then the timer never times out and the blinking will stop. But, if the corresponding RB program is not running then the first time through the loop we will go into the second Repeat loop. But since RB is not running there will never be a byte received. This means the program flow will stay in the inner loop and the timer would not be reinitialized except every time it overflows. But when RB is run it will start to send bytes. This will cause the outer loop to be executed, which resets the timer without ever blinking the LED.

> This kind of error is something to watch out for. It is not an easy error to debug due to the nature of microcontroller programming.

5.4.3 Achieving Initial Parallelism

The corrected Program_04_B.Spin is now in a format that will allow us to easily move over to real parallel processing by using **COGS** (sub-microcontrollers). Remember in Section 5.4.1 we defined the three logical modules. In Section 5.4.2 we developed the program to make use of subroutines (methods) and also some multitasking using the polling technique. Since now we have the program divided up into its logical parts, we can assign each logical part to run in its own microcontroller (COG). This way we can achieve Parallelism. Because the various parts need to send data back and forth we will use the shared memory model. This means that each cog is doing its work but is also reading data in the shared memory stored by other modules or writing data for other cogs to use.

Program_05.Spin

```
'Use Program_03.BAS as the RB program
'Use F11 to upload to EEPROM
CON
  _clkmode = xtal1 + pll16x
  _xinfreq  = 5_000_000
  RB_TX     = 30
  RB_RX     = 31
  RB_BAUD   = 115200
  Blink_Time = 160_000_000    '2 secs

Var
  byte ReceivedByte, ByteToSend
  Long Stacks[20]

OBJ
  RB     : "FullDuplexSerial"

PUB Main|x,t
  RB.Start(RB_RX,RB_TX,0,RB_BAUD)
  dirA[16..23]~~
  cogNew(SetLEDs(@ReceivedByte),@Stacks[0])   'put method in its own cog
  cogNew(ReadPins(@ByteToSend) ,@Stacks[10])  'put method in its own cog
  t := cnt   'init timer
  repeat
    repeat
      x := RB.RXcheck
      if (cnt-t)> Blink_Time
        !outA[23]    'toggle LED
        t := cnt      'reset timer
    until x <> -1
    ReceivedByte := x
    'Notice there is no more calling of the methods
    RB.TX(ByteToSend)

Pri SetLEDs(ReceivedByteAddr)
  outA[22..16] := Byte[ReceivedByteAddr]

Pri ReadPins(ByteToSendAddr)
  Byte[ByteToSendAddr] := inA[7..5]
```

Look at Program_05.Spin. What we have are the following 4 cogs (sub-microcontrollers) working in parallel:

1. The **Main** cog receives data from RB and stores it into a RAM location, also it will send data stored in another memory location to RB (see the next section for more details).
2. The FDS object does the low level work of bit-banging the bytes over the serial port.

   So far whenever we used the FDS (or SM) object we have been actually implicitly assigning it its own cog without realizing it using the object's **Start()** method (highlighted line). We will discuss this later when we create our own objects. But for now note that calling the **RB.Start()** method is in fact assigning the FDS to its own cog.
3. The **SetLEDs()** cog reads a memory byte to set the status of the LEDs.
4. The **ReadPins()** cog reads the pushbuttons status and stores the value in a memory location.

Notice how the **CogNew()** Spin function is used (bold lines) to assign the **SetLEDs()** and **ReadPins()** methods to a cog each. This is ***extremely powerful***. With this one statement we start a new microcontroller and program it with the code in the method and then let it go on doing its work in Parallel with the other cogs. We now have two more microcontrollers doing the work specified in the methods assigned to the cogs.

Compile and upload the program (F11). Notice how the LED on P23 is blinking fine which indicates to us that the program is functioning. Now run Program_03.Bas and click the checkboxes and press the pushbuttons on the board. What is wrong? Why is the program not working? We will debug the program in Section 5.4.4, but first let's look at a few details.

The Relationship Between Cogs, Methods and Objects

When the Propeller boots up, it will use the first cog to run a Spin interpreter which will look at the ***top-level-object*** (main program file) and will start executing the ***first Pub method*** in the object. In the above program that was the **Main** method. There is no explicit action needed to assign **Main** to a cog; this was achieved by the Propeller boot up procedure. See the Propeller Manual V1.1 pp 18-19.

When we talk about assigning a method to a cog what we really mean is that the method will be run by a copy of the Spin interpreter in that cog. When we **Cognew()** a method, Spin will (in effect) load a copy of itself into a cog and then start it running. This ***clone*** cog will know where in RAM is the code for the method it was passed the name of and will start running that code. The whole arrangement is as if a new Propeller microcontroller with its copy of Spin and its assigned method as a program were booted up. It will become an independent Propeller running in parallel to the original cog. See the Propeller Manual pp 78-83.

> ⚠️It is important to realize that it is the ***method*** that is assigned to the cog, not the object that contains the method. However, since the object owns the method, the cog running this method has access to the variables and other methods in the object and ***in a manner of speaking*** the object owns the cog. So we can ***loosely say*** the object is assigned to the cog. But, it is not, strictly speaking, the case. It is not the object that is assigned to the cog it is the method in the object.

> ⚠️The **Cognew()** function assigns a particular method to a cog. This method will then be run by the cog and any action it takes will pertain to the cog running it. However, it is also possible to call the same method from another cog as an explicit invocation of the method. The method will then do actions but these actions will pertain only to the ***caller cog*** and not the cog that owns the method.

> ⓘIn the program above, the methods to be assigned to cogs were inside the same object as **Main** which invoked the **Cognew()** function to start the methods in their own cogs. However, if these methods were in their own separate objects we would need the container object to provide a method that we can call from **Main**. This is what we did with the FDS and SM objects. Whenever we called their **Start()** methods we were implicitly starting a cog. But since the object hides everything from the outside it will have to do its own housekeeping. We will see how this works later when we create our own objects.

Cogs and Stack Space

There is one more complication that we need to appreciate. The first bold line is declaring an array variable we are calling **Stacks[]**. This is basically setting aside a block of RAM in the main memory that will be used exclusively by the cogs. We made it 20 Longs because we need 10 Longs for each cog and we have 2 cogs. When we start the cog we give it a *pointer* (the address) to this area of RAM. That is the purpose of the **@Stacks[0]** and **@Stacks[10]**. In the first one we are telling the cog to use the top of the stacks area. In the second we are telling it to start at the 11th long down from the top. Spin indexes arrays starting with 0 for the first element just like in RobotBASIC. This means that the first element in an array is element number 0; the eleventh element is element number 10.

The program uses 4 cogs, but we only needed to assign stack space for the two cogs that *we* explicitly started in our program. The **Main** cog is started by the boot up procedure and its stack space is assigned by the Spin interpreter. The FDS cog was started internally by the object which takes care of its own stack space. You will see in Section 5.5 how when we create our own objects each will have its own stack space. Also see PP 78-83 in the Propeller Manual V1.1. Cogs need some scratch pad RAM to do temporary work like expression evaluation and so forth. How many Longs they will need is not easy to determine. This is a complex topic and there are things you can do to optimize the size. However for our purposes it is not that important if we assign more than we need. But if we use less than needed *weird errors* will occur. It is advisable to be generous here.

⚠ It is important to realize that sometimes you may guess wrongly and assign too little stack space. If your program is not working and you feel that it should, always, keep in mind this stack problem. Try to increase the stack size and see if that helps. Assigning too small a stack size is a major source of head scratching buggy behavior that can drive you astray going off on all sorts of wild goose chases trying to figure out why a perfectly sound looking program is not working when it should be. Just remember to eliminate stack overflow as a source of error by increasing the stack size to some ridiculous number (e.g. 50) and then when your program is working experiment with decreasing it to some realistic value. Most of the time 10 to 25 should be fine unless your method is doing some deeply nested calling of sub-sub routines or evaluating really complex expressions.

ⓘ The reason too little stack space causes trouble is that the cog will start using the memory at the area you point it to. However if the space assigned is too small the cog does not really care, it will just keep on going using as much space as it needs. But if that space is used by other actions then the data stored there will be clobbered and all sorts of mayhem will result. If you are a C programmer you are all too familiar with this.

5.4.4 Systematic Debugging of Complex Programs

There are various problems with Program_05.Spin; to figure out what they are we are going to embark on a journey of systematic and gradual debugging.

What is the program supposed to do?
- ❑ Blink an LED on P23 every 4 seconds for 2 seconds **(working)**.
- ❑ Whenever we click on a checkbox in RB a corresponding LED on the PDB should light up **(not working)**.
- ❑ Whenever we press a pushbutton on the PDB a simulated LED should light up on the RB screen **(not working)**.

What do we know?
- ❑ We know the problem is not in the RB program since we used it with Program_04_B.Spin and it worked.
- ❑ We also know that Program_04_B.Spin was working and all we did was to move things over to cogs.

Could it be the Stack size? Try to increase the stack size to **Stacks[100]** and also use **@Stacks[50]** instead of [10]. Does it work? No still same as before.

Now it is time to insert a few debug lines to send some data to the PST so that we can examine the insides of the program while it is running on the Propeller.

> (i) So far we have only used the PST and RB concurrently in Test_06.Spin (Chapter 3.7) just to see how it is done. Now, we will see the real need for this and the power of it.

From this point onwards we are going to move the RB communications to use the Propeller Plug (PP) port as we did back in Test_06.Spin in Chapter 3.7. We are going to simultaneously use the PST and RB. The new Program_05.BAS will communicate with our program as before but now through a different port (also one less checkbox). Additionally, we will use the PST to output telltale indicators to help us gradually narrow down the problems with Program_05.Spin. We will be using the configuration of Figure 2.15.

Program_05.Bas

```
//works with Program_05_B/C/D/E.Spin
//same as Program_03.BAS but using the PP port and one less Checkbox
//because the Spin program is only using 7 LEDs to be set since now
//the P23 LED is the blinker one
Port = 8   //change this as per your system
Main:
    setcommport Port,br115200   //set serial comms
    xystring 10,10,"Click on the checkbox to light up the corresponding LED"
    xystring 10,70,"Press the buttons on the Propeller and see the "+\
                "corresponding checkbox change"
    for i=0 to 6 //only 7 boxes
        AddCheckBox "DS"+i,60+20*i,40," "   //add checkboxes as bits to form the
    next                                    //number to send
    while true
        x =0
        for i=0 to 6   //form the byte from the individual bits
            if GetCheckBox("DS"+i) then x += 1<<(6-i)
        next
        serialout x  \ xystring 240,40,"=",x,spaces(20)
        repeat
            CheckSerBuffer x //wait for data in the buffer
        until x
        serin s
        x = ~GetStrByte(s,Length(s))   //value of the last byte and invert it
        for i=0 to 2
            if GetBit(x,i)
                circlewh 60+i*40,100,30,30,red,red  //simulate LED on
            else
                circlewh 60+i*40,100,30,30,red       //Simulate LED off
            endif
        next
    wend
end
```

Program_05_B.Spin

```
'Use Prgram_05.Bas as a companion RB program
'Use F10 to upload to RAM
CON
  _clkmode = xtal1 + pll16x
  _xinfreq  = 5_000_000
  RB_TX     = 1
```

```
RB_RX      = 0
RB_BAUD    = 115200
D_TX       = 30
D_RX       = 31
D_BAUD     = 115200
Blink_Time = 160_000_000    '2 secs

Var
  byte ReceivedByte, ByteToSend
  Long Stacks[100]
OBJ
  RB      : "FullDuplexSerial"
  D       : "SerialMirror"
PUB Main|x,t
  D.Start(D_RX,D_TX,0,D_BAUD)
  RB.Start(RB_RX,RB_TX,0,RB_BAUD)
  dirA[16..23]~~
  cogNew(SetLEDs(@ReceivedByte),@Stacks[0])
  cogNew(ReadPins(@ByteToSend),@Stacks[50])
  t := cnt   'init timer
  repeat
     repeat
        x := RB.RXcheck
        if (cnt-t)> Blink_Time   'if timed out
           !outA[23]             'toggle LED
           t := cnt              'reset timer
     until x <> -1
     D.Str(string(13,"Received="))
     D.Dec(ReceivedByte)
     D.Str(string("   , Sending="))
     D.Dec(ByteToSend)
     ReceivedByte := x
     RB.TX(ByteToSend)

Pri SetLEDs(ReceivedByteAddr)
  outA[22..16] := Byte[ReceivedByteAddr]

Pri ReadPins(ByteToSendAddr)
  Byte[ByteToSendAddr] := inA[7..5]
```

Let's make sure that the byte coming from RB is the correct one. Also let's make sure the byte we send to it is the correct one. Notice the highlighted lines in Program_05_B.Spin. They send some information to the PST for us to see what the values of the bytes are. Compile and upload Program_05_B.Spin (use F10 no need for F11 any longer) then run the PST. In the PST, click on the *Pref.* button and select the *Functions* tab. Now **uncheck** the "*Automatically Disable...*" checkbox (see Figure 2.14). This is because we want the PST to remain active when we go to the RB program and interact with the checkboxes. If we do not uncheck the above then we would not see the output from the Spin program since the PST will deactivate when we switch over to RB.

⚠ Remember always to 'Disable' the PST before you try to program the Propeller. If you see the message in Figure 2.13, make sure the PST is deactivated and then try again.

Size your windows so that you have the setup in Figure 5.1. Now go over to RB and run program_05.Bas and press the checkboxes.

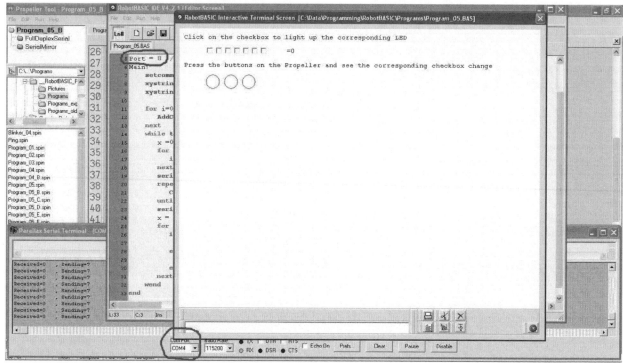

Figure 5.1: The Arrangement of the windows during the debugging session of Program_05_B.Spin

We are going to do a session of intricate debugging observing the output and input in RB and at the same time observing the output in the PST. First notice that there is no output on the PST before you run the RB program. Is this a problem? No, because we have designed the spin program so that it would wait for a byte to come in from RB before it falls out of the inner repeat-until loop and therefore reach the debug statements. So this is OK.

Run the RB program. The PST output will now scroll and also notice that the checkboxes are all un-checked and the output on the PST says "Received = 0". On the PST it says "Sent=7" and the three LEDs on the RB screen are off (Figure 5.1).

Check some checkboxes on the RB screen. The corresponding LED on the PDB is *still not* lighting up. But, the output from the PST is showing the correct value. See the top hand drawn circular marking (red or gray in B&W) on the RB side and its associated one on the PST side in Figure 5.2. Now press a bush button on the PDB and notice that the PST output is not reflecting any change and of course neither is the RB output. See Figure 5.2 the second set of hand drawn circles (blue or dark gray in B&W).

Why is it that even though the value says 7 the LEDs on the RB screen are off? Remember that in RB we are inverting the byte when received from the Propeller (see the highlighted line in the listing of Program_05.Bas).

So what do we know now?
- ❑ The RB program is sending the right byte and the Propeller is receiving the right byte.
- ❑ The propeller is not reading the pushbuttons' status correctly since it is not correct on the PST output.
- ❑ There is a problem in setting the LEDs on the Propeller but not in receiving the byte. Also there is a problem with reading the pushbuttons' status but not in sending them.
- ❑ So we can conclude that **Main** is OK.
- ❑ We now think there is a problem with both the cogs since no setting and no reading is occurring.
- ❑ However, it seems that the reading of the pushbuttons must have worked momentarily because the PST is showing 7 not 0 for the **ByteToSend** value. If there was never a reading then that should be zero. So we must have managed to read at least once.

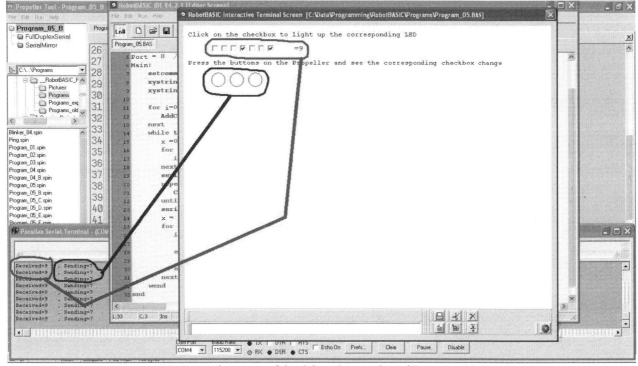

Figure 5.2: Example output of the debugging session of Program_05_B.Spin

Program_05_C.Spin

```
'Use Prgram_05.Bas as a companion RB program
'Use F10 to upload to RAM
CON
  _clkmode = xtal1 + pll16x
  _xinfreq  = 5_000_000
  RB_TX     = 1
  RB_RX     = 0
  RB_BAUD   = 115200
  D_TX      = 30
  D_RX      = 31
  D_BAUD    = 115200
  Blink_Time = 160_000_000    '2 secs

Var
  byte ReceivedByte, ByteToSend
  Long Stacks[100]
OBJ
  RB    : "FullDuplexSerial"
  D     : "SerialMirror"
PUB Main|x,t
  D.Start(D_RX,D_TX,0,D_BAUD)
  RB.Start(RB_RX,RB_TX,0,RB_BAUD)
  dirA[16..23]~~
  cogNew(SetLEDs(@ReceivedByte),@Stacks[0])
  cogNew(ReadPins(@ByteToSend),@Stacks[50])
  t := cnt  'init timer
  repeat
    repeat
      x := RB.RXcheck
```

```
            if (cnt-t)> Blink_Time   'if timed out
                !outA[23]            'toggle LED
                t := cnt             'reset timer
        until x <> -1
        ReceivedByte := x
        RB.TX(ByteToSend)

Pri SetLEDs(ReceivedByteAddr)
  outA[22..16] := Byte[ReceivedByteAddr]
   'D.Str(string(13,"Received="))
   'D.Dec(byte[ReceivedByteAddr])

Pri ReadPins(ByteToSendAddr)
  Byte[ByteToSendAddr] := inA[7..5]
  D.Str(string(13,"Sending="))
  D.Dec(byte[ByteToSendAddr])
```

Let's debug the **ReadPins()** cog next. Load Program_05_C.Spin and do the same as before. Do not forget to disable the PST before compiling the program. Now run the PST and observe. There is no output whatsoever. Even when RB is run there is no output. If the cog were working there would be a continuous stream of output on the PST. No output indicates that in fact the cog is not running. Why?

It is due to a little oversight. Remember back in Program_04_B.Spin, we had the program *call* the methods and that occurred every time around the loop. This ensured that the methods did their work (but not in parallel of course). Now, however, we put them in cogs and we thought that the cog will keep running and do the work. Unfortunately, there is a problem in the code. Notice that once the cog is started it will execute the line of code but then there are no more lines. This means the cog will just stop after the last line of code (one line in this case). This actually accounts for why we managed to set the **ByteToSend** value correctly once and never again.

What we need is a way to make the line execute over and over. Of course, we do that with a Repeat-statement. The same is obviously true also for the **SetLEDs()** method. Prove that (in Program_05_D.Spin) by commenting the bold lines and un-commenting the highlighted line and run the program again. The same thing happens, there is no output.

So now we will correct this with the insertion of a Repeat-statement at the top of each of the methods as shown in the listing of Program_05_D.Spin (lines in reverse). Now run Program_05_D.Spin and observe the output on the PST when you press the pushbuttons on the PDB. Also notice that the RB screen is actually working at least as far as the LEDs on it are concerned. We are now finished with debugging the **ReadPins()** cog; it is working fine.

However, the **SetLEDs()** method seems to be still not working, since when we press the checkboxes we do not see the corresponding LEDs light up on the PDB. So let's debug it and see. Comment the bold lines out and uncomment the highlighted lines. Now run the program and also the RB program and click some of the checkboxes. Observe that in fact the method is receiving the right value for the LEDs as shown by the PST but it is not setting the LEDs for some reason.

Let's try another thing. Change the second highlighted line inProgram_05_D.Spin to say:
```
    D.Dec(outA[22..16])
```

This change checks whether the **outA[]** register is being set correctly. Try the program again and click checkboxes on RB's screen. Interesting! The pins are in fact being set to the correct value and we can see that the **outA[]** register is in fact set correctly. But the LEDs are still not lighting up. Why?

Program_05_D.Spin

```
'Use Prgram_05.Bas as a companion RB program
'Use F10 to upload to RAM
CON
  _clkmode = xtal1 + pll16x
  _xinfreq  = 5_000_000
  RB_TX     = 1
  RB_RX     = 0
  RB_BAUD   = 115200
  D_TX      = 30
  D_RX      = 31
  D_BAUD    = 115200
  Blink_Time = 160_000_000    '2 secs

Var
  byte ReceivedByte, ByteToSend
  Long Stacks[100]
OBJ
  RB      : "FullDuplexSerial"
  D       : "SerialMirror"
PUB Main|x,t
  D.Start(D_RX,D_TX,0,D_BAUD)
  RB.Start(RB_RX,RB_TX,0,RB_BAUD)
  dirA[16..23]~~
  cogNew(SetLEDs(@ReceivedByte),@Stacks[0])
  cogNew(ReadPins(@ByteToSend),@Stacks[50])
  t := cnt   'init timer
  repeat
    repeat
      x := RB.RXcheck
      if (cnt-t)> Blink_Time   'if timed out
        !outA[23]              'toggle LED
        t := cnt              'reset timer
    until x <> -1
    ReceivedByte := x
    RB.TX(ByteToSend)

Pri SetLEDs(ReceivedByteAddr)
  repeat
    outA[22..16] := Byte[ReceivedByteAddr]
    'D.Str(string(13,"Received="))
    'D.Dec(byte[ReceivedByteAddr])

Pri ReadPins(ByteToSendAddr)
  repeat
    Byte[ByteToSendAddr] := inA[7..5]
    D.Str(string(13,"Sending="))
    D.Dec(byte[ByteToSendAddr])
```

5.4.5 Sources For Obtaining Help With Difficult Problems

Ok now, this a head-scratcher, what is going on? To all appearances the cog is working (it is outputting to the PST). It is receiving the correct value (as indicated earlier) and it is setting the **outA[]** register correctly (as we just saw). Nothing is wrong. Why are the LEDs not lighting up? Could it be the LEDs are bad.?

Let's check that out; run Test_01.Spin (Chapter 3.1). No all is OK. Run Program_01.Spin with its companion RB program Program_01.Bas (Chapter 4.1). Again all is OK.

What is it? This is a major problem. Where can you get help?
> At the Parallax Propeller Forum[23]
> At the RobotBASIC web site[2]
> At the RobotBASIC forum[22]

This is one of these problems where if you have not read the Propeller Chip manual *very carefully* you would miss the information. Something like this is best suited for help from the above resources.

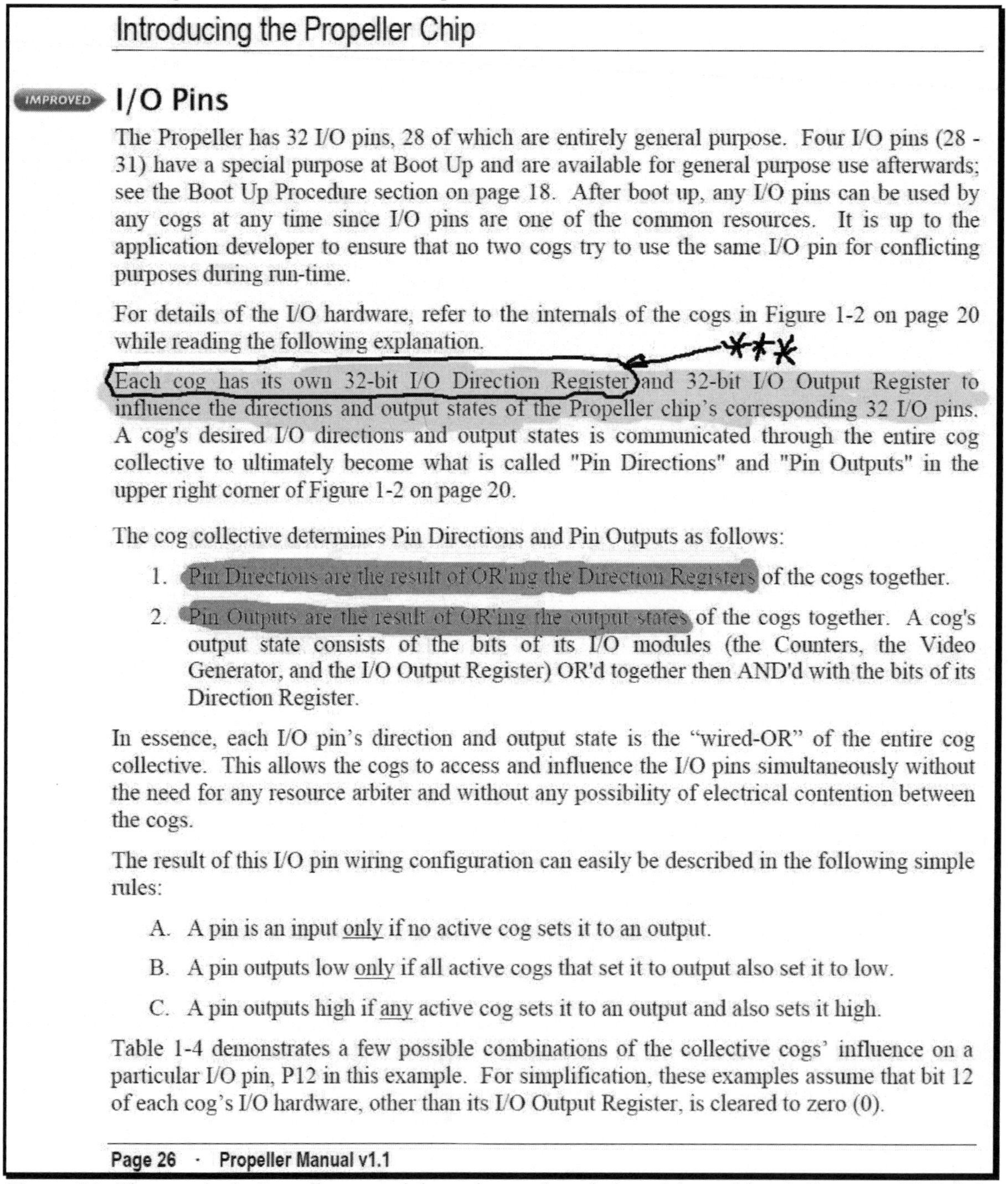

Introducing the Propeller Chip

IMPROVED I/O Pins

The Propeller has 32 I/O pins, 28 of which are entirely general purpose. Four I/O pins (28 - 31) have a special purpose at Boot Up and are available for general purpose use afterwards; see the Boot Up Procedure section on page 18. After boot up, any I/O pins can be used by any cogs at any time since I/O pins are one of the common resources. It is up to the application developer to ensure that no two cogs try to use the same I/O pin for conflicting purposes during run-time.

For details of the I/O hardware, refer to the internals of the cogs in Figure 1-2 on page 20 while reading the following explanation. ***

Each cog has its own 32-bit I/O Direction Register and 32-bit I/O Output Register to influence the directions and output states of the Propeller chip's corresponding 32 I/O pins. A cog's desired I/O directions and output states is communicated through the entire cog collective to ultimately become what is called "Pin Directions" and "Pin Outputs" in the upper right corner of Figure 1-2 on page 20.

The cog collective determines Pin Directions and Pin Outputs as follows:

1. Pin Directions are the result of OR'ing the Direction Registers of the cogs together.
2. Pin Outputs are the result of OR'ing the output states of the cogs together. A cog's output state consists of the bits of its I/O modules (the Counters, the Video Generator, and the I/O Output Register) OR'd together then AND'd with the bits of its Direction Register.

In essence, each I/O pin's direction and output state is the "wired-OR" of the entire cog collective. This allows the cogs to access and influence the I/O pins simultaneously without the need for any resource arbiter and without any possibility of electrical contention between the cogs.

The result of this I/O pin wiring configuration can easily be described in the following simple rules:

A. A pin is an input only if no active cog sets it to an output.

B. A pin outputs low only if all active cogs that set it to output also set it to low.

C. A pin outputs high if any active cog sets it to an output and also sets it high.

Table 1-4 demonstrates a few possible combinations of the collective cogs' influence on a particular I/O pin, P12 in this example. For simplification, these examples assume that bit 12 of each cog's I/O hardware, other than its I/O Output Register, is cleared to zero (0).

Page 26 · Propeller Manual v1.1

Figure 5.3: The page in the Propeller manual that points to the solution of the problem in Program_05_D.Spin

On page 26 of the Propeller Manual V1.1 (see Figure 5.3) it states the solution to our dilemma. Each cog has its own **dirA[]** register. So now the problem is obvious. We have not set the **dirA[]** to be an output register. So even though we are setting **outA[]** correctly it will not influence the LEDs since the pins are not configured to be outputs. Now the solution is obvious. Just add **dirA[22..16]**~~ to the top of the method (line in reverse). The final Program_05_E.Spin should now be a working program. Try it out.

Program_05_E.Spin

```
'Use Prgram_05.Bas as a companion RB program
'Use F10 to upload to RAM
CON
  _clkmode = xtal1 + pll16x
  _xinfreq   = 5_000_000
  RB_TX      = 1
  RB_RX      = 0
  RB_BAUD    = 115200
  D_TX       = 30
  D_RX       = 31
  D_BAUD     = 115200
  Blink_Time = 160_000_000    '2 secs

Var
  byte ReceivedByte, ByteToSend
  Long Stacks[100]
OBJ
  RB    : "FullDuplexSerial"
  D     : "SerialMirror"
PUB Main|x,t
  D.Start(D_RX,D_TX,0,D_BAUD)
  RB.Start(RB_RX,RB_TX,0,RB_BAUD)
  dirA[16..23]~~
  cogNew(SetLEDs(@ReceivedByte),@Stacks[0])
  cogNew(ReadPins(@ByteToSend),@Stacks[50])
  t := cnt   'init timer
  repeat
    repeat
        x := RB.RXcheck
        if (cnt-t)> Blink_Time  'if timed out
           !outA[23]             'toggle LED
           t := cnt              'reset timer
    until x <> -1
    ReceivedByte := x
    RB.TX(ByteToSend)

Pri SetLEDs(ReceivedByteAddr)
  dirA[22..16]~~
  repeat
    outA[22..16] := Byte[ReceivedByteAddr]
    D.Str(string(13,"Received="))
    D.Dec(byte[ReceivedByteAddr])

Pri ReadPins(ByteToSendAddr)
  repeat
    Byte[ByteToSendAddr] := inA[7..5]
    'D.Str(string(13,"Sending="))
    'D.Dec(byte[ByteToSendAddr])
```

5.4.6 Parallel Processing Contention for Resources

Now that we have a working program (Program_05_E.Spin) that also accomplishes the concept of parallel processing we are going to make it do more things in parallel but this will be in the next section. For now, let's examine a hitch with Parallel programming that can be a problem if not accounted for. To see this effect make sure the highlighted lines *and* bold lines in Program_05_E.Spin are *not* commented. You will see that the output on the PST screen is working from both cogs. But, there is a problem. Notice how the output from both is *jumbled up*. The program is otherwise working perfectly and the RB screen LEDs as well as the PDB LEDs are all working. So why do you think the letters from the two cogs are shuffled on the PST screen like that?

Give it a bit of thought for a moment! Can you now see why? It is the Parallel processing. The two cogs are streaming out their respective data to go to the PST but since they are not waiting until the other finishes, the bytes arrive at the PST in jumbled up order as each cog is sending its bytes without any synchronization and the letters become shuffled up like two halves of a deck of cards.

We will solve this problem in the next section. For now also consider another issue. So far we have kept the **Stacks[100]** and are using 50 Longs for each cog. This is most likely wasteful. However, we will not tackle this for now. We will try later to use the *reduce-and-try methodology* mentioned earlier to reduce the stack size. But for now it is of no consequence.

5.5 Objects, Semaphores and Flags

In Section 5.4 we achieved a major step forward towards our objective. We managed to create parallelism with three processes (5 really with the FDS and SM) running independently and truly simultaneously:
1. The **Main** cog doing the byte receiving and sending as well as blinking an LED on P23.
2. The **SetLEDs()** cog setting the LEDs according to the byte received by **Main**.
3. The **ReadPins()** cog reading the pushbuttons and setting the byte to be sent by **Main**.
4. The FDS cog doing serial data bit banging to and from RB.
5. The SM cog doing serial data bit banging to the PST.

In fact though, we really do not get a full appreciation for the parallelism since cog 2 and 3 are not really doing much that truly requires the power of parallelism. Of course we are still in the process of advancing towards a useful and powerful system and we have to proceed gradually. Nevertheless, we did get a feel for this parallelism when we allowed cog 2 and 3 to output to the PST, albeit in an intermingled manner.

In this section we are going to press forward, adding more complexity. We are still in the learning process, so don't worry we will proceed in small surmountable steps. We will:
➢   Divide the project into objects, adding some more parallel actions.
➢   Solve the problem of jumbled output to the PST by using Semaphores.
➢   Manage the Parallelism further with Flags.

5.5.1 Creating Objects

We looked briefly at the concept of object-based-programming in Section 5.4.1 and some more related details in Section 5.4.3. Here, we will recap on some of this information and go further by creating our own objects; one for each of the **SetLEDs()** and **ReadPins()** methods of the previous program.

An *object* is really just a Spin file like any of the programs we have developed so far. The purpose of an object is to *encapsulate* the *methods* and *variables* that are related to a task. This encapsulation helps hide variables and *non-public* (*private*) methods. Another advantage of objects is *reusability*. If you create some kind of useful object correctly you can then use it in other projects without having to worry about the details again. In a way the object becomes much like a *black box* or actually a better description would be like the *helper modules* we talked about in

Section 5.3 but in firmware rather than hardware. If you examine what hardware helper modules really are you will see that objects for the Propeller are very much like helper modules.

We have been using objects quite a lot in our programs so far, but not ones we created. The FDS and SM are objects. And in the **OBJ** section of our programs we *instantiated* the object and gave it a name. Thus the lines:

```
OBJ
  RB      : "FullDuplexSerial"
  D       : "SerialMirror"
```

They are the way we created an *instance* of the object and also *named* it. Later when we wanted to use a method in the object we used the name of the instance. So for example, to transmit we did:

```
RB.Tx(ByteToSend)
```

Using the methods of an object is much like using the dials on a black box. We really do not care how they work behind the scenes, we just want to interact with the object and use any *functionality* (methods) it provides for us to use. Therefore, it is a good programming practice to create objects. There are quite a few rules for creating objects to be used by other people. We are not going to learn about this here. We just want to use Spin Objects that are useful and provided to us by the ObEx[15] and also to organize our own projects using ones we create.

If you noticed, at the beginning of any programs that use the FDS we always use the **Start()** method to start the object working. This is also what we will have to do to our objects. The **Start()** method should do all sorts of initialization needed by the object and it is also the way we pass the object information (e.g. variable addresses) that will determine how we want the object to be configured and where to put data that we might need from it or pass to it. Another thing that a **Start()** method should do *if* the object will be doing some work in an independent cog, is to take care of calling the **CogNew()** Spin function like we did in our programs so far.

One thing you must always keep in mind with objects is the encapsulation aspect. To use the object you must provide public methods to give access to variables in the object and to functionalities. The object may have private methods which will not be usable by anything from outside the object.

Not all objects have to start a cog. Some objects are just like a library of routines that you can use without having to worry about their internal design. We will use such an object in Chapter 7.4. Also some objects may call other objects and those may start a separate cog. So some objects may require two cogs.

It is possible to run out of cogs if you use too many objects that use their own cogs. If your objects also require cogs then you may not have enough for your requirement.

Strictly speaking objects that use cogs should provide a **Start()** and a **Stop()** method. In the design of our objects we have not bothered with the **Stop()** method because we really will not require to stop the cogs in our operations. So we left things simple. *We will show how to do this in the final version of our firmware.* Another thing you must do is check if in fact the cog was started and return its number so as to use it in the **Stop()** method later, and if the cog could not be started take action. Since in our case if cogs are not started the entire system will not work we take this fact as an indication that things have gone amiss. Again to keep things simple we do not bother to do any tighter checking than that.

With all this in mind study Program_06.Spin and its companion Program_06.Bas and then proceed to the discussion below. Don't forget to also study the sub-objects Program_06_Set.Spin and Program_06_Read.Spin.

Program_06.Spin

```
'Use Program_06.Bas as the companion RB program
'Use F10 to upload to RAM
CON
  _clkmode = xtal1 + pll16x
  _xinfreq = 5_000_000
  RB_TX       = 1
  RB_RX       = 0
  RB_BAUD     = 115200
  D_TX        = 30
  D_RX        = 31
  D_BAUD      = 115200
  Blinker     = 23


OBJ
  RB      : "FullDuplexSerial"
  D       : "SerialMirror"
  Set     : "Program_06_Set"      'our object
  Read    : "Program_06_Read"     'our object

PUB Main|x,t
  RB.Start(RB_RX,RB_TX,0,RB_BAUD)
  D.Start(D_RX,D_TX,0,D_BAUD)
  Set.Start(@ReceivedByte,@Blink_Time) 'start our object
  Read.Start(@ByteToSend,@Blink_Time)  'start our object
  dirA[Blinker]~~
  t := cnt                             'init timer
  repeat
    repeat
      x := RB.RXcheck
      if (cnt-t)> Blink_Time    'if time out
        !outA[Blinker]          'toggle LED
        t := cnt                'reset timer
    until x <> -1
    ReceivedByte := x
    RB.TX(ByteToSend)

Dat
  ReceivedByte Byte 0
  ByteToSend   Byte 0
  Blink_Time   Long 80_000_000    '1 sec
  Blink1_Time  Long 160_000_000   '2 secs 2*80_000_000
  Blink2_Time  Long 240_000_000   '3 secs 3*80_000_000
```

Program_06_Read.Spin

```
'Object used by Program_06.Spin
CON
  Blinker    = 22

Var
  long Stacks[50]


PUB Start(ByteToSend,Rates)
  cogNew(ReadPins(ByteToSend,Rates),@Stacks[0])
```

```
Pri ReadPins(ByteToSend,Rates)|t
  dirA[Blinker]~~
  t := cnt                          'initialize the timer
  repeat
      if (cnt-t) => Long[Rates][1]  'blinker time out 2 secs
          !outA[Blinker]            'toggle the LED
          t :=cnt                   'reset the timer
     Byte[ByteToSend] := inA[7..5]
```

Program_06_Set.Spin

```
'Object used by Program_06.Spin
CON
  Blinker    = 21

Var
  long Stacks[50]

PUB Start(ReceivedByte,Rates)
  cogNew(SetLEDs(ReceivedByte,Rates),@Stacks[0])

Pri SetLEDs(ReceivedByte,Rates)|t
  dirA[20..16]~~
  dirA[Blinker]~~
  t := cnt                          'initialize timer
  repeat
     if (cnt-t) => Long[Rates][2] 'blinker time out
       !outA[Blinker]             'toggle the LED
       t := cnt                   'reset timer
    outA[20..16] := Byte[ReceivedByte]
```

Program_06.BAS

```
//works with Program_06.Spin
Port = 8  //change this as per your system
Main:
    setcommport Port,br115200   //set serial comms
    xystring 10,10,"Click on the checkbox to light up the corresponding LED"
    xystring 10,70,"Press the buttons on the Propeller and see the "+\
                "corresponding checkbox change"
    for i=0 to 4
      AddCheckBox "DS"+i,60+20*i,40," "  //add checkboxes as bits to form the
    next                               //number to send
    while true
      x =0
      for i=0 to 4   //form the byte from the individual bits
        if GetCheckBox("DS"+i) then x += 1<<(4-i)
      next
      serialout x  \ xystring 240,40,"=",x,spaces(20)
      repeat
        CheckSerBuffer x //wait for data in the buffer
      until x
      serin s
      x = ~GetStrByte(s,Length(s))  //value of the last byte and invert it
      for i=0 to 2
        if GetBit(x,i)
            circlewh 60+i*40,100,30,30,red,red  //simulate LED on
```

```
            else
                 circlewh 60+i*40,100,30,30,red        //Simulate LED off
            endif
        next
    wend
end
```

What Program_06.Spin performs is similar to Program_05_E.Spin except:

> We added a blinker to each of the objects. So instead of just blinking P23 in the **Main** method, we now also blink P22 and P21 in each of the objects. Also, since now we use P23..P21 as blinkers then there will only be P20..P16 (5 pins) available as LEDs to correspond to the checkboxes on the RB screen. This is why in Program_06.Bas we have setup only 5 checkboxes.

> We moved variables to a **Dat** section. This is more convenient and allows us to initialize the variables.

> Instead of using **CogNew()** in the **Main** method to start the cogs (we cannot any way since they are in other objects) we now use the **Start()** method of each new object.

> Each object has its own **Stack[]** variable defined in the object, so no needed for it in the **Main** object.

> ⓘ In a program that uses objects the main object used to instantiate the other objects and also to be compiled as *the* program when we press F10 or F11 is called the *top-level-object*. Its *first Pub method* is also used to be the method called by the Spin interpreter when it first boots up. See Propeller Manual V1.1 PP 18, 141-142

That is all there is to it. We have just created two objects (and the top-level object is the third) and made them start their own cogs running methods in the object. Also we now have three independent blinkers each blinking at its own rate. These blinkers indicate that the cogs are active and continually doing their work without using the PST or RB to do any output. This way we get visual feedback for the status of the cogs. If any of the blinking LEDs stop blinking we would know that something is awry with the related cog.

Before we proceed we will make use of a great feature in the Propeller Tool IDE (PT). Our project is quite simple so far, but projects may become quite complex and objects could be calling objects and we may need some kind of *map* for how the objects are interacting. Fortunately the PT provides a mechanism to obtain this map. In the *Files* menu there is a menu option called *Archive*. This option will create a zip file that packages all the objects and files needed for the project together. Additionally it creates a file called _ReadMe_.Text which has in it the following information:

```
Parallax Propeller Chip Project Archive

 Project :   "Program_06"
Archived :   Monday, October 25, 2010 at 2:56:16 PM
    Tool :   Propeller Tool version 1.2.7
             Program_06.spin
                 ├──FullDuplexSerial.spin
                 ├──SerialMirror.spin
                 ├──Program_06_Set.spin
                 └──Program_06_Read.spin


Parallax, Inc.
www.parallax.com
support@parallax.com
USA 916.624.8333
```

If the project is more complex the above tree (map) would be invaluable in tracking what object utilizes what, and the tree would be quite complex too. In our case the tree is very flat and the whole thing is simple. Nevertheless, it is a valuable tool you should utilize with your projects. See Appendix B for the tree of the books final firmware.

5.5.2 Utilizing Semaphores

Recall how in Program_05_E.Spin (Section 5.4.4) we used output to the PST but when we let both cogs stream out to the PST we had a problem with the bytes from each being intermingled with the other and the output was a useless jumble of data from each shuffled up into an unreadable mess.

In this improvement of our program we are going to use PST debugging and we will let both cogs as well as the **Main** cog output messages to the PST while also working the LEDs and pushbuttons and receiving and sending data to RB as well as keeping the LEDs blinking. With all this action we will make decisive use of parallelism and multitasking. See Figure 5.4 for a conceptual schematic of the system.

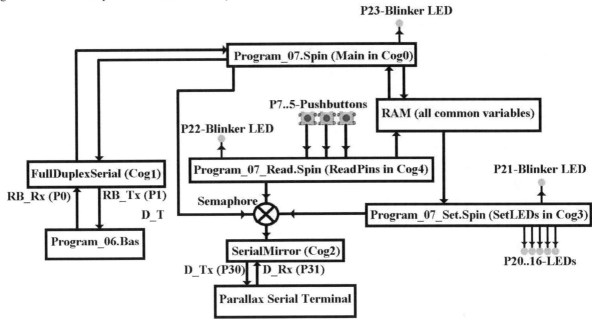

Figure 5.4: A schematic of the various objects and cogs in the new system showing how they interact. Cog numbers are just for reference, they are not necessarily the actual order.

Notice how **Main**, **ReadPins()** and **SetLEDs()** are all using the SerialMirror object. Because every object must instantiate its own version of any other objects it uses, we must instantiate the SM object in all the objects. However, only one of them must call the **Start()** method of the SM object. This should be done by the top-level-object (**Main**).

This is why we used SM for debugging with the PST instead FDS. It is because SM can handle multiple objects using it with only *one* cog, while the FDS has to have multiple cogs. So the FDS is wasteful of cogs. However, notice that SM will only do this for the same RX/TX pins for all the objects using it. Since we want different pins for sending to RB we use the FDS as the object for that. We cannot use SM with another call to its **Start()** method with different pins.

Also notice that the FDS and SM objects do not share RAM with the other objects. They have their own RAM area that does not need to be accessed by outside objects because the objects provide getters and setters (for example the **Tx()**, **Rx** and **Dec()** method). Strictly speaking all the objects share the same RAM but in *logical* terms the RAM for the FDS and for SM are not accessible or visible to the other objects.

Study Figure 5.4 well. It is a good way of understanding what we have achieved so far and for developing a feel for the way parallel processing is going on and appreciating how the shared RAM is a great way for connecting the **Main** cog with the **SetLEDs** and **ReadPins** cogs. The next thing we need to do in Program_07.Spin is to create a mechanism where only one of the three independent and parallel cogs can send through the SM object at a time.

ⓘ It is possible to use SM over multiple ports if we need to, but we would have to make a copy of the Spin file and rename it a different name and then instantiate that object and call its **Start()** method to make it run in another cog and use different pins for the Rx/Tx pins. There is no advantage in this over using the FDS object.

ⓘ The reason SM can be instantiated and used from multiple objects (with only one call to **Start()**) is that it places its variables in the **Dat** section of its object. So the RAM for the send and receive buffers is shared among all instances of the object. In fact as far as the Spin interpreter is concerned there is only one version of the object in RAM altogether. The Spin compiler will only create one copy in RAM of the methods of an object regardless of how many times it is instantiated. Also any variables in the **Dat** section are only created in RAM once too. However, any **Var** section variables are duplicated in RAM for each instance. Therefore instances can share the variables in the **Dat** section but not the ones in the **Var** section. This is why SM works with multiple instantiations as long as its **Start()** method is called only one time to initiate the needed cog.

What is a Semaphore?

The word *Semaphore* means *an apparatus for signaling, such as the arrangement of lights, flags, and mechanical arms on railroads.*

Imagine the three cogs are like trains trying to use a *single* crossing. You obviously need a signal to tell the trains to wait before they cross while another train is using the crossing. No train can attempt to move through the crossing until it has a green light to do so. Once it has acquired the green light it should then cross and once clear of the crossing it should release the green light. Other trains will then be able to attempt to turn the green light on. Only one train can have the green light at a time.

The above mechanism of Semaphores is exactly what we will use to stop data jumbling when cogs are trying to send data simultaneously to the PST. Only the top-level object should create the semaphore (**LockNew**) and then it must pass the address of the signal to the other cogs so that they can try to lock it (**LockSet**). A cog will only send data through the PST if it has managed to acquire the lock. Once it finishes sending it should then release the lock (**LockClr**). This way, the three cogs will be guaranteed a turn to send data through this one *shared resource*.

⚠ The three Spin statements used to utilize semaphores are:

LockNew(): to create the required semaphore and store its ID in a variable. *This is only performed once for each semaphore (maximum of 8)* by the top-level-object and then it makes the *address* of the ID variable available to all other cogs that need to manipulate the semaphore.

LockSet(): to try to capture the semaphore. If the semaphore is in use by another cog then the function will return true, if it is not then it will return false, but that also means that it is now captured by the calling cog. There is no specific need to take any other action. If **LockSet()** returns false then it is now captured by the calling cog. If it returns true then it is not captured by the calling cog. *Note the logic*.

LockClear(): to release the semaphore when it is no longer needed by the cog. A cog that acquires a semaphore *must also release it*. If it does not release it then other cogs that may require it will never be able to do their action. Even the cog that has the semaphore may not be able to do any more work again if it does not release the semaphore before it tries to lock it again (e.g. in a loop).

Using a Semaphore

In the new Program_07.Spin and Program_07_Set.Spin and Program_07.Read.Spin, the lines in bold are the lines we have changed or added to the Program_06 equivalent. We will still use Program_06.Bas with the new suite. As far as RB is concerned nothing is changed. The only new thing is sending to the PST. So when you run the RB program all should be the same as far as clicking the checkboxes and pushbuttons. But now with the same arrangement of windows as we had in Figure 5.1 you should see that the output from the program is not garbled.

There is still a problem, however. Seeing the output from **Main** is very hard. This is because **Main** only tries to send to the PST whenever it receives a byte from RB while the other cogs are attempting a lot more often. Whenever **Main** sends an output it immediately scrolls up off the screen because of the very frequent stream from the other two. However the data is orderly and each line has bytes from only one of the cogs. Watch carefully and when you see the output from **Main** flick by, immediately press *Pause* on the PST and scroll the window up and you will see how **Main** managed to output, albeit very rarely. In the next section we will see how to manage the streaming of data to the PST in a more controlled manner where **Main** gets to have its say more often.

Program_07.Spin

```
'Use Program_06.BAS as the companion RB program
'Use F10 to upload to RAM
CON
  _clkmode = xtal1 + pll16x
  _xinfreq = 5_000_000
  RB_TX       = 1
  RB_RX       = 0
  RB_BAUD     = 115200
  D_TX        = 30
  D_RX        = 31
  D_BAUD      = 115200
  Blinker     = 23

OBJ
  RB    : "FullDuplexSerial"
  D     : "SerialMirror"
  Set   : "Program_07_Set"      'our object
  Read  : "Program_07_Read"     'our object

PUB Main|x,t
  RB.Start(RB_RX,RB_TX,0,RB_BAUD)
  D.Start(D_RX,D_TX,0,D_BAUD)
  Semaphore := LockNew                              'create Semaphore
  Set.Start(@ReceivedByte,@Blink_Time,@Semaphore)  'start our object
  Read.Start(@ByteToSend,@Blink_Time,@Semaphore)   'start our object
  dirA[Blinker]~~
  t := cnt                              'init timer
  repeat
    repeat
      x := RB.RXcheck
      if (cnt-t)> Blink_Time   'if time out
        !outA[Blinker]          'toggle LED
        t := cnt               'reset timer
    until x <> -1
    ReceivedByte := x
    RB.TX(ByteToSend)
    if Not LockSet(Semaphore)            'only send if can acquire the semaphore
      D.Str(string(13,"Main:"))
```

```
            D.Dec(ReceivedByte)
            D.Str(string("   , "))
            D.Dec(ByteToSend)
            LockClr(Semaphore)                'clear the semaphore


Dat
  ReceivedByte Byte 0
  ByteToSend   Byte 0
  Semaphore    byte 0
  Blink_Time   Long 80_000_000    '1 sec
  Blink1_Time  Long 160_000_000   '2 secs 2*80_000_000
  Blink2_Time  Long 240_000_000   '3 secs 3*80_000_000
```

Program_07_Set.Spin

```
CON
  Blinker    = 21

Var
  long Stacks[50]

Obj
  D      : "SerialMirror"

PUB Start(ReceivedByte,Rates,Semaphore)
  cogNew(SetLEDs(ReceivedByte,Rates,Semaphore),@Stacks[0])

Pri SetLEDs(ReceivedByte,Rates,Semaphore)|t
  dirA[20..16]~~
  dirA[Blinker]~~
  t := cnt                          'initialize timer
  repeat
     if (cnt-t) => Long[Rates][2] 'blinker time out
       !outA[Blinker]                'toggle the LED
       t := cnt                      'reset timer
     outA[20..16] := Byte[ReceivedByte]
     if Not LockSet(byte[Semaphore])       'only send if can acquire the semaphore
        D.Str(string(13,"Set:"))
        D.Dec(byte[ReceivedByte])
        LockClr(byte[Semaphore])            'clear the semaphore
```

Program_07_Read.Spin

```
CON
  Blinker    = 22

Var
  long Stacks[50]

Obj
  D      : "SerialMirror"

PUB Start(ByteToSend,Rates,Semaphore)
  cogNew(ReadPins(ByteToSend,Rates,Semaphore),@Stacks[0])

Pri ReadPins(ByteToSend,Rates,Semaphore)|t
  dirA[Blinker]~~
```

```
    t := cnt                              'initialize the timer
  repeat
      if (cnt-t) => Long[Rates][1]  'blinker time out 2 secs
         !outA[Blinker]                  'toggle the LED
         t :=cnt                          'reset the timer
      Byte[ByteToSend] := inA[7..5]
      if Not LockSet(byte[Semaphore]) 'only send if can acquire the semaphore
         D.Str(string(13,"Read:"))
         D.Dec(byte[ByteToSend])
         LockClr(byte[Semaphore])        'clear the semaphore
```

5.5.3 Tighter Control With Flags

In the previous section we resolved the problem of intermingling bytes sent from the cogs simultaneously by using a very clever technique that the Propeller + Spin make extremely easy to implement. Another technique related to semaphores is *flagging*. Using flagging, a process signals another to go ahead and do something that should only be performed when flagged and once it's finished doing so it should clear the flag which also serves the purpose of telling the signaling process that the task is finished.

A flag serves as a two way signal between two processes where one raises the flag and the other lowers it.

With this mechanism even though the two processes might be running in parallel and at different speeds, the controller process can signal the other to tell it that some data is ready or that it is ok to do something. The other process can check for the flag state (polling) and if it is raised the process does what it is supposed to do and then lowers the flag. This indicates to the master process that the work is done. Sometimes, depending on the task, the process may lower the flag before it finishes doing the work if the action permits that kind of synchronization. This way the flag raiser can go on doing something else while the flagged process can be working at its pace processing the flagged action.

In Progam_08.Spin (and its subordinate objects) we will use flags between the **Main** cog and the two other cogs (2 flags). The flags are basically to let the other cogs know that **Main** has output data to the PST and so the other cogs can output their data too. In this manner **Main** can get in a word edge wise instead of being outspoken by the much more verbose other cogs. When you run Program_08.Spin and observe the output on the PST window you will see that now the **Main** message is visible a lot more often and that the output from all the cogs is taking place in a lot more orderly manner. Also observe that the RB interaction is quite timely too and that the three Blinker LEDs are also blinking on time.

Program_08.Spin

```
'Use Program_06.BAS as the companion RB program
'Use F10 to upload to RAM
CON
  _clkmode = xtal1 + pll16x
  _xinfreq = 5_000_000
  RB_TX         = 1
  RB_RX         = 0
  RB_BAUD       = 115200
  D_TX          = 30
  D_RX          = 31
  D_BAUD        = 115200
  Blinker       = 23
  SetFlagMask  = %0000_0010
  ReadFlagMask = %0000_0001

OBJ
  RB     : "FullDuplexSerial"
  D      : "SerialMirror"
```

```
  Set    : "Program_08_Set"    'our object
  Read   : "Program_08_Read"   'our object

PUB Main|x,t
  RB.Start(RB_RX,RB_TX,0,RB_BAUD)
  D.Start(D_RX,D_TX,0,D_BAUD)
  Semaphore := LockNew                              'create Semaphore
  Set.Start(@ReceivedByte,@Blink_Time,@Semaphore)  'start our object
  Read.Start(@ByteToSend,@Blink_Time,@Semaphore)   'start our object
  dirA[Blinker]~~
  t := cnt                              'init timer
  repeat
    repeat
        x := RB.RXcheck
        if (cnt-t)> Blink_Time     'if time out
           !outA[Blinker]          'toggle LED
           t := cnt                'reset timer
    until x <> -1
    ReceivedByte := x
    RB.TX(ByteToSend)
    if Not LockSet(Semaphore)              'only send if semaphore acquired
       D.Str(string(13,"Main:"))
       D.Dec(ReceivedByte)
       D.Str(string("  , "))
       D.Dec(ByteToSend)
       Flags |= SetFlagMask | ReadFlagMask 'set flags
       LockClr(Semaphore)                          'clear the semaphore

Dat
  ReceivedByte Byte 0
  ByteToSend   Byte 0
  Semaphore    byte 0
  Flags        byte 0
  Blink_Time   Long 80_000_000    '1 sec
  Blink1_Time  Long 160_000_000   '2 secs 2*80_000_000
  Blink2_Time  Long 240_000_000   '3 secs 3*80_000_000
```

Program_08_Set.Spin

```
CON
  Blinker    = 21
  FlagMask   = %0000_0010

Var
  long Stacks[50]

Obj
  D      : "SerialMirror"

PUB Start(ReceivedByte,Rates,Semaphore)
  cogNew(SetLEDs(ReceivedByte,Rates,Semaphore),@Stacks[0])

Pri SetLEDs(ReceivedByte,Rates,Semaphore)|t
  dirA[20..16]~~
  dirA[Blinker]~~
  t := cnt                          'initialize timer
  repeat
```

```
        if (cnt-t) => Long[Rates][2] 'blinker time out
          !outA[Blinker]                'toggle the LED
          t := cnt                      'reset timer
      outA[20..16] := Byte[ReceivedByte]
      if byte[Semaphore][1] & FlagMask    'only output to PST if flagged
          if Not LockSet(byte[Semaphore]) 'only send if semaphore acquired
              D.Str(string(13,"Set:"))
              D.Dec(byte[ReceivedByte])
              byte[Semaphore][1] &= !FlagMask  'clear the flag
              LockClr(byte[Semaphore])         'clear the semaphore
```

Program_08_Read.Spin

```
CON
  Blinker     = 22
  FlagMask    = %0000_0001

Var
  long Stacks[50]

Obj
  D       : "SerialMirror"

PUB Start(ByteToSend,Rates,Semaphore)
  cogNew(ReadPins(ByteToSend,Rates,Semaphore),@Stacks[0])

Pri ReadPins(ByteToSend,Rates,Semaphore)|t
  dirA[Blinker]~~
  t := cnt                           'initialize the timer
  repeat
      if (cnt-t) => Long[Rates][1]  'blinker time out 2 secs
          !outA[Blinker]             'toggle the LED
          t :=cnt                    'reset the timer
      Byte[ByteToSend] := inA[7..5]
      if byte[Semaphore][1] & FlagMask    'only output to PST if flagged
          if Not LockSet(byte[Semaphore]) 'only send if semaphore acquired
              D.Str(string(13,"Read:"))
              D.Dec(byte[ByteToSend])
              byte[Semaphore][1] &= !FlagMask 'clear the flag
              LockClr(byte[Semaphore])        'clear the semaphore
```

Using Semaphores and Flags we managed to tame the chaos caused by unbridled parallel processing. We utilized the power and convenience of multiple microcontrollers doing their work in *parallel but yet in orchestrated unison*.

Semaphores are also a great mechanism for coordinating memory access. Imagine if two processes share a buffer in RAM. One writes to it and the other reads from it. Imagine if the buffer is a few bytes long. If a process reads the buffer while another is still writing to it then it is possible that the reader would be reading jumbled data of old and new bytes. Semaphores should be used to synchronize this process.

Notice in the program how we used a byte variable in the **Dat** section of the top-level-object. The individual flags are the Least Significant (first from the right) two bits of the byte variable.

Rather than passing yet one more parameter to the other cogs we made use of the fact that the **Flags** variable in the **Dat** section comes directly after the **Semaphore** variable. And since we are already passing the *address* of the **Semaphore** variable to the other cogs, we obtain the **Flags** variable by reading the byte after the **Semaphores** variable. Thus the use of **Byte[Semaphore][1]** since **Byte[Semaphore][0]** would be the byte which is the **Semaphore** variable itself then [1] is the byte right after and therefore is the **Flags** variable

ⓘ When sharing RAM variables between cogs, we need to pass the addresses of these variables from the object that contains them to the cogs in the other objects. This can be achieved by passing an address for *each* variable, but this is wasteful. A better mechanism is to ensure that all the necessary variables are arranged in a *contiguous* block of RAM we will call a *buffer*. Then the address of the top of the buffer is passed to the other cogs. This buffer can then be used as an *array* of data. The cog using the buffer can *index* into the buffer as it needs to obtain the **Longs**, **Word** or **Bytes** it needs. Of course the arrangement has to be known so that the correct indexing can be used. However, not all the variables in the buffer have to be of the same type. But care has to be taken to ensure that they are *aligned properly*.

Notice the use of the **FlagMask** constants. These are used to check if the flag is set in the respective cogs by masking out the appropriate bit from the byte that contains all the flags. Also the inverted mask is used to reset the flag.

The flags are not set until **Main** has actually sent some data to the PST. When the flags are set, the other cogs contend between each other for the semaphore to write to the PST. Also the cog does not clear its flag until after it has already written out to the PST. This assures that the cog will continue to contend for the Semaphore until it has written data out to the PST. **Main** also needs to contend for the Semaphore because the two cogs might still be trying to write out and we do not want it to clash.

Semaphore ensures that no two cogs can write out at the same time. The flags are a way for the less frequent writer (**Main**) to not be swamped out and rarely be able to get hold of the Semaphore.

5.6 Parallel-Parallel Processing

The Propeller Chip has a mechanism to create even more parallelism. It is like parallel processing on top of parallel processing. This mechanism is called *counters*. Every cog has two of them. Each counter can do all sorts of actions that once configured can be left alone and they will continue to do their action while the cog is free to do other actions. So this is like two parallel processes going on within the cog and the cog is doing its work in parallel to the others; *Parallel-Parallel processing*.

There are numerous things these counters can do. As a useful example we are going to modify the top-level-object (Program_08.Spin) instead of blinking the LED on P23 to slowly vary the brightness of the LED from off to full brightness and then gradually dimmer until off again. This will continue as long as the cog is active.

We modified Program_08.Spin to make Program_09.Spin. However the sub-objects remain the same. This illustrates the use of making objects since the Program_08_Set.Spin and Program_08_Read.Spin will be used again with Program_09.Spin.

The accompanying RB program remains to be Program_06.Bas since the new system is the same as far as the RB program is concerned. The only difference is that instead of blinking the P23 LED on/off **Main** will use a counter in the *duty mode* to control the level of voltage on P23. This causes the LED to vary in brightness. We will set it so that the LED will repeatedly increase in brightness from off to fully bright in 255 steps over 1 second and then dim back to off in 255 steps over 1 second.

ⓘ The principle is something similar to Pulse Width Modulation (PWM). It is similar in effect but not the same in action. In action it is more aptly called Pulse Frequency Modulation (PFM). Rather than vary the duty of a constant frequency signal we vary the frequency of a constant duty signal.

Even though this sounds complicated, in practice it is quite simple thanks to Spin and the Propeller. Each cog has two Counters **ctrA** and **ctrB**. Assuming we want to use **ctrA**, then what we need to do is:

- ctrA[31..26] := %00110 'set the counter to the code for the Duty mode.
- ctrA[5..0]   := 23   'the pin number in this case 23.
- Setup the frqA register with the right number (see later).
- dirA[PinNumber]~~   'set the pin as an output pin.
- In a loop vary the frqA value to the appropriate number for the desired DAC output level.

That is all there is to it. The only aspect that is not totally simple is the value to place in the **frqA** register. The Propeller documentation explains this very well (pp95-98 in the Propeller Manual V1.1). In this mode the Propeller will add the value inside the **frqA** register to the **phsA** register every time the clock ticks. When the **phsA** register overflows (becomes bigger than $FFFFFFFF) the pin associated with the counter (P23 in this case) will be pulsed on for one clock tick. The more often the pin is pulsed the higher the average voltage level at the pin. So what we need is to calculate the value to place in the **frqA** register to ensure that the **phsA** register keeps overflowing at the right rate.

Here we are going to have the DAC create 256 voltage levels. Since the Propeller is a 32-bit system then $2^{32}/256 =$ 16_777_216. This means that **frqA := Level *Scale** where **Scale = 16_777_216** and Level will be varied from 0 to 255.

To cause the P23 pin to be pulsed every clock tick (i.e. continuously) and therefore create a full average voltage (3.3V) we would set **Level := 255**. This means that now **frqA** will be $FF00_0000. So when, with every clock tick, **frqA** is added to the **phsA** the result will cause the **phsA** register to overflow, which pulses the P23 pin every clock tick.

If we set **Level := 128** then **frqA** will be $8000_0000 which means that it will take two clock ticks for **phsA** to overflow. The pin will be pulsed every other tick resulting in an average voltage of 1.65V. This is the same for all the levels from 0 to 255.

> The above might be confusing but the final outcome is that all we need to do is set **Level** to a value between 0 and 255 and the value of **Scale** is set as a constant in the **Con** section to be 16_777_216 and **frqA** is set to be **Level * Scale**.

Here is the program. Remember it needs the objects which were listed before. Also the accompanying RB program is Program_06.Bas.

Program_09.Spin

```
'Use Program_06.Bas as the companion RB program
'Use F10 to upload to RAM
CON
  _clkmode = xtal1 + pll16x
  _xinfreq = 5_000_000
  RB_TX         = 1
  RB_RX         = 0
  RB_BAUD       = 115200
  D_TX          = 30
  D_RX          = 31
  D_BAUD        = 115200
  Blinker       = 23
  SetFlagMask   = %0000_0010
  ReadFlagMask  = %0000_0001
  DimmerScale   = 16_777_216 ' 2³²÷ 256   for DAC counter
                             ' to make dimming to be 0 to 255
OBJ
  RB    : "FullDuplexSerial"
  D     : "SerialMirror"
```

```
  Set      : "Program_08_Set"        'our object
  Read     : "Program_08_Read"       'our object

PUB Main|x,t,c
  RB.Start(RB_RX,RB_TX,0,RB_BAUD)
  D.Start(D_RX,D_TX,0,D_BAUD)
  Semaphore := LockNew                            'create Semaphore
  Set.Start(@ReceivedByte,@Blink_Time,@Semaphore) 'start our object
  Read.Start(@ByteToSend,@Blink_Time,@Semaphore)  'start our object
  ctra[30..26] := %00110              'Set ctra to DUTY mode
  ctra[5..0]   := Blinker             'Set ctra's APIN
  frqa := DimmerLevel* DimmerScale    'Set frqa register for off to start with
  dirA[Blinker]~~
  t := cnt                            'init timer
  c := 1                              'incrementer for the dim level
  repeat
    repeat
      x := RB.RXcheck
      if (cnt-t)> Blink_Time                'if time out
         DimmerLevel += c                   'increment level
         if DimmerLevel == 255              'if top change incrementr to be -1
            c := -1
         elseif DimmerLevel == 0            'if lowest level change decrementer to 1
            c := 1
         frqA := DimmerLevel*DimmerScale    'set frqA to effect the right Duty
         t := cnt                           'reset timer
    until x <> -1
    ReceivedByte := x
    RB.TX(ByteToSend)
    if Not LockSet(Semaphore)      'only send if can acquire the semaphore
        D.Str(string(13,"Main:"))
        D.Dec(ReceivedByte)
        D.Str(string("  ,  "))
        D.Dec(ByteToSend)
        Flags |= SetFlagMask | ReadFlagMask 'set flags
        LockClr(Semaphore)                   'clear the semaphore
Dat
  ReceivedByte  Byte 0
  ByteToSend    Byte 0
  Semaphore     byte 0
  Flags         byte 0
  DimmerLevel   byte 0                 'Duty level 0-255
  Blink_Time    Long 80_000_000/256    'take a second to brighten/dim all the way
  Blink1_Time   Long 160_000_000       '2 secs 2*80_000_000
  Blink2_Time   Long 240_000_000       '3 secs 3*80_000_000
```

5.7 Stack Overflow

Now that we have the program all working let's see if we can reduce the **Stack[50]** in the **SetLEDs()** cog and the **ReadPins()** cog to something smaller and not so wasteful.

The easiest and quickest approach (there is another) is to just change the 50 to 10 to start with. This is most likely too small. But this way you will gain an appreciation for what happens when you have too small a stack buffer and it overflows causing *memory clobbering*.

See how the program stops working correctly and how the PST is now showing some garbage output. This alone is enough to lead you astray. You might conclude all sorts of possible causes for such behavior that may be valid causes in other situations but in this case are not the cause.

Now try to increase the number by steps of 5 until you get the program working again. This should be sufficient but you may if you really want refine the steps to narrow down the value to a more optimal one.

So the strategy to determine a good value for stack size is:
- ❑ Use a huge number (e.g. 50 or 100).
- ❑ Develop the program and make sure it is working fine.
- ❑ Reduce the number with something obviously too small.
- ❑ Keep increasing it by small steps (e.g. 5) until it works again as before.

> ⓘ Make sure to always keep in mind that stack-overflow is a possible reason for the buggy and weird behavior of your program and try to eliminate this possibility. See Propeller Manual PP 78-83.

5.8 A Musical Keyboard

As you saw in Section 5.6 the counters in the Propeller Chip can be quite interesting. One of the modes for using the **ctrA** or **ctrB** counters in a cog is to generate a signal of a particular frequency. In this section we will make use of this ability to make musical sounds on a Piezoelectric Speaker (Part#900-00001)[27].

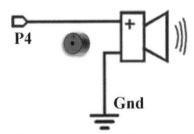

Figure 5.5: Piezoelectric Speaker Connection Schematic.

We will use RB and the Propeller Chip to allow a user to play music on a Piano Keyboard by clicking with the mouse on a graphical representation of the keyboard. Furthermore, there will be a button that when pushed will start playing a tune. The new program Piano.Spin is a modification of Program_09.Spin. We will still use Program_08_Read.Spin but we will not use Program_08_Set.Spin. Instead we will make a new object called Piano_Set.Spin.

Piano.Spin is a major modification of the original object in that we now will receive 4 bytes not one as before. These bytes will be used to create a Long integer (32 bits) using the Little-Endian arrangement since that is what the Propeller uses to store its 32-bit integers. Other actions are as before in changing the brightness of the LED on P23 and everything else as in Section 5.6.

5.8.1 A Different Way of Sharing RAM

Other changes from the old program are that we no longer need the **ReceivedByte** buffer area and also when we **Set.Start()** we no longer need to pass along the buffer address either. This is because we are using a new style of passing the value to the other object and thus to the other cog (see discussion about objects in Section 5.4.1). This is achieved with the *Public* **PlayNote()** method in the **Piano_Set** object. We use the method to pass the value of the frequency to the *object*. But this does not pass it to the *cog*; to make it available to the cog, the method has to store the value into a variable in the RAM to which the cog has access (**Frequency**). This variable is accessible to the cog since it is in the same object as the cog's method. But the variable is not accessible to other objects.

This new method of passing parameters to other objects and on to the cog in the object is effective because it achieves tighter encapsulation. Nevertheless, it is a bit wasteful in that there are function calls to be made and stacks to be pushed and popped and so forth. This can be wasteful in both stack size requirement and in speed. However, encapsulation and hiding of variables may be a desirable property in certain situations.

In this case we will use this method just as an illustration of this option. It would have been more efficient to have given **Main** access to the shared variable and let it set the variable and then the sub-object would see the change. Nonetheless, in certain situations using this methodology might be desirable for other than encapsulation. Sometimes calling methods provides *sequencing control* where some actions are only performed when the method is called as opposed to when the variable changes value which has to be monitored (polled) or by using flagging as we have been doing.

> The Propeller is a 32-bit processor and a Long in its memory is a 32-bit number (4 bytes). You can also access the 4 bytes as individual bytes. If you have a variable **f** declared as a Long you can access its individual 4 bytes using **f.Byte[n]** where **n** ranges from 0 to 3.
>
> The Propeller uses the Little-Endian format to store integers. So if we have an integer in memory that is $A3\_12\_BC\_45$ then in RAM it is actually stored as 4 bytes where the first byte (byte 0) is $45 and the next byte (byte 1) is $BC and so forth. So when we look at **f.Byte[0]** we will see $45 and so on.

Piano.Spin will wait for 4 bytes to arrive from the RB program one by one. When the first one comes in it will be set in the **f.Byte[0]**. The next received will be saved in the next byte (1) and so on. When all 4 arrive the Long value would then be fully formed as a 32-bit integer and it will be passed to the **Piano_Set** object using the **PlayNote()** method which uses it to set the **Frequency** variable in its RAM space where the cog has access to it.

We will still use the **Program_08_Read** object just as before to read the status of the pushbuttons. **Main** will send that value back to RB to serve as a signal to proceed with sending the next 4 bytes and also the RB program may use the pushbuttons' status if needed like before.

The new **Piano_Set** object will not set the LEDs on P20..P16 any longer. Instead it will use the **Frequency** value to set the **frqB** register of a counter as will be explained shortly.

5.8.2 Creating Frequencies (Numerically Controlled Oscillator)

The new object will setup the **ctrB** counter to be in the NCO (Numerically Controlled Oscillator) mode. In this mode the counter will make a pin go high as long as the 32nd bit (bit 31) on the **phsB** register is high and low when it is low. And since the counter will add the value of **frqB** to **phsB** every clock tick then we need to set the **frqB** value so that bit 31 of the **phsB** register will go high and low to generate the right frequency. The formula is:

$$\text{frqB} = \text{Required Frequency} * 2^{32} / \text{clock-frequency.}$$

Since the clock-frequency we are using is 80_000_000 (80 MHz) then $2^{32}/80\_000\_000 = 53.678$

To generate a frequency of say 1708 we need to set **frqB** to the value **round(1708*(2.0^32)/80e6)**. When we send this value to the Propeller, it assigns it to **frqB** and also sets P4 to be an output pin. If P4 is connected to a Piezoelectric Speaker the right tone would be generated.

The object will also blink an LED on P21 (as before). When **Frequency** is other than -1 it will be assigned to **frqB** and P4 will be set as an output pin to allow the oscillations to start. It will also set **Frequency** to -1 to prevent replaying the same note for ever. When the **PlayNote()** method is invoked it will also start a stopwatch timer. This timer is used to stop the note playing if no new note (frequency value) is received before a certain timeout (5 secs)by makingP4 an input pin which will disable the oscillation, effectively stopping the signal. If a new value is received before the timeout then of course it will change the **frqB** value which starts a new frequency and reset the timer.

The new firmware is much like the old system but now RB will have to send the 32-bit (long Integer) frequency value as 4 bytes with the LSByte first and the firmware will receive those bytes and then send a byte back to RB (the pushbuttons status as before).

5.8.3 Testing the Speaker Firmware

The RB program needs to calculate the value to be sent to the Propeller using:

```
N = (2.0^32)/80e6
FreqValue = round(ActualFrequency*N)
```

FreqValue will then be sent using:
```
Serialout BuffWrite("",0,FreqValue)
```

The function **BuffWrite()** is used to create a byte buffer with the 4-byte (32 bits) integer in it. RB also uses the Little-Endian format and so byte 0 is also the LSByte. When **SerialOut** sends the byte buffer all 4 bytes would be sent to the send buffer and then RB would take care of sending these 4 bytes to the Propeller one at a time.

Examine the program Speaker_Tester.Bas to see how this is implemented in the **PlayNote()** subroutine. Also notice how the main program generates random frequencies. The program will not do much else for the sake of simplicity. Notice all the bold code lines to see how the discussion above is implemented in code.

> (i) The Propeller is a 3.3V chip, so the Speaker will not be very loud. You may have to be close to it to hear the sounds well. We will see how to increase the volume of the sound in Chapter 8.

> (i) If you are running on an Me or XP machine you will be able to hear the sounds generated on the PC speaker if you set the variable **Port** to 0 and also uncomment the highlighted line. Do not do this if you have a Vista machine because it may give you an error.

> (i) Another way we can send the 4 bytes of the Long Integer value is to use the **GetByte()** function in a loop:
> ```
> N = (2.0^32)/80e6 \ FreqValue = Round(ActualFrequency*N)
> For I=0 to 3
>     SerialOut GetByte(FreqValue,I)
> Next
> ```

Speaker_Tester.Bas

```
//Speaker_Tester.Bas
//works with Piano.Spin
Port = 8 //change this as per your system
Main:
    setcommport Port,br115200
    while true
        call PlayNote(random(3000)+500,600)
    wend
End
//--------------------------------
sub PlayNote(F,D,&B)
    xystring 1,1,"Note = ",F;"Duration = ",D,spaces(10) //display data
    B = 0 \ c = 1
    if Port == 0                     //if not serial
        //sound F,D                  //play on speaker...only XP machines
```

```
    else                        //otherwise
       N = round(F*2.0^32/80e6)    //convert to frqA values
       SerialOut BuffWrite("",0,N) //send the 4 bytes of the Long LSByte first
       /****this is another way to do the same thing but is commented out
       for i = 0 to 3              //send the 4 bytes of the Long
          serialout getbyte(N,i)   //LSByte first
       next
       ***************************/
       delay D                  //delay
       serbytesin 1,m,c          //get the confirmation byte (buttons state)
       if c then B = getstrbyte(m,1) //get the value
    endif
Return (c==1) //return true or false if there was a byte received
//===================================================================
```

Piano.Spin

```
CON
  _clkmode = xtal1 + pll16x
  _xinfreq = 5_000_000
  RB_TX         = 1
  RB_RX         = 0
  RB_BAUD       = 115200
  D_TX          = 30
  D_RX          = 31
  D_BAUD        = 115200
  Blinker       = 23
  SetFlagMask   = %0000_0010
  ReadFlagMask  = %0000_0001
  DimmerScale   = 16_777_216 ' 2³²÷ 256   for DAC counter
                             ' to make dimming to be 0 to 255


OBJ
  RB      : "FullDuplexSerial"
  D       : "SerialMirror"
  Read    : "Program_08_Read"    'our object
  Set     : "Piano_Set"          'our object

PUB Main|x,t,c,n,f
  RB.Start(RB_RX,RB_TX,0,RB_BAUD)
  D.Start(D_RX,D_TX,0,D_BAUD)
  Semaphore := LockNew                              'create Semaphore
  Set.Start(@Blink_Time,@Semaphore)                'start our object
  Read.Start(@ByteToSend,@Blink_Time,@Semaphore)   'start our object
  ctra[30..26] := %00110                           'Set ctra to DUTY mode
  ctra[5..0]   := Blinker                           'Set ctra's APIN
  frqa := DimmerLevel* DimmerScale                 'Set frqa off to start with
  dirA[Blinker]~~
  t := cnt                                          'init timer
  c := 1                                            'incrementer for dim level
  repeat
    f~
    repeat n from 0 to 3                            'receive the 4 bytes of the Long
      repeat
          x := RB.RXcheck
          if (cnt-t)> Blink_Time                    'if time out
             DimmerLevel += c                       'increment level
```

```
                if DimmerLevel == 255              'if top change incrementer to -1
                  c := -1
                elseif DimmerLevel == 0            'if lowest level decrementer =1
                  c := 1
                frqA := DimmerLevel*DimmerScale    'set frqA to effect the new Duty
                t := cnt                           'reset timer
          until x <> -1
          f.byte[n] := x 'when byte received put it in right byte of the Long
        Set.PlayNote(f)                     'when all bytes received set the Frequency
      RB.TX(ByteToSend)                  'send buttons status
      if Not LockSet(Semaphore)          'only send if can acquire the semaphore
        D.Str(string(13,"Main:"))
        D.Dec(f)
        D.Str(string("  , "))
        D.Dec(ByteToSend)
        Flags |= SetFlagMask | ReadFlagMask 'set flags
        LockClr(Semaphore)                        'clear the semaphore


Dat
  ByteToSend   Byte 0
  Semaphore    byte 0
  Flags        byte 0
  DimmerLevel  byte 0                    'Duty level 0-255
  Blink_Time   Long 80_000_000/256       'take a second to brighten/dim all the way
  Blink1_Time  Long 160_000_000          '2 secs 2*80_000_000
  Blink2_Time  Long 240_000_000          '3 secs 3*80_000_000
```

Piano_Set.Spin

```
CON
  Speaker    = 4
  Blinker    = 21
  FlagMask   = %0000_0010


Var
  long Stacks[50],Frequency,tt


Obj
  D      : "SerialMirror"


PUB Start(Rates,Semaphore)
  cogNew(SetLEDs(Rates,Semaphore),@Stacks[0])


Pub PlayNote(Freq)
  Frequency := Freq
  tt := cnt          'start timeout timer


Pri SetLEDs(Rates,Semaphore)|t
  dirA[20..16]~~
  dirA[Blinker]~~
  t := cnt                            'initialize blinker timer
  ctrB[30..26] := %00100              'set ctrb to NCO
  ctrb[5..0]   := Speaker             'Set ctrb's APIN
  frqB~
  dirA[Speaker]~                      'speaker off for now
  tt := cnt                           'init speaker timer
  repeat
```

```
    if (cnt-tt) > 400_000_000          'if no frequency setting in 5 secs
      dirA[Speaker]~                   'set pin as input to turn sound off
      tt := cnt                        'prevent too many timeouts
    if (cnt-t) => Long[Rates][2]       'blinker time out
      !outA[Blinker]                   'toggle the LED
      t := cnt                         'reset blinker timer
    if Frequency <> -1                 'if value is received
      frqB := Frequency                'set frqB
      'phsB~                           'clear phsB causes clicking if uncommented
      dirA[Speaker] := (frqB <> 0)     'make the pin output allowing sound
      Frequency~~                      'reset to -1 to prevent replaying note

    if byte[Semaphore][1] & FlagMask   'only output to PST if flagged to do so
      if Not LockSet(byte[Semaphore])  'only send if can acquire the semaphore
        D.Str(string(13,"Set:"))
        D.Dec(frqB)
        byte[Semaphore][1] &= !FlagMask 'clear the flag
        LockClr(byte[Semaphore])        'clear the semaphore
```

5.8.4 A Piano Keyboard Player

Now that we tested the new firmware we will write an interesting program utilizing the new firmware to allow a user to interact with a graphical Piano Keyboard on the PC screen. The user can click on the key and will hear the notes playing on the Piezoelectric Speaker on the Propeller. Additionally, there will be a button on the screen that will allow the user to hear a tune playing repeatedly until the button is pushed again. The tune is "Jingle Bells". See Figure 5.6.

The program is a complex one but it basically uses the **PlayNote()** subroutine we saw in Speaker_Tester.Bas to play the note that the user clicks the mouse over. The program will have to determine the following:

1. Which key the user is pushing. This is determined by:
    a. The position of the mouse when clicked.
    b. The color of the key under the mouse.
2. What the frequency of that key is. This is calculated from:
    c. The key's scale.
    d. The Key's position within the scale (Note).

Remember that there are seven normal notes and five sharps in each scale. Also there are 5 scales as drawn on the screen with the middle scale being the middle C-scale. Once the key's scale and note are determined, the actual frequency value is determined from an array of frequencies.

All the code in the program is to draw the keyboard and to determine the key being pushed and its frequency. Once the frequency is determined, it is played by sending it to the Propeller.

Another action the program provides is the ability to play a tune. This is *similar* to the RTTTL tunes on cell phones. The tune is defined as a series of notes and durations with also the ability to define the scale and pauses. The tempo and the code of the duration determine the actual time in milliseconds the note will play. Again, the note's frequency is determined from the scale and the note's position in the scale. These two as before determine the frequency value from the array of frequencies.

Examine the listing below to see how all the above logic is implemented.

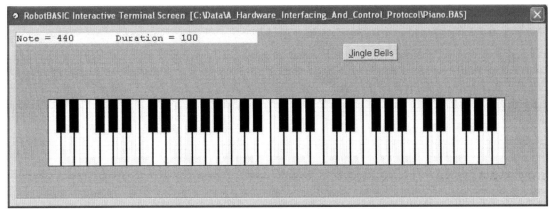

Figure 5.6: Screenshot of Piano.Bas in action

⚠️In Piano.Bas and many of the programs to come we use RB's Call/Sub subroutines with variable parameters, by reference parameters, local variable scoping and global variables with the use of the _ operator. See RobotBASIC_Subroutines.PDF[72] for a tutorial on this powerful feature of RB.

Piano.Bas

```
//Piano.Bas
//Works with Piano.Spin
Port = 0 //set this as per your system
Main:
   GoSub Initialization
   while true
      call CheckMouse()
      while PlayTune
         call Play_Tune(Tempo)
      wend
   wend
end
//=======================================================
Initialization:
   GoSub SetUpNotes
   GoSub SetUp_Jingles
   clearscr gray
   WOffset = 50 \ WW=20
   for i=0 to 7*5-1  //draw the normal keys
      rectanglewh WOffset+WW*i,100,WW,100,rgb(0,0,50)
   next
   BW = 14 \ BOffset = 63
   for i=0 to 7*5-1  //draw the sharp keys
      rectanglewh BOffset+WW*i,100,BW,50,black,black
      if i#7 == 1 || i#7 == 5 then i++ //some sharps not allowed
   next
   data NoteMap; 0,2,4,5,7,9,11
   data SharpMap; 1,3,0,6,8,10
   setcommport Port,br115200
   clearserbuffer
   PlayTune = false
   AddButton "&Jingle Bells",500,20
   onButton bHandler
Return
//=================================================================
```

```
sub bHandler()   //button interrupt handler
   lb = LastButton()
   if left(lb,3) == "&Ji"
      RenameButton lb,"&Stop"
      _PlayTune = true
   else
      RenameButton lb,"&Jingle Bells"
      _PlayTune = false
   endif
   onbutton bHandler
return
//==================================================================
SetUpNotes: //frequencies array
   data Notes;32.703,34.648,36.708,38.891,41.203,43.654
   data Notes;46.249,48.999,51.913,55.0,58.27,61.735
   data Notes;65.406,69.296,73.416,77.782,82.407,87.307
   data Notes;92.499,97.999,103.83,110.0,116.54,123.47
   data Notes;130.81,138.59,146.83,155.56,164.1,174.61
   data Notes;185.0,196.0,207.65,220.0,233.08,246.94
   data Notes;261.63,277.18,293.66,311.13,329.63,349.23        'middle C
   data Notes;369.99,391.99,415.31,440.0,466.16,493.88
   data Notes;523.25,554.37,587.33,622.25,659.26,698.46
   data Notes;739.99,783.99,830.61,880.0,932.33,987.77
   data Notes;1046.5,1108.7,1174.7,1244.5,1318.5,1396.9
   data Notes;1480.0,1568.0,1661.2,1760.0,1864.7,1975.5
   data Notes;2093.0,2217.5,2349.3,2489.0,2637.0,2793.8
   data Notes;2960.0,3136.0,3322.4,3520.0,3729.3,3951.1
   S=-2 \ P=-1\ C=0 \ CS=1 \ D=2 \ DS=3 \ E=4
   F=5 \ FS=6 \ G=7 \ GS=8 \ A=9 \ AS=10 \ B=11
Return
//==================================================================
SetUp_Jingles: //RTTTL codes for the tune
   Tempo = 1500
   data Song;S,5,E,8,E,8,P,32,E,4,P,32,E,8,E,8,P,32,E,4,P,32
   data Song;E,8,G,8,P,32,C,4,D,16,P,32,E,2,P,16
   data Song;F,8,F,8,P,32,F,8,F,16,P,32,F,8,E,8,P,32
   data Song;E,8,E,16,P,32,G,8,G,8,F,8,D,8,P,32,C,2
Return
//==================================================================
sub Play_Tune(Tempo)   //play all the notes in the tune list
  Scale = 4
  FOR i = 0 TO MaxDim(Song,1)-1 step 2
    if Song[i] = _P  //if a pause
      Frequency = 0
      Duration = Tempo/Song[i+1]
    elseif Song[i] = _S   //if scale change
      Scale = Song[i+1]
      continue
    else
      Frequency = Notes[Song[i]+12*Scale]   //determine freq from scale & note
      Duration = Tempo/Song[i+1]            //determine duration from tempo
    endif
    call PlayNote(Frequency,Duration)
    if !_PlayTune || !PlayNote__Result then _PlayTune = false \ break
  next
Return
```

```
//===================================================================
sub PlayNote(F,D,&B)
   xystring 1,1,"Note = ",F;"Duration = ",D,spaces(10) //display data
   B = 0 \ c = 1
   if _Port == 0                        //if not serial
       //sound F,D                       //play on PC speaker...only XP machines
   else
       N = round(F*2.0^32/80e6)      //convert to frqA values
       SerialOut BuffWrite("",0,N) //send the 4 bytes of the Long LSByte first
       delay D                           //delay
       serbytesin 1,m,c                 //get the confirmation byte (buttons state)
       if c then B = getstrbyte(m,1) //get the value of the buttons' states
   endif
Return (c==1) //return true or false if there was a byte received
//===================================================================
sub CheckMouse() //determine which key is pushed
       readmouse x,y,b                       //read mouse
       if !b then call PlayNote(0,1) \ return //if no click then no sound
       c = pixelclr(x,y)                     //get the color under the mouse
       if c == white
         x = (x-_WOffset)/_WW                //convert x to key number
         Scale = 1+x/7 \ Note = NoteMap[x#7] //convert to note number & scale
       elseif c == black
         x = (x-_BOffset)/_WW                //convert to key number
         Scale = 1+x/7 \ Note = SharpMap[x#7] //convert to note number & scale
       endif
       if c == white || c == Black           //if there is a note
           Frequency = Notes[Note+12*Scale]  //convert to frequency
           call PlayNote(Frequency,100)      //play it
       endif
Return
```

An Exercise

In Piano.Bas above, when you press the button on the screen to start playing the tune you can stop the tune by pushing the button again. Is it possible to accomplish the same action with the hardware pushbuttons? The firmware returns the status of the pushbuttons on the hardware; therefore it is possible to have the tune start/stop by pushing a button on the hardware – say the one on P5. If the tune is already playing, pushing the pushbutton on P5 should stop it, and if the tune is not already playing then it should be started; P5 will behave like the button on the RB screen. The tune can be started or stopped (toggled) by pushing either the RB screen button or the hardware P5 pushbutton.

Can you implement the required software changes in the program Piano.Bas to apply the above improvements? What is needed is to use the byte returned by the Propeller with the status of the pushbuttons to decide whether to play the tune if it is not already playing or to stop it if it is already playing. Try to do so without reading the hints. The solution is given below.

The above interaction illustrates how the software can be made to act as a surrogate for the hardware but also augment and enhance it (e.g. the piano GUI keyboard). Also imagine if you had a library of tunes and you wanted to allow the user to select one from a list of tunes. In the software it would be easy to do this (see **AddListBox** command in RB). However, in the hardware you would need additional hardware.

Hint: The buttons are active low.

Hint: Remember that the RB pushbutton needs to be renamed to reflect the state. If the tune is playing it should say **Stop** and if the tune is not playing it should say **Jingle Bells**. This way the button will continue to work correctly in conjunction with the hardware button.

Hint: Look at the **Main** section in the RB program and see what determines if a tune is to be played or not.

Hint: A few lines of code are needed in the subroutine **PlayNote()** just above the **endif** statement. These lines should check to see if the hardware button is pushed and also check what the current condition of play is – if playing then stop, if not then start.

Solution

In the **PlayNote()** subroutine just after the line:

```
if c then B = getstrbyte(m,1) //get the value of the buttons' states
```

Add the following lines:

```
if (~B) & 0%001  //the buttons are active low and P5 is the LSBit
    if _PlayTune
        RenameButton "&Stop","&Jingle Bells"
    else
        RenameButton "&Jingle Bells","&Stop"
    endif
    _PlayTune = ! _PlayTune
    delay 200  //delay to eliminate button bounce
endif
```

5.8.5 Some Thoughts and Considerations

Sections 5.8.3 and 5.8.4 highlight something very interesting. Consider what we did. In Section 5.8.3 we used a **hardware** setup with a **firmware** and a **protocol** to play some random notes by using simple **software**. The protocol allowed the software to send values which the firmware knew what to do with and that caused the hardware to generate an audible frequency on the speaker.

In Section 5.8.4 we used the very same hardware, firmware and protocol; *nothing changed*. The hardware does not know anything about how to play a tune. It does not have any user interface (only the pushbuttons). It has no means of organizing tempo or determining if the user wanted to play Jingle Bells or not. There was nothing in the hardware that even told it what to do if the user did push the pushbuttons. *The hardware and firmware knew nothing except how to play a note of a particular specified frequency and read a pushbutton status*. Yet, when we changed the software we had a sophisticated overall system.

The PC did not have the means of generating the sound. It had no speaker and no frequency generator. However, when combined with the hardware it had the means to do so. The hardware had no means of effecting a user interface, yet when combined with the PC it had the means to do so.

Later in the exercise we saw how powerful the cooperation between the software and firmware can be. The firmware had absolutely nothing to relate the press of a pushbutton to any action other than to send it on the serial port. It had no logic to make it into a toggle switch for playing a musical tune. As far as the hardware is concerned there is absolutely no relationship between the speaker and the pushbuttons. But, with the addition of a few lines of software we made it possible for the hardware to become an intelligent device.

Think about this for a moment. If you are standing away from the PC and do not see the screen while the RB program is running, you can push the button on P5 and hear the song play. You push it again and it stops. The hardware is now doing something intelligent. It knows when you push the button whether to play a song or not. It knows whether a song is already playing to stop it and vice versa. How can it even know that? There is nothing in the firmware that tells it that. *It has decision abilities that were not even programmed at all in the firmware*. The firmware is doing something it was never specifically programmed to do. This is a powerful concept. Three different version of software, using the very same hardware, accomplished different actions. The behavior of the very same hardware changed drastically *only by changing the software*.

This is what we are trying to accomplish here. We want to be able to make hardware do different things but without having to reprogram the firmware on it. Without having to keep changing the low-level Operating System of the hardware we can add new software to make it do new actions.

> (i) The hardware and firmware know *how* to do a low-level action. The software knows the *when* and *why* the hardware needs to do something without having to be hindered with the details of how. It is like a company. The boss knows why she needs a certain product and when it has to be created. The boss has the bigger picture in view; she knows what she wants done to be able to make the company successful. However, she does not know how to create the product. She has no idea how to use a lathe or how to weld. So she employs people who do. She knows the why and when. The employees know the how. Alone the boss could not accomplish her vision. Alone the employees do not have the drive. Together they form a successful endeavor beneficial to all (at least most of the time).

5.9 Parallel Programming Can Create Puzzling Errors

Programming for parallel processing has many pitfalls that can cause quite a lot of puzzling bugs. Often the cause is a lack of appreciation for what can occur when parallel processes are interacting. Other times the cause can be misunderstanding what the mechanisms provided by a system such as the Propeller Chip can do.

Coming from the traditional linear flow programs it is often hard to switch over to a mode of thinking that allows for the nuances of parallel processing. The Propeller Chip enables the creation of parallelism with ease, nonetheless, there are things the Propeller cannot do for you. You still have to consider carefully all the intricacies of interaction that are required to assure proper sequencing and orchestration of the various independent processes.

You have to remember that despite the programs in each cog being linear programs, the overall system is not. Each cog can be in a totally undeterminable state in as far as another cog is concerned. We have already seen one type of this problem where parallelism can be puzzling. When we finally had the program working in Section 5.4 we had the problem of the PST output being a jumble of letters where the messages from all the cogs were *shuffled* together. The fact that the cogs were sending their messages simultaneously through the one serial port was the problem and we devised a mechanism for orchestrating them using semaphores in Section 5.5. We also had to use flags to further control the output of the cogs to stop one swamping and obscuring the output of the others.

5.9.1 An Example of a Parallel Processing Trap

Consider the program Trap_1.Spin. The secondary cog outputs to the PST a message saying that it is working, along with the value of a variable being incremented. When the variable overflows, it causes an LED to be toggled. This is continuing on in parallel to the main cog that is monitoring the status of the P7 and P5 pushbuttons.

If you push the P7 button the main cog changes the value of a variable being monitored by the other cog. The other cog is supposed to terminate its work if the P7 button is pushed because that sets the variable to -1 to signal the cog to stop. Also a message is displayed on the PST indicating that the cog is not working any more. If you push the P5 button the variable will be reset to 0 to allow the secondary cog to start working again.

Try the program and push and release the P7 button. Make sure the PST is active and that you can watch its output. You will notice that the program is not responding properly. You may have to push the button several times before the cog stops. You may even have to push the button and keep it pushed for a while.

Trap_1.Spin

```
CON
  _clkmode = xtal1 + pll16x
  _xinfreq = 5_000_000
  D_TX      = 30
  D_RX      = 31
  D_BAUD    = 115200

OBJ
  D    : "SerialMirror"    'serial driver

Var
  Long Stack[20], sharedVar
PUB Main
  dirA[23..16]~~
  D.Start(D_RX,D_TX,0,D_BAUD)    'start the serial driver
  CogNew(CogProcess,@Stack)
  repeat
     if not inA[7]
        sharedVar := -1
     if not inA[5]
       sharedVar :=0

Pri CogProcess|x
   dirA[23..16]~~
   repeat
      if sharedVar <> -1
         outA[23]~~
         x := (x+1)// $1_0000
         if x == 0
            !outA[16]
         D.Str(string(13,"Working "))
         D.Dec(x)
         waitcnt(clkfreq+cnt)
         sharedVar := 2
      else
         outA[23]~
         outA[16]~
         D.Str(string(13,"not doing anything "))
         D.Dec(x)
```

The Problem

The problem is bad design for a parallel processing system. The secondary cog uses an if-statement to determine whether to stop or not. The condition depends on the value in **sharedVar**. The main cog is attempting to change the variable to signal the other cog to stop. However, within the if-block of the second cog the variable is modified. When the if-statement is evaluated the next time around the main cog may or may not have had time to modify the variable to be –1 in time for the if-statement to fail. Since you are pushing the button and releasing it the main cog would change the variable however the secondary cog might be inside the if-block and is about to execute the line that modifies the shared variable.

Coming from a traditional linear programming environment you may consider that since the main cog has changed the variable the other would not execute the if-block since now the value is -1. But this is not the case. The secondary cog could have *just* finished its conditional statement evaluation when the main cog changed the variable and so the evaluation fails to take into account the new value of the variable. Since the code within the block also changes the variable then things are not as orderly or linear or predictable as you might have thought.

The Solution

The system's design is a bad one and is an illustration of a design not well suited for parallel processing. Nevertheless, there are solutions that would allow the program to work. One solution is to remove the **Waitcnt()** statement. Another is to move the bold line to above the **WaitCnt()** statement; another is to remove the bold line altogether.

The best way is to redesign the system with consideration for the *logistical* actions and keeping in mind the fact that shared variables that are changed by separate cogs may cause *contention* or unpredictable results due to wrong *orchestration*.

5.9.2 An Example of a Propeller Specific Trap

There are also traps that are specific to the Propeller Chip itself. In addition to the pitfall we considered in Section 5.4.4 regarding the fact that each cog has its own direction and output and input registers, there are other traps. Since the I/O lines are shared by all the cogs, you have to be aware of what is the effect on an I/O line if one cog is trying to set it as an output high while the other tries to set it as low. What will happen if one pin is set as an output in one cog and an input in another? The manual points to the answers (Figure 5.3), the I/O pins are ORed together.

Consider the program Trap_2.Spin and its sub-object Trap_Tester_Faulty.Spin. The program is supposed to blink an LED on P16 at the rate of 10 Hz. If you push the pushbutton on P7 and keep it pressed it will become 1Hz and if you push the button on P5 and keep it pressed it will become 3 Hz.

But the program is faulty. Can you figure out why? Study the programs well and see if you can figure out the problem.

Trap_2.Spin

```
CON
  _clkmode = xtal1 + pll16x
  _xinfreq = 5_000_000

OBJ
  T    : "Trap_Tester_Faulty"
  'T   : "Trap_Tester_Working"

PUB Main
  T.Start(10)
  repeat
    if not inA[7]
        T.SetFreq(1)
    elseif not inA[5]
        T.SetFreq(3)
    else
        T.SetFreq(10)
```

Trap_Tester_Faulty.Spin

```
Var
  Long Stack[20]

PUB Start(Initial)
   Cognew(Blink(Initial),@stack)

Pub SetFreq(f)
  frqB := f*54

Pri Blink(Init)
  dirA[23..16]~~
  ctrB[30..26] := %00100          'set ctrb to NCO
```

```
ctrb[5..0]    := 16              'Set ctrb's APIN
frqB := Init*54
repeat
    !outA[23]
    waitcnt(clkfreq/10+cnt)
```

The Problem

The problem is in the way we effect the frequency change. The method **SetFreq()** in the sub-object looks like it should work. It is setting the **frqB** register to the value passed to it. The problem is a lack of appreciation for how a cog is related to the object that starts it.

Think of a cog as a truly independent microcontroller. The only thing it shares with other cogs is the RAM and nothing else. Each cog has its own RAM too and has its own registers. The I/O lines are ORed with the I/O lines of the other cogs.

When Trap_2.Spin calls the method **SetFreq()** and the method sets the **frqB** register it is in fact setting the **frqB** of the cog that called the method which in this case is the main cog and not the cog that is blinking the LED and therefore the frequency is never changed.

The Solution

Uncomment the second line in the **Obj** section of Trap_2.Spin and comment out the first one. This will make it use the Trap_Tester_Working.Spin object. This new object solves the problem by storing the frequency value passed to it in a memory variable that the cog can access. The cog itself then will effect the frequency change by setting *its own* **frqB** register.

Trap_Tester_Working.Spin

```
Var
  Long Stack[20], Freq

PUB Start(Initial)
    Freq := Initial*54
    Cognew(Blink(Initial),@stack)

Pub SetFreq(f)
  Freq := f*54

Pri Blink(Init)
  dirA[23..16]~~
  ctrB[30..26] := %00100          'set ctrb to NCO
  ctrb[5..0]   := 16              'Set ctrb's APIN
  frqB := Init*54
  repeat
      !outA[23]
      waitcnt(clkfreq/10+cnt)
      if frqB <> Freq
          frqB := Freq
```

5.10 Logistical Planning for Parallelism With the Propeller

Here are some points to consider towards a successful parallel system design with the Propeller:

> Always plan a parallel system with consideration for the *logistics* of the various processes being performed. In a true parallel system processes are running independently and *contention* in the usage of resources such as memory and serial ports and so forth are always a possibility.

> Always keep in mind that despite the cogs of the Propeller being encapsulated within the one chip, they are really independent and separate microcontrollers that only share RAM. Therefore design your programs to communicate the cogs using this RAM as the only communications conduit between the cogs.

> Keep in mind that Objects encapsulate variable names and methods. Public methods are available to other objects. You can use methods to communicate objects together or you can use RAM addresses.

> *Objects are not cogs*. An object may encapsulate a cog and the cog has the variables and methods of the object available to it. However, if a cog calls public methods available in another object the actual execution of those methods occurs within the caller cog and does not in any way apply to any cogs encapsulated by the object.

> Remember that every cog is an independent processor. I/O pin directions and states should be set within the cog. They cannot be set by other cogs.

> The Propeller provides *contention resolution* for RAM on the basis of reading one Long. But if you need to read/write multiple Longs/Bytes/Words then you need to consider using Semaphores.

> Always remember that the top-level-object in fact starts a cog implicitly. Other objects if they need to run a cog need to explicitly start it with the **CogNew()** function, however the top-level-object (the main program) does not do so since this is achieved by the boot-loader process when the Propeller starts.

> Do not forget that the when the cog starts it will execute the code given to it in the method that is passed to it. If this method runs out of code to execute, the cog will stop and will go to sleep, and any I/O lines driven by it will be released. To maintain the states of any I/O lines driven by the cog you must keep it running even if that is by adding an endless empty repeat-loop.

5.11 Summary

In this chapter we:

❑ Studied Multitasking using interrupts in RobotBASIC.
❑ Created Parallelism using Polling in RobotBASIC and Spin.
❑ Learned about timing in Spin.
❑ Learned about variable addresses (pointers) in Spin.
❑ Learned about some object-based programming in Spin.
❑ Learned how to start cogs working in Parallel.
❑ Examined the relationship between cogs, methods and objects.
❑ Learned how to debug puzzling problems.
❑ Learned how to use Semaphores and Flags to avoid contentions.
❑ Learned about Stack Space.
❑ Learned about using counters in the Duty and NCO modes.
❑ Utilized a counter to generate sound.
❑ Seen how the PC and Propeller can create synergetic relationship through the protocol, firmware and software.
❑ Learned about some possible traps in using the Propeller and parallelism.
❑ Considered some aspects of the logistics of planning for parallel programs.

A Communications Protocol

Program_09.Spin in Chapter 5 performs quite a lot of actions in parallel, yet effectively synchronized. Figure 5.4 (P23 LED is now a dimmer not a blinker) is a schematic for the actions going on. However, you may argue that the experiment is not really doing much. The reason we have restricted the actions to only LEDs and pushbuttons is that we did not want to be bogged down with wiring and debugging hardware at the same time we were still learning the principles. Also, since the PDB is a ubiquitous and convenient platform it is simple for most to try out and follow along with all the experiments up to this point without too much investment in time and equipment. Moreover, it is the principle that we want to concentrate on at this stage.

What we want is to appreciate the details of programming RB and the Propeller to achieve an effective control system where RB programs can control an array of various hardware systems that carry out parallel, simultaneous and independent actions. Specifically, on a robot these systems are motors and sensors with the *RB programs* performing the *Artificial Intelligence* (thinking) that coordinates all the *hardware* by communicating with the onboard *firmware*.

We have already achieved a modicum of effectiveness and we will add more soon. Consider that in the system of Figure 5.4 we can substitute the LEDs with all sorts of hardware. For instance instead of the LED being dimmed it could be a motor to be driven using PWM. The pushbuttons can be replaced with bumpers or line sensors or infrared proximity sensors. We will eventually add more to the system using more substantial hardware. For example we will add an ultrasonic ranger and servomotors.

Before we start working with a more realistic system, we must develop the principles sufficiently to cope with the intricacies of a real system. It is more important to learn the *principles* than the details. The *overall methodology and principles* are not affected by the details of the hardware. In this chapter we want to expand on the system of Chapter 5 by developing a more effective communications protocol that will make it more versatile and better able to cope with a variety of hardware.

6.1 A Better Protocol?

In the system of Chapter 5 the RB program continuously monitored the status of the checkboxes and sent a byte to the Propeller and then waited for a byte to come back before sending the next byte. This mechanism was developed as a means for synchronizing the exchange of data back and forth in an orderly manner to avoid swamping and loss of bytes. Therefore, in fact we have been using a *protocol* all along, albeit a simple and ad hoc one.

A communications protocol is a *procedure* for an agreed upon sequence of actions to be performed by the sender and the receiver. It provides the means for assuring an orderly and effective data exchange between the sender and receiver.

A serial communications protocol can be a very involved and sophisticated system. Some protocols provide ack/nack, error checking, packet re-sending, and many such details. For our purposes we will not go that far. What we require is a way for:

> ➢ Synchronizing the order of communications.
> ➢ The RB program to know that the data it sent to the Propeller has arrived.
> ➢ The Propeller program to know what it should do in response to and with the received data.
> ➢ The Propeller to send data to the RB program when the RB program asks for it.
> ➢ Handling changes in the firmware without requiring changes in the software.
> ➢ Handling dropped communications and effect graceful recovery.

We will not go so far as to implement CRCs and error checking and other nuances. The reason is that if the serial link is established over a wireless link such as Bluetooth or XBee then all those details are in fact carried out by the hardware in the link. If we use TCP or UDP then again that *layer* of the protocol is handled by the hardware/firmware of the TCP and UDP protocols. If the link is a direct link through wires then the reliability of transmission is quite high. Moreover, if our protocol can deal with the occasional failed communication in an effective manner then we do not really need to go further to assure error free communications.

However, if you feel that your system requires more rigorous checking than what we will develop here then by all means do so. Again, it is the principle that we are trying to impart. If you understand the methodology and appreciate the strategy then you can supply the details for your system's requirements.

6.1.1 A Protocol Enables More Control

Think about the system in Chapter 5 and consider the various parameters we used in it. Here is the **Dat** section from Program_09.Spin:

```
Dat
  ReceivedByte  Byte 0
  ByteToSend    Byte 0
  Semaphore     byte 0
  Flags         byte 0
  DimmerLevel   byte 0                'Duty level 0-255
  Blink_Time    Long 80_000_000/256  'take a second to brighten/dim all the way
  Blink1_Time   Long 160_000_000     '2 secs 2*80_000_000
  Blink2_Time   Long 240_000_000     '3 secs 3*80_000_000
```

The bold lines show the various parameters that so far have been fixed. **DimmerLevel** was varied but in a predetermined manner and the blinking rates of the other LEDs were fixed.

If we want to make those blinking rates controllable by the RB program in addition to sending the status of the checkboxes, what can we do? Also, so far the Spin program has been sending to RB the status of the three pushbuttons using the one byte. What if we had more information that needs to be sent to the RB program? As designed so far our protocol is not sufficiently versatile. If we add more hardware and if we require more control it becomes necessary to change the protocol.

The above actions are not dissimilar to controlling a robot. A robot control program needs to send commands to make the robot perform actions. How should we send these commands? The system also needs to collect information such as the status of the robot's bumpers, infrared sensors and the like. So the program needs to receive all that information too. How and when should we send them?

6.1.2 Specifying the protocol

The protocol we had so far is not sufficient to allow *interactive modification of the parameters* of the system. One way we can extend the protocol is to send control bytes from RB to the Propeller, say one byte for each parameter we want to control. If we want to extend the amount of data to send back to RB from the Propeller we just send as many bytes as we need for the information.

One problem with this strategy is that as the requirements change we would have to reprogram the Propeller with a different protocol to allow for sending/receiving the extra bytes. Another problem is that as the amount of data increases so does the time spent on sending and receiving. Eventually data transmission time will become too long for *real-time* control. In our system so far this is not a major factor but for a robot, for instance, it is of paramount importance that control information arrive in a timely manner and that the response of the system is fast. So increasing the number of bytes to send every time the requirements change is not an efficient or versatile option.

A more effective mechanism would be to send two bytes. The first byte is an action code and the second byte is a parameter. This way RB can command the Propeller to do up to 256 different actions. The second byte is a parameter to specify how to do the action. So for example, in our system, RB sends a byte value of say 1 and the second byte has the value 100. This means to the Propeller that RB wants to carry out command #1 and that the parameter is 100. Let's say command #1 is to set the blink duration for the P22 LED to the level 100. So the Propeller uses that value and converts it using an appropriate formula to represent a timing value and then save it in the Blink1_Time variable. And as the cog uses that value the blink duration will be changed.

This is effective but there is no way for the RB program to know the command has arrived and has been acted upon. One way to do this is to have the Propeller program always send a byte back after receiving the command to acknowledge (Ack) the receipt and completion of the command.

In our simple system, the LEDs on the RB screen need to be updated to reflect the state of the pushbuttons on the Propeller. However, with the above mechanism there is no way to do this. We could of course have RB always send a command to request the value, but then how would the Propeller send that value? Maybe we can use the Ack byte? But another consideration is, how would RB know that the pushbuttons have been changed to know to request the new value? We could make RB always send the command to request the value.

There is another problem to be addressed. What if there are more things that RB requires on regular basis than can fit in the Ack byte. Let's say on a robot there are bumpers, infrared and line sensors. These are time critical data for effective control of a robot for instance and RB needs to have an up-to-date value for them all the time. To request these three bytes of data RB will have to send three commands (3x2 = 6 bytes) and receive three Acks where we use the Ack as the value. That is a total of 9 bytes and since we desire the fastest possible response we need a better way to achieve this with fewer bytes since timing is important.

Consider this better protocol. RB sends two bytes (command and parameter) and then waits with a time out for the Propeller to respond with 5 bytes. If the 5 bytes do not arrive RB would know that something went wrong. RB can then take action accordingly. If the 5 bytes arrive then RB uses these bytes to update some time critical data. But also in some situations RB would request values to be returned other than the standard time sensitive data. Depending on the number of bytes needed to send that data they could also be in the returned bytes.

You may ask why 5 bytes, why not 6, 10 or 2? Remember, we need a minimal number of bytes to send so as to optimize the time response. Conversely, we also want a sufficient number to be able to send all the data that needs to be sent. We will shortly see why 5 is an *adequate compromise*.

Our aim here is to develop a protocol for controlling a complex hardware system. Let's consider what needs to be returned as data from a robot as an example of such a system. A well-designed robot should have bumpers, perimeter infrared or sonar sensors and, for doing things such as line following, line sensors. These sensors are usually the on/off kind (1 bit) or at least can be designed to be so. To be useful, there have to be a few around the perimeter of the robot. To send the status of these arrays of sensors we might need a few bits. A byte (8 bits) for each type should be adequate.

Since these are time sensitive they will have to be transmitted in the first three of the 5 bytes all the time. Some commands may return data. Things like compasses or ultrasonic rangers and the like will return a value. Most of these do not require more than a 16-bit number so two bytes in the 4th and 5th bytes should be sufficient. If a command requires more than 16 bits to return data then we will use all 5 bytes and RB would know then that all 5 bytes are the returned value since it knows what it asked for.

Here is the proposed protocol (see Figure B.5 in Appendix B for the Protocol's State Diagrams):

1. RB sends the command and parameter bytes.
2. The Propeller will sit waiting for the first byte forever. When it arrives, it will wait for the second byte with a timeout. If the second byte comes in within the timeout it will then proceed as below. If no second byte arrives then the Propeller will go back to waiting for the first byte discarding the previously arrived byte.
3. The Propeller receives these two bytes and decides what RB wants done and how depending on the command and its parameter.
4. Within a timeout period the Propeller carries out the command then fills the first three critical bytes that will always be returned with almost every command (for example the values of the bumper, infrared and line sensors).
5. If the executed command also returns a value then the 4th and 5th bytes are used to return the value.
6. If the command requires to return values of more than 2 bytes then it uses all the 5 bytes from the top and forgoes sending the three critical bytes.
7. If RB does not receive the 5 bytes within a timeout it will assume a communications failure and will take action accordingly.
8. If the command is not one that fills all 5 bytes then when RB receives the 5 bytes it will use the first three to update its three critical values in its own memory and discard the extra bytes.
9. If the command also sends data back in the last two bytes RB will extract that from the last two bytes and create the number (Using Most Significant Byte First standard) and use it accordingly.
10. If the command uses all 5 bytes then RB will use all 5 bytes depending on the command and data expected and will not update the three critical data since now the first three bytes are for a different process.

It is possible to vary this protocol to make RB send more than two bytes and also to make the Propeller send back more than 5 bytes. However, this increases the traffic volume and the response time. Additionally we could send back to RB more than 5 bytes to include a CRC for error correction. However, this is not really needed with transceivers such as Bluetooth or XBee. With direct wire connection it is usually not necessary to perform error detection. Besides, this will again just increase the traffic volume and decrease response speed.

As a compromise between the most optimal and the most comprehensive the above protocol is quite adequate and provides sufficient versatility and utility. In the next section we will implement this protocol with the system in Figure 5.4. This will enable us to test the protocol in a proven system. In Chapter 7 we will use the protocol to control another system with real hardware.

6.1.3 Implementing the Protocol

Program_10_Main.Spin, Program_10_Reader.Spin and Program_10_Others.Spin together implement the new protocol described in Section 6.1.2 to control the system in Figure 5.4 (with P23 as a dimmer).

In the firmware implemented by Program_09.Spin we used the **Main** cog's counter (**ctrA**) in the Duty mode as a DAC (Digital to Analog Converter) to control a Dimmer LED on P23 and we had it continuously change brightness. In the new firmware we will have it so that it is controllable by a command that sets the brightness level.

In the old firmware the **ReadPins** cog did the reading of the pushbuttons on the hardware independently and continuously in parallel and saved the value of the bits in one byte that was used by **Main** to send back to RB. In the new firmware, the **Reader** cog will perform a similar action but it will save the pushbuttons separately each in a byte on its own with the first bit being the button's status. It will also blink an LED on the P22 pin as before using time polling to set the on/off duration. But now the duration can be changed using a command from RB with the parameter specifying the duration time (255 steps between off and 2 seconds with 0 being off).

The **SetLEDs** cog in the old firmware did the work of setting 5 LEDs according to a byte value received from RB. We also had it blink an LED on the P21 pin using time polling. The new **Others** cog firmware will perform many more actions. One of the things it will do is to set the 5 LEDs according to a value received from RB but now in a command.

Additionally, instead of blinking the P21 LED using time polling we will use the **ctrB** counter of the **Others** cog in the NCO (Numerically Controlled Oscillator) mode to blink P21 on/off with a frequency between 1 and 255 Hz (0 is off). Again the frequency can be changed using a command from RB with the parameter of the command specifying the frequency.

So the system in Figure 5.4 is slightly changed in that:
  ➢ The brightness of the P23 LED is controlled by the DAC output of the **ctrA** counter of the **Main** cog.
  ➢ The on/off (50% duty) rate of the P21 LED is controlled by the NCO frequency of the **ctrB** counter in the **Others** cog.
  ➢ The On duration (and off) of the P22 LED is controlled by a *Poll timer* (using **cnt**) in the **Reader** cog.

According to the description in Section 6.1.2 we will provide the following Command Codes:
  0: Do nothing but still return the 5 bytes with pushbutton states in the first three.
  255: Reset the Propeller (soft reboot).
  1: Set the LEDs on P16..P20 per the parameter byte.
  2: Set the Blink frequency for the P21 LED per the parameter byte (0 to 255 Hz, 0 is off).
  200: Set the brightness of the P23 LED per the parameter byte (0 to 255 i.e. in 256 steps between 0 and 3.3V).
  201: Set the blink duration of the P22 LED per the parameter byte (255 steps between 0 and 2 secs, 0 is off).
  192: A Command to simulate one of the type where two bytes are retuned in the 4th and 5th bytes. Ignores the parameter byte.
  66: A command to simulate one that returns values in all 5 bytes. Ignores the parameter byte.

In all commands that do not use all 5 bytes to return values the first three bytes will return the status of the pushbuttons. The 1st byte [ie byte 0] = P5, 2nd byte [byte 1] = P6 and 3rd byte [byte 2] = P7. *Inversion is performed on the Propeller side to make the buttons appear to be active high*.

The **Main** cog will wait forever for the first byte to come in. The second byte is awaited with a timeout. If it times out then **Main** goes back to waiting for the first byte again. This assures a graceful recovery from a loss of communications. All RB has to do in the event of loss of synchronization is to wait the timeout periods after which synchronization is reestablished.

Once both (command and parameter) bytes arrive, **Main** will execute the command using the **ExecuteCommand** method. There are 3 kinds of commands:
  1. Commands that change settings that can be changed by the **Main** cog.
     Main will execute these commands and then send the *primary* 5 bytes buffer that are already filled with the three critical bytes by the **Reader** cog.

  2. Commands that return two bytes of data or do not return any data.
     Main will *set a flag* to signal the **Others** cog to handle the command. The **Others** cog will, upon seeing the set flag, execute the command and (if needed) put data in the last two bytes in the *primary* send buffer. Then the cog will *reset the flag*. This will signal **Main** that everything is completed. So it will then proceed to sending the primary send buffer which would have the top three bytes filled with data from the **Reader** cog as normal and the last two bytes having data (if any) from the **Others** cog.

     If the **Others** cog does not reset the flag *within a timeout* period **Main** will not send the buffer and will go back to the top to start receiving commands again after resetting the flag itself. This will cause the RB program to timeout and signal an error, which RB can handle as desired.

  3. Commands that return more than two bytes of data.
     Main will *set a flag* to signal the **Others** cog to handle the command. The **Others** cog will, upon seeing the set flag, execute the command and put data in a *secondary* send buffer. Then the cog will *reset the flag*. This will signal **Main** that everything is completed. So it will then proceed to send the *secondary* send buffer instead of the primary since it now knows that the command was of this type.

If the **Others** cog does not reset the flag *within a timeout* period **Main** will not send the buffer and will go back to the top to start receiving commands again after resetting the flag itself. This will cause the RB program to timeout and signal an error, which RB can handle as desired.

Reading of the pushbutton status is continuously and independently performed all the time filling the top three bytes of the primary send buffer with the results. It is sometimes desirable before we send the send buffer that we should lock a semaphore to assure that the bytes sent are not changed while sending them since the **Reader** cog is running in parallel and it can do so independently. **Main** waits until it gets hold of a semaphore then sends the data assured that they will not be changed and then releases the semaphore. In this way, the **Reader** cog will not write the top three bytes of the primary send buffer until it has locked the semaphore, clearing it after updating the bytes.

In our new firmware we will have this action already programmed but it will be commented out. In our case we really do not care that the **Reader** cog updates the bytes while **Main** is sending them since they are independent sensory data that needs to be as up to date as possible and there is no contention if one or more of the bytes has more recent data than the others. Nevertheless you can always uncomment these lines of code to implement the semaphore and assure the *congruity* of the three bytes.

> ⓘ **Main** may signal any number of cogs to handle commands, and even many simultaneously, but they should also use semaphores to evade writing/reading memory or using exclusive resources concurrently. Additionally, cogs are still doing actions while not handling a flagged command, so cogs can be updating PWM signals or reading special sensors or blinking LEDs or sounding Piezoelectric speakers and so forth. In this section we are only using the **Others** cog for this type of action; later we will add one more cog.

A cog that receives a flag to handle a command will know what the command and its parameter are from a shared memory area. There are two ways to handle a command:
1. Carry out the action and fill the bytes (last two or all 5 or none) and then lower the flag.
2. Store the command and its parameter in local variables, lower the flag and then handle the command by doing what is needed (no data is returned) on its own time without holding up **Main** until it finishes.

The **Others** cog will handle commands of the first type. So the flag will be lowered only after the command is handled and data is put in the bytes to send back to RB if there is a need for that. In Chapter 7 we will see how the second type is used.

> ⚠ All handling of commands of the first type must be completed within the timeout period. For now this timeout period is not changeable. In later improvements we will provide commands to set the timeout.

> ⓘ In summary, there are commands that are handled within **Main** and commands that are handled by other cogs. **Main** will raise a flag that corresponds to the cog it wants to handle the command and then waits with a timeout for the flag to be lowered. One type of cog (e.g. **Others**) handles the command and then lowers the flag and may return data. Another kind of cog stores the command and its parameter then lowers the flag and then handles the command on its time independently *but must not return data*. Other cogs (e.g. **Reader**) do not wait for any flags and will continuously and in parallel perform actions that can fill certain data buffers as agreed upon with **Main**.

In the light of all this, study the listings below. Notice the lines that output to the PST. A semaphore is used just as in Chapter 5 to prevent output clashing. However, swamping may occur if you have the **Reader** output in conjunction with the others since **Reader** is running all the time. You may wish to comment the output lines and have only one cog at a time outputting to the PST. It is useful to study the output in conjunction with interacting with the RB program as we did in Chapter 5. This action of outputting to the PST illustrates yet another level of how the system is nicely multitasking in parallel. See the PST output pointed to by arrows in Figure 6.1 in Section 6.3.

Program_10_Main.Spin

```
'Use Program_10_A.Bas or Program_10_B.Bas as the companion RB program
'Use F10 (or F11) to upload to RAM (or EEPROM)
'Use F11 if you want to try resetting the Propeller while RB is still
'running to see how error tolerance and recovery works
CON
  _clkmode = xtal1 + pll16x
  _xinfreq = 5_000_000
  RB_TX            = 1
  RB_RX            = 0
  RB_BAUD          = 115200
  D_TX             = 30
  D_RX             = 31
  D_BAUD           = 115200
  DimmerPin        = 23
  OthersFlagMask = %0000_0001    'flag mask for flagging the Others Cog
  DimmerScale      = 16_777_216  ' 2³²÷ 256    for DAC counter
                                 ' to make dimming to be 0 to 255

Var
   byte SendBufferOffset
OBJ
  RB     : "FullDuplexSerial"
  D      : "SerialMirror"
  Others : "Program_10_Others"
  Reader : "Program_10_Reader"


PUB Main|x
  Initialization
  repeat
    SendBufferOffset~      'reset data buffer pointer
    ReceiveCommand         'receive 2 bytes command, parameter
    OutputToPST_1          'output some info to the PST
    ExecuteTheCommand      'Execute the Command
    SendTheBuffer          'send the data buffer (either the
                           'normal or the secondary depending
                           'on the command just executed
    OutputToPST_2          'output some info to the PST

Dat
  Command         Byte 0,0             'command and parameter from RB
  PrimaryBuffer   Byte 0,0,0,0,0       'primary 5 bytes to send to RB
  SecondaryBuffer Byte 0,0,0,0,0       'secondary 5 bytes to send to RB
  Sems_Flags      byte 0,0,0           'semaphore1,flags,semaphore2
  Settings        Long 80_000_000      'various settings buffer
                                       '[0] is Reader blinker duration
  TimeOut1        Long 240_000_000 '3 secs time out for receiving second byte
  TimeOut2        Long 320_000_000 '4 secs timeout to be allowed to send data

Pri Initialization
  RB.Start(RB_RX,RB_TX,0,RB_BAUD)      'start FDS serial driver
  D.Start(D_RX,D_TX,0,D_BAUD)          'start SM driver (only need to do once)
  Sems_Flags[0] := LockNew             'create Semaphore for SendBuffer
  Sems_Flags[2] := LockNew             'create Semaphore for PST output
  Others.Start(@Command,@Settings,@Sems_Flags)        'start Others Cog
  Reader.Start(@PrimaryBuffer,@Settings,@Sems_Flags)  'Start Reader Cog
  'create a dimmer LED on P23
```

```
  ctra[30..26]  := %00110        'Set ctra to DUTY mode
  ctra[5..0]    := DimmerPin     'Set ctra's APIN
  frqA := 127 *DimmerScale       'Set frqa register to mid level to start with
  dirA[DimmerPin]~~              'make output pin

Pri ReceiveCommand|t,x
  repeat
    Sems_Flags[1]~              'reset flags
    repeat                     'wait forever to receive command byte
        Process0               'call process that need to be done always
        x := RB.RXcheck
    until x <> -1
    Command[0] := x
    t := cnt                   'init timer
    repeat                     'wait with timeout to receive parameter
        Process0               'call process that needs to be done always
        x := RB.RXcheck
        if cnt-t > TimeOut1
            quit
    until x <> -1
    if x == -1                 'if no byte received loop back to the top
      Next                     'gracefully recover from receive error
    Command[1] := x
    quit                       'exit to return to Main

Pri SendTheBuffer|x
  if Not Sems_Flags[1]        'if flags clear then send bytes
   'if SendBufferOffset == 0 'if using primary buffer wait for semaphore
   '                          'to ensure data congruity
   '    repeat until Not LockSet(Sems_Flags[0])
   '        'wait for semaphore forever, may need to do timeout but
   '        'uncomment these lines to assure data congruity
   '        'also the LockClr() below
    repeat x from 0 to 4        'transmit the 5 bytes of data
      RB.TX(PrimaryBuffer[x+SendBufferOffset])
    'if SendBufferOffset == 0   'if data congruity with semaphore is used
   '    LockClr(Sems_Flags[0])  'then also uncomment out these two line also

Pri Process0
  'can do anything here.
  'but there is nothing to do in this case
  'but could be anything that requires polling or updating etc.

Pri ExecuteTheCommand
  case Command[0]
    255: 'reset the propeller
      Reboot

    200:'set the Dimmer level on P23
      frqA := Command[1] *DimmerScale

    201:'set blinker duration for Reader cog(P22)
        '256 levels between 0 to 2 secs (0=off)
      Settings[0] := Command[1]*(2_000/255)*(ClkFreq/1_000)

    1,2,192:'commands in the Others cog that may fill the
```

```
              'the last two bytes in the primary send buffer
       Sems_Flags[1] |= OthersFlagMask      'set flag
       WaitForFlagResetWithTimeOut(OthersFlagMask)


    66:'commands in the Others cog that fill the secondary send buffer
       SendBufferOffset := 5              'command uses the secondary buffer
       Sems_Flags[1] |= OthersFlagMask  'set flag to signal the cog
       WaitForFlagResetWithTimeOut(OthersFlagMask)

Pri WaitForFlagResetWithTimeOut(Flag)|t
  t:=cnt
  repeat until cnt-t > TimeOut2 'wait for flag to clear with time out
     Process0
     if Not(Sems_Flags[1] & Flag)
        quit

Pri OutputToPST_1
  if Not LockSet(Sems_Flags[2])  'output info to the PST if semaphore acquired
    D.Str(string(13,"Main Received:"))
    D.Dec(Command[0])
    D.Str(string(","))
    D.Dec(Command[1])
    LockClr(Sems_Flags[2])

Pri OutputToPST_2|x
  if Not LockSet(Sems_Flags[2]) 'output info to the PST if semaphore acquired
    D.Str(string(13,"Main Sending:"))
    repeat x from 0 to 4          'show the bytes sent
       D.Dec(PrimaryBuffer[x+SendBufferOffset])
       D.Str(string(","))
    LockClr(Sems_Flags[2])
```

Program_10_Reader.Spin

```
CON
  Blinker     = 22
Var
  long Stacks[50]
  long t, SendBuffer,Settings,Sems_Flags
  byte LocalBytes[3]
Obj
  D      : "SerialMirror"

PUB Start(SendBufferAddr,SettingsAddr,Sems_FlagsAddr)
  SendBuffer  := SendBufferAddr    'save all passed addresses as
  Settings    := SettingsAddr      'local variables to be used
  Sems_Flags  := Sems_FlagsAddr    'by all processes
  cogNew(Reader,@Stacks[0])        'start the cog

Pri Reader
  Initialization
  repeat
    Process0
    ReadByte0
    ReadByte1
    ReadByte2
    PutBytesInSendBuffer
```

```
Pri Initialization
  'initialize variables I/O direction etc.
  dirA[Blinker]~~
  t := cnt                                    'initialize the timer

Pri Process0
  'can do anything here that requires polling or regular updating
  'For example we are blinking an LED on P22 using a stop watch
  'action with the variable t that hast to be initialized before
  'calling this process for the first time.
  if Long[Settings][0] == 0                   'if duration is 0 then off
    outA[Blinker]~
  elseif (cnt-t) => Long[Settings][0]         'blinker time out
    !outA[Blinker]                            'toggle the LED
    t :=cnt                                   'reset the timer

Pri ReadByte0
  'could do all sorts of actions here that are needed
  'to read the byte from any source eg. Bumpers
  'for now just read the pushbutton on P5 invert it
  'and mask it to make sure it is and active high not low
  'and in the LSbit
  LocalBytes[0]:= !inA[5] & $01

Pri ReadByte1
  'could do all sorts of actions here that are needed
  'to read the byte from any source eg. Bumpers
  'for now just read the pushbutton on P6 invert it
  'and mask it to make sure it is and active high not low
  'and in the LSbit
  LocalBytes[1]:= !inA[6] & $01

Pri ReadByte2
  'could do all sorts of actions here that are needed
  'to read the byte from any source eg. Bumpers
  'for now just read the pushbutton on P7 invert it
  'and mask it to make sure it is and active high not low
  'and in the LSbit
  LocalBytes[2]:= !inA[7] & $01

Pri PutBytesInSendBuffer|i
  if Not LockSet(byte[Sems_Flags][0]) the bytes to send if got semaphore
    repeat i from 0 to 2
      byte[SendBuffer][i] := LocalBytes[i]
    LockClr(byte[Sems_Flags][0])             'clear the semaphore
    OutputToPST                              'send some info to the PST

Pri OutputToPST|i
  if Not LockSet(byte[Sems_Flags][2]) 'write debug messages to the PST
    D.Str(string(13,"Reader:"))       '    if semaphore acquired
    repeat i from 0 to 2
      D.Dec(byte[SendBuffer][i])
      D.Str(string(","))
    LockClr(byte[Sems_Flags][2])
```

Program_10_Others.Spin

```
CON
  Blinker       = 21
  FlagMask      = %0000_0001     'mask for flag for this cog
  BlinkerScale  = 54             ' 2³²÷ 80_000_000 for NCO counter
  Offset_1      = 5      'offset for location of 2 byte data buffer
  Offset_2      = 7      'offset for location of 5 byte data buffer

Var
  long Stacks[50], t
  Long Command,Settings,Sems_Flags

Obj
  D       : "SerialMirror"

PUB Start(CommandAddr,SettingsAddr,Sems_FlagsAddr)
  Command    :=    CommandAddr    'save all passed addresses as
  Settings   :=    SettingsAddr   'local variables to be used
  Sems_Flags :=    Sems_FlagsAddr 'by all processes
  cogNew(Others,@Stacks[0])       'start the cog

Pri Others
  Initialization
  repeat
    Process0
    if Not(byte[Sems_Flags][1] & FlagMask) 'if flag not set then no action
      Next                                 'required, just loop back
    case byte[Command][0]      'execute the command
        1: Set_LEDs
        2: Set_BlinkRate
       66: Action_66
      192: Action_192
    OutputToPST                           'output some info to the PST
    byte[Sems_Flags][1] &= !FlagMask   'clear flag to signal Main to proceed

Pri Initialization
  'initialize variables I/O direction etc.
  ctrB[30..26] := %00100          'Set ctrB for "NCO single-ended"
  ctrB[5..0]   := Blinker         'Set ctrB's APIN
  frqB         := 10*BlinkerScale 'set rate
  dirA[20..16]~~
  dirA[Blinker]~~
  t := cnt                        'initialize timer

Pri Process0
  'can do anything here.
  'but there is nothing to do in this case
  'but could be anything that requires polling or updating etc.

Pri Set_LEDs
  'set the LEDs on P20..P16 per the parameter byte
  outA[20..16] := Byte[Command][1]

Pri Set_BlinkRate
  'set the blink rate  for P21
  frqB := byte[Command][1] * BlinkerScale 'set rate
```

```
  if frqB == 0
    phsB~    'make sure the pin is low if it to be off

Pri Action_192
  'simulate a command that returns some data in
  '4th and 5th bytes in the normal send buffer
  'for now doing nothing but could do any process here
  'to obtain the bytes
  byte[Command][Offset_1]    := 4
  byte[Command][Offset_1+1]  := 5

Pri Action_66
  'simulate a command that returns some data in the
  'secondary send buffer. For now it is doing nothing
  'but can do any process here to obtain the data
  byte[Command][Offset_2]    := 10
  byte[Command][Offset_2+1]  := 20
  byte[Command][Offset_2+2]  := 30
  byte[Command][Offset_2+3]  := 40
  byte[Command][Offset_2+4]  := 50

Pri OutputToPST
  if Not LockSet(byte[Sems_Flags][2]) 'output some info to the PST
    D.Str(string(13,"Others:"))        'if semaphore acquired
    D.Dec(byte[Command][0])
    D.Str(string(","))
    D.Dec(byte[Command][1])
    LockClr(byte[Sems_Flags][2])
```

Program_10_A.Bas is a modification of Program_06.Bas to work with the new protocol. Study it and try to figure out where and why the changes were made in comparison to 06. It is a simple program that exercises the new system. But, now that we can do a lot more than just set the LEDs we need a program to reflect this. See Program_10_B.Bas in Section 6.3, it is a fully GUI program that provides full control over the various parameters and variables of the system.

Program_10_A.BAS

```
//Program_10_A.BAS
//work with Program_10_Main.Spin
Port = 8  //change this as per your system
Main:
    setcommport Port,br115200   //set serial comms
    xystring 10,10,"Click on the checkbox to light up the corresponding LED"
    xystring 10,70,"Press the buttons on the Propeller and see the "+\
                "corresponding checkbox change"
    for i=0 to 4
      AddCheckBox "DS"+i,60+20*i,40," "   //add checkboxes as bits to form the
    next                                  //number to send
    while true
      x =0
      for i=0 to 4   //form the byte from the individual bits
         if GetCheckBox("DS"+i) then x += 1<<(4-i)
      next
      serialout 1,x  \ xystring 240,40,"=",x,spaces(20)
      serbytesin 5,s,x
      if x < 5 then continue
      for i=0 to 2
         if Getstrbyte(s,i+1)
```

```
            circlewh 60+i*40,100,30,30,red,red   //simulate LED on
        else
            circlewh 60+i*40,100,30,30,red       //Simulate LED off
        endif
      next
   wend
end
```

6.2 Fault Tolerance With Recovery

One of the important things in a communications process is the ability of the system to ***properly recover from a fault***. Communication can lose synchronization due to a fault on either side of the communications process. For example a power outage on the Propeller side will cause the Propeller to reset. Similarly the RB side of things can drop the link.

It is important if this happens that the non-fault side be able to reset itself to a position in the program flow so that when the faulty side resolves the problem and tries to reestablish the exchange, it would be able to do so without having to reset both systems.

The way we achieve this with the protocol in Section 6.1 is with the way the Propeller program always goes back to receiving the first byte if anything goes wrong and that it remains there waiting for the first byte. So the Propeller is always guaranteed to be at a ***known state*** after a timeout period if communications are interrupted for any reason. Therefore all RB has to do if there is a fault is to wait a little then go back to transmitting the first byte again.

Due to the nature of our protocol both sides know when a fault occurs. RB knows because it won't receive the 5 bytes in response to the two bytes it sent. The Propeller also knows something is wrong if it receives the first byte and does not receive the second byte within the timeout period. It is also possible for the Propeller process requested by the command to fail and not finish its task on time. The fact that the protocol prevents the Propeller from sending the response 5 bytes ensures that RB knows that some fault occurred. RB can then take appropriate measures. But always knowing that it can reestablish the link because the Propeller is guaranteed to be again waiting for the command.

You can see that with the design of the protocol we have an effective way for both sides to be able to know when a fault has occurred and to be able to ***recover*** from the fault and to ***resynchronize*** and reestablish communications. Do the following exercise to prove the fact:

- ❑ Compile Program_10_Main.Spin and upload it to EEPROM (F11).
- ❑ Run Program_10_A.BAS.
- ❑ Try clicking the checkboxes on RB and pressing the pushbuttons on the Propeller.
- ❑ Establish that all is working properly. Keep the state of the check boxes on the RB screen in some combination other than all unchecked.
- ❑ Now reset the Propeller.
- ❑ Notice that when the Propeller reboots it turn the LEDs on corresponding to the state of the checkboxes on the still running RB program. Notice that we did not have to restart the RB program or even stop it.
- ❑ Keep some LEDs lit on the Propeller by clicking some checkboxes.
- ❑ Now quit the RB program.
- ❑ Restart the RB program.
- ❑ Notice that the Propeller will turn off the LEDs to reflect the unchecked boxes upon starting the RB program again.
- ❑ Click some boxes.
- ❑ Notice how the RB program can control the Propeller without having to reset it.

As you can see from this there is a very strong fault tolerance and recovery built in the protocol.

6.3 GUI Instrumentations

With the new protocol we can now control numerous things in the hardware and firmware on the Propeller. It is not like before where we just set the LEDs and received the pushbutton status. Now we can carry out a few other interactions. We can:

 ➢ Change the Blink duration of the P22 LED.
 ➢ Change the Blink frequency of the P21 LED.
 ➢ Change the brightness level of the P23 LED.
 ➢ Change the on/off state of the LEDs on P20..P16.
 ➢ Press pushbuttons on P7..P5.
 ➢ Execute two additional commands that return data.

What we need is a program that gives us control over these actions, like systems you may have seen in factories or other places, where a computer with a Graphical User Interface (GUI) provides visual feedback on the status of some sensors (transducers) and allows for control of motors and such (i.e. actuators).

The new Program_10_B.BAS illustrates the power and advantage of using the protocol in the system as we have developed it so far. It shows how we can do all sorts of hardware actions using the power of a Graphical User Interface to provide a visual and effective feedback and control (see Figure 6.1).

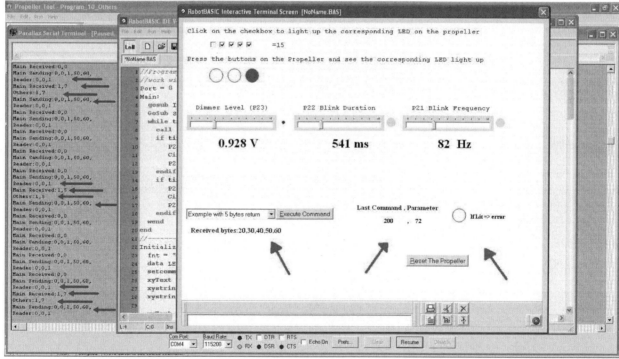

Figure 6.1: A screenshot of Program_10_B.Bas in action. The arrows point to areas of interest as discussed in the text.

Notice that this RB program is using Event-Handlers (interrupts as in Chapter 5.1). It uses a lot of RB's abilities and is a good illustration of the kind of power you can achieve with RB. You should study the program carefully to get an appreciation for its logic. It also employs a few interesting programming tricks to make the code more efficient and generic. Compare Figure 6.1 to Figures 7.9 and 8.15 which show how this program is evolved as the hardware grows in complexity.

Figure 6.1 also shows some debug information that the system outputs to the PST screen. Study the output on the PST and observe the order of the display from the various cogs. This should be quite informative and instructive in how Parallel Processing takes place.

Also notice how the RB program is designed to give us *diagnosis* information. For instance we can always see the last command and parameter bytes sent to the Propeller. Change some things and see how this helps study the actions of the program. Also notice how the Error LED gives us an interesting indicator. Turn the Propeller off and see what happens. Make sure you have the program in the EEPROM so that when you reset or restart the Propeller the program will still be rebootable.

The RB program uses some simple Graphics to simulate blinking LEDs that reflect the blinking rate of the LEDs on the Propeller. Also the dimmer on the RB screen emulates the one on the Propeller. It is made red so that you can see the very dim state easier since yellow is hard to see when the LED is very dim.

Note how the list box on the bottom left of the screen allows us to select one of the emulation commands. These commands don't actually do anything other than return data. They are there to exercise the action of issuing a command that will return data in the last two bytes of the primary send buffer and data in the secondary send buffer. For now the data is just numbers set by the methods in the Spin program. In Chapter 7 we will use these commands to return real data from reading real hardware. For now just use the list box to select one and press the execute button to see how the returned bytes are printed underneath the list box (pointed to by the arrow in Figure 6.1).

Program_10_B.Bas

```
//Program_10_B.BAS
//work with Program_10_Main.Spin
Port = 8  //change this as per your system
Main:
  gosub Initialization
  GoSub SetAllLevels
  while true
    call SendCommand(Command,Parameter,true)
    if timer()-P22_Timer > sValue[1]  //if P22 blinker time out
        P22_State = !P22_State \if !sValue[1] then P22_State=0
        CircleWH 455,205,20,20,FactorColor(ConsToClr(yellow),\
              -20),LEDState[P22_State*2]
        P22_Timer = timer() //reset timer
    endif
    if timer()-P21_Timer > 500.0/Limit(sValue[2],1,255)//if P22 blinker timeout
        P21_State = !P21_State \if !sValue[2] then P21_State=0
        CircleWH 695,205,20,20,FactorColor(ConsToClr(yellow),\
              -20),LEDState[P21_State*2]
        P21_Timer = timer() //reset timer
    endif
  wend
end
//----------------------------------------------
Initialization:
  fnt = "Times New Roman"
  data LEDState;white,red,yellow
  setcommport Port,br115200   //set serial comms
  xyText 390,390,"Last Command , Parameter",fnt,11,fs_Bold
  xystring 10,10,"Click on the checkbox to light up"+
                  " the corresponding LED on the propeller"
  xystring 10,70,"Press the buttons on the Propeller and see the "+\
                  "corresponding LED light up"
  xyText 640,410,"If Lit => error",fnt,10,fs_Bold
  for i=0 to 4
```

```
      AddCheckBox "DS"+i,60+20*i,40," "    //add checkboxes as bits to form the
    next                                    //number to send
    data sLabel;"Dimmer Level (P23)","P22 Blink Duration","P21 Blink Frequency"
    data sCommand; 200,201,2
    data sValue; 0,0,0,127,127,10
    for i=0 to 2
      xyString 240*i+30,175,sLabel[i]
      AddSlider "P"+(23-i),10+240*i,200,200,0,255
      SetSliderPos "P"+(23-i),sValue[i+3]
      call MakeValue(i,sValue[i+3])
      xyText 80+240*i,245,MakeValue__Result,fnt,20,fs_Bold
    next
    call DrawDimmer(sValue[3])
    CheckBoxes = 0
    Command = 0 \ Parameter = 0
    P22_Timer = timer() \ P22_State = 0
    P21_Timer = timer() \ P21_State = 0
    LastSlider()   'clear any slider events
    AddButton "&Reset The Propeller",500,500
    AddButton "&Execute Command",210,400
    data OtherCommands;"Example with 2 bytes return"
    data OtherCommands;"Example with 5 bytes return"
    data OtherCommandsV;192,66
    data OtherCommandsP;2,5
    AddListBox "Commands",10,402,200,mToString(OtherCommands)
    SetListBox "Commands",1
    onCheckBox cbHandler \ onSlider sHandler \ onButton bHandler
Return
//-------------------------------------------------
SetAllLevels:
    serialout 1,_CheckBoxes     //force checkboxes to be reflected
    for i=0 to 2                //force blinkers and dimmers to be set
       serialout sCommand[i],getsliderpos("P"+(23-i))
    next
Return
//-------------------------------------------------
sub SendCommand(Command,Parameter,SetLeds)
    if Command
        xyText 450,420, Format(Command,"##0"+spaces(10))+\
             ", "+Format(Parameter," ##0         "),_fnt,10,fs_Bold
    endif
    ClearSerBuffer \ serialout Command,Parameter
    _Command = 0 \ _Parameter = 0  //clear last command
    serbytesin 5,s,x
    circlewh 600,400,30,30,red,LEDState[(x<5)]  //set the error LED
    if x < 5 || !SetLeds then return s
    for i=0 to 2
      circlewh 60+i*40,100,30,30,red,LEDState[Getstrbyte(s,i+1)&1]//set the LED
    next
Return s
//-------------------------------------------------
sub bHandler()
  lb = LastButton()
  msg="Are you sure you want to reset the Propeller"+crlf()+\
              "If the program is in RAM you will lose it!"
  if left(lb,2) == "&R"
```

```
        if ErrMsg(msg,"RobotBASIC",MB_YESNO|MB_ERROR)==MB_YES
            serialout 255,0                  //reset
            delay 2000
            GoSub SetAllLevels
        endif
    elseif left(lb,2) == "&E"
        n = GetListBox("Commands")-1 \ x = (OtherCommandsP[n] <3)
        call SendCommand(OtherCommandsV[n],0,x)
        s = SendCommand__Result
        n = 1 \ if x then n=4
        ss = "Received bytes:"
        if Length(s)
            for i=n to 5
                ss += ""+getstrbyte(s,i)+","
            Next
        else
            ss += "Error "
        endif
        xyText 20,440,left(ss,length(ss)-1)+spaces(50),_fnt,,fs_Bold
    endif
    onbutton bHandler
return
//-----------------------------------------------
sub cbHandler()
    lcb = LastCheckBox()
    _CheckBoxes = MakeBit(_CheckBoxes,4-ToNumber(right(lcb,1)),GetCheckBox(lcb))
    xystring 200,40,"=",_CheckBoxes,spaces(20)
    _Command = 1 \ _Parameter = _CheckBoxes
    onCheckBox cbHandler
Return
//-----------------------------------------------
sub sHandler()
    ls = LastSlider()
    _Parameter = GetSliderPos(ls)
    n = 23-tonumber(substring(ls,2))
    _Command = sCommand[n]
    if n == 0 then Call DrawDimmer(_Parameter)
    call MakeValue(n,_Parameter)
    xyText 80+240*n,245,MakeValue__Result,_fnt,20,fs_Bold
    onSlider sHandler
return
//-----------------------------------------------
sub MakeValue(which,Level)
    if which == 0   'dimmer
        n = Level/256.0*3.3
        Level = Format(n,"0.000 V  ")
    elseif which == 1   'P22 blink duration
        n = Level*2000/256
        Level = Format(n,"####0 ms  ")
    else
        n = Level
        Level = Format(n,"##0  Hz  ")
    endif
    sValue[which] = n
return Level
//-----------------------------------------------
```

```
sub DrawDimmer(Level)
     CircleWH 212,202,26,26,white,white
     if !Level then return
     x = 1+(20*Level/256)/2
     Circle 225-x,215-x,225+x,215+x,red, RGB(Limit(Level,70,255),0,0)
return
```

6.4 Versatility of the Protocol

Another advantage of the protocol is that regardless of the hardware on the Propeller the protocol can be used to control it. As long as the Propeller program is able to execute the commands agreed upon:

➢ The system can be expanded to allow new commands.
➢ The implementation of the hardware that carries out the actual actions can use different hardware as long as the data returned is the expected one. For example the first bye in the 5 bytes can be data from up to 8 bumper switches or it can be data from 8 infrared proximity sensors acting as bumper switches. Maybe you are not running a robot at all. You can still use the protocol to, for example, return a temperature value in the first byte as an 8-bit number.
➢ The RB program that interacts with the Propeller can be changed to do new things or to do the same things in a different way. But due to the protocol the firmware (Propeller program) does not have to be changed every time we want the system to do different actions. We just change the RB program.

We have seen how a different RB programs can interact with the same firmware program without having to change anything on the Propeller. Proram_10_A.Bas and Program_10_B.Bas are a great example of that.

We can also show how the same is true with the Propeller side. A different firmware can be made to run and still use the very same RB program. We are not going to give a listing of this program. However in the downloadable Zip file there is a program (and its associated objects) called Program_10_Main_Simple.Spin. Use that and run it with either of the RB programs above. See how even though the Spin program is quite a different one it still functions perfectly with the same RB program. This is due to the protocol.

> ⓘNeither the RB program (*software*) nor the Spin program (*firmware*) matter and to a certain extent not even the *hardware*. Even the details of how they *implement* the protocol are not crucial. What matters is that they *perform* the actions required by the protocol.

6.4.1 A Thought Exercise

As an illustration of how a well-designed system should allow for changes with ease we will do a small exercise. The solution will be given later as part of a future improvement. If you look at Program_10_Main.Spin there is a section called **Dat**. In the bottom of the list of variables there are two: **TimeOut1** (set to 3 secs 240_000_000) and **TimeOut2** (set to 4 secs 320_000_000).

In the system there is no way to change the values of these timeouts without changing the Spin program and recompiling it to the Propeller. If the protocol allowed us to change these two values by sending a command then we could change the responses of the system without recompiling. How can we expand Program_10_Main.Spin to allow for this? We can just use a new command code and then use the parameter byte to send the new desired value. However, there is a snag. The value is a LONG (32-bit Integer). We can only send a value of a BYTE (8-bit Integer). So how can we do this? How can we transmit using 1 command byte with 1 parameter byte to set the value of the timeout that is a Long value?

Think about what it would take to implement the new command. How can we send a 1-byte value that would translate into the 4-byte value required to set the system parameter TimeOut1 or TimeOut2? We will show the solution in Chapter 7.7.3.

For now look at the following lines from the **ExecuteTheCommand** method in Program_10_Main.Spin:

```
201:'set blinker duration for Reader cog(P22)
    '256 levels between 0 to 2 secs (0=off)
  Settings[0] := Command[1]*(2_000/256)*(ClkFreq/1_000)
```

See how the parameter for the command #201 is used to set the on/off duration of the P22 LED. It maps the byte value ranging from 0 to 255 to a value that ranges between 0 and 2000 (milliseconds). So, it effectively achieves being able to specify a parameter that can be bigger than one byte with only one byte.

This is another example of **_data remapping_** but on the firmware side this time. When the Propeller receives a byte, which can only have a value between 0 and 255, it uses a formula to transform it into a value that can range between 0 and 2000. If we had to send a value of 1000 say we would normally need two bytes. But with this scheme of data remapping we can send the byte value 128; we are able to command a value bigger than one byte with only one byte.

There is a catch, however. What should the parameter be if we wanted to send 1045? It should be:
1045*256/2000 = 133.76 (133 in integer math)

If we recalculate back what 133 would result in, we obtain 1039. There is a slight loss in resolution and accuracy. But, this is a very small price to pay for being able to only send one byte and still command a value that needs two bytes or more to send. In many applications the loss of resolution is acceptable in comparison to the increase in time required to send the data otherwise. If the loss in accuracy is unacceptable then another solution is needed. See Chapter 11.1.1 for one such solution.

6.4.2 Another Exercise

In the firmware as implemented by Program_10_Main.Spin we do not *zero* the send buffers between commands. This means that if one command fills the buffer with data the next time the buffer is sent it might still hold data from the previous command if the current one does not fill the buffer with sufficient bytes to overwrite all the 5 bytes in the buffer.

For the primary buffer the first three bytes are **_always_** filled with the latest data from the **Reader** cog, and in fact, we should not zero these because we might interfere with the data. However the last two bytes are left holding data from a previous command if the current one does not fill them; likewise with the secondary buffer.

Normally this does not matter; the RB program would know what bytes to read and it would only read the bytes that are filled by the latest issued command. Nevertheless, there is an advantage in zeroing the buffers before filling them up again. The RB program can use the non-filled bytes as a **_simple data integrity check_**. The software can check the bytes it knows should not be filled and thus should be zeros. If they are not zeros, the program concludes that some data corruption has occurred and takes action accordingly (e.g. discard the data altogether and try again).

There are two ways to achieve this:
   ➢ Every command, whether it uses the last two bytes of the primary buffer or not should either zero them or fill them with data as needed. If the command is a secondary send buffer type then it should zero any unused bytes.
   ➢ Zero the buffers in the **Main** cog before issuing the commands.

The first three bytes of the primary buffer **_should not_** be zeroed. This is because the **Reader** cog is always filling them with data regardless, and if we zero them **Main** may send the buffer before **Reader** has had a chance to fill them with the right data.

The first option is more versatile because each command zeroes the bytes, but if we wish we can have the command fill the bytes with other than 0 to allow for other possibilities. This is not different from actually filling the bytes with data anyway; whether the data is 0 or not. So it is easy to implement just as we have done so far.

The second option is more rigorous and ensures a zeroed buffer regardless of what the commands do. This does however add a very slight overhead due to the time it takes to fill the buffer even though it might be filled again with the command – a little less efficient.

The first option is easily implemented in the code that carries out each command. But, how would you go about implementing the second option? Think about it before you see the solution below.

The solution

In Spin there is a very convenient command to help us accomplish zeroing the buffers with maximum efficiency. The command is **ByteFill()**. If we want to fill the secondary buffer with 0 we would say:

ByteFill(@SecondaryBuffer,0,5)

Remember the first three bytes of the primary buffer should not be filled. Also, it would be less efficient to issue two commands to fill each buffer in turn. Notice that the buffers are *contiguous* in the **Dat** section. So the best way to accomplish this as efficiently as possible is to insert the following line in the **Main** method of Prgoram_10_Main.Spin just under the repeat statement:

```
ByteFill(@PrimaryBuffer + 3 , 0, 7)
```

We index to the 4th byte in the primary buffer and fill 7 bytes, which fills the 4th and 5th bytes of the primary buffer and all 5 bytes of the secondary buffer since they come right after the 5th byte of the primary buffer. Notice how we added 3 to **@PrimaryBuffer** to start at the 4th byte into the primary buffer area.

We won't implement either option in our firmware since it is not necessary for our purposes. If you feel that you need to do so, then by all means go ahead using either of the suggested options above or any other method of your devising. This, after all, is the idea. You should be able to implement any improvements, additions, and/or modifications to meet your own requirements.

6.5 Summary

In this chapter we:
- Saw why a protocol is necessary.
- Specified a practical protocol.
- Implemented the protocol in Spin.
- Saw how the protocol provides versatility and fault tolerance.
- Used the protocol in a complex GUI system.
- Examined how data mapping can also be useful in giving more versatility to the protocol.
- Seen how easy it can be to modify the firmware to add more processes when needed.

Chapter 7

Adding More Hardware

The hardware we utilized so far was deliberately kept relatively simple for two reasons:

> To concentrate on strategies and principles.
> To be amenable to a wide range of readers who may not have a particular type of hardware.

Nonetheless, we have developed a good understanding for system requirements. We utilized Input and Output. We used PFM (DAC) output. We used asynchronous serial communications with buffering. In fact, with microcontrollers, that is almost all you need. Everything on most microcontrollers boils down to *digital* I/O. And we have exercised that quite well. It was not our aim to be mired in details and minutia of hardware. Our aim is to develop the software and firmware to enable a PC running an RB program to communicate with a complex and multifaceted hardware system and to control it according to information obtained from the system about its environment (*feedback control*).

Even though we are using the Propeller Chip as our microcontroller we could in reality use any other microcontroller with similar powerful and easy to utilize abilities. Furthermore, despite using RB (for its facility and utility), we really could be using any other programming language on the PC. The aim is to have the PC communicate with firmware onboard a hardware platform and control it effectively and with versatility. In Chapter 6 we developed a protocol for doing so.

Now that we have a solid and flexible foundation on which to build infrastructure we will evolve our system to incorporate more interesting hardware. We will add servomotors, an ultrasound ranger, and two potentiometers. In Chapter 8 we will add even more interesting devices.

We have chosen this hardware for three reasons:
> They have utility.
> They are illustrative of most classes of hardware.
> They are affordable and easily acquired.

Servomotors are obviously useful for robots. An ultrasound ranger is typical in that it is a type of hardware that requires signaling the device and capturing signals returned from the device. Moreover it is quite useful for robots. Potentiometers are typical of devices where the microcontroller will need to do some interesting interaction with a device to read its value and is illustrative of Analog to Digital Conversion (ADC). A pot could be a joystick or a position/level encoder or a thermostat and for robots it could be replaced with a photoresistor to detect light intensities or a thermistor to detect heat sources.

More important is that the hardware is attainable and typical. Once you learn how to use this type of hardware with our protocol it is not much of a step up to handle other hardware in a similar manner. Once you see how you can incorporate this hardware into the protocol of Chapter 6 you can venture on by yourself to add other devices as you need, armed with the experience and knowledge of how to effectively and easily add it to the versatile protocol we have developed for the purpose, or even to an entirely different protocol of your own devising. In Chapter 8 we will utilize more hardware to illustrate other principles you may need for your projects.

The methodologies we developed are useful in any application. A robot is nothing more than an intricate system of *actuators* and *transducers* combined with a capable *microcontroller* and appropriate *firmware*. The protocol and strategies developed here are certainly applicable to any similar system. It could be a satellite, a house, a car, an airplane, an elevator, a factory, or just about anything you can envision that requires an effective *feedback control system*.

A well-designed protocol should be sufficiently versatile to be able to accommodate additional requirements with easy modifications. As we will soon see, adding all the above hardware will in fact be surprisingly simple. Nevertheless, before we go on to the step of integrating all the various devices into one project, we need to understand the hardware and to acquire a feel for how to control it without worrying about other devices that would complicate the process of learning about the device under consideration.

In any software or mechanical systems, whenever you do new designs or add new functionalities you should do so one at a time. Thus any faults are easily diagnosed since the new stuff is the most likely cause, not the well-proven and exercised preexisting systems. Additionally, when you join two proven systems and there is a fault it is logical to assume that the fault lies in the interfacing not the systems themselves.

In keeping with this sound strategy, we will develop the firmware and software for the new hardware one at a time. Armed with that experience we will then see how simple it is to incorporate them into our protocol of Chapter 6.

See Appendix B for the complete details of the final setup of the system as it will be once we complete adding all the hardware in this chapter and the next. Also see Figure B.3 for schematics of all the hardware connections. See Figure B.2 for a layout of how the Propeller pins will be utilized. Table B.1 has a list of all the commands we will eventually implement. Figure B.1 is a conceptual schematic of the system's software hierarchy. Figure 8.15 in Chapter 8 is a screenshot of one of the more complex RB programs that will be developed to utilize the hardware and firmware based on our protocol.

Before adding hardware to an overall system it is best to experiment with the hardware on a separate board all by itself. This way you can hone your experience with the device and be assured that it will not interfere with other devices or itself be interfered with by other devices. Once you establish the requirements for controlling, wiring, and communicating with the device you can then incorporate it into a larger overall system.

7.1 Utilizing the PPDB

From this point onwards we will use the Propeller Professional Development Board. We will use the Propeller Plug to communicate to the RB programs and the programming port to communicate with the Parallax Serial Terminal (as we have been doing so far with the PDB).

Initially we want to prove the PPDB as we did with the PDB. Wire the PPDB as illustrated in Figure 2.4. Once we have established that the PPDB will in fact behave like the PDB we will gradually build more hardware (see Figure 7.1) onto this extremely handy and well-equipped board. A really useful feature of the PPDB is that it already has all the components that we need, like pushbuttons and LEDs, wired with the correct resistors and all we have to do is add wires between the Propeller pins and the components. It also has correctly wired servomotor headers, potentiometers and more (refer to Figure 2.2). It even has a secondary RS232 DB-9 serial port all ready with the FTDI chip. If your computer does not have the old style RS232 ports then you will need to use a USB2Serial[67] converter to use it; rather than do that, we will use the Propeller Plug which achieves the same purpose.

Make sure you have wired the PPDB as in Figure 2.4 and check the following:
- ❏ Make sure the 3.3V and Ground are wired to the top bus lines of the breadboard, and also that the two halves of the bus lines are connected as shown.
- ❏ Make sure that the 5V and Ground are wired to the bottom bus lines of the breadboard and also that the two halves of the bus lines are connected as shown.
- ❏ 8 Wires going from the headers of P23..P16 to the headers of 8 LEDs.
- ❏ Three wires going from the headers of P7..P5 to the headers of three pushbuttons.
- ❏ A wire from the header of P0 to the header of the TX on the PP.
- ❏ A wire from the header of P1 to the RX on the PP.
- ❏ A wire from the Ground Bus to the Vss on the PP.

Connect the Programming port to a USB port on the PC and connect the PP to another USB port on the PC.

> ⓘ If you are using a PC that does not have USB ports, use a USBToSerial (Pasrt#28030)[67] converter to connect between the PC's DB-9 serial port and the programming port on the PPDB. Use a second DB-9 serial port on the PC and connect it to the DB9 on the PPDB and connect P0 to the RX header on the DB-9 and P1 to the TX header .*This is opposite to the PP*.

Now, let's perform the following tests:
- ❏ Test_01.Spin, Test_02.Spin and Test_03.Spin.
- ❏ Test_04.Spin+Test_04.Bas, but make sure to compile the program and upload to EEPROM (F11). Also change the **Port=4** in the RB program to be the programming port number on the PPDB. You can determine this by pressing the F7 function key in the PT IDE.
- ❏ Test_05.Spin +Test_04.Bas. In the RB program change **Port** to be the port that is *not* the programming port but the one for the PP.

Now that we know the communications, LEDs and pushbuttons work let's test the protocol in Chapter 6. Compile and upload (F10 no need for F11 since we are using the PP) Program_10_Main.Spin and run Program_10_B.BAS. Make sure to change **Port** to be the one corresponding to the PP on your system.

All should work. However, there are three small problems:
1. If you change the voltage level on the Dimmer slider (first on the left in the RB screen) you will notice that the LED wired to P23 seems to not be working until the voltage level is above about 1.95 volts. This is not actually a fault. It is because the PPDB uses Blue LEDs and these have a threshold voltage of 1.95 Volts, unlike the Yellow LEDs on the PDB which have a threshold level of about 0.01 volts. If you have a Volt Meter, disconnect the wire from the LED and connect it to the DMM and verify that in fact the voltage is changing correctly from 0 to 3.3V when you move the slider on the RB program. This is not the same as the voltage drop across the LEDs. It is to do with how the LEDs respond to the PWM (or rather the PFM) signal.
2. The LEDs are in reverse order to what is represented by the checkboxes on the RB screen. But this is only if we view the LEDs from the right side of the PPDB as depicted in Figure 2.4. If we view the LEDs from the left of the picture they are OK. This is another situation for *Data Remapping*. We can change the wiring (doable but we don't really want to do that), or we can change the firmware (Spin program) or we can do it in RB. Which is the easiest? We will do it in the firmware later when we modify the system. But for now, consider what can you do to the Spin program to make the LED correspond correctly to the checkboxes on the RB screen as when you view the PPDB from the right side of Figure 2.4? **Hint:** See the **Set_LEDs** method in Program_10_Others.Spin object.
3. The Pushbuttons on the PPDB when pushed are lighting up the LEDs on the RB screen in the reverse order. Again this is easily fixed in the RB program. We will fix this in a later version of the firmware. But for now try and think about what changes to the RB program are needed to do this. **Hint:** See the For-Loop in the **SendCommand()** subroutine in Program_10_B.Bas.

> ⓘ Both problems 2 and 3 above were solved as an exercise in Chapter 4.3.

Now that we have verified that the system is performing correctly and that all the programs we have developed so far work exactly the same on the PPDB (wired as in Figure 2.4) as they do on the PDB (wired as in Figure 2.5) we will progressively modify it to accommodate the new hardware as shown in Figure 7.1.

> (i) Figure 7.1 shows the new hardware but does not show the remainder of the wiring in Figure 2.4. It should be the same except for P16 and P17 which will be disconnected from the LEDs and connected to the servomotors. See Figure B.3 in Appendix B for connections schematics.

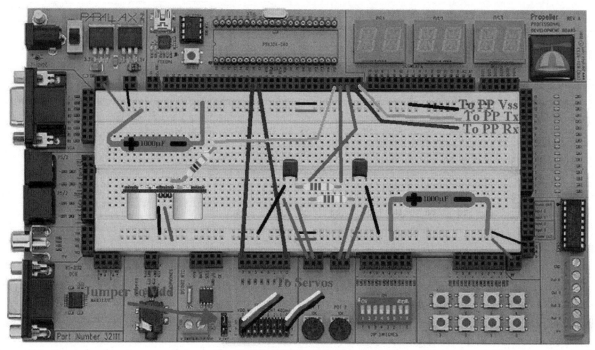

Figure 7.1: Some hardware connections on the PPDB. LED and Pushbutton connections are not shown; see Figure 2.4, but P16 and P17 are now used for Servomotors. Also see Figure B.3 for connection schematics.

7.2 Controlling Servomotors

We will use the Parallax continuous rotation Servo Motors (Part# 900-00008) [11] as are on the Boe-Bot or other such robots. These motors will turn in one direction if they receive a pulse of duration greater than 1.5 milliseconds every 20 milliseconds and the other direction if the duration of the pulse is less than 1.5 ms. Also, it rotates faster the bigger the difference of the pulse duration from the center duration of 1.5 ms (up to a limit).

The problem with such motors is that we have to maintain the signal or else the motor will stop. Even when stopped the signal (1.5 ms) still has to be maintained all the time otherwise the motor will lose torque. Controlling servomotors is best suited to the Propeller and parallel processing since we can have one cog maintain the continuous signal while the other cogs are carrying out other tasks.

To do the experiments in this section connect the P16 and P17 headers with a wire to the headers of two of the servomotor 3-pin male connectors on the PPDB (see Figure 7.1). Connect a Servomotor to the servomotor 3-pin connector. Make sure the jumper just to the left of the servomotor header pins is jumped to the Vdd side.

You will also need a 1000 µF capacitor across the 3.3V power line and ground and one across the 5V power line and ground. This will prevent the Propeller from resetting due to *Brownout* when the motors surge.

⚠️Using the Vdd power supply for driving the servomotors in our experiments is fine since the motors are not loaded (i.e. not under any torque) and we are only using 2 for now and one more later. However, if the motors are to be loaded or more motors are used then the Jumper should be jumped to the external power supply side. An external power supply of 5 volts and able to supply a few amps should be used.

ⓘContinuous rotation servomotors when paired and installed on a robot such as the Boe-Bot, serve as a very convenient propulsion mechanism. When the motors are turned simultaneously but in opposite directions and are mounted on either side of the robot they will drive the robot forward/backward. When they are turned together in the same direction the robot will turn left/right on the spot about the centre of the wheels' axis.

ⓘThe PPDB is very convenient platform since it has all we need at this stage. Normally you need to connect a 150Ω resistor between the Propeller pin and the signal line of the servomotor. This is already done on the PPDB so all we need is a wire to connect the pin's header and header of the 3-pin servomotor connector.

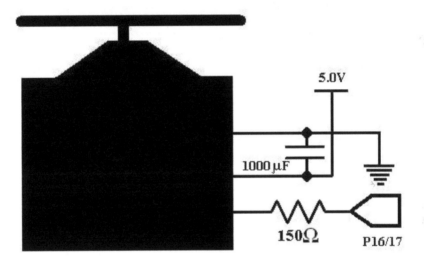

Figure 7.2: Schematic of the Servomotor connection.

⚠️ Make sure you connect the Servomotor's wires as shown in Figure 7.1. White is the signal (S) and Black is Ground (-) and Red is the power (+) as marked on the PPDB. The schematic is shown in Figure 7.2.

⚠️ When we add the servomotors we will also put large capacitors across the power line and ground to prevent resetting the Propeller when the motors draw too much current and cause a voltage drop. But it is still possible for too large a drop on occasion to cause the Propeller to experience a brownout condition.

⚠️ Make sure the Capacitor's negative is connected to Ground if you are using an electrolytic capacitor.

⚠️ The capacitor may still hold a charge even after you have switched the power off. So be careful while wiring new hardware and connecting things to the power busses. You may want to discharge the capacitors across a resistor (10KΩ) before you rewire things. ***Do not short it***.

ℹ️ To be able to tell if the Propeller has reset, upload Test_01.Spin (or a similar program) to the EEPROM (F11). All the programs we will use from now on should be compiled to RAM (F10). If the Propeller resets, Test_01.Spin will reload from the EEPROM and start blinking the LEDs in the distinctive pattern we saw before. This will help in recognizing a reset situation.

7.2.1 A Simplistic Method For Driving a Servomotor

Servomotor_01.Spin is a simple program that will keep a pulse of 2.0 ms (2_000 micro seconds) appearing every 20 ms (20_000 micro seconds) on P16. Run the program and watch the servo. Now change the value of the variable **Pulse0** from 2000 to 700 and rerun the program. Watch how the motor turns the other way.

Servomotor_01.Spin

```
CON
  _clkmode = xtal1 + pll16x
  _xinfreq = 5_000_000

  ServoPin0 = 16

Var
   long Pulse0

PUB Main
  dirA[ServoPin0]~~                        'set pins as output
  Pulse0 := 2000
  repeat
    outA[ServoPin0]~~
    waitcnt(cnt+Pulse0*(clkFreq/1_000_000))
    outA[ServoPin0]~
    waitcnt(cnt+(20_000 - Pulse0)*(clkfreq/1_000_000))
```

What is the problem with this program? Consider what is going on. The program turns the pin high then waits using **Waitcnt()** for the desired pulse duration. Then it puts the pin low and then waits for (20_000 - n) microseconds where n is the time the pin was high.

This is of course what is required, but what can we do if we want to drive two motors say on P17 and P16? Think about this for a minute. Look at the new program Servomotor_02.Spin; it can drive two motors. Notice how instead of delaying 20_000-n we now delay 20_000-n1-n2 since of course when we waited to keep the second pulse high the other pulse was already low for that duration.

Servomotor_02.Spin

```
CON
  _clkmode = xtal1 + pll16x
  _xinfreq = 5_000_000

  ServoPin0 = 16
  ServoPin1 = 17

Var
   long Pulse0,Pulse1

PUB Main
  dirA[ServoPin0]~~                        'set pins as output
  dirA[ServoPin1]~~
  Pulse0 := 2000
  Pulse1 := 1000
```

```
repeat
  outA[ServoPin0]~~
  waitcnt(cnt+Pulse0*(clkFreq/1_000_000))
  outA[ServoPin0]~
  outA[ServoPin1]~~
  waitcnt(cnt+Pulse1*(clkFreq/1_000_000))
  outA[ServoPin1]~
  waitcnt(cnt+(20_000-Pulse0-Pulse1)*(clkfreq/1_000_000))
```

The Limitation of This Methodology

There is a major problem with the methodology used in the above two programs. Consider for a moment, how would the program be able to do anything useful while it is driving the motors? The problem is the **WaitCnt()** function which is a total waste of time ☺. While we are waiting for 20 ms there is nothing being achieved by the program. Twenty ms is a huge amount of time with respect to microcontrollers and they can do scads of things in that time; so why waste it? But more to the point is that using this methodology there is nothing else the program can do. For instance what can you do with this program to make it blink an LED on P23?

One way to resolve the above problem is with Polling and Timers similar to what we did in Chapter 5.2. This way instead of using **Waitcnt()** we use a loop with a counter and within the loop we perform other tasks and when the timer expires we attend to the servo's signal. We do this for both the on and the off delays using two timers. If we need to drive 2 motors then we use three timers. For blinking the LED on P23 we use a fourth timer and so on. Another method is to use timer interrupts where a timer will cause a regular interrupt and in the interrupt handler we can drive the servomotor signals.

Using Helper Modules

The above strategy is likely to be a major headache to implement, and you'll have to do quite a bit of finagling to get the program to work and do additional useful tasks (even with interrupts). Also you will have to be quite careful with timing and even though you can achieve a lot in 20ms it is not sufficient time to do everything else a complex system requires from a microcontroller.

A normal microcontroller driving two servomotors is likely to be over-tasked. This is why using *helper modules* such as Servo Pal (Part#28824) [24] or PWM Pal (Part#28020) [25] (for DC motors) to maintain the required signals is indispensable with normal microcontrollers.

7.2.2 The Propeller Advantage

The strategy of driving the servos one after the other for a bit of time then go do something else then come back and drive the motors will cause a jerky robot that stops and goes all the time. A much better method is to drive the robot *while* other things are being performed like reading sensors and the like.

With the Propeller, fortunately, we can create our own helper module using a cog. We use a cog drive the pins high and low with all the required delays. To tell the cog what direction and speed we need we use shared RAM variables. The program Servomotor_03.Spin below achieves this and more.
  ➢ It blinks an LED on P23 at a constant rate (on 1 sec off 1 sec).
  ➢ It drives *two* servomotors with ramping slowly increasing the speed up to a maximum and then back slowing down to a stop and then in the other direction and so on.

Notice how simple it is to do such a complex action with the Propeller. With other microcontrollers you would have to do a lot of fiddling to carry out the work performed by Servomotor_03.Spin. We use two timers and time polling in the **Main** cog to accomplish ramping of the motors and blinking the P23 LED. The **Servos** cog drives the servomotor using the code we had before but it now uses the *address* of the shared array variable (**Pulse[]**) to obtain the desired pulse time value. Because we use a cog, all the work is performed in parallel with other tasks.

Servomotor_03.Spin

```
CON
  _clkmode = xtal1 + pll16x
  _xinfreq = 5_000_000

  Blinker = 23
  Steps   = 10
  MinVal  = 1000
  MaxVal  = 2000
  MidVal  = 1500


Var
   long Stack[10],Pulse[2],Inc[2]

PUB Main|i,t[2]
  Pulse[0] := Pulse[1] := MidVal
  Inc[0] := Steps
  Inc[1] := -Steps
  cognew(Servos(16,17,@Pulse),@Stack) 'start the servomotor driver
  dirA[Blinker]~~
  t[0] := t[1] := cnt
  repeat
    if cnt - t[0] > clkfreq
      t[0] := cnt
      !outA[Blinker]
    if cnt-t[1] > clkfreq/10
      t[1] := cnt
      repeat i from 0 to 1
        Pulse[i] += inc[i]
        if Pulse[i] => MaxVal or Pulse[i] =< MinVal
          Inc[i] := -Inc[i]

Pri Servos(ServoPin0,ServoPin1,Pulses)
  dirA[ServoPin0]~~                      'set pins as output
  dirA[ServoPin1]~~
  repeat
    outA[ServoPin0]~~
    waitcnt(cnt+Long[Pulses][0]*(clkFreq/1_000_000))
    outA[ServoPin0]~
    outA[ServoPin1]~~
    waitcnt(cnt+Long[Pulses][1]*(clkFreq/1_000_000))
    outA[ServoPin1]~
    waitcnt(cnt+(20_000-Long[Pulses][0]-Long[Pulses][1])*(clkfreq/1_000_000))
```

7.2.3 Control With RobotBASIC

Servomotor_04.Spin is a redesign of the previous program to communicate with Servomotor_04.Bas, which provides a GUI interface to drive the motors forwards/backwards or left/right and to stop them. You can click the mouse button over the arrows on the screen or you can press the arrow keys on the keyboard. Use the spacebar to stop the motors or click the mouse on the center white square between the arrows (see Figure 7.3).

The firmware Servomotor_04.Spin is a simple one. It expects one byte from the RB program which is the code for how to drive the motors. It will return one byte back to the RB program as an indicator of having received the command (set to be the command code). Once the command is received it is acted upon depending on the code. Notice that we stop the motors before changing direction. This is to minimize a huge current draw on the motors due to sudden changes in direction. This also makes it a smoother running robot if the motors are mounted on one. Remember that to tell the servo driver cog how to drive the motors we need to change the shared variables' values. These values will be changed depending on the required command to effect the required movement. The motors are driven at full speed.

> ⓘ The protocol used in this firmware is similar to what we developed in Chapter 6 but simpler. The reason we are keeping things simple for now is to be able to test the servomotor and how to control it from an RB program without all the complications of the firmware in Chapter 6. We will of course later on incorporate the principles learned here into the full protocol along with the other hardware to be developed in later sections.

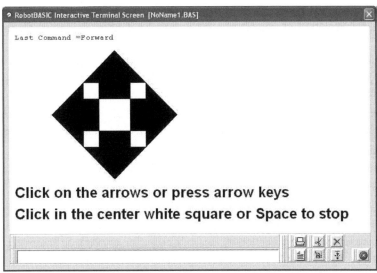

Figure 7.3: Screenshot of Servomotor_04.Bas in action.

Servomotor_04.Spin

```
'Uses Servomotor_04.Bas as a companion RB program
CON
  _clkmode = xtal1 + pll16x
  _xinfreq = 5_000_000

  RB_TX   = 1
  RB_RX   = 0
  RB_BAUD = 115200

  Blinker = 23
  MidVal  = 1500
  MinVal  = 1000
  MaxVal  = 2000

Var
   long Stack[10],Pulse[2]

Obj
  RB: "FullDuplexSerial"

PUB Main|t,x
  Pulse[0] := Pulse[1] := MidVal
  RB.Start(RB_RX,RB_TX,0,RB_BAUD)          'start the serial driver
  cognew(Servos(16,17,@Pulse),@Stack)      'start the Servos driver
  dirA[Blinker]~~
  t := cnt
```

```
  repeat
    if cnt-t > clkfreq
      !outA[Blinker]
      t := cnt
    x := RB.RxCheck
    if x == -1
      Next
    case x
      0: StopMotors(0)                    'stop
      1: StopMotors(1)
         Pulse[0] := MinVal               'forward
         Pulse[1] := MaxVal
      2: StopMotors(1)
         Pulse[0] := MaxVal               'backward
         Pulse[1] := MinVal
      3: StopMotors(1)
         Pulse[0] := Pulse[1] := MinVal 'right
      4: StopMotors(1)
         Pulse[0] := Pulse[1] := MaxVal  'left
    RB.Tx(x)

Pri StopMotors(wait)
  Pulse[0] := Pulse[1] := MidVal          'stop motors
  if wait
    waitcnt(cnt+(clkfreq/1_000_000)*50)   'wait 50 microsecs

Pri Servos(ServoPin0,ServoPin1,Pulses)
  dirA[ServoPin0]~~                       'set pins as output
  dirA[ServoPin1]~~
  repeat
    outA[ServoPin0]~~
    waitcnt(cnt+Long[Pulses][0]*(clkFreq/1_000_000))
    outA[ServoPin0]~
    outA[ServoPin1]~~
    waitcnt(cnt+Long[Pulses][1]*(clkFreq/1_000_000))
    outA[ServoPin1]~
    waitcnt(cnt+(20_000-Long[Pulses][0]-Long[Pulses][1])*(clkfreq/1_000_000))
```

In Servomotor_04.Bas, the subroutine **DriveMotors()** takes care of sending the byte for the command code and receiving the response byte. The rest of the program draws the arrows then monitors the user's input to determine the appropriate command code. The function **Within()** is used to determine if the mouse cursor is within a certain area of the screen when the mouse was clicked and from that we determine which arrow was clicked.

Servomotor_04.Bas

```
//Servomotor_04.BAS
//works with Servomotor_04.Spin or Servomotor_05.Spin
Port = 8  //change this as per your system
Main:
  GoSub Initialization
  while true
    K=-1
    if keydown(kc_UArrow) then K = 1
    if keydown(kc_DArrow) then K = 2
    if keydown(kc_RArrow) then K = 3
    if keydown(kc_LArrow) then K = 4
    if keydown(kc_Space)  then K = 0
```

```
      readmouse x,y,mb
      if mb==1 then Call WhichIsIt(x,y,Ax,Ay,As,K)
      if K > -1 then call DriveMotors(K)
   wend
end
//----------------------------------------------------------
Initialization:
   setcommport Port,br115200
   data Commands;"Stop","Forward","Backward","Right","Left"
   fnt = "Time New Roman"
   xytext 10,400,"Click on the arrows or press arrow keys",fnt,20,fs_Bold
   xytext 10,440,"Click in the center white square or Space to stop" \
               ,fnt,20,fs_Bold
   Ax = 200 \ Ay = 200 \ As = 30
   Call DrawArrows(Ax,Ay,As)
Return
//----------------------------------------------------------
sub DrawArrows(Cx,Cy,Scale)
   arrow = "UlulwwssldlU"
   for i=0 to 3
       drawshape RotShape(arrow,i),Cx,Cy,Scale
       floodfill ,,black
   next
return
//----------------------------------------------------------
sub WhichIsIt(x,y,Cx,Cy,Scale,&n)
   f2 = Scale*2 \ f4=Scale*4
   if within(x,Cx-f2,Cx+f2)     && within(y,Cy-f4,Cy-Scale)    then n=1
   if within(x,Cx-f2,Cx+f2)     && within(y,Cy+Scale,Cy+f4)    then n=2
   if within(x,Cx+Scale,Cx+f4)  && within(y,Cy-f2,Cy+f2)       then n=3
   if within(x,Cx-f4,Cx-Scale)  && within(y,Cy-f2,Cy+f2)       then n=4
   if within(x,Cx-Scale,Cx+Scale) && within(y,Cy-Scale,Cy+Scale) then n=0
return
//----------------------------------------------------------
sub DriveMotors(K)
   xystring 10,10,"Last Command =",Commands[K],spaces(20)
   serialout K
   serbytesin 1,s,x
return
```

7.2.4 Using Servo32V7.Spin

Just like the readymade FDS and SM objects, there is an object available in the ObEx[15] that is a very powerful servomotor driver made by professionals at Parallax. It is better than our simple attempt in the previous sections. You can download Servo32V7.Spin[26] from the Obex or you can find the object in the downloadable Zip file with all the programs in this book.

The new program Servomotor_05.Spin is the same as the previous one and will work with Servomotor_04.Bas in exactly the same way but now it uses the object from the ObEx. The only difference is that instead of having our own method in a cog and passing it the desired motor states by setting variables we now use the method from the Servo32V7 object (we have to **Start()** it). The method **Set()** is used to pass the desired motor setting to the object which uses its own cog to drive the motor.

Servo32V7 is a lot more sophisticated than our driver and is able to drive 32 motors and allows for ramping and other details we may need later. We definitely will need to drive a third motor in the next chapter.

> (i) This is another illustration of how the same RB program can be used with a different firmware on the Propeller as long as the communications method is the same.

Servomotor_05.Spin

```
'Uses Servomotor_04.Bas as a companion RB program
CON
  _clkmode = xtal1 + pll16x
  _xinfreq = 5_000_000
  RB_TX    = 1
  RB_RX    = 0
  RB_BAUD  = 115200
  Blinker = 23
  MidVal  = 1500
  MinVal  = 1000
  MaxVal  = 2000
  Servo1  = 16
  Servo2  = 17


Obj
  RB     : "FullDuplexSerial"
  Servo  : "Servo32V7"


PUB Main|t,x
  RB.Start(RB_RX,RB_TX,0,RB_BAUD)       'start the serial driver
  Servo.Start                           'start the object
  dirA[Blinker]~~
  t := cnt
  repeat
    if cnt-t > clkfreq
      !outA[Blinker]
      t := cnt
    x := RB.RxCheck
    if x == -1
      Next
    case x
      0: StopMotors(0)                  'stop
      1: StopMotors(1)
         Servo.Set(Servo1,MinVal)       'forward
         Servo.Set(Servo2,MaxVal)
      2: StopMotors(1)
         Servo.Set(Servo1,MaxVal)       'backward
         Servo.Set(Servo2,MinVal)
      3: StopMotors(1)
         Servo.Set(Servo1,MinVal)       'right
         Servo.Set(Servo2,MinVal)
      4: StopMotors(1)
         Servo.Set(Servo1,MaxVal)       'left
         Servo.Set(Servo2,MaxVal)
    RB.Tx(x)

Pri StopMotors(wait)
  Servo.Set(Servo1,MidVal)
  Servo.Set(Servo2,MidVal)
  if wait
    waitcnt(cnt+(clkfreq/1_000_000)*50)  'wait 50 microsecs
```

7.3 Using an Ultrasonic Ranger

A sensor often used on robots is the <u>Ping))) Ultrasonic Sensor(Part#28015)</u>[10]. We will add this to our system as shown in the schematic in Figure 7.4 also see the way it fits on the PPDB in Figure 7.1; it will be connected to P4. In Chapter 8 we will mount it on a Turret (standard servomotor) and make behave like a RADAR (SONAR) of sorts.

The principle of how the Ping))) works is straightforward. Set P4 to high output for a little over 2 µs and then turn the pin into an input. Then wait for the pin to read high and note the value of **cnt** then wait again for it to read low and note the new **cnt** value. The difference between these two counts gives us the time the returned signal stayed high. This is the time it took for the ultrasound signal to go to the object and return.

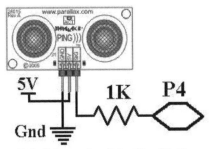

Figure 7.4: Schematic of the Ping))) Connection

Notice that we wait for the pin to go high with a timeout mechanism. This prevents the cog from waiting for ever if the pin never goes high, which can happen if for instance the echo comes back too quickly for the Propeller to have caught it in time due to an object being extremely close, or due to stray echo returns from a previous burst. Waiting for the pin to go low again is performed with the **WaitPeq()** function. This function can lock the cog if the pin never goes low again, but this is not likely to occur. We use **WaitPeq()**because it is implemented in PASM (Propeller's Assembly Language) so we do not have to do our own code which will be slower to execute. As soon as the pin goes low the function exits and we can be assured that we measured the time the pin went low as quickly as possible, eliminating the time delay it takes to execute Spin commands which will introduce a slight error.

> ⚠️Keep in mind that the **WaitPeq()** and **WaitPne()** wait for ever for the required pin state. If the pin never goes to that state the cog executing the command *will lock up*. So if there is ever a possibility of the pin not attaining the awaited state do not use these functions despite their speed advantage. We use **WaitPeq()** because if the pin goes high then it definitely will eventually be driven low by the Ping))). However we do not use **WaitPne()** to wait for a high since the pin may have already gone high and low before the Propeller could catch the pulse due to execution speed.

Since now we know the time it took for the ultrasound signal to go to the object and back at the speed of sound, we can calculate the distance to the object from $D = Vs*t/2$. Where **t** is the time we measured and **Vs** is the speed of sound through air. But **Vs** depends on the temperature and pressure of the air. If we assume sea level then we can get the speed in terms of temperature in °C where $Vs = 331.5+0.6*Tc$. Where **Tc** is the temperature in centigrade, and **Vs** is in meters per second.

If the Propeller returns the time **t** it took to go to the object and then back in microseconds and we want the distance in mm, the formula for the distance to the object becomes:

$$D = 0.5 *t * [331.5+0.6 * Tc] / 1000 \quad (D \text{ millimeters} , t \text{ microseconds} , Tc \text{ °C})$$

You can use the above formula in RB with ease. Spin reports to RB the time it took for the signal to go and come back in microseconds. How many bytes do we need? From the documentation of the Ping))), the maximum value for the time is 18500 microseconds. So the maximum possible returned value can fit in a 16 bit number and as per our protocol in Chapter 6 this value can be sent to RB as two bytes using the MSByte first method.

The documentation states that the minimum possible time is 115 μs and the maximum is 18500 μs. So what are these distances if we assume Tc is 22.2°C? Let's use RB to find out:

MaxMinPing.Bas

```
//MaxMinPing.Bas
//calculates the maximum and minimum distances the Ping))) can measure
Main:
    call mmDistance(,115,Dmin)
    call mmDistance(,18500,Dmax)
    print "Min=",Dmin," mm";"";"   Max=",Dmax," mm"
    print "Min=",Convert(Dmin/1000,cc_MTOIN)," in";"Max=",\
       Convert(Dmax/1000,cc_MTOIN)," in"
    print "Min=",Convert(Dmin/1000,cc_MTOIN)/12," ft";"Max=",\
       Convert(Dmax/1000,cc_MTOIN)/12," ft"
End
//----------------
sub mmDistance(Tc,t,&D)
    if !vType(Tc) then Tc = 22.2  //if temp not given then 22.2 C
    D = 0.5*t*(331.5 + 0.6* Tc)/1000
Return D
```

The program above gives the output

```
Min=19.78575 mm          Max=3182.925 mm
Min=0.77896656036 in     Max=125.312011884 in
Min=0.06491388003 ft     Max=10.442667657 ft
```

The maximum distance the Ping))) can measure is just over 3 meters (10 feet). Also notice the highlighted subroutine. This is a useful and quite versatile subroutine that you can use to convert the output from the Spin program to millimeters distance. Notice the **Convert()** function in RB that allows you to convert various measurements to different units.

> ⚠The subroutine **mmDistance()** uses some of the powerful feature of RB's Call/Sub subroutines with variable parameters, by reference parameters, local variable scoping. See RobotBASIC_Subroutines.PDF[72] for a tutorial on this powerful feature of RB.

7.3.1 Showing the Ping))) Values on the PST

To test the above principles we will use Ping_01.Spin, which will continually measure the Ping))) time and return that value to the PST to be displayed as a test number. Use it to get a feel for the range of your Ping))). It should be 115 to 18500 but it seems that in our case sometimes it can return a little over 22000.

Ping_01.Spin

```
'Uses the PST for output
CON
  _clkmode = xtal1 + pll16x
  _xinfreq = 5_000_000
  D_TX     = 30
  D_RX     = 31
  D_BAUD   = 115200
  PngPin   = 4
```

```
OBJ
  D     : "SerialMirror"

PUB Main|x
  D.Start(D_RX,D_TX,0,D_BAUD)
  repeat
    x := Ping(PngPin)
    D.Dec(x) 'send the number
    D.Tx(13) 'carriage return
    waitcnt(clkfreq/100+cnt) 'delay for a bit

Pri Ping(Pin) : MS| x,time[2]
  outA[Pin]~                'set Pin low
  dirA[Pin]~~               'make Pin Output
  outA[Pin]~~               'Set Pin high
  outA[Pin]~                'Set Pin low ( results in a > 2 µs pulse)
  dirA[Pin]~                'make Pin Input
  x:=cnt                    'start timing for timeout
  repeat until inA[Pin]     'wait for Pin to go high
    if cnt-x > clkfreq/100  'with a 10ms time out
      return 0              'if timed out then return 0
  time[0] := cnt            'store Current Counter Value
  waitpeq(0, |< Pin, 0)     'wait For Pin To Go LOW
  time[1] := cnt            'store New Counter Value
  MS :=||(time[0] - time[1])/(clkfreq / 1_000_000) ' Return Time in µs
```

7.3.2 Using the Ping))) With an RB Program

Again, we will use a simplified protocol at this stage to test the workings of the Ping))). The firmware waits for a byte from RB to indicate it is requesting a reading. The firmware then reads the ping and sends the result as two bytes, then goes back, waiting for the next byte. We need to send *two bytes* since the result is a 16-bit value. We need to agree on a standard for that. What we use is the MSByte First (MSBF) order. If the number is 0x3AF4 ($3AF4 in Spin), we will send the 3A byte first then the F4 byte. So when RB receives the buffer there will be the bytes 3A and 4F in that order in the buffer.

In Spin, to extract the first bytes to send (MSByte), the number will be right-shifted 8 bits then ANDed with $FF to mask off higher bytes. To obtain the second byte we just AND the number with $FF. So the code will be:

```
RB.Tx((x>>8) & $FF)
RB.Tx(x & $FF)
```

When RB receives the bytes using **SerBytesIn** we will extract them from the buffer using **getstrbyte()** and then reconstitute the 16-bit value by shifting the first byte left by 8 bits and adding the second byte:

```
SerBytesIn 2,s,n
X = (GetStrByte(s,1) << 8) + GetStrByte(s,2)
```

We will see how this works with Ping_02.Spin and Ping_02.Bas. The RB program signals the Spin program to send it the value (two bytes). When received the value is reconstituted and used to draw a graphical representation of the reported distance to the object (Figure 7.5). Notice the bold lines in the listings that reflect the above logic. Also study how the units of the displayed distance can be selected by the user and how the program achieves this.

The software uses a screen back buffer to draw the signal in order to make the animation flicker free. This is achieved with the **Flip On** command and the **Flip** command. The **mmDistance()** subroutine is used as before to convert the returned value to millimeters.

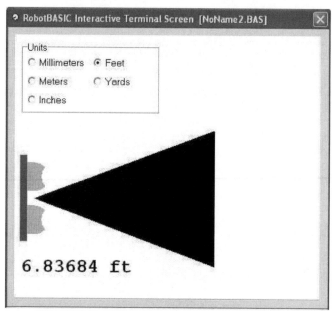

Figure 7.5: Screenshot of Ping_02.Bas in action.

Ping_02.Spin

```
'Use Ping_02.Bas as the companion RB program
CON
  _clkmode = xtal1 + pll16x
  _xinfreq = 5_000_000
  RB_TX    = 1
  RB_RX    = 0
  RB_BAUD  = 115200
  D_TX     = 30
  D_RX     = 31
  D_BAUD   = 115200
  RCPin1   = 3
  RCPin2   = 2
  PngPin   = 4

OBJ
  RB     : "FullDuplexSerial"
  D      : "SerialMirror"

PUB Main|x
  RB.Start(RB_RX,RB_TX,0,RB_BAUD)
  D.Start(D_RX,D_TX,0,D_BAUD)
  waitcnt(ClkFreq/10+cnt)
  repeat
    RB.RX                       'wait for signal from RB
    x := Ping(PngPin)           'read the Ping
    D.Dec(x)                    'send to the PST
    D.Tx(13)                    'carriage return
    RB.Tx((x>>8) & $FF)         'send MSByte to RB
    RB.TX(x & $FF)              'send LSByte to RB

Pri Ping(Pin) : MS| x,time[2]
  outA[Pin]~                    'set Pin low
  dirA[Pin]~~                   'make Pin Output
```

```
  outA[Pin]~~              'Set Pin high
  outA[Pin]~               'Set Pin low ( results in a > 2 µs pulse)
  dirA[Pin]~               'make Pin Input
  x:=cnt                   'start timing for timeout
  repeat until inA[Pin]    'wait for Pin to go high
    if cnt-x > clkfreq/100 'with a 10ms time out
      return 0             'if timed out then return 0
  time[0] := cnt           'store Current Counter Value
  waitpeq(0, |< Pin, 0)    'wait For Pin To Go LOW
  time[1] := cnt           'store New Counter Value
  MS :=||(time[0] - time[1])/(clkfreq / 1_000_000) ' Return Time in µs
```

Ping_02.Bas

```
//works with Ping_02.Spin
Port = 8  //change this as per your system
Main:
  gosub Initialization
  while true
    call ReadPing(t)                     //get the time value from the propeller
    if !ReadPing__Result then continue //if failed loop back
    call mmDistance(,t,D)                //convert to mm
    n=getrbgroup("Units")-1              //get desired units
    x=Format(D*factors[n],"0.0####")    //convert to units and format
    call DrawSignal(Px,Py,t,x+unitn[n])//draw beam and display value in units
  wend
end
//-------------------------------------------
Initialization:
  setcommport Port,br115200
  data units;"Millimeters","Meters","Inches","Feet","Yards"
  data unitn; " mm"," m"," in"," ft"," Yrds"
  data factors;1.,.001,Convert(.001,cc_MTOIN)
  data factors;Convert(.001,cc_MTOIN)/12
  data factors;Convert(Convert(.001,cc_MTOIN)/12,cc_FTTOYRD)
  AddRBGroup "Units",10,10,200,100,2,mToString(units)
  SetRBGroup "Units",1
  Px = 10 \ Py = 300
  call DrawPing(Px,Py)
  savescr
  Flip on
Return
//-------------------------------------------
sub ReadPing(&P)
  P = -1
  serialout 1               //signal the Propeller
  serbytesin 2,s,n          //receive the value bytes
  if n < 2 then return false //if error just return false
  P = (getstrbyte(s,1)<<8)+getstrbyte(s,2) //reconstitute the value
Return true
//-------------------------------------------
sub mmDistance(Tc,t,&D)
  if !vType(Tc) then Tc = 22.2      //if no temp specified assume 22.2c
  D = 0.5*t*(331.5 + 0.6* Tc)/1000  //convert time to mm
Return D
//-------------------------------------------
```

```
sub DrawPing(x,y)    //draw picture of Ping device
  s = 30
  for i=-1 to 1 step 2
    line x,y+s*i,x+20,y+s*i,40,gray
    circlewh x+30,y-20+s*i,40,40,white,white
  next
  rectanglewh x-20,y-2*s,25,s*4,white,white
  rectanglewh x-2,y-s*2,10,s*4,green,green
Return
//-------------------------------------------
sub DrawSignal(x,y,d,str)
  d *= 500.0/22000      //scale value to screen coordinates
  restorescr
  xx1 = x+20+CartX(d,dtor(20))
  yy1 = y+CartY(d,dtor(20))
  Line x+20,y,xx1,yy1
  xx2 = x+20+CartX(d,dtor(-20))
  yy2 = y+CartY(d,dtor(-20))
  Line x+20,y,xx2,yy2
  Line xx1,yy1,xx2,yy2
  if d > 3 then floodfill x+20+d/2,y,black
  xytext x,y+80,str,,20,fs_bold
  flip
return
```

7.4 Using Two Potentiometers

To illustrate other sensors and functionalities that can be incorporated in a major system, we will use two potentiometers (connected as rheostats). Reading a pot is not a trivial process. It is illustrative of how to do an Analog to Digital Conversion (ADC) with only one digital I/O pin. We have already seen with the dimmer in Chapter 5.6 how to do Digital to Analog Conversion (DAC). The pots will be wired as shown in Figure 7.6, and see Figure 7.1 for how the components fit on the PPDB. We will use P2 and P3 to be the pots' pins.

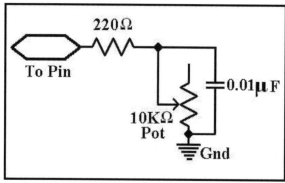

Figure 7.6: The Schematic for wiring a Potentiometer for an R-C A/D Measurement.

A potentiometer can be a joystick, a position/level encoder or a thermostat. A potentiometer can be replaced with a Photo Resistor[60] with an appropriate value capacitor, or even better with a Photo Diode[61] (this requires a slight change in the circuit but it is still an RC circuit just with a slightly different setup). These devices can be utilized in many interesting application (e.g. light following for a robot or for detecting night and day time).

The principle of reading the value of the resistance of a pot is to use it in conjunction with a capacitor (Figure 7.6). This R-C circuit has a property that if we apply a voltage to charge the capacitor and wait a while to give it time to fully charge then short it, the capacitor will discharge over a period of time determined by the value of the capacitor and the resistor. Thus, if we know the value of the capacitor and the time it took to discharge, we can calculate the value of the resistor. Here is the formula:

$$V(t) = Vo*exp(-t/R/C)$$ V(t) is the voltage level at a time t and Vo is the initial voltage.

With the Propeller the maximum voltage is 3.3V and the Off-voltage is 1.65V which implies that Vo is 3.3 and the pin goes off when the V(t) is 1.65. So:

$$1.65 = 3.3*exp(-t/R/C) \rightarrow 0.5 = exp(-t/R/C) \rightarrow exp(t/R/C) = 2$$

Taking the natural log of both sides. ➔ t = ln(2)*R*C ➔

$$R = t/(ln(2)*C)$$

If we know **C** (Farads) and **t** (seconds) we can calculate the value of **R** (Ohms). The problem is it's not quite easy to get an accurate value for **C** and also the value **t** is not extremely accurate either. Additionally, all this requires floating point math (the **Ln()** function). Fortunately, most of the time we are not so much interested in the actual value as an Ohms value. We are just interested in the *position* of the pot. So what we do is get a value for t_{max} when the pot is at its maximum position and a value for t_{min} when the pot is at its minimum position and then when we do a reading of the time at any other position say **t**, we can calculate the position of the pot as a percentage from 0 to 100%.

Because **R=t/(ln(2)*C)** is a linear formula and since **Ln(2)*C** is a constant (say **K**) then $R_{min} = t_{min}/K$ and $R_{max} = t_{max}/K$ and R(t) = t/K. ➔

$Pos\% = 100*(R(t)-R_{min})/(R_{max}-R_{min}) = 100*(t-t_{min})/(t_{max}-t_{min})$…. The K cancels out and ➔

$$Pos\% = 100*(t-t_{min})/(t_{max}-t_{min})$$

Thus we can use the pot as a *Joystick* where we can determine whether it is left or right or anywhere in between, similar to a slider or a thermostat setting and other proportional devices. All we have to do is obtain the reading of the time without having to do any of the math above and since we are just interested in the relative position then the time reading does not have to be accurate and we do not even need to know the value of the capacitor at all.

One thing we do need to know is if we have a 10KΩ pot, what is a good capacitor value to use to obtain a reasonable charge/discharge time. We do not want the RC-circuit to take too long to charge and discharge and also we do not want it to discharge too quickly either so the Propeller can measure the discharge time. So not too slow so a reading can be taken as quickly as possible and not too fast so the Propeller would be able to read the discharge time.

For a 10 KΩ pot and a 0.01 μF capacitor the time constant τ = R*C is 100 microseconds. This is pretty fast for the operation not to be too long and since the Propeller is a very fast processor, this time is within its abilities to measure.

The algorithm performed by the Propeller is: charge the circuit by turning the Pin high, wait for 100 microseconds, then turn the pin into a counter pin (**ctrA**) that counts the time the pin remained high. That is the time it took for the capacitor to discharge enough to turn the pin back to low. This will be the value to send to RB.

⚠️The value sent back to RB is not in fact a time value. Rather it is a count of clock ticks. If you do need to change it to a time then divide it by the frequency of the clock of the Propeller (80 MHz) to obtain the time in seconds. However, there is no need to do this since we just need a position indication.

To do all this we will use an object we developed in another project and is quite a versatile object. It can be used to do a onetime reading of the pot whenever it is needed. The object is used as a library of routines to do the work and return a value. It makes use of the **ctrB** counter so the calling cog must have that counter free.

Another way the object can be used is to call its **Start()** method and let it launch itself in a separate cog. In this mode it does its work in parallel, reading the pot level all the time and putting its value in a shared memory variable. So whenever you need to read the pot level just read the variable. This is a great way to use the object but will waste a cog and if you do not need to read the Pot *continuously* then the former method is better as long as the calling cog has the **ctrB** counter free. The point though is that the object Pots_RCTime.Spin is a versatile one that you can use in either way and obtain a reading for the *position* of the potentiometer. Since we have two pots and we only need to read their positions when required (not continuously), we will use the object in the static way (saving on cogs).

Pots_01.Spin uses the object and reports the values of the two pots to the PST. You can use the reported values for the maximum and minimum in the formula above.

> (i) You have already seen how to use cog counters in two different manners – The NCO mode (Chapter 5.8.2) and in the Duty mode (Chapter 5.6). The Pots_RCTime object hides the fact from you, but it is in fact using the cog counters in yet another mode called the Edge Detection mode (positive or negative). There are many other useful counter modes.

7.4.1 Testing the Pots

Pots_01.Spin is a simple program that will test the Pots_RCTime object and the pots. It will continuously print out on the PST screen the values of the pots. Use this to test the range of values your pots return.

Pots_01.Spin

```
' uses the PST
Con
  _clkmode = xtal1 + pll16x
  _xinfreq = 5_000_000
  D_TX     = 30
  D_RX     = 31
  D_BAUD   = 115200
  RCPin1   = 3
  RCPin2   = 2


Var
  Long RCTime[2]

Obj
  RC   : "Pots_RCTime"
  D    : "SerialMirror"

Pub Main
  D.Start(D_RX,D_TX,0,D_Baud)
  waitcnt(ClkFreq/10+cnt)
  repeat
    RC.RCTime(RCPin1,1,@RCTime[0])    'use Pots_RCTime in direct mode ...no cog
    RC.RCTime(RCPin2,1,@RCTime[1])    'to get one-time reading...
    D.Tx(16)                          'clear the PST screen
    D.Dec(RCTime[0])                  'output first pot's time value
    D.TX(13)                          'line feed
    D.Dec(RCTime[1])                  'output second pot's time value
    waitcnt(ClkFreq/2+cnt)
```

This is how simple it is to use the Pots_RCTime object. Notice that we never called its **Start()** method because we just want to use it in the static mode (no cog) using its **RCTime()** method to acquire a one shot reading. Also notice how we acquired the reading by passing the *address* of a variable in which the method will put the reading. You can use Pots_01.Spin to obtain readings for the values of the maximum and minimum.

If you look inside the Pots_RCTime object you will see that the values reported are not *really* time values. Rather they are *clock-ticks* values. That is how many clock-ticks it took for the pin to go off. Of course this is easily converted into a time value if we know how often the clock ticks – in the Propeller this is normally 80 MHz. So if we really want the value in actual time we would divide the value reported by 80_000_000. Of course we do not need to do this since all we want is a relative position and in the formula above if you look at the math the 80_000_000 will cancel out. Therefore, if only the relative position is required we do not even need to know the clock frequency either. However, to perform a quick check, the maximum value we obtained for one of the pots was 5496. Notice that

$$5496/80\_000\_000 = 68.7 \text{ microseconds}$$

This is within our time constant of 100 microseconds and it checks out. The minimum value is 0 as expected too. So for this pot to acquire a position reading in terms of 0-100% we would use:

$$P\% = 100*t/5496$$

At any time we need to know where the pot is positioned within its range we take a reading and use the above formula. Another method is to not care about the position percentage and just use the reading itself as a value.

7.4.2 Using the Pots With an RB Program

If you have used joysticks on a PC you are familiar with the procedure for calibrating them. Above, we performed a manual calibration. Pots_02.Spin and Pots_02.Bas demonstrate how to use an automatic calibration method. The RB program will let you calibrate the pot using software by moving it to either end of its range a few times. When finished it reports the maximum and minimum settings. Afterwards the program uses those values to show the correct position of the pot as you move it (See Figure 7.7).

> (i) Pots_02.Bas demonstrates again how a GUI can be of an advantage when interacting with hardware.

We will use a simplified protocol for now to test the system. The values of the pots are 16 bit numbers and we will use the MSByte First standard to send the values to RB. The RB program signals the Spin program to send it the values of the two pots and then waits for the 4 bytes to arrive (with time out). When the bytes are received the values are reconstituted for each pot. See the bold code in both listings.

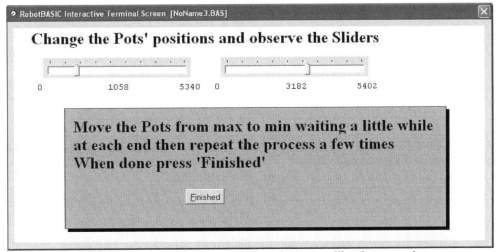

Figure 7.7: Screenshot of Pots_02.Bas during a calibration operation.

Pots_02.Spin

```
'Use Pots_02.Bas as the companion RB program
Con
  _clkmode = xtal1 + pll16x
  _xinfreq = 5_000_000
  RB_TX    = 1
  RB_RX    = 0
  RB_BAUD  = 115200
  D_TX     = 30
  D_RX     = 31
  D_BAUD   = 115200
  RCPin1   = 3
  RCPin2   = 2


Var
  Long RCTime[2]


Obj
  RB    : "FullDuplexSerial"
  D     : "SerialMirror"
  RC    : "Pots_RCTime"


Pub Main|i
  RB.Start(RB_RX,RB_TX,0,RB_Baud)
  D.Start(D_RX,D_TX,0,D_Baud)
  waitcnt(ClkFreq/10+cnt)
  repeat
    RB.RX
    RC.RCTime(RCPin1,1,@RCTime[0])    'use Pots_RCTime in direct mode ...no cog
    RC.RCTime(RCPin2,1,@RCTime[1])    'to get onetime reading...
    D.Tx(16)                          'clear the PST screen
    D.Dec(RCTime[0])                  'output first pot's time value
    D.TX(13)                          'line feed
    D.Dec(RCTime[1])                  'output second pot's time value
    repeat i from 0 to 1
      RB.Tx((RCTime[i]>>8)&$FF)
      RB.Tx(RCTime[i] & $FF)
    waitcnt(ClkFreq/2+cnt)
```

Pots_02.BAS

```
//Pots_02.Bas
//works with Pots_02.Spin
Port = 8  //change this as per your system
Main:
  gosub Initialization
  while true
    call ReadRC(P1,P2)
    setsliderpos "Pot0",P1
    setsliderpos "Pot1",P2
    for i=0 to 1
        xystring 150+300*i,90,Format(GetSliderPos("Pot"+i),"####0")
    next
  wend
end
//----------------------------------------------
```

```
Initialization:
  setcommport Port,br115200
  dim P[2,3] \  mconstant P,0
  fnt = "Times New Roman"
  xytext 30,2,"Change the Pots' positions and observe the Sliders",\
            fnt,20,fs_bold
  AddButton "&Calibrate",290,120
  AddButton "&Finished",290,420
  HideButton "&Finished"
  AddSlider "Pot0",50,50,250,0,6000
  AddSlider "Pot1",350,50,250,0,6000
  enableslider "Pot0",false \ enableslider "Pot1",false
  call WriteLabels()
  onbutton bHandler
Return
//----------------------------------------------
sub bHandler()
  lb = lastbutton()
  Hidebutton lb
  HideButton "&Finished",false
  savescr
  w = 650 \ h = 200
  rectanglewh 90,290,w,h,black,black
  rectanglewh 85,285,w,h,,gray
  xytext 100,300,"Move the Pots from max to min waiting a little while",\
               _fnt,20,fs_Bold,,gray
  xytext 100,330,"at each end then repeat the process a few times",\
              _fnt,20,fs_Bold,,gray
  xytext 100,360,"When done press 'Finished'",_fnt,20,fs_Bold,,gray
  call Calibrate()
  restorescr
  call WriteLabels()
  Hidebutton lb,false
  HideButton "&Finished"
  onbutton bHandler
return
//----------------------------------------------
sub Calibrate()
  mconstant P,0
  while true
     if LastButton() != "" then return
     call ReadRC(P1,P2)
     if !ReadRC__Result then continue
     P[0,1] = P1 \ P[1,1] = P2
     for i=0 to 1
        P[i,2] = MaxV(P[i,2],P[i,1])
        P[i,0] = MinV(P[i,0],P[i,1])
        SetSliderMax "Pot"+i,P[i,2]
        SetSliderMin "Pot"+i,P[i,0]
        SetSliderPos "Pot"+i,P[i,1]
     next
     Call WriteLabels()
  wend
return
//----------------------------------------------
```

```
Sub WriteLabels()
  for i=0 to 1
     xystring 40+300*i,90,GetSliderMin("Pot"+i)
     xystring 280+300*i,90,GetSliderMax("Pot"+i)
     xystring 150+300*i,90,Format(GetSliderPos("Pot"+i),"####0")
  next
return
//----------------------------------------
sub ReadRC(&P1,&P2)
   P1 = -1 \ P2 = -1
   serialout 1
   serbytesin 4,s,n
   if n < 4 then return false
   P1 = (getstrbyte(s,1)<<8)+getstrbyte(s,2)
   P2 = (getstrbyte(s,3)<<8)+getstrbyte(s,4)
Return true
```

7.5 Putting It All Together

In Sections 7.1 to 7.4 we learned how to use all the hardware on an ***individual*** basis and how to control and interact with it through GUI RB programs and ***simple*** firmware on the Propeller. Next, we want to incorporate all this into one system and allow for control of all these subsystems through one program using our protocol as developed in Program_10_Main.Spin in Chapter 6.

Let's examine what we have as ***new*** hardware
  ➢ Servomotors x 2 on P16, P17.
  ➢ Ping))) on P4.
  ➢ Potentiometers x 2 on P2,P3.
What we had before:
  ➢ Three Pushbuttons on P7, P6, P5.
  ➢ Dimmer LED on P23 (using DAC counter).
  ➢ Blinker LED on P22 (using Time Polling).
  ➢ Blinker LED on P21 (using NCO counter).
  ➢ Five on/off LEDs on P16..P20.

Due to the new hardware we are using P16 and P17 for driving Servos. So now P16 and P17 are no longer available for LEDs and we only have 3 LEDs (P20..P18) as on/off LEDs.

Since one of our aims is to be able to control complex systems then combining all the above hardware in one project will certainly qualify as a complex system. A specific type of complex system is a robot. Let's see how all this relates to a robot.
  ➢ Motors are for driving the robot or for turrets and so forth.
  ➢ Ping))) is an ultrasonic ranger in front of the robot to measure distances to objects.
  ➢ Pushbuttons can represent bumpers, infrared proximity detectors, and line sensors. We only have one bit for each, but since we use an 8 bit variable to report each, we can use up to 8 of each type.
  ➢ Dimmer LED could be any kind of device that requires an analog output.
  ➢ Blinker with NCO could be any kind of frequency output like a Piezoelectric speaker.
  ➢ Blinker with time polling, represents any system that requires a regular attention where we need to do something. Here we just blink the LED but it could be anything.
  ➢ 3 On/Off outputs (LEDs here) can be just about anything that requires turning on/off. For instance turning on a dispenser for watering plants.
  ➢ Potentiometers are similar to any device that is an analog input. However, the idea is that the action of reading these devices simulates the action of reading just about anything else. For instance it could be a color sensor.

Pots can be quite useful as position indicators (e.g. Joysticks or Temperature setting). A pot can also be replaced with a photoresistor for detection and measurements of light intensity levels.

In Chapter 6.3 Program_10_B.Bas allowed us to control all the aspects of Program_10_Main.Spin. What we need now is to incorporate all the new hardware with the implemented protocol and to modify the RB program to allow us to read and control the new equipment.

We will gradually build up to the final program Program_11_Main.Spin (Section 7.6.1) and its associated sub-objects to implement the integration of all the new hardware. We will test the new firmware with the old RB program, and afterwards, we will make a new RB program that will let us drive the motors like we did in Section 7.2.4 and also to read the Ping))) and the Pots in the same way as we did in Sections 7.3 and 7.4, altogether in one program along with all the other hardware from the previous chapters.

Let's ponder for a moment how we would incorporate all the new hardware into our protocol from Chapter 6:
- ❑ The Ping))) can be implemented in the **Others** cog and will return the reading in the 4th and 5th bytes of the primary send buffer.
- ❑ The two pots can also be put in **Others** to return the data in the last two bytes of the primary buffer, each pot as a separate command. Another possibility is to return the values of both pots together in the secondary send buffer.
- ❑ The motors may be integrated into **Others**. However, driving motors does not need to return any data. Also it may be necessary to drive the motors and do other related tasks such as measuring wheel travel (quadrature encoder) and other related processes. It would be advisable to create a new object and cog to control motors and motor related duties. Let's call it **Motors**.

When we experimented with the hardware, we developed firmware for each system on its own. However, now we want to put them altogether and it is possible for clashing to occur. For instance we may run out of cogs, or out of I/O pins or if we are using counters maybe an object requires to use a counter while the calling object also requires the same counter in a different manner. Also, we need to make sure we are not using the same I/O pins for different outputs or even worse the same pin as output in one place and as input in a different section.

We have already checked the usage of pins above, and all is ok. Let's check the number of cogs.
1. Main
2. Others
3. Reader
4. Motors
5. FDS
6. SM (can be dispensed with if another cog becomes necessary)
7. Servo32V7 (no ramping)

We have one spare cog. We will only use Pots_RCTime in the static mode. The Servo driver will need another cog if we use ramping; we can afford it, but we won't require it for now.

Let's examine the **Others'** ctrA and ctrB usage. Pots_RCTime will need **ctrB**. The Blinker is using **ctrB** too. *Oops, we have a clash*. Can we fix it? Yes, just let the blinker use **ctrA** since it is free. Ok, a good thing we checked. But, had we not checked what could have happened? You can always try to deliberately cause the clash and see what happens.

Notice that **Main** will need to flag the new **Motors** object to signal it to do its work. So we need to create a new flag, but fortunately we have the flags as bits in a byte. So we do not really need to add a flag. Just use the second bit in the **Flags** byte; we will also need to define a mask for it.

> ⓘ As an engineer you should always design then build. Always measure and check and measure again then cut. You should always check and check again and again before turning the power on. Always read the schematics. Check the wiring against the schematic. ***Repeat all this twice***.

7.5.1 Modifying the Others Object

To demonstrate how simple it is to expand our system of Chapter 6 we are going to integrate the Ping))) and the two potentiometers into the **Others** cog. If you look at the listing of Program_10_Others.Spin in Chapter 6.1.3 you will notice that we already have **Action_3** and **Action_4** that can serve as templates for what we want to do. **Action_3** as it is right now does nothing but serve as a template. If we modify it to read the Ping))) and then put the two bytes in the 4th and 5th bytes of the primary send buffer we would achieve what we need; we will do exactly that, but we will also rename it **Read_Ping**.

Action_4 is also similar to what we want to do with the pots. If we make it read the two pots and then set the 1st and 2nd bytes of the secondary send buffer with the first pot's data and the 3rd and 4th bytes with the second pot's data (5th byte is not needed) we would have exactly what we need. We will change this method to do exactly that and rename it **Read_Pots**.

If you look at the method **RCTime()** inside the object Pots_RCTime.Spin we used in the program Pots_01.Spin in Section 7.4 you will notice that it uses the **ctrB** counter to do its work. Also if you look at the **Initialization** and the **Set_LEDs** methods in Program_10_Others.Spin you will notice that they use the **ctrB** counter too.

Since we are going to incorporate the reading of the Pots into the **Others** cog and since we will use the Pots_RCTime in the same cog (static mode not a separate cog) then if **ctrB** is being used, Pots_RCTime will not be able to use it as well. Of course we could go inside Pots_RCTime.Spin and modify it. However, this is not a good idea in general. Usually we use objects and do not really want to go inside them tinkering with how they do their work. We do not want to spend the time to study them and consider all the details to understand the implications if we do change things. It is a lot easier to change our own objects that we designed ourselves.

We are going to change the **Initialization** and **Set_LEDs** methods to use the **ctrA** instead of **ctrB**. Also **Set_LEDs** needs changing to allow for the fact that P16 and P17 will be used for the Servomotors. We need to change the setting from **outA[20..16]** to **outA[18..20]**. Why are we reversing the order? <u>**Hint:**</u> See third problem in the discussion at the end of Section 7.1 just above the first warning box.

We will add the **Ping()** method we used in Ping_01.Spin in Section 7.3 to the new **Others** object. Also, the constants to define the pin numbers in the **Con** section and also the instantiation of the Pots_RCTime object in the **Obj** section. Additionally, in the **Var** section we will add the **RCTime[]** array to use with the **RCTime()** method for its reading.

See the listing below for Program_11_Others.Spin. The highlighted code is modified code. The bold code is new code.

Program_11_Others.Spin

```
CON
  Blinker       = 21
  PingPin       = 4
  RCPin1        = 2
  RCPin2        = 3
  FlagMask      = %0000_0001    'mask for flag for this cog
  BlinkerScale  = 54            ' 2³² ÷ 80_000_000 for NCO counter
  Offset_1      = 5    'offset for location of 2 byte data buffer
  Offset_2      = 7    'offset for location of 5 byte data buffer
Var
  long Stacks[50], t
  Long Command,Settings,Sems_Flags,RCTime[2]

Obj
  D       : "SerialMirror"
  RC      : "Pots_RCTime"

PUB Start(CommandAddr,SettingsAddr,Sems_FlagsAddr)
  Command      :=    CommandAddr    'save all passed addresses as
```

```
  Settings    :=    SettingsAddr    'local variables to be used
  Sems_Flags :=    Sems_FlagsAddr  'by all processes
  cogNew(Others,@Stacks[0])          'start the cog

Pri Others
  Initialization
  repeat
     Process0
     if Not(byte[Sems_Flags][1] & FlagMask) 'if flag not set then no action
       Next                                 'required, just loop back
     case byte[Command][0]                 'execute the command
         1: Set_LEDS
         2: Set_BlinkRate
        66: Read_Pots
       192: Read_Ping

     OutputToPST                           'output some info to the PST
     byte[Sems_Flags][1] &= !FlagMask 'clear flag to signal Main to proceed

Pri Initialization
  'initialize variables I/O direction etc.
  ctrA[30..26] := %00100            'Set ctrA for "NCO single-ended"
  ctrA[5..0]   := Blinker           'Set ctrA's APIN
  frqA         := 10*BlinkerScale 'set rate
  dirA[20..18]~~
  dirA[Blinker]~~
  t := cnt                          'initialize timer

Pri Process0
  'can do anything here.
  'but there is nothing to do in this case
  'but could be anything that requires polling or updating etc.

Pri Set_LEDs
  'set the LEDs on P20..P18 per the parameter byte
  outA[18..20] := Byte[Command][1]

Pri Set_BlinkRate
  'set the blink rate  for P21
  frqA := byte[Command][1] * BlinkerScale 'set rate
  if frqA == 0
    phsA~   'make sure the pin is low if it to be off

Pri Read_Ping |x
  'read the Ping time and return its 2 byte value in the
  '4th and 5th bytes of the primary buffer. MSByte first.
  x := Ping(PingPin)
  byte[Command][Offset_1]   := (x >> 8) & $FF
  byte[Command][Offset_1+1] := x & $FF

Pri Read_Pots
  'Read the two Pots and returns the readings in the
  'secondary send buffer. Use MSByte first for both
  'the 16 bit values
  RC.RCTime(RCPin1,1,@RCTime[0])   'use Pots_RCTime in direct mode ...no cog
  RC.RCTime(RCPin2,1,@RCTime[1])    'to get one-time reading...
```

```
  byte[Command][Offset_2]    := (RCTime[0]>>8)& $FF
  byte[Command][Offset_2+1]  := RCTime[0] & $FF
  byte[Command][Offset_2+2]  := (RCTime[1]>>8)& $FF
  byte[Command][Offset_2+3]  := RCTime[1] & $FF
  byte[Command][Offset_2+4]  := 0

Pri OutputToPST
  if Not LockSet(byte[Sems_Flags][2]) 'output some info to the PST
    D.Str(string(13,"Others:"))         'if semaphore acquired
    D.Dec(byte[Command][0])
    D.Str(string(","))
    D.Dec(byte[Command][1])
    LockClr(byte[Sems_Flags][2])

Pri Ping(Pin) : MS| x,time[2]
  outA[Pin]~                 'set Pin low
  dirA[Pin]~~                'make Pin Output
  outA[Pin]~~                'Set Pin high
  outA[Pin]~                 'Set Pin low ( results in a > 2 µs pulse)
  dirA[Pin]~                 'make Pin Input
  x:=cnt                     'start timing for timeout
  repeat until inA[Pin]      'wait for Pin to go high
    if cnt-x > clkfreq/100   'with a 10ms time out
      return 0               'if timed out then return 0
  time[0] := cnt             'store Current Counter Value
  waitpeq(0, |< Pin, 0)      'wait For Pin To Go LOW
  time[1] := cnt             'store New Counter Value
  MS :=||(time[0] - time[1])/(clkfreq / 1_000_000) ' Return Time in µs
```

7.5.2 Modifying the Reader Object

No change is required. We will just copy it as it is and rename it as Program_11.Reader.Spin.

7.5.3 Checking the New Hardware + Firmware + System So Far

We have just performed some major changes. As prudent engineers we should now check that the system is still working and that the new additions are working fine. If you do too many changes before you test and there are problems you will have too may variables to check out. Always vary one thing at a time and then check. That way at any stage if there is trouble, you know that the only changed part is the one you just did; you can concentrate your troubleshooting to that area instead of being overwhelmed with too many possibilities due to too many changes before the last verification.

We will copy Program_10_Main.Spin and rename it **Program_11_Main_A.Spin** (notice the _A, this is an interim step towards our final program). Also change the **Obj** section to instantiate the _11_ objects. Like this *(no other changes are required)*:

```
Others : "Program_11_Others"
Reader : "Program_11_Reader"
```

We now have a new system with the Pots and Ping))). We will test it with an extremely simple RB program. Afterwards, we will use Program_10_B.Bas without any modification whatsoever. After that we will modify the programs we used earlier (Ping_02.BAS and Pots_02.Bas) to work with the new system.

All this will demonstrate four things:
1. All the old stuff still functions as before.
2. The new hardware + firmware work as they should.

3. How simple it is to modify the hardware + firmware and yet due to the versatility of the protocol a software written for the older hardware + firmware should still work the same way *without* modification.
4. The power and advantages of using our system because software written for an entirely different hardware setup can still work with our protocol with *minor* changes.

A Simple Test RB Program

Compile the new Program_11_Main_A.Spin (F10 or F11) resulting from the modifications above. Then run Program_11_A.Bas and see how it works.

Notice how the RB program gets the data for the Ping and Pots from the protocol. Remember the protocol requires the RB program to send two bytes. The first is the code for the command and the second as a parameter for the command. In this case the commands do not require a parameter so we just send a 0. If you read the listings for the **Others** and **Main** objects you will notice that the code for the Ping is 192 and the value is returned as part of the primary send buffer with the value in the last two bytes of the 5 bytes returned from the protocol.

For the Pots the command is 66 and it is a command that returns its value in the secondary send buffer. As far as RB is concerned secondary or primary is immaterial. It is the 5 bytes that it receives that matters. But to be able to understand what the data in the 5 bytes mean RB has to know which commands will return the result in the 4th and 5th bytes, and which will return the results using all 5 bytes or at least more than two bytes that start at the 1st byte. In this case, per our protocol and as agreed upon, the first two bytes are one pot's reading and the second two are the other; the 5th byte is not used. Also, the order is MSByte First.

When you run the program you will notice that the readings for the pots are in reverse order if you look at the PPDB as depicted in Figure 7.1. The first reading on the left is the pot on the right and vice versa for the right reading. This is another situation for *data re-mapping*. You can always change the hardware or firmware or the RB program. Which is the easiest? Yes, it is the RB program. Do you know what to do? What changes are needed in Program_11_A.Bas to change the display so that the pot on the right of the PPDB (as in Figure 7.1) is on the right of the RB screen display of Program_11_A.Bas? The highlighted lines in the listing are one possibility where you can swap L1 and L2. But the bold lines are a better place to do the change (swap P1 and P2). Also, if you had to, do you know what to change in the Spin programs? It is very simple matter of swapping the pins allocation in the **Con** section in the **Others** object.

Note the **GetPing()** and **GetPots()** subroutines are where all the work takes place for requesting the values. Notice how they implement the protocol of Chapter 6.

Program_11_A.Bas

```
//work with Program_11_Main_A.Spin
Port = 8  //change this as per your system
Main:
   setcommport Port,br115200
   xystring 10,10,"Ping Reading";"";"Pot1";"";"Pot2"
   while true
      Call GetPing(P)
      Call GetPots(L1,L2)
      xystring 10,40,P;spaces(10);L1;"";L2;spaces(10)
   wend
End
//------------------------------------------
sub GetPing(&d)
   d = 0
   serialout 192,0    //code for ping is 192, no parameter is needed
   serbytesin 5,s,n   //get the 5 bytes
   if n < 5 then  return false
   d = getstrbyte(s,5)+(getstrbyte(s,4)<<8)  //reading is in last 2 bytes
return true
//------------------------------------------
```

```
sub GetPots(&P1,&P2)
   P1 = 0 \ P2 = 0
   serialout 66,0     //code for pots in protocol is 66, no parameter is needed
   serbytesin 5,s,n  //get the 5 bytes
   if n < 5 then return false
   P1 = getstrbyte(s,2)+(getstrbyte(s,1)<<8)   //1st is in bytes 1 and 2
   P2 = getstrbyte(s,4)+(getstrbyte(s,3)<<8)   //2nd is in bytes 3 and 4
Return true
```

Using Program_10_B.Bas

Now that we know the hardware is actually working and that the protocol is in fact giving us the data we need. Let's prove that even a program written for the *old* hardware + firmware system still works with the *new* configuration without modification whatsoever. The old Program_10_B.Bas was written for the old system in Chapter 6 (Program_10_Main.Spin), will it work with the new Program_11_Main_A.Spin? Yes, it will. However since the program had no idea about what to do with Commands 192 and 66 all it did was display the bytes as individual bytes. So when we use this program and issue Command 192 and 66 by selecting them from the list box we will get 2 bytes (former) and 5 bytes (latter) as individual valued bytes (see Figure 6.1 first arrow on the left in the RB screen).

To verify these values, run Program_11_A.Bas above, and set the Pots at a particular position and note the values returned from them. Also set an object in front of the Ping and note the value. Keep everything the same. Now run the system with Program_10_B.Bas. Choose the first option in the list box and press the '*Execute Command*' button. Take a calculator (or run another instance of RB and write a one line program) and multiply the first byte by 256 and add the 2nd byte. This value should be very close to the Ping reading you noted earlier. Now execute the second option in the list box and do the same for the first two bytes as above and then also do the same for the 3rd and 4th bytes. The two numbers should be the same (or close) as the ones you noted earlier for the pots.

Change some of the blinking LEDs' rates and the dimmer (remember the dimmer will now only work with voltage threshold level of 1.95). Also change some of the checkboxes. All should now be in the correct orientation, but we have too many checkboxes. The last two that correspond to P16 and P17 are of no use now since we use these as servomotor signals. Also of course they are not even sent to the pins due to the change we did to the **Set_LEDs** method in the **Others** object.

An Exercise in Versatility

So far we have seen how *simple* it is to write a barebones RB program to interact with the protocol (Program_11_A.Bas). We have seen how *resilient* the protocol is because despite major changes to the hardware and firmware a program written for the older version still worked with the new version without any modifications (Program_10_B.Bas). You have also seen in Chapter 6.2 that the protocol provides *error tolerance and recovery* too.

We now want to see if programs written to work with the devices on their own would still work with the same hardware while integrated in a complex and multifaceted overall system. In Sections 7.3 and 7.4 we developed interesting GUI programs to interact with the respective hardware. At the time there was only the hardware we needed to work with and the programs Ping_02.Bas and Pots_02.Bas were written for a different interface with a different Spin program (firmware). These two programs are quite nice. Can we still use them to access the hardware despite being merged with different hardware and despite having to go through a different *protocol layer*?

Indeed we ought to be able to do so, and with ease. In fact we have already done this in Program_11_A.Bas. Therefore we leave it as a challenge for you to modify Ping_02.Bas and Pots_02.Bas to make them work in exactly the same manner they did but through the protocol. That is using Program_11_Main_A.Spin.

In the downloadable zip file that contains the source code for all the programs in this book you will find Ping_03.Bas and Pots_03.Bas that are the solution to this challenge.

Do attempt to do this and do give it your best effort! It should give you a good indicator of how well you have grasped the principles and more importantly that you can go further than what you have learned here. If you need a hint read the next paragraph. But please try to do it without the hints. Finally if you give up and/or to verify your efforts you can compare your work with the programs given in the zip file.

Hint #1: Look at the two subroutines in Program_11_A.Bas.

Hint #2: Look at the subroutine **ReadPing(&P)** in Ping_02.Bas and **ReadRC(&P1,&P2)** in Pots_02.BAS.

Hint #3: Remember that in the protocol (see **Others** object) the command to access the pots is code 66 and for the ping is code 192.

Hint #4: Consider carefully the requirements of each program. While you are creating Ping_03.Bas you would not be able to just replace the **ReadPing()** with the **GetPing()** from Program_11_A.Bas. Likewise for the **ReadRC()** and **GetPots()** for Pots_03.BAS.

7.6 Adding the Motors Object

We are about to create a whole new object. This object is similar to the **Others** object in that it will be *flagged* to do something by the **Main** object. Since it is designed to drive the motors we will not for now require that it return any data in either of the send buffers. However, in keeping with flexibility and future adaptability, we will keep the mechanism just in case we may need it in a future adaptation.

If you look at Servomotor_05.Spin in Section 7.2.4 you will see what we need to add to the new **Motors** object. We will use **Others** as a *template* and modify it to allow the control of the servomotors as we did in Servomotor_05.Spin.

Copy Program_11_Others.Spin and rename it to Program_11_Motors.Spin. Then do the following changes:
- ❑ Change the **FlagMask** constant in the **Con** section to %000_0010.
- ❑ Add the constants for the pins and the servomotor signal durations as in Servomotor_05.Spin.
- ❑ Instantiate the Servo32V7 object in the **Obj** section.
- ❑ Rename the method to be run by the cog as **Motors** instead of **Others**. Also change the **Cognew()** statement to reflect that.
- ❑ The Initialization method does not need to do most of the stuff related to starting a counter to blink an LED, so delete that code, but now we also need to **Servo.Start** the servos object.
- ❑ Cut and paste the **StopMotors()** method form Servomotors_05.Spin.
- ❑ Add a new method called **MoveMotors()**.
- ❑ Modify the Case statement. We will use different codes than we did in Servo_05.Spin. This is because in the new system we are already using the codes we were using in Servomotors_05.Spin. The codes chosen could have been anything from 0-255 other than the numbers already used for the other things in the protocol.

See the code listing below for Program_11_Motors.Spin. It should be obvious from the list above what we did for this new object. It really is just a few easy modifications and additions and removing no longer needed code from a copy of the **Others** object and cutting and pasting from Servomotors_05.Spin. Pay attention to the bold lines. In the next section we will further modify Program_11_Main_A.Spin to create a new Program_11_Main.Spin (notice no _A) object to allow for the **Motors** object.

Program_11_Motors.Spin

```
CON
  FlagMask   = %0000_0010    'mask for flag for this cog
  Offset_1   = 5    'offset for location of 2 byte data buffer
  Offset_2   = 7    'offset for location of 5 byte data buffer
  MidVal     = 1500
  MinVal     = 1000
  MaxVal     = 2000
  Servo1     = 16
  Servo2     = 17
Var
  long Stacks[50], t
  Long Command,Settings,Sems_Flags
```

```
Obj
  D      : "SerialMirror"
  Servo  : "Servo32V7"

PUB Start(CommandAddr,SettingsAddr,Sems_FlagsAddr)
  Command    :=    CommandAddr    'save all passed addresses as
  Settings   :=    SettingsAddr   'local variables to be used
  Sems_Flags :=    Sems_FlagsAddr 'by all processes
  cogNew(Motors,@Stacks[0])        'start the cog

Pri Motors
  Initialization
  repeat
    Process0
    if Not(byte[Sems_Flags][1] & FlagMask) 'if flag not set then no action
      Next                                  'required, just loop back
    case byte[Command][0]                   'execute the command
      0:   StopMotors(0)
      6:   MoveMotors(MinVal,MaxVal) 'forward
      7:   MoveMotors(MaxVal,MinVal) 'back
      12:  MoveMotors(MinVal,MinVal) 'right
      13:  MoveMotors(MaxVal,MaxVal) 'left
    OutputToPST                             'output some info to the PST
    byte[Sems_Flags][1] &= !FlagMask   'clear flag to signal Main to proceed

Pri Initialization
  'initialize variables I/O direction etc.
  'none needed here
  t := cnt                        'initialize timer
  Servo.Start

Pri Process0
  'can do anything here.
  'but there is nothing to do in this case
  'but could be anything that requires polling or updating etc.

Pri StopMotors(wait)
  Servo.Set(Servo1,MidVal)
  Servo.Set(Servo2,MidVal)
  if wait
    waitcnt(cnt+(clkfreq/1_000_000)*50)  'wait 50 microsecs

Pri MoveMotors(Val1,Val2)
  StopMotors(1)
  Servo.Set(Servo1,Val1)
  Servo.Set(Servo2,Val2)

Pri OutputToPST
  if Not LockSet(byte[Sems_Flags][2]) 'output some info to the PST
    D.Str(string(13,"Motors:"))          'if semaphore acquired
    D.Dec(byte[Command][0])
    D.Str(string(","))
    D.Dec(byte[Command][1])
    LockClr(byte[Sems_Flags][2])
```

7.6.1 Further Modifications of the Main Object

We will copy Program_11_Main_A.Spin and rename it Program_11_Main.Spin (no _A). We will then modify it to accommodate the new **Motors** object. Here is the list:

- ❑ Instantiate the new **Motors** object in the **Obj** section.
- ❑ Add the new flag for the **Motors** cog (**MotorsFlagMask = %0000_0010**) in the **Con** section.
- ❑ Add the **Motors.Start()** statement to the **Initialization** method.
- ❑ Add a case in the case block in the **ExecuteTheCommand** method to allow for the new commands that will be run by the **Motors** cog. This should be very similar to the other cases.

That is really how simple it is. With just a few changes we now have an entirely new object that will drive the motors. See the listing below, specifically the bold lines.

Program_11_Main.Spin

```
CON
  _clkmode = xtal1 + pll16x
  _xinfreq = 5_000_000
  RB_TX           = 1
  RB_RX           = 0
  RB_BAUD         = 115200
  D_TX            = 30
  D_RX            = 31
  D_BAUD          = 115200
  DimmerPin       = 23
  OthersFlagMask = %0000_0001    'flag mask for flagging the Others Cog
  MotorsFlagMask = %0000_0010    'flag mask for flagging the Motors Cog
  DimmerScale    = 16_777_216    ' 2³²÷ 256   for DAC counter
                                 ' to make dimming to be 0 to 255
Var
  byte SendBufferOffset

OBJ
  RB     : "FullDuplexSerial"
  D      : "SerialMirror"
  Others : "Program_11_Others"
  Reader : "Program_11_Reader"
  Motors : "Program_11_Motors"

PUB Main|x
  Initialization
  repeat
    SendBufferOffset~       'reset data buffer pointer
    ReceiveCommand          'receive 2 bytes command,parameter
    OutputToPST_1           'output some info to the PST
    ExecuteTheCommand       'Execute the Command
    SendTheBuffer           'send the data buffer (either the
                            'normal or the secondary depending
                            'on the command just executed
    OutputToPST_2           'output some info to the PST


Dat
  Command         Byte 0,0              'command and parameter from RB
  PrimaryBuffer   Byte 0,0,0,0,0        'primary 5 bytes to send to RB
  SecondaryBuffer Byte 0,0,0,0,0        'secondary 5 bytes to send to RB
  Sems_Flags      byte 0,0,0            'semaphore1,flags,semaphore2
```

```
Settings          Long 80_000_000  'various settings buffer
                                   '[0] is Reader blinker duration
TimeOut1          Long 240_000_000 '3 secs timeout for receiving second byte
TimeOut2          Long 320_000_000 '4 secs timeout for sending data

Pri Initialization
  RB.Start(RB_RX,RB_TX,0,RB_BAUD)   'start FDS serial driver
  D.Start(D_RX,D_TX,0,D_BAUD)       'start SM serial driver (only do once)
  Sems_Flags[0] := LockNew          'create Semaphore for SendBuffer
  Sems_Flags[2] := LockNew          'create Semaphore for PST output
  Others.Start(@Command,@Settings,@Sems_Flags)        'start Others Cog
  Reader.Start(@PrimaryBuffer,@Settings,@Sems_Flags)  'Start Reader Cog
  Motors.Start(@Command,@Settings,@Sems_Flags)        'Start Motors Cog

  'create a dimmer LED on P23
  ctra[30..26] := %00110      'Set ctra to DUTY mode
  ctra[5..0]   := DimmerPin   'Set ctra's APIN
  frqA := 127 *DimmerScale    'Set frqa register to mid level to start with
  dirA[DimmerPin]~~           'make output pin

Pri ReceiveCommand|t,x
  repeat
    Sems_Flags[1]~              'reset flags
    repeat                      'wait forever to receive command byte
      Process0                  'call process that need to be done always
      x := RB.RXcheck
    until x <> -1
    Command[0] := x
    t := cnt                    'init timer
    repeat                      'wait with timeout to receive parameter
      Process0                  'call process that needs to be done always
      x := RB.RXcheck
      if cnt-t > TimeOut1
        quit
    until x <> -1
    if x == -1                  'if no byte received loop back to the top
      Next                      'gracefully recover from receive error
    Command[1] := x
    quit                        'exit to return to Main

Pri SendTheBuffer|x
  if Not Sems_Flags[1]          'if flags clear then send bytes
  'if SendBufferOffset == 0 'if using primary buffer wait for semaphore
  '                            'to ensure data congruity
  '    repeat until Not LockSet(Sems_Flags[0])
  '        'wait for semaphore forever, may need to do timeout but
  '        'uncomment these lines to assure data congruity
  '        'also the LockClr() below
    repeat x from 0 to 4        'transmit the 5 bytes of data
      RB.TX(PrimaryBuffer[x+SendBufferOffset])
  'if SendBufferOffset == 0   'if data congruity with semaphore is used
  '    LockClr(Sems_Flags[0])  'then also uncomment out these two line also

Pri Process0
  'can do anything here.
  'but there is nothing to do in this case
```

```
    'but could be anything that requires polling or updating etc.

Pri ExecuteTheCommand
  case Command[0]
    255: 'reset the propeller
      Reboot

    200:'set the Dimmer level on P23
      frqA := Command[1] *DimmerScale

    201:'set blinker duration for Reader cog(P22)
        '256 levels between 0 to 2 secs (0=off)
      Settings[0] := Command[1]*(2_000/256)*(ClkFreq/1_000)

    1,2,192:'commands in the Others cog that may fill the
            'the last two bytes in the primary send buffer
      Sems_Flags[1] |= OthersFlagMask     'set flag
      WaitForFlagResetWithTimeOut(OthersFlagMask)

    66:'commands in the Others cog that fill the secondary send buffer
      SendBufferOffset := 5              'command uses the secondary buffer
      Sems_Flags[1] |= OthersFlagMask   'set flag to signal the cog
      WaitForFlagResetWithTimeOut(OthersFlagMask)

    6,7,12,13,0:'commands in the Motors cog
      Sems_Flags[1] |= MotorsFlagMask      'set flag
      WaitForFlagResetWithTimeOut(MotorsFlagMask)

Pri WaitForFlagResetWithTimeOut(Flag)|t
  t:=cnt
  repeat until cnt-t > TimeOut2  'wait for flag to clear with time out
    Process0
    if Not(Sems_Flags[1] & Flag)
       quit

Pri OutputToPST_1
  if Not LockSet(Sems_Flags[2])  'output info to PST if semaphore acquired
    D.Str(string(13,"Main Received:"))
    D.Dec(Command[0])
    D.Str(string(","))
    D.Dec(Command[1])
    LockClr(Sems_Flags[2])

Pri OutputToPST_2|x
  if Not LockSet(Sems_Flags[2]) 'output info to the PST if semaphore acquired
    D.Str(string(13,"Main Sending:"))
    repeat x from 0 to 4          'show the bytes sent
      D.Dec(PrimaryBuffer[x+SendBufferOffset])
      D.Str(string(","))
    LockClr(Sems_Flags[2])
```

7.6.2 Verifying the Motors Object

We will use the motors in the next section in an interesting manner, but before doing so we need to verify that everything is functioning correctly. We need a simple RB program that talks to the new firmware and tells it to move the motors to try out all the new commands (0,6,7,12,13). Again, please give this a bit of thought before you read on.

Can you write a simple program to make the motors go forward and then wait for the user to press enter on the keyboard and then move to the right and then backwards then to the left. Entirely simple for now; just to demonstrate that the **Motors** object is working and how simple and effective the protocol is.

> ⓘ You should also test the new firmware with Program_10_B.Bas, Program_11_A.Bas, Ping_03.Bas and Pots_03.Bas

Simple Test For The Motors

Here is a listing of a simple program to test the motors:

Program_11.Bas

```
//Program_11.Bas
//works with Program_11_Main.Spin
Port = 8  //change as per your system
Main:
  setcommport Port,br115200
  while true
    call DriveMotors(6)
    waitkey K
    call DriveMotors(7)
    waitkey K
    call DriveMotors(12)
    waitkey K
    call DriveMotors(13)
    waitkey K
    call DriveMotors(0)
    waitkey K
  wend
end
//-----------------------------------
sub DriveMotors(how)
  serialout how,0
  serbytesin 5,s,x
return
```

Another Exercise In Versatility

Try to change Servomotor_04.Bas in Section 7.2.3 to function exactly in the same way but with the new firmware and protocol. Remember that the commands are now different codes. Look at the listing below to see an efficient and effective application of *data-remapping* to avoid changing the program too extensively. Remember, for example, that the program is using one code for forward while the protocol requires another. Rather than change the program all over the place for the new codes, why not remap the codes just before sending them to the Propeller. See the listing for Servomotr_06.Bas below and look at the bold lines.

The only difference between Servomotor_06.Bas and Servomotor_04.Bas is the **DriveMotors()** subroutine. Mainly the new version obeys the protocol of sending the command and parameter bytes and receiving the 5 bytes sent back. But the main program is going to try to send the command codes from the old version since we did not change anything there. The new **DriveMotors()** will also have to perform the mapping of these old command codes to the new ones.

The old commands were 0,1,2,3,4. This is convenient and the value can be used to index into an array where the value of the array element contains the new command code. Notice the use of the **vType()** function. This function is a very convenient one. It checks to see if the global variable exists or not. The variable is global not local because there is a _ before its name. If the variable does not exist then the array is defined and its elements are added using the **data** statement. Also the variable is defined and assigned a value. This way the next time the subroutine is called it does not define the array again.

Servomotor_06.Bas

```
//Servomotor_06.BAS
//works with Program_11_Main.Spin
Port = 8  //change this as per your system
Main:
  GoSub Initialization
  while true
    K=-1
    if keydown(kc_UArrow) then K = 1
    if keydown(kc_DArrow) then K = 2
    if keydown(kc_RArrow) then K = 3
    if keydown(kc_LArrow) then K = 4
    if keydown(kc_Space)  then K = 0
    readmouse x,y,mb
    if mb==1 then Call WhichIsIt(x,y,Ax,Ay,As,K)
    if K > -1 then call DriveMotors(K)
  wend
end
//------------------------------------------------------------
Initialization:
  setcommport Port,br115200
  data Commands;"Stop","Forward","Backward","Right","Left"
  fnt = "Time New Roman"
  xytext 10,400,"Click on the arrows or press arrow keys",fnt,20,fs_Bold
  xytext 10,440,"Click in the center white square or Space to stop" \
            ,fnt,20,fs_Bold
  Ax = 200 \ Ay = 200 \ As = 30
  Call DrawArrows(Ax,Ay,As)
Return
//------------------------------------------------------------
sub DrawArrows(Cx,Cy,Scale)
  arrow = "UlulwwssldlU"
  for i=0 to 3
    drawshape RotShape(arrow,i),Cx,Cy,Scale
    floodfill ,,black
  next
return
//------------------------------------------------------------
sub WhichIsIt(x,y,Cx,Cy,Scale,&n)
  f2 = Scale*2 \ f4=Scale*4
  if within(x,Cx-f2,Cx+f2)      && within(y,Cy-f4,Cy-Scale)    then n=1
  if within(x,Cx-f2,Cx+f2)      && within(y,Cy+Scale,Cy+f4)    then n=2
  if within(x,Cx+Scale,Cx+f4)   && within(y,Cy-f2,Cy+f2)       then n=3
  if within(x,Cx-f4,Cx-Scale)   && within(y,Cy-f2,Cy+f2)       then n=4
  if within(x,Cx-Scale,Cx+Scale) && within(y,Cy-Scale,Cy+Scale) then n=0
return
//------------------------------------------------------------
sub DriveMotors(K)
   xystring 10,10,"Last Command =",Commands[K],spaces(20)
   if !vType(_FirstTime)
      data remap;0,6,7,12,13
      _FirstTime = false
   endif
   serialout remap[K],0
   serbytesin 5,s,x
return
```

7.7 RB Programs to Exercise the Entire System

Let's examine what we have so far. See Figure 7.8, which is a modification of Figure 5.4. The diagram is a conceptual schematic for the system as it is now.

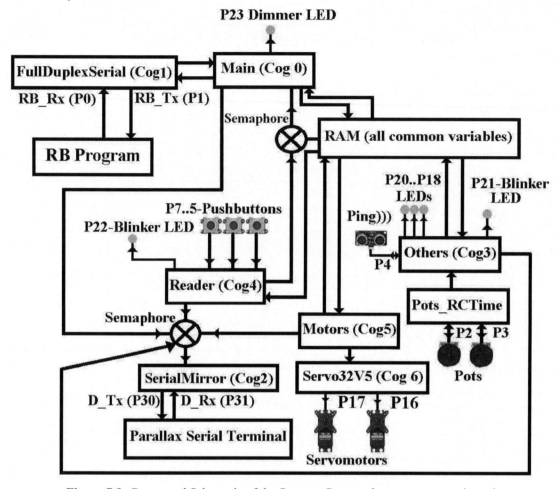

Figure 7.8: Conceptual Schematic of the System. Cog numbers are not actual numbers.

Program_11_Advanced.Bas below is a quite complex and intricate program (See Figure 7.9 for a screen shot). It:
- Allows a user to set the LEDs on P20..P18 on/off.
- Allows a user to define the brightness of the P23 LED.
- Allows a user to define the blink duration of the LED on P22.
- Allows a user to define the frequency for the LED on P21.
- Allows a user to command the servomotors in all directions.
- Continuously displays on the screen, representations of the states of all the LEDs above.
- Simulates LEDs on the Screen to reflect the states of the three pushbuttons on P7..P5.
- Shows the state of the potentiometers.
- Allows the user to calibrate the pots.
- Shows the reading of the Ping))).
- Allows the user to define the units for the Ping))) reading.
- Lights a simulated LED on the screen if there is a communications error.
- Shows in text the last command executed and its parameter.

In addition to all the above the firmware will also output information to the PST to reflect what cog is working and doing what.

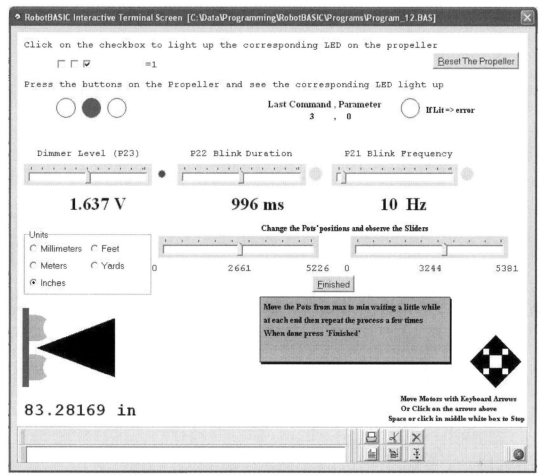

Figure 7.9: Screen Shot of Program_11_Advanced.Bas in action. Notice that a pots calibration is currently taking place.

Program_11_Advanced.Bas demonstrates how to use the power of our protocol to interact with numerous subsystems to set parameters, change states, read information, and animate instrumentation on the screen. Generally this is not a different situation from a factory control panel. The user is given ergonomic and pertinent feedback indicating the status of various ***transducers*** (sensors) in the system. The user is also able to effect changes to the system by controlling ***actuators*** (motors, relays, solenoids); this is the ***essence of a GUI Instrumentation and Feedback Control System***.

We will not discuss the program. It is basically an integration of all the programs you have seen so far. However, it is not that simple. Many details had to be considered to integrate the subroutines and make them work together. You should be able to recognize elements from Servomotor_06.Bas, Ping_03.Bas, Pots_03.Bas and Program_10_B.Bas. In most cases there were modifications to make the systems behave in concordance without clashing and also to make the ***screen animation*** of the simulated instrumentation work well together.

Do not worry if you find this program overwhelming. Just study it as far as you can. It is not really the objective here that you learn ***this*** program. The point is that you can see what ***can be*** achieved and to know that you can have a very impressive system using RB and the Propeller programmed with the right firmware and software.

Another point to note is the way things are all happening in parallel. Also notice how the motors can be turning while you are pushing buttons and so forth. All this illustrates a level of sophistication that would hardly be possible without a really versatile and effective protocol such as we have developed so far. To illustrate another level of parallelism, activate the PST and observe its output.

Program_11_Advanced.Bas

```
//Program_11_Advanced.BAS
//work with Program_11_Main.Spin
Port = 8  //change this as per your system
Main:
  gosub Initialization
  GoSub SetAllLevels
  while true
    call CheckMouseKeyboard()
    if Command == -1 then call DoPing(PX,PY)
    if Command == -1 then call DoPots()
    call SendCommand(Command,Parameter)
    if timer()-P22_Timer > sValue[1]  //if P22 blinker time out
        P22_State = !P22_State \if !sValue[1] then P22_State=0
        CircleWH 455,205,20,20,FactorColor(ConsToClr(yellow),\
            -20),LEDState[P22_State*2]
        P22_Timer = timer() //reset timer
    endif
    if timer()-P21_Timer > 500.0/Limit(sValue[2],1,255)  //if blinker timeout
        P21_State = !P21_State \if !sValue[2] then P21_State=0
        CircleWH 695,205,20,20,FactorColor(ConsToClr(yellow),\
            -20),LEDState[P21_State*2]
        P21_Timer = timer() //reset timer
    endif
  wend
end
//--------------------------------------------
Initialization:
  fnt = "Times New Roman"
  data LEDState;white,red,yellow
  setcommport Port,br115200   //set serial comms
  xyText 390,100,"Last Command , Parameter",fnt,11,fs_Bold
  xystring 10,10,"Click on the checkbox to light up the corresponding LED"+\
              " on the propeller"
  xystring 10,70,"Press the buttons on the Propeller and see the "+\
              "corresponding LED light up"
  xyText 640,110,"If Lit => error",fnt,10,fs_Bold
  for i=0 to 2
     AddCheckBox "DS"+i,60+20*i,40," "   //add checkboxes as bits to form the
  next                                    //number to send
  data sLabel;"Dimmer Level (P23)","P22 Blink Duration","P21 Blink Frequency"
  data sCommand; 200,201,2
  data sValue; 0,0,0,127,127,10
  for i=0 to 2
    xyString 240*i+30,175,sLabel[i]
    AddSlider "P"+(23-i),10+240*i,200,200,0,255
    SetSliderPos "P"+(23-i),sValue[i+3]
    call MakeValue(i,sValue[i+3])
    xyText 80+240*i,245,MakeValue__Result,fnt,20,fs_Bold
  next
  call DrawDimmer(sValue[3])
  CheckBoxes = 0
  Command = 0 \ Parameter = 0
  P22_Timer = timer() \ P22_State = 0
  P21_Timer = timer() \ P21_State = 0
  LastSlider()  'clear any slider events
```

```
   AddButton "&Reset The Propeller",650,30
   GoSub InitPing \ GoSub  InitPots \ GoSub InitMotors
   onCheckBox cbHandler \ onSlider sHandler \ onButton bHandler
Return
//-----------------------------------------------
SetAllLevels:
  serialout 1,_CheckBoxes      //force checkboxes to be reflected
  for i=0 to 2                 //force blinkers and dimmers to be set
     serialout sCommand[i],getsliderpos("P"+(23-i))
  next
Return
//-----------------------------------------------
sub SendCommand(Command,Parameter,&s)
   if Command < 0 then s="" \ return false
   xyText 450,120, Format(Command,"##0"+spaces(10))+\
           ", "+Format(Parameter," ##0          "),_fnt,10,fs_Bold
   ClearSerBuffer \ serialout Command,Parameter
   _Command = -1 \ _Parameter = -1
   serbytesin 5,s,x
   circlewh 600,100,30,30,red,LEDState[(x<5)]  //set the error LED
   if x < 5 then s = "" \ return false
   if Command == 66 then return true
   for i=0 to 2
     circlewh 60+i*40,100,30,30,red,LEDState[Getstrbyte(s,3-i)&1]  //set LEDs
   next
Return true
//-----------------------------------------------
sub CheckMouseKeyboard()
   readmouse x,y,mb
   if mb=1
     call WhichIsIt(x,y,_MX,_MY,_MS,n)
     _Command = n \ _Parameter = 0
   elseif KeyDown()
     _Parameter = 0
     if keydown(kc_UArrow) then _Command = 6
     if keydown(kc_DArrow) then _Command = 7
     if keydown(kc_RArrow) then _Command = 12
     if keydown(kc_LArrow) then _Command = 13
     if keydown(kc_Space)  then _Command = 0
   endif
return
//-----------------------------------------------
sub bHandler()
  lb = LastButton()
  msg="Are you sure you want to reset the Propeller"+crlf()+\
            "If the program is in RAM you will lose it!"
  if left(lb,2) == "&R"
     if ErrMsg(msg,"RobotBASIC",MB_YESNO|MB_ERROR)==MB_YES
         serialout 255,0               //reset
         delay 2000
         GoSub SetAllLevels
     endif
  elseif left(lb,2) == "&C"
     Hidebutton lb
     HideButton "&Finished",false
     mconstant P,0
```

```
      CopyScr ,350,400
      rectanglewh 380,405,300,100,black,black
      rectanglewh 378,402,300,100,black,gray
      xytext 384,410,"Move the Pots from max to min waiting a little while",\
             _fnt,10,fs_Bold,,gray
      xytext 384,430,"at each end then repeat the process a few times",_fnt,\
             10,fs_Bold,,gray
    xytext 384,450,"When done press 'Finished'",_fnt,10,fs_Bold,,gray
      _Calibrate = true
   elseif left(lb,2) == "&F"
      HideButton lb
      HideButton "&Calibrate",false
      _Calibrate = false
      copytoscr ,350,400
      call WriteLabels()
   endif
   onbutton bHandler
return
//------------------------------------------------
sub cbHandler()
   lcb = LastCheckBox()
   _CheckBoxes = MakeBit(_CheckBoxes,2-ToNumber(right(lcb,1)),GetCheckBox(lcb))
   xystring 200,40,"=",_CheckBoxes,spaces(20)
   _Command = 1 \ _Parameter = _CheckBoxes
   onCheckBox cbHandler
Return
//------------------------------------------------
sub sHandler()
   ls = LastSlider()
   if left(ls,3) !="Pot"
      _Parameter = GetSliderPos(ls)
     n = 23-tonumber(substring(ls,2))
      _Command = sCommand[n]
      if n == 0 then Call DrawDimmer(_Parameter)
      call MakeValue(n,_Parameter)
      xyText 80+240*n,245,MakeValue__Result,_fnt,20,fs_Bold
   endif
   onSlider sHandler
return
//------------------------------------------------
sub MakeValue(which,Level)
   if which == 0   'dimmer
      n = Level/256.0*3.3
      Level = Format(n,"0.000 V   ")
   elseif which == 1   'P22 blink duration
      n = Level*2000/256
      Level = Format(n,"####0 ms   ")
   else
      n = Level
      Level = Format(n,"##0   Hz   ")
   endif
   sValue[which] = n
return Level
//------------------------------------------------
sub DrawDimmer(Level)
   CircleWH 212,202,26,26,white,white
```

```
  if !Level then return
  x = 1+(20*Level/256)/2
  Circle 225-x,215-x,225+x,215+x,red, RGB(Limit(Level,70,255),0,0)
return
//---------------------------------------------
//---------------------------------------------
InitPing:
  data units;"Millimeters","Meters","Inches","Feet","Yards"
  data unitn; " mm"," m"," in"," ft"," Yrds"
  data factors;1.,.001,Convert(.001,cc_MTOIN)
  data factors;Convert(.001,cc_MTOIN)/12
  data factors;Convert(Convert(.001,cc_MTOIN)/12,cc_FTTOYRD)
  AddRBGroup "Units",10,300,200,100,2,mToString(units)
  SetRBGroup "Units",1
  PX = 10 \ PY = 480
  call DrawPing(PX,PY)
  savescr 0,400,350
Return
//---------------------------------------------
sub DoPing(Px,Py)
  call SendCommand(192,0,s)
  if !SendCommand__Result then  return
  t = (getstrbyte(s,4)<<8)+getstrbyte(s,5) //reconstitute the value
  call mmDistance(,t,D)                    //convert to mm
  n=getrbgroup("Units")-1                  //get desired units
  x=Format(D*factors[n],"0.0####")         //convert to units and format
  call DrawSignal(Px,Py,t,x+unitn[n])  //draw beam and display value in units
Return
//---------------------------------------------
sub mmDistance(Tc,t,&D)
   if !vType(Tc) then Tc = 22.2        //if no temp specified assume 22.2 C
   D = 0.5*t*(331.5 + 0.6* Tc)/1000  //convert time to mm
Return D
//---------------------------------------------
sub DrawPing(x,y)    //draw picture of Ping device
  s = 30
  for i=-1 to 1 step 2
    line x,y+s*i,x+20,y+s*i,40,gray
    circlewh x+30,y-20+s*i,40,40,white,white
  next
  rectanglewh x-20,y-2*s,25,s*4,white,white
  rectanglewh x-2,y-s*2,10,s*4,green,green
Return
//---------------------------------------------
sub DrawSignal(x,y,d,str)
  d *= 200.0/19000        //scale value to screen coordinates
  restorescr 0,400
  xx1 = x+20+CartX(d,dtor(20))
  yy1 = y+CartY(d,dtor(20))
  Line x+20,y,xx1,yy1
  xx2 = x+20+CartX(d,dtor(-20))
  yy2 = y+CartY(d,dtor(-20))
  Line x+20,y,xx2,yy2
  Line xx1,yy1,xx2,yy2
  if d > 3 then floodfill x+20+d/2,y,black
  xytext x,y+80,str,,20,fs_bold
```

```
  //flip
return
//-------------------------------------------
//-------------------------------------------
InitPots:
  dim P[2,3] \ mconstant P,0
  xytext 380,290,"Change the Pots' positions and observe the Sliders",\
                 fnt,9,fs_bold
  AddButton "&Calibrate",460,370
  AddButton "&Finished",460,370
  HideButton "&Finished"
  AddSlider "Pot0",220,310,250,0,6000
  AddSlider "Pot1",520,310,250,0,6000
  enableslider "Pot0",false \ enableslider "Pot1",false
  call WriteLabels()
  Calibrate = false
Return
//-------------------------------------------
sub DoPots()
  call SendCommand(66,0,s)
  if !SendCommand__Result then return
  P2 = (getstrbyte(s,1)<<8)+getstrbyte(s,2)
  P1 = (getstrbyte(s,3)<<8)+getstrbyte(s,4)
  setsliderpos "Pot0",P1
  setsliderpos "Pot1",P2
  for i=0 to 1
     xystring 320+300*i,350,Format(GetSliderPos("Pot"+i),"####0")
  next
  If _Calibrate then Call Calibration(P1,P2)
Return
//-------------------------------------------
sub WriteLabels()
  for i=0 to 1
     xystring 210+300*i,350,GetSliderMin("Pot"+i)
     xystring 450+300*i,350,GetSliderMax("Pot"+i)
     xystring 320+300*i,350,Format(GetSliderPos("Pot"+i),"####0")
  next
return
//-------------------------------------------
sub Calibration(P1,P2)
     P[0,1] = P1 \ P[1,1] = P2
     for i=0 to 1
        P[i,2] = MaxV(P[i,2],P[i,1])
        P[i,0] = MinV(P[i,0],P[i,1])
        SetSliderMax "Pot"+i,P[i,2]
        SetSliderMin "Pot"+i,P[i,0]
        SetSliderPos "Pot"+i,P[i,1]
     next
     Call WriteLabels()
return
//-------------------------------------------
//-------------------------------------------
InitMotors:
  arrow = "UlulwwssldlU"
  MX = 750 \ MY = 500 \ MS = 10
  for i=0 to 3
```

```
      drawshape RotShape(arrow,i),MX,MY,MS
      floodfill ,,black
  next
  xyText 600,550,"Move Motors with Keyboard Arrows",fnt,8,fs_Bold
  xyText 600,565,"Or Click on the arrows above",fnt,8,fs_Bold
  xyText 580,580,"Space or click in middle white box to Stop",fnt,8,fs_Bold
Return
//----------------------------------------
sub WhichIsIt(x,y,Cx,Cy,Scale,&n)
  n = -1
  f2 = Scale*2 \ f4=Scale*4
  if within(x,Cx-f2,Cx+f2)     && within(y,Cy-f4,Cy-Scale)    then n=6
  if within(x,Cx-f2,Cx+f2)     && within(y,Cy+Scale,Cy+f4)    then n=7
  if within(x,Cx+Scale,Cx+f4)  && within(y,Cy-f2,Cy+f2)       then n=12
  if within(x,Cx-f4,Cx-Scale)  && within(y,Cy-f2,Cy+f2)       then n=13
  if within(x,Cx-Scale,Cx+Scale) && within(y,Cy-Scale,Cy+Scale) then n=0
return
```

7.7.1 Flexibility, Facility and Simplicity

Program_11_Advanced.Bas tests the new Program_11_Main.Spin (and its objects) quite thoroughly. The program is complex and may appear overwhelming. Notwithstanding, it is the type and level of program you should expect to eventually create for your own systems.

In the interest of clarity and simplicity we will develop a second test program that will test the system but in a simpler and less GUI manner. Moreover, this exercise will serve another purpose. Think about this for a moment. We have programmed our Propeller with a system that in conjunction with the right RB program gave us the actions and interactions we had in Program_11_Advanced.Bas. Normally in a system of just firmware and hardware, to change the purpose of the system we would have to reprogram the microcontroller all over again. Not to mention the fact that we would be very hard pressed to achieve the level of GUI with just a microcontroller on its own.

With the arrangement we have we can, with minimal effort, change the behavior of the system entirely and still not need to reprogram the Propeller at all. This is not something to gloss over. You really need to reflect on this carefully. With the very same firmware and hardware, we can now make the system do something different by just changing the easily reprogrammable software. In fact the system as it is right now could function as a simple robot if you had it sitting on a chassis with wheels driven by the motors. The system still needs a little more improvement and we will also incorporate wireless later but regardless, as it is, we could actually make a viable robot out of it.

7.7.2 A Really Simple Program

Just to illustrate how simple a program can be and yet do interesting things, let's make one that would keep the motors turning forward unless the Ping value is less than 500 mm at which time it will reverse and keep reversing until the Ping returns a value greater than 1000mm. If you press *Esc* on the keyboard the motors stop and the program halts. Notice in the listing the subroutine **SendCommand()** which facilitate the sending of a command. Notice that besides sending the command and receiving the 5 bytes it also prints a message if there is a communications error. Also if the command is the Ping one (192) it converts the last two received bytes from the 5 bytes into the Ping value. But further it converts the Ping value to a millimeter value using **mmDistance()** which you have seen before. The main program becomes quite simple due to the support provided by the **SendCommand()** subroutine.

Program_11_ReallySimple.Bas

```
// Program_11_ReallySimple.Bas
//works with Program_11_Main.Spin
Port = 8 //change this as per your system
Main:
  Gosub Initialization
  while true
```

```
        if keydown(kc_Esc) then call SendCommand(0,0) \ break
        call SendCommand(6,0)    //set forward
        call SendCommand(192,0) //get ping
        if Ping < 500
            repeat
                if keydown(kc_Esc) then call SendCommand(0,0) \ break
                call SendCommand(7,0)    //set backward
                call SendCommand(192,0) //get ping
            until Ping > 1000
        endif
  wend
End
//---------------------------------------------
Initialization:
  setcommport Port,br115200
  Ping = 0
Return
//---------------------------------------------
sub SendCommand(C,P)
   clearserbuffer
   serialout C,P
   serbytesin 5,s,n
   if n < 5
      s=""
      xystring 500,40,"Comms Error"
      return false
   endif
   if C ==192  //if command is ping make up number and convert to mm
      call mmDistance(,GetStrByte(s,5)+(getstrbyte(s,4)<<8),x)
      _Ping = x
      xystring 10,30,"Ping = ",x,spaces(20)
   endif
return true
//---------------------------------------------
sub mmDistance(Tc,t,&D)                  //convert ping to mm
   if !vType(Tc) then Tc = 22.2          //if no temp specified assume 22.2 C
   D = 0.5*t*(331.5 + 0.6* Tc)/1000  //convert time to mm
Return D
```

7.8 Improving the Motors Object

Program_11_Advanced.Bas is impressive indeed in the way it allows so many tasks to be performed in parallel and yet under control of the visually pleasing and functionally effective GUI System. The new **Motors** object, however, is not quite sufficient. In this section we will improve it to behave in a more useful manner.

If you examine how **Motors** works you will notice a glaring omission. The problem is two fold:
1.   There is no allowance for step size or turn amount. It just keeps the motors on until a new command comes in.
2.   There is no speed control; the motors just go at top speed.

We will rectify these two problems, but this is not as simple a matter as you might think at first glance.

7.8.1 Allowing For Distance and Angle

Think for a moment about what would happen when we command the motors to move forward or backwards a particular distance:

➢ How do we specify the distance?
➢ Should it move the distance then stop?

If we had wheel counters then specifying a distance would be easy. We know the wheel's circumference, so we can measure the distance in terms of the number of turns. This is one way you can achieve this; you would turn on the motors and then keep interrogating a wheel counter system (e.g. a quadrature encoder) until the required number of turns is achieved. Another possible solution is to use a Global Navigation System (GPS) or Local Navigation System (LPS) or Inertial Navigation System (INS) using accelerometers and gyroscopes. With all these we would use the same strategy of turning the wheels on then waiting for the correct value to be reported by the system.

In our hardware we have none of these and therefore we will use timing. It is a similar strategy to the above one in that we will start the wheels and wait for a particular value. However, there is no system to interrogate for a value; instead, we will use a time delay. But how do we know how long to wait? Simply use the required distance as a multiplier for a time interval. So if a distance of 1 is required then delay X milliseconds. If a distance of 10 is required then delay 10*X milliseconds. We should then do some experimenting and tweaking to adjust the value X so that it results in a traveled distance that is 1 unit of what we need. So if we are going to specify the units in inches then commanding the wheels to move forward (command 6) with a parameter of 1 will result in the wheels turning for a duration such that 1 inch is the resulting forward movement. It is up to you to change the X parameter to achieve this.

It would be nice however if, instead of building this factor into the firmware as a fixed value, we allow this factor to be specified by a command from the software. Remember, though that the parameter is limited to one byte (0-255). Therefore we will have to do some data mapping to be able to specify a number 0-255 and convert it into an X that is an acceptable time (e.g. milliseconds). We will discuss this later.

The same applies for turning. If we have a compass or some navigation system, we can use that to provide the value to wait for while the wheels are turning. But, since we have none of these, we will use a timed turn where a degree is Y milliseconds and n degrees is n*Y milliseconds. Also we will need to allow for specifying this parameter with a command from RB to be able to vary the system without reprogramming the firmware.

> In the firmware so far the motors are always controlled *together*. For a forward/backward command the motors are rotated in *opposite directions*. This ensures that they would cause a robot to move forward/backward when they are mounted on either side of a robot as in a Parallax Boe-Bot. Also for turning, the motors rotated together in the *same direction* which will make the robot turn on the spot about the center of the wheels' axis. In Chapter 8 we will add more commands to allow for rotating the motors individually and to even keep them rotating until commanded to stop.

7.8.2 Eliminating Jitter

Another aspect we need to consider is what should be done upon the completion of the required distance. Should we turn the motors off or should we keep them on? You may think that it is obvious that they should be turned off. However, keeping the motors turning might be a good strategy. Why?

The problem with stopping after every move is that the continuous stop-move action causes the robot to be *"jerky"* it keeps moving in fits of stops and starts and this will translate into a jittery robot. One way to solve this is to use ramping. Ramping is the action of slowly increasing/decreasing the speed of the motor to avoid sudden accelerations. This however is not effective for short distances since there is not enough time to ramp up the motor in an effective way. Nevertheless, ramping is an effective strategy in general and should be applied for longer commanded distances. This is why we are using the Servo32V7 object. It has a ramping option that makes using ramping very simple. We will not use this option however for our system. It is an improvement you can implement if you wish on your own.

The strategy we will use is a simple one. Think about how robot control is applied most of the time. It is rare that we would command the robot to move a long distance because we do not want the robot to move any appreciable distance without checking its environment. For instance in line following we do not want the robot to move without checking if the line is still under the robot or if it has veered right or left. We need to command the robot to move a small step then check the sensors then either continue in the same direction or turn.

Accordingly, the best way to stop jitter is to keep the robot moving and when the new command arrives the robot will either stop and turn or will continue to move in the same direction. This will result in a much smoother movement.

There is a further issue to consider. What happens if a new command does not arrive? What if the communications link is severed or the control program goes haywire? Obviously we should have a timeout. If a new command does not arrive within a certain period the motors would be turned off. Again, we need to be able to specify and modify this period without having to recompile the firmware.

Determining the Command Turnaround Frequency

Obviously every command may take slightly more or slightly less time to execute but what we want is to have a feel for how long it takes to send out a command with its parameter to the firmware and then receive the 5 bytes. Obviously it takes time to send and receive bytes over the serial link. Moreover, the code itself that carries out the work in both RobotBASIC and Spin would add further time to that. But even further, the time it takes to create the data to be sent/received and the time it takes to carry out the command and the time it takes to interpret the data received, all add further delays. For now we are using a direct wire link. This will of course be the fastest possible link. Later in Chapter 9 we will make the link wireless and/or over a LAN link which itself could be wireless or wired and within a local LAN or over a wider WAN or even the Internet.

We want to develop a RobotBASIC program that will give an average value for the ***command turnaround*** so we can see how long it takes on average to carry out a command. You can use this program to test the wireless command frequency later in Chapter 9 but for over the LAN we will present a slightly different version in Chapter 9.2.8. Command_Turnaround.Bas will send out command code 0 with parameter 0 and then will receive the 5 bytes. To simulate using the 5 bytes we will extract the top three bytes and assign them to variables and then we will also use the 4th and 5th bytes to make a 16-bit number and assign it to a variable. All this will be repeated 100 times and the total time will be averaged to determine the average turnaround time in milliseconds. You can then use this value to gain insight for how to set the motors' timeout discussed in the previous section.

For our configuration, with a direct wire connection (through the PP) the average was about 31 ms (32 Hz). With the XBee at 115200 baud it was 51 ms (19 Hz) and over the TCP with LAN and Wi-Fi it was 52 ms (19Hz). You can use the program below to test your own setup.

Command_Turnaround.Bas

```
//Command_Turnaround.Bas
//works with Program_11_Main.Spin or Program_12.Spin
Port =8  //change this as per your system
Main:
  setcommport Port,br115200
  t = timer()
  C = 0 \ P = 1   //modify the command code and parameter to see
                  //how long a particular command takes to execute
  for i=1 to 100
    call SendCommand(C,P,s,n)
    if !SendCommand__Result then continue
    a = getstrbyte(s,1) \ b= getstrbyte(s,2)
    c = getstrbyte(s,3)
    x = (getstrbyte(s,4) << 8) +getstrbyte(s,5)
    xystring 10,50,a;b;c;x;timer()-t
  next
  t = (timer()-t)/100
  clearscr
```

```
  print "Average Turnaround = ",t," millisecs"
  print "Frequency          = ",1000/t," Hz"
end
//----------------
sub SendCommand(C,P,&s,&x)
  m = ""
  serialout C,P
  SerBytesIn 5,s,x
  if x != 5 then m = "Comms Error"
  xyText 500,10,m,,,red
Return (x==5)
```

7.8.3 Modifying the System Parameters

So far we have these required parameters:
1. Time factor for a step of linear movement (**StepTime**).
2. Time factor for a degree of rotation movement (**TurnTime**).
3. Timeout for keeping the motors on after a forward step (**L_TimeOut**).
4. Timeout for keeping the motors on after a turning (**T_TimeOut**).
5. Speed factor for a linear movement (**L_Speed**).
6. Speed factor for a turning movement (**T_Speed**).

Also if you remember in the **Main** object we had two parameters we never bothered to allow to be changed. These are (see the **Dat** section)
7. **Timeout1** for the timeout period for receiving the second byte (the parameter of the command).
8. **Timeout2** for the timeout period to allow a command to finish its works before the **Main** cog will ignore it and not send the send buffer and go back to receiving another command. This will have to be slightly less than the Timeout in the software expecting the 5 bytes back. So if we change this we must also change the timeout in the RB program to be always slightly longer (see the **SetTimeOut** command in RobotBASIC).

In the light of all the above let's modify the **Motors** object and the **Main** object to accommodate the new strategies and to allow for specifying the parameters from the RB program.

> The ability to modify the operational parameters of the firmware without having to modify and recompile it is a powerful and convenient feature. You will see this soon where we will experiment with the timeouts to arrive at a good value. If we had to recompile the firmware every time we changed the value, then try, then recompile to change it and so on we would soon grow weary and may not arrive at an optimal value.

7.8.4 Timeout Range Remapping

With our protocol we send a byte to hold the command code and then a byte as a parameter for the code. So parameters are limited to a value of 0 to 255. Therefore we have to be careful as to how we are going to interpret the parameters for the commands that will change the timeouts because we need to know if they are seconds or milliseconds and we may want to data-map the byte value into the required range for the desired parameter.

For instance, if you want a range from 10 to 5000 milliseconds, we obviously cannot specify that with only one byte. At this point you might ask why we can't extend the protocol to allow for sending two bytes for the parameter. Well, you can definitely do this; but consider that most of the time while using the protocol you will only need a byte value. It is only for a few rarely used commands where you require the full 16 bits. So if you always send two bytes you are increasing the traffic volume by 33% all the time for the sake of the 1% of the time that you may need two. You may use this option, but there are other ways we can get around this (also see Chapter 11).

One way is to use two consecutive commands. So for instance you can have the firmware whenever it sees the command XXX store the parameter and then expect a second consecutive occurrence of the command to come in and when that comes in it would then use the second parameter with the stored one to reconstitute the 16 bit number and then set the variable in the system; this is a viable option if there is no alternative (See Chapter 11.1). A better solution that is acceptable in all our cases is to use *data-mapping*. We would lose some resolution but that is usually not a problem. For example, to map to a range of 10 to 5000 milliseconds we would use a formula like this

$$Value = 10+ 4990*(Received\_Parameter/255)$$

This formula will map the 0-255 received value to a value between 10 and 5000. The resolution will then be almost 20 ms. Thus you cannot set the required variable except in steps of 20 milliseconds. This might be unacceptable and then you would have to resort to the consecutive commands option above (or see Chapter 11). However for most of our requirements this has proven to be quite acceptable.

> ⚠️ The formula above is just an example. For our mapping we will simply use a multiplying factor.

Hence we will use for the:
1. **StepTime** a map of 10 ms   (i.e. 0 to 2550 ms for a range of 0-255).
2. **TurnTime** a map of 10 ms   (i.e. 0 to 2550 ms for a range of 0-255).
3. **L_TimeOut** a map of 10 ms   (i.e. 0 to 2550 ms for a range of 0-255).
4. **T_TimeOut** a map of 10 ms   (i.e. 0 to 2550 ms for a range of 0-255).
5. **L_Speed** a map of 1   (i.e. range 0 to 255, see the Spin listing for how this is utilized).
6. **T_Speed** a map of 1   (i.e. range 0 to 255, see the Spin listing for how this is utilized).
7. **Timeout1** a map of 500 milliseconds (i.e. 0 to 127.5 secs for a range of 0-255).
8. **Timeout2** a map of 500 milliseconds (i.e. 0 to 127.5 secs for a range of 0-255).

Items 1-4 have a range from 0 to 2550 ms; this is quite acceptable. Also when you consider that the servomotor's signal is 20 ms then a resolution of 10 ms is probably too fine anyway. To have a step value longer than 2.55 seconds is too long and usually a much shorter time is required.

For 7 and 8 we have a range of 500 ms to 127.5 seconds. Obviously we do not need all this range since 500 ms is too short and 127.5 secs is too long, but a resolution of 0.5 secs is good to have. RB has a default serial communications time out set at 5000 milliseconds. Usually this is more than sufficient. If you keep this default in RB, you have to keep **Timeout2** at slightly shorter than that (4 secs is good). However, as we will see shortly, you may need to extend this time; in which case you must also set the RB program to also expect a longer timeout.

7.8.5 Avoiding Serial Communications Timeout

Notice that if we set the **StepTime** to 50 ms and command the motors to go forward for 255 steps we will get a delay of 12.75 seconds. This is way over the **Timeout2** value and also RB's timeout. So in this case **Main** will timeout and not send the 5 bytes back to RB which will also timeout and cause an error situation.

If we determine that the motors need to stay on for 50 ms to move a step as an acceptable distance in our scaling then to allow for a full 255 steps we will have to extend the **Timeout2** period in **Main** and therefore also the timeout in the RB program. Alternatively, we can limit the RB program to never command more than 80 steps at a time, which requires 4 seconds to complete and is therefore within the timeout.

In a real program where RB is commanding the robot to do real actions it is almost never going to command the robot to move more than a few steps. This is because the AI control program will need to keep track of obstacles or lines to follow or beacons to look for. Almost, 99.9% of the time an AI program should not make the robot move more than few step before reexamining the sensory reports to avoid the robot falling off edges, crashing into obstacles, or missing a line being followed. It is on the very rare occasion indeed where an AI program will command the robot to move for more than 4 seconds without sensory feedback.

Additionally, there is another way we can keep the motors moving without causing a timeout. This is with the **L_TimeOut** value. Remember this is a value that determines when the motors will be stopped after a forward/backward command has finished and before the next command comes in. So if we set this to 255 (ie 2550 ms according to our mapping) then after executing the forward/backward command for the number of steps commanded the motors will keep turning another 2.55 seconds unless a new command is received to change that. Again, in an AI program for controlling a robot you won't need **L_TimeOut** to be that long, but in other application you may need this.

> ⓘ The point is that you have flexibility and controllability and you can change the parameters as you need. Also see Chapter 8.2.3 where we add new commands to activate the motors independently from each other with an option to keep them on until commanded to stop.

7.8.6 The Modified Firmware

Program_12_Main.Spin and its associated sub-objects implement all the new requirements. Notice that only **Main** and **Motors** are new objects the other two are still the same as in _11. In **Main** we changed the instantiation of Motors_12 and also allowed for the new command codes. Only the changes are listed below with the bold lines being the new code. **Motors** is changed extensively so all of it is listed with the bold lines being the new code.

We will use Timeout_Tester.Bas to experiment with various values for the step time and timeout parameters so as to tweak the system. This will illustrate how we can modify the behavior of the system without having to recompile the firmware every time we want to change a parameter. This is a major advantage made available to us because of the protocol. Trying out various settings using the firmware alone is a tedious process of modifying-compiling-uploading-trying and then repeating the entire process. The tedium of doing this can force us to accept less than optimal parameters due to not trying sufficient variations. However, with an RB program we can easily and interactively try out as many variations and combinations as we need. Once an acceptable set of parameters are determined, we can then put them as default values in the firmware (**Dat** section). This will make it possible to have the system behave as we desire without having the RB program always setting the parameters. The RB program would then only change things when situations other than the default are required.

> ⓘ See Chapter 8.3 for another way we can save the parameters without recompiling the firmware by saving them to the Propeller EEPROM.

Notice all the new command codes that are now handled by the **Main** and **Motors** objects and allow you to modify how the motors move by setting the various parameters. Remember these new command codes because we will use them in Timeout_Tester.Bas.

> ⓘ See Table B.1 in Appendix B for the command codes; also Table 8.2 in chapter 8.2.1.

Use Timeout_Tester.Bas to experiment with various settings. Your goal is to determine a value for the **L_TimeOut** and **StepTime** so that you get an acceptable step size (distance wise) and also to have the motors keep moving smoothly between commands. Initially, try **L_StepTime** of 1 and **L_TimeOut** of 0. Then use command 6 with a parameter of 1. Keep pressing the space bar or keep it pressed. Notice how the motors jitter and jerk. Also only press the space bar slowly. Notice how the motors do not move except every other press of the space bar. Why is that?

When we set the **StepTime** to 1 we are setting it to 10 ms (remember the mapping). Remember that this is a servomotor and the signal required to move it has to be repeated every 20ms. So by setting the step time to 10ms we are not allowing the motor to move except every two steps.

Now try **StepTime** of 4 (resulting in 40ms). See how far the motors move. Keep trying until the amount of movement of the motors translates to an acceptable distance as you need. Then change **L_Timeout** to say 10 (i.e. 100 ms). Now see what happens when you keep the space bar pressed down. Notice how the motors move in a lot smoother fashion. This is because now there is no stopping between receiving one command and the next. The motors will keep moving and when a new command comes that is another move forward then there is no change. If the new command is a turn then the movement will still be smoother than before.

Do remember though that if the communication is interrupted or no command arrives then the motors will stop only after the timeout. This is important in order to avoid a runaway robot. What you need is the shortest possible timeout that would still result in a smooth movement. You may need to change this time for instance if the communications baud rate is changed.

> (i) As determined using Command_Turnaround.Bas in the previous section, for direct wired communications the maximum rate of commands is 1 every 31 ms and for wireless 1 every 51 ms. So if we keep the motors turning for say 100 ms after completion of a command then we are guaranteed that the motor would stay turning until the next command arrives; 100 ms might be an acceptable amount.

Do the same for **TurnTime** until you have the robot turning about 1 degree. Also change **T_Timeout** to obtain smooth turning just as we did for the linear movement.

There is a crucial difference between turning and going straight. Even though it is rare that we would command the robot to move more than few steps at a time, it is very possible to require the robot to turn many degrees at a time. If **TurnTime** is set to 2 (20 ms) we would be allowed a maximum of 200 degrees before the **TimeOut2** period is exceeded. Also anything less than 20ms is not likely to be effective.

Since 200 degrees is in fact 160 degrees the other way around, having a limit of 200 is acceptable. We would make our programs always turn in the appropriate direction so that if we ever require to turn more than 180 degrees we should in fact turn the other way around; so we should never need to turn more than 180 degrees. This means that we can afford a **TurnTime** of at most 22 ms and since we have a resolution of 10 then we should not set **TurnTime** to more than 2 (20ms) if we are to keep the **TimeOut2** at 4 seconds as it is by default. If you need to set **TurnTime** to more than 2 then you will need to either limit the turning to less than 180 degrees or to extend the **TimeOut2** value (*and also the Timeout in RB*). You can always issue two consecutive turns of say 90 to get 180. As you can see you have many alternatives.

Timeout_Tester.Bas

```
//Timeout_Tester.Bas
//works with Program_12_Main.Spin
Port = 8  //change this as per your system
Main:
  setcommport Port,br115200
  call DoCommand(241,10)  'L_Timeout
  call DoCommand(242,3)   'StepTime
  call DoCommand(243,2)   'TurnTime
  call DoCommand(245,3)   'T_Timeout
  while true
     'for i=1 to 10  //uncomment this loop to try out many steps
                     //in succession to see how smooth the motors are
        call DoCommand(12,1) 'change the 6 to 12 for turning
        'delay 10     //simulates some processing that causes a delay
                      //before the next command
     'next
     waitkey k
  wend
end
//-----------------------------
sub DoCommand(C,P,&s,&x)
   serialout C,P
   serbytesin 5,s,x
return (x==5)
```

Program_12_Main.Spin (only changes)

```
OBJ
  RB     : "FullDuplexSerial"
  D      : "SerialMirror"
  Others : "Program_11_Others"
  Reader : "Program_11_Reader"
  Motors : "Program_12_Motors"

Pri ExecuteTheCommand
  case Command[0]
    255: 'reset the propeller
      Reboot

    200:'set the Dimmer level on P23
      frqA := Command[1] *DimmerScale

    201:'set blinker duration for Reader cog(P22)
        '256 levels between 0 to 2 secs (0=off)
      Settings[0] := Command[1]*(2_000/256)*(ClkFreq/1_000)

    202: 'set the TimeOut1 for waiting for parameter byte in seconds
        TimeOut1 := (clkfreq/1000)*Command[1]*500
    203: 'set TimeOut2 for waiting for a command to finish its actions
        'before sending the send buffer. It should reflect and be in relation
        'to the PC system's time out in seconds
        TimeOut2 := (clkfreq/1000)*Command[1]*500

    1,2,192:'commands in the Others cog that may fill the
            'the last two bytes in the primary send buffer
      Sems_Flags[1] |= OthersFlagMask    'set flag
      WaitForFlagResetWithTimeOut(OthersFlagMask)

    66:'commands in the Others cog that fill the secondary send buffer
      SendBufferOffset := 5            'command uses the secondary buffer
      Sems_Flags[1] |= OthersFlagMask  'set flag to signal the cog
      WaitForFlagResetWithTimeOut(OthersFlagMask)

    0,6,7,12,13,240,241,242,243,244,245:'commands in the Motors cog
      Sems_Flags[1] |= MotorsFlagMask    'set flag
      WaitForFlagResetWithTimeOut(MotorsFlagMask)
```

Program_12_Motors.Spin

```
CON
  FlagMask = %0000_0010   'mask for flag for this cog
  Offset_1 = 5   'offset for location of 2 byte data buffer
  Offset_2 = 7   'offset for location of 5 byte data buffer
  MidVal   = 1500
  MinVal   = 1000
  MaxVal   = 2000
  Servo1   = 16
  Servo2   = 17

Var
  long Stacks[50], t, onTimer, MotorsOn, MotorsTimeOut
  Long Command,Settings,Sems_Flags
```

```
Dat
  L_Speed       long 255    'speed factor for moving forward/backward
  T_Speed       long 255    'speed factor for turning
  StepTime      long 30
  TurnTime      long 20
  L_TimeOut     long 100    'motor keep on time after forward/backward
  T_TimeOut     long 0      'motor keep on time after turning

Obj
  D     : "SerialMirror"
  Servo : "Servo32V7"

PUB Start(CommandAddr,SettingsAddr,Sems_FlagsAddr)
  Command     :=    CommandAddr    'save all passed addresses as
  Settings    :=    SettingsAddr   'local variables to be used
  Sems_Flags  :=    Sems_FlagsAddr 'by all processes
  cogNew(Motors,@Stacks[0])        'start the cog

Pri Motors
  Initialization
  repeat
    Process0
    if Not(byte[Sems_Flags][1] & FlagMask) 'if flag not set then no action
      Next                                  'required, just loop back
    case byte[Command][0]                   'execute the command
        0:   StopMotors(0)
        6:   MoveMotors(1)  'forward
        7:   MoveMotors(-1) 'back
        12:  TurnMotors(1)  'right
        13:  TurnMotors(-1) 'left
      240:   L_Speed   := byte[Command][1]    'set speed
      241:   L_TimeOut := byte[Command][1]*10 'set timeout in steps of 10ms
      242:   StepTime  := byte[Command][1]*10 'set step time in steps of 10ms
      243:   TurnTime  := byte[Command][1]*10 'set turn time in steps of 10ms
      244:   T_Speed   := byte[Command][1]    'set speed
      245:   T_TimeOut := byte[Command][1]*10 'set timeout in steps of 10ms

    OutputToPST                             'output some info to the PST
    byte[Sems_Flags][1] &= !FlagMask  'clear flag to signal Main to proceed

Pri Initialization
  'initialize variables I/O direction etc.
  'none needed here
  t := cnt                          'initialize timer
  Servo.Start
  MotorsOn~


Pri Process0
  'can do anything here that requires polling or updating etc.
  'We will use this to turn motors off after a certain timeout
  if MotorsOn And cnt-onTimer > MotorsTimeOut*(clkfreq/1000)
    StopMotors(0)
```

```
Pri StopMotors(wait)
  Servo.Set(Servo1,MidVal)
  Servo.Set(Servo2,MidVal)
  MotorsOn~
  if wait
    waitcnt(cnt+(clkfreq/1_000_000)*50)   'wait 50 microsecs

Pri MoveMotors(Dir)|Val1,Val2
  StopMotors(1)
  Val1 := MidVal+Dir*1000*L_Speed/255
  Val2 := MidVal-Dir*1000*L_Speed/255
  if byte[Command][1]
    MotorsOn~~
    Servo.Set(Servo1,Val1)
    Servo.Set(Servo2,Val2)
    WaitForDistance

Pri WaitForDistance
  'this will use whatever system needed to evaluate the
  'the distance moved. For now we will just use a timed step
  waitcnt(clkfreq/1000*StepTime*byte[Command][1]+cnt)
  MotorsTimeOut := L_TimeOut
  OnTimer := cnt

Pri TurnMotors(Dir)|Val1,Val2
  StopMotors(1)
  Val1 := MidVal+Dir*1000*T_Speed/255
  Val2 := MidVal+Dir*1000*T_Speed/255
  if byte[Command][1]
    MotorsOn~~
    Servo.Set(Servo1,Val1)
    Servo.Set(Servo2,Val2)
    WaitForAngle

Pri WaitForAngle
  'this will use whatever system needed to evaluate the
  'the angle turned. For now we will just use a timed turn
  waitcnt(clkfreq/1000*TurnTime*byte[Command][1]+cnt)
  MotorsTimeOut := T_TimeOut
  OnTimer := cnt

Pri OutputToPST
  if Not LockSet(byte[Sems_Flags][2]) 'output some info to the PST
    D.Str(string(13,"Motors:"))          'if semaphore acquired
    D.Dec(byte[Command][0])
    D.Str(string(","))
    D.Dec(byte[Command][1])
    LockClr(byte[Sems_Flags][2])
```

7.8.7 Testing the New Firmware

Program_12_Main.Spin is now a real and complex system. However before we move on to test it with new programs let's test it with the old programs. As you know by now, the versatility of the protocol is that:

> Different RB programs work with the same firmware/hardware.
> Different hardware/firmware works with the same RB program.

However, in the latest improvement we have made a lot of changes to the way the **Motors** object is driving the motors. If you remember before, when the command to move the motors was sent the parameter did not matter and it was not even looked at by the firmware. But the new firmware now takes into account the parameter as well as the command and the parameter is used to drive the motors for a certain number of steps. If the parameter is 0 it will actually cause the motors to stop. Keep in mind this fact while we are testing the old programs with the new system. Let's see which programs will work and which program will have a snag.

We need to test
> Ping_03.Bas, Pots_03.Bas, Program_10_B.Bas, Program_11_A.Bas, Program_11.Bas, Servomotor_06.Bas, Program_11_Advanced.Bas, and Program_11_ReallySimple.Bas.

Compile and upload Program_12_Main.Spin and then run the programs above with the new system. Test all the aspects of the program and if there are any that are not working. Make the changes that would make the program work again. Please do not look at the answers below until you have attempted the modifications (if any) yourself.

The following programs did not work. Can you tell why?
> Program_11.Bas, Servomotor_06.Bas, Program_11_Advanced.Bas, and Program_11_ReallySimple.Bas.

They all did not work for exactly the ***same reason***. The reason is that now with the new firmware you cannot send a motor command (e.g. 6) with a parameter of 0. In all these programs the parameter is being set to 0 because in the old firmware the parameter for the motor commands was immaterial and so was set to 0. Now however, the parameter of the motor commands is very important. If it is 0 it actually causes the motors to stop.

⚠The new firmware in the **Motors** object will not return from the commanded motor action (turning or straight) until the time corresponding to the commanded number of steps has elapsed. This means that the RB program statement that command the robot to move will also wait for the movement to finishes before proceeding to the next statement. This is how it should be for this kind of work. See Chapter 8 for a way to command the motors to move separately and in the background without halting the program flow.

To correct all the programs you need to go through them and change the parameter for any of the motor commands (6,7,12,13) to a number other than 0. We have done this for you in the Zip file that contains all the source code in this book. The new programs are:
> Program_12.Bas, Servomotor_12.Bas, Program_12_Advanced.Bas, and Program_12_ReallySimple.Bas.

Have a look at these files for the solution ***if you cannot do it yourself***. But please do attempt the changes for at least one of the programs.

7.8.8 Robot Moves

The new hardware and firmware as we now have it can be placed on the chassis of a robot which would make a ***rudimentary*** real robot. Moreover, if you modify the pushbuttons to be a combination of bumpers around the robot and/or infrared sensors you would in fact have an ***almost viable*** robot.

The idea is not to concentrate on a particular hardware combination. Rather our aim is that after reading the book you should be able to organize ***any hardware*** to be working in a coordinated and parallel manner and to be controllable through a PC running an RB program.

To prove that this can be a real robot let's see the program RobotMoves_12.Bas. What it achieves is quite a feat made extremely simple and readily achievable because of our protocol. It should be quite straightforward to see what the program accomplishes. In **Initialization** there are four lines that are commented out. These lines will set some system parameters to control the step size and latency times as discussed in Section 7.8.3. You may want to modify these numbers if they are not according to the numbers you determined for your system in the previous section.

The subroutine **DisplayData()** is called after each motor movement is completed to display the Ping and Pots as well as the three hardware pushbuttons' status. Notice how it explicitly sends out the commands to read the Ping and the Pots. However, it does nothing about reading the bumpers, infrared sensors and line sensors. Remember these are not really bumpers and so forth on our hardware; rather they are the pushbuttons on P5..P7 emulating the sensors. In Chapter 8 we will add real line sensors but for now we are using P7 to emulate them. **DisplayData()** does not need to call any additional commands to read these data because they are always in the first three bytes of the 5 bytes returned whenever any command is called (except for certain ones that use all 5 bytes to return their data).

The **SendCommand()** subroutine takes care of sending the command and receiving the 5 bytes and creating the data for the bumpers and so on from the first three bytes (unless the command is 66). It also checks if the command was a 192 (Ping) and if so, the 4th and 5th bytes are used to reconstitute the value (MSBF). If the command is 66 (Pots) then the 1st and 2nd bytes are used to make up the first pot reading and the 3rd and 4th bytes to make up the second value.

RobotMoves_12.Bas

```
//RobotMoves_12.Bas
//works with Program_12_Main.Spin
Port =8  //change this as per your system
Main:
  Gosub Initialization
  while true
     call SendCommand(6,20)      'forward
     call DisplayData()
     call SendCommand(12,90)     'turn right
     call DisplayData()
     call SendCommand(7,20)      'backward
     call DisplayData()
     call SendCommand(13,90)     'turn left
     call DisplayData()
  wend
end
//----------------------------
Initialization:
  Bumper = 0 \ Feel = 0 \ Sense = 0
  GPSx = 0 \ GPSy = 0 \  Ranger = 0
  setcommport Port,br115200
  //call DoCommand(240,255) 'L_Speed
  //call DoCommand(241,10)  'L_TimeOut
  //call DoCommand(242,5)   'StepTime
  //call DoCommand(243,2)   'TurnTime
Return
//----------------------------
sub SendCommand(C,P,&s)
   serialout C,P
   serbytesin 5,s,x
   if x != 5 then xystring 10,100,"Comms Error" \ return false
   if C != 66
      _Bumper = getstrbyte(s,1)
      _Feel   = getstrbyte(s,2)
      _Sense  = getstrbyte(s,3)
   endif
   if C==192
      _Ranger = getstrbyte(s,5)+(getstrbyte(s,4)<<8)
   elseif C==66
      _GPSx = getstrbyte(s,2)+(getstrbyte(s,1)<<8)
      _GPSy = getstrbyte(s,4)+(getstrbyte(s,3)<<8)
   endif
```

```
return true
//-------------------------------
sub DisplayData()
  xystring 10,10,"Bumper";"Feel";"Sense";"Ranger";"GPSx";"GPSy"
  Call SendCommand(66,0)      'pots
  Call SendCommand(192,0)     'ping
  xystring 10,30,_Bumper;_Feel;_Sense;_Ranger;_GPSx;_GPSy,spaces(10)
return
```

7.9 An Exercise

It is now time for you to try it out; just a simple program to experiment with the **L_Speed** parameter. What we want is a program that will keep driving the motors in the forward direction. At the same time it will also monitor the keyboard. If an up arrow is pressed it will increment the speed (limit 255), if the down arrow is pressed it will decrement the speed (limit 0). You may want to set the **L_TimeOut** so that the motors will be smooth while the program is processing key presses etc.

Remember that the command to set the speed is code 240 (see Table B.1 in Appendix B or look in the listing of the **Motors** object). The command to set the motors forward is code 6. To set **L_Timeout** is 241. Before reading the solution, try to do it for yourself.

7.9.1 The Solution

Speed_Tester.Bas

```
//Speed_Tester.Bas
//works with Program_12_Main.Spin
Port = 8  //set this as per your system
Main:
  setcommport Port,br115200
  n = 3  //initial speed
  call SendCommand(240,n)   //set L_Speed
  call SendCommand(241,20) //set L_TimeOut
  while true
      xystring 10,10,"speed=",n;spaces(10)
      call SendCommand(6,5)   //forward
      if keydown(kc_UArrow) || keydown(kc_DArrow)
         if keydown(kc_UArrow) then n = Limit(n+10,0,255)
         if keydown(kc_DArrow) then n = Limit(n-10,0,255)
         waitnokey 150
         call SendCommand(240,n)   //set Lspeed
      endif
  wend
end
//----------------------------------------
sub SendCommand(C,P,&s)
   m = ""
   serialout C,P
   serbytesin 5,s,x
   if x < 5 then m = "comms error"
   xystring 500,20,m,spaces(30)
return (x==5)
```

7.10 Summary

In this chapter we have achieved numerous changes and improvements:
- ❑ Moved over to using the PPDB and tested it with the programs from Chapter 3.
- ❑ Experimented with controlling Servomotors in various ways.
- ❑ Experimented with the ultrasound ranger Ping))).
- ❑ Experimented with using potentiometers.
- ❑ Integrated all of the above hardware into the protocol of Chapter 6 and had it working under control of RB programs interacting with the new firmware through the protocol.
- ❑ Developed a complex GUI Instrumentation control program to interact with the hardware.
- ❑ Improved the firmware by allowing for step and latency times for motor movements.
- ❑ Studied various intricacies of timing and timeouts and command turnaround frequencies.
- ❑ Developed programs to use the hardware as if it were a robot.

More Advanced Hardware

In Chapter 7 we added some interesting hardware. In this chapter we will add more hardware that despite being slightly more complicated than what we had so far, is nonetheless easy to integrate into our system due to the versatility and robustness of the protocol. The actual hardware used is immaterial and your requirements may dictate a different set of devices. What is important, are the ***principles*** involved in incorporating the hardware within the system. Section 8.2 will expound a ***procedural strategy*** that makes adding any hardware to the ***protocol*** a simple endeavor. The details will differ from one device to another, but the overarching principle for how the ***firmware*** makes the devices available to ***software*** by means of a protocol is what interests us here. We will add:

- ➢ A compass.
- ➢ Ability to control the motors individually.
- ➢ A turret for the ultrasound ranger.
- ➢ A mechanism to save the system's parameters to the EEPROM and to reset them to factory settings.
- ➢ An accelerometer.
- ➢ Three Infrared line sensors.
- ➢ A speaker.

> To keep track of all the modifications and hardware, see Appendix B for the complete details of the final setup of the system as it will be once we complete adding all the hardware in this chapter. See Figures B.1, B.2 and Table B.1. Also see Figure 8.15.

> See Section 8.2 for a ***procedural strategy*** for adding hardware to a system that implements our protocol.

8.1 Adding a Compass

So far our firmware always had the hardware corresponding to a particular command available and when the command is invoked it would interact with the device with the assumption that there is one actually onboard and can be utilized. It is possible to have firmware that allows for more commands than there is actual hardware available. The firmware is designed to be all-inclusive and to allow for various devices that users may not opt to install on their version of the hardware configuration to cut costs.

Rather than have a different firmware for every different combinations of hardware, we would have one firmware designed so that when compiled to the particular configuration some constants (flags) are set to indicate that the hardware is implemented or reset if it is not. We may have a collection of these constants and all we have to do is set them to 1 or 0 before we compile and upload the firmware to the specific board.

The firmware is also written in such a way that it skips interacting with the hardware and just returns a value of 0 or some other value to indicate the fact that there is no hardware. If the hardware is available then it interacts with the firmware and returns the results. The firmware also should provide a mechanism so that the software communicating with it can ascertain if the hardware is available by returning the status of the relevant constant.

To illustrate this we will add the Honeywell HMC6352 Compass Module (Part#29323) [12] (Figure 2.9). A command that uses the compass module will return 0 unless the compass is available. Additionally, there will be a mechanism with which the RB program can ask the firmware if the compass is available. The wiring schematic for the compass will be as shown in Figure 8.1. The way it should look like on the PPDB is in Figure 8.2.

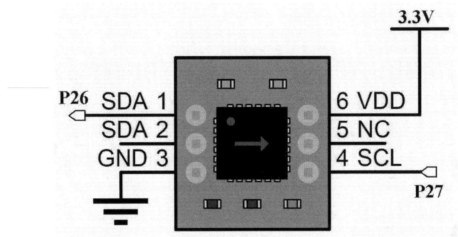

Figure 8.1: HMC6352 Connection Schematic. Notice the reference axis of the module is important.

> The reference direction of the PPDB board will depend on how you place the compass module on it. In our application we placed the module as shown in Figure 8.2 with Pin 1 on the bottom half of the breadboard and the HMC6352 reference axis (arrow on the chip in Figure 8.1) pointing upwards towards the top side of the PPDB towards the Propeller chip. Also see Figure 8.10 for a better perspective. The compass readings will be in relation to this direction.

Just as we did with the Pots_RCTime.Spin object we will use an object from the ObEx called HMC6352.Spin[28] that we also provide for you in the Zip file with all the source code. This object does not need to start a cog, so it is quite efficient. We will add the code to handle the reading of the compass to the **Others** object. The command code will be 24 and it will return its reading in the 4th and 5th bytes of the primary buffer. We will also need to change the **Main** object to allow for the new **Others** object as well as for the new commands.

The command 24 will do different things depending on the parameter passed to it:
    0 =   Read the compass and return its value in the 4th and 5th bytes.
    1 =   Report if there is a compass available or not in the 5th byte (4th always 0), 1 means yes, 0 means no.
    2 =   Calibrate the compass using the manual mode.
    3 =   Calibrate the compass using the automatic mode.

> The RB programs using the compass should always check if there is one available. The firmware will always report a heading of 0 if you try to read it and there isn't one available on the hardware.

In order to report accurate headings The HMC6352 has to be calibrated before it is used for the first time in a particular hardware environment. The command 24 with parameters 2 or 3 will allow for that. The implementation adds a level of complexity to the system that is quite an interesting issue. We will discuss it after you get a chance to study the listing of the new programs.

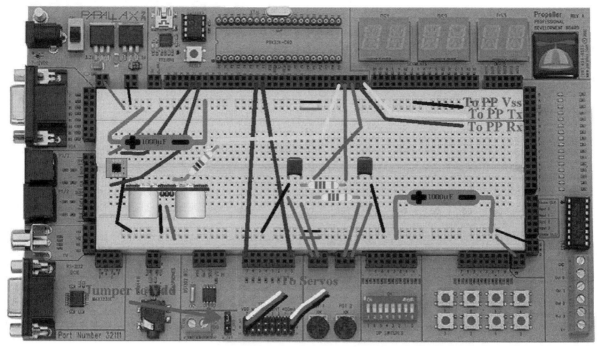

Figure 8.2: PPDB With the HMC6352 and all the previously installed hardware. LED and Pushbutton connections are not shown, see Figure 2.4, but P16 and P17 are now used for Servomotors.

For the sake of completeness we will also rename the other objects so that the whole firmware suite will have the same name. It will now be called Firmware_XXXX.Spin where the XXXX will be Main, Others, Reader and Motors. The new system is now as depicted in Figure 8.3. The only objects substantially changed for this improvement are **Main** and **Others**. The **Motors** and **Reader** objects are just renamed but also with the minor addition of a **Stop** method to allow for stopping the object's cog if ever required (for completeness). See how this is achieved in the listing of **Others** with the **Stop** method (highlighted lines).

Note that the **Cognew()** function is used in a different manner to allow the **Start()** method to return the number of the cog the method successfully started (1 to 8) or 0 if the method failed to start a cog. This way you can always check the return value when you invoke **Start()** to see if it has succeeded. To stop the cog, just call the **Stop** method. This modification is for the sake of following professional standards established at Parallax for the design of objects to be used by programmers. However, our objects are not of interest except in the context of our overall system design and to implement our protocol. So we would not require these features; they are implemented as an example.

In the code we prevent reading the compass module if the **Compass_On** constant in the **Con** section is 0. If your hardware has a compass then set the **Compass_On** constant to 1 when you compile and upload the firmware to the Propeller. If you do not have the compass module installed then just set the constant to 0. This way the same firmware is used. The software can interrogate the hardware to see if there is a compass by using the command code 24 with the parameter 1.

Only the **Main** and **Others** objects are listed below. In the zip file you have all the files. For **Main** we will list only the sections in the code that have undergone changes or additions.

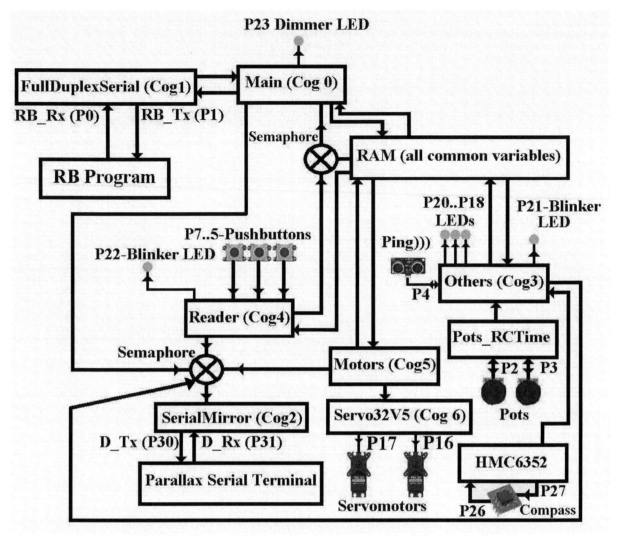

Figure 8.3: The Conceptual Schematic of the system with all the new hardware.

Firmware_Main.Spin (only changes)

```
OBJ
  RB      : "FullDuplexSerial"
  D       : "SerialMirror"
  Others  : "Firmware_Others"
  Reader  : "Firmware_Reader"
  Motors  : "Firmware_Motors"

Pri ExecuteTheCommand
  case Command[0]
    255: 'reset the propeller
      Reboot

    200:'set the Dimmer level on P23
      frqA := Command[1] *DimmerScale

    201:'set blinker duration for Reader cog(P22)
       '256 levels between 0 to 2 secs (0=off)
      Settings[0] := Command[1]*(2_000/256)*(ClkFreq/1_000)
```

```
202: 'set the TimeOut1 for waiting for parameter byte (second command byte)
     'in seconds
     TimeOut1 := (clkfreq/1000)*Command[1]*500
203: 'set the TimeOut2 for waiting for a command to finish its actions
     'it should reflect and be related to the PC system's timeout (secs)
     TimeOut2 := (clkfreq/1000)*Command[1]*500

1,2,24,192:
   'commands in the Others cog that may fill the
   'the last two bytes in the primary send buffer
   Sems_Flags[1] |= OthersFlagMask    'set flag
   WaitForFlagResetWithTimeOut(OthersFlagMask)

66:'commands in the Others cog that fill the secondary send buffer
   SendBufferOffset := 5             'command uses the secondary buffer
   Sems_Flags[1] |= OthersFlagMask  'set flag to signal the cog
   WaitForFlagResetWithTimeOut(OthersFlagMask)

0,6,7,12,13,240,241,242,243,244,245:'commands in the Motors cog
   Sems_Flags[1] |= MotorsFlagMask    'set flag
   WaitForFlagResetWithTimeOut(MotorsFlagMask)
```

Firmware_Others.Spin

```
CON
  Blinker        = 21
  RCPin1         = 2
  RCPin2         = 3
  PingPin        = 4
  FlagMask       = %0000_0001    'mask for flag for this cog
  MotorsFlagMask = %0000_0010    'Mask For Motors Flag
  BlinkerScale   = 54            ' 2³² ÷ 80_000_000 for NCO counter
  Offset_1       = 5    'offset for location of 2 byte data buffer
  Offset_2       = 7    'offset for location of 5 byte data buffer
  Compass_SDA    = 26
  Compass_SCL    = 27
  Compass_On     = 1 'if there is no compass make this 0
Var
  long CogN,Stacks[50], t
  byte Compass_Calibration
  Long Compass_Timer
  Long Command,Settings,Sems_Flags,RCTime[2]

Obj
  D      : "SerialMirror"
  RC     : "Pots_RCTime"
  Compass: "HMC6352"

PUB Start(CommandAddr,SettingsAddr,Sems_FlagsAddr)
  Compass.Init(Compass_SDA, Compass_SCL)
  Command    :=    CommandAddr    'save all passed addresses as
  Settings   :=    SettingsAddr   'local variables to be used
  Sems_Flags :=    Sems_FlagsAddr 'by all processes
  Compass_On~
  Compass_Calibration~
  CogN := Result :=cogNew(Others,@Stacks[0])+1      'start the cog
```

```
Pub Stop
  If CogN
    CogStop(CogN~ -1)

Pri Others
  Initialization
  repeat
    Process0
    if Not(byte[Sems_Flags][1] & FlagMask) 'if flag not set then no action
      Next                                 'required, just loop back
    case byte[Command][0]                  'execute the command
        1: Set_LEDS
        2: Set_BlinkRate
       24: 'compass commands
           case byte[Command][1]
               1: Is_Compass_Enabled 'return if compass is available or not
               2: Calibrate_Compass(0) 'manual
               3: Calibrate_Compass(1) 'auto
               other: Read_Compass
       66: Read_Pots
      192: Read_Ping
    OutputToPST                            'output some info to the PST
    byte[Sems_Flags][1] &= !FlagMask       'clear flag to signal Main to proceed

Pri Initialization
  'initialize variables I/O direction etc.
  ctrA[30..26] := %00100           'Set ctrA for "NCO single-ended"
  ctrA[5..0]   := Blinker          'Set ctrA's APIN
  frqA         := 10*BlinkerScale 'set rate
  dirA[20..18]~~
  dirA[Blinker]~~
  t := cnt                         'initialize timer

Pri Process0
  'can do anything here.
  'but there is nothing to do in this case
  'but could be anything that requires polling or updating etc.
  if Compass_Calibration                   'if calibration is in progress
    if cnt-Compass_Timer > ClkFreq*20      'and time is out
      Compass.EndCalibration               'send end command
      Compass_Calibration~                 'clear indicator

Pri Set_LEDs
  'set the LEDs on P20..P18 per the parameter byte
  outA[18..20] := Byte[Command][1]

Pri Set_BlinkRate
  'set the blink rate  for P21
  frqA := byte[Command][1] * BlinkerScale 'set rate
  if frqA == 0
    phsA~  'make sure the pin is low if it to be off

Pri Read_Ping |x
  'read the Ping time and return its 2 byte value in the
  '4th and 5th bytes of the primary buffer. MSByte first.
```

```
  x := Ping(PingPin)
  byte[Command][Offset_1]   := (x >> 8) & $FF
  byte[Command][Offset_1+1] := x & $FF

Pri Read_Pots
  'Read the two Pots and returns the readings in the
  'secondary send buffer. Use MSByte first for both
  'the 16 bit values
  RC.RCTime(RCPin1,1,@RCTime[0])   'use Pots_RCTime in direct mode ...no cog
  RC.RCTime(RCPin2,1,@RCTime[1])   'to get one-time reading...
  byte[Command][Offset_2]   := (RCTime[0]>>8)& $FF
  byte[Command][Offset_2+1] := RCTime[0] & $FF
  byte[Command][Offset_2+2] := (RCTime[1]>>8)& $FF
  byte[Command][Offset_2+3] := RCTime[1] & $FF
  byte[Command][Offset_2+4] := 0

Pri OutputToPST
  if Not LockSet(byte[Sems_Flags][2]) 'output some info to the PST
    D.Str(string(13,"Others:"))       'if semaphore acquired
    D.Dec(byte[Command][0])
    D.Str(string(","))
    D.Dec(byte[Command][1])
    LockClr(byte[Sems_Flags][2])

Pri Is_Compass_Enabled
  byte[Command][Offset_1]   := 0
  byte[Command][Offset_1+1] := Compass_On

Pri Read_Compass |x
  'read the Compass and return its 2 byte value in the
  '4th and 5th bytes of the primary buffer. MSByte first.
  x~
  if Compass_On and Not Compass_Calibration
    x := Compass.Heading / 10
  byte[Command][Offset_1]   := (x >> 8) & $FF
  byte[Command][Offset_1+1] := x & $FF

Pri Calibrate_Compass(Mode)
  'Starts the compass calibration
  'If the Mode is <> 0 then it will also
  'rotate the motors  while doing it. RB must
  'not do anything else in the meantime since
  'the system would not respond for 20 secs.
  'The RB program must do a 20 seconds delay
  'to allow for it
  'If the Mode is 0 then the command will
  'return immediately. RB can then do its own
  'motor turning if it wants.
  'The calibration will be done in the background.
  if Not Compass_On  or Compass_Calibration
    return
  Compass.StartCalibration
  if Mode == 0
    Compass_Timer := cnt                'start timer for end of calibration
    Compass_Calibration~~               'indicate that calibration is on
    'the endcalibration is executed when the time finishes
```

```
        'in the Process_0 method
    else
        Compass_Timer := cnt
        repeat until cnt-Compass_Timer > ClkFreq*20
            byte[Command][0] := 12
            Byte[Command][1] := 10
            byte[Sems_Flags][1] |= MotorsFlagMask    'Flag the Motors Cog
        Compass.EndCalibration

Pri Ping(Pin) : MS| time[2]
  outA[Pin]~                 ' Clear I/O Pin
  dirA[Pin]~~                ' Make Pin Output
  outA[Pin]~~                ' Set I/O Pin
  outA[Pin]~                 ' Clear I/O Pin (> 2 µs pulse)
  dirA[Pin]~                 ' Make I/O Pin Input
  waitpne(0, |< Pin, 0)      ' Wait For Pin To Go HIGH
  time[0] := cnt             ' Store Current Counter Value
  waitpeq(0, |< Pin, 0)      ' Wait For Pin To Go LOW
  time[1] := cnt             ' Store New Counter Value
  MS :=||(time[0] - time[1])/(clkfreq / 1_000_000) ' Return Time in microsecs
```

8.1.1 Using the Compass

We will now write the simplest possible program to test the new firmware. All the RB programs that ran with the old _12 firmware from Chapter 7 should also run with this new firmware and you should verify this fact. The only things that changed are to do with the compass readings.

Before reading further do a mental exercise. Try to think about writing a simple program to read the compass heading using our new addition to the protocol. Remember the command is code 24 and the parameters allowed are:

1:      To determine if there is a compass. The result will be in the 5th byte of the returned 5 bytes (0=no, 1=yes).
0:      To return the compass reading in the 4th and 5th bytes.
2 or 3: To go through the calibration process of the compass 2=manual, 3=automatic.

We will send command 24 with a parameter of 1. If the fifth byte in the returned 5 bytes is 1 then there is a compass and we will go on to reading it repeatedly. If it is a 0 then there is no compass and a message will be printed to that effect and the program terminated.

See Section 8.1.4 for a more sophisticated display of the compass heading (Figure 8.4). Also see Section 8.4.3 (Figure 8.11) for another application using the compass.

Run the program while rotating the PPDB board to see how the value changes. You may have noticed that the value returned is not quite the correct compass heading because we have not yet performed a calibration. In the program there are lines of code that are commented out. They will be used to calibrate the compass using the manual mode.

How the calibration process is implemented in the firmware needs additional explanation. We will leave it for the next two sections. However, for now, uncomment the bold lines and run the program. The calibration process will take 20 seconds. During this time try to rotate the PPDB two complete rotations while maintaining it level. When the readings start, notice how they are now more accurate. Orient the PPDB (see Figure 8.10 in Section 8.4.3) to a known compass heading and verify that indeed a correct reading is being returned.

Any motors or electrical hardware close to the compass will affect its readings. For best accuracy you should mount the compass module as far away from other hardware or metal as possible.

Compass_Tester.Bas

```
//Compass_Tester.Bas
//works with Firmware_Main.Spin
Port = 8 //change this as per your system
Main:
    setcommport Port,br115200
    call SendCommand(24,1,s)  //see if there is a compass
    if SendCommand__Result
        if !getstrbyte(s,5) then print "no compass available" \Terminate
    endif
    //uncomment the following three lines to invoke a manual calibration
    //print "Calibration in progress...rotate two turns while level"
    //call SendCommand(24,2)  //calibrate the compass
    //delay 20000
    while true
        call SendCommand(24,0,s)  //read the compass
        if !SendCommand__Result then continue
        x = (getstrbyte(s,4)<<8)+getstrbyte(s,5)
        xystring 10,30,"Heading=",x,"°",spaces(10)
    wend
end
//-----------------------------------------
sub SendCommand(C,P,&s)
  m = ""
  serialout C,P
  serbytesin 5,s,x
  if x < 5 then m= "Comms Error"
  xystring 500,20,m,spaces(30)
return (x == 5)
```

8.1.2 Inter-Cog Communications and Complex Object Interaction

You already know that one cog can influence another cog by sharing variables in RAM and they can communicate by passing data between them using shared RAM variables or buffers. This, as you already have seen, is the way **Main** communicates with all the cogs. So far we only had **Main** controlling the other modules. They are subordinate cogs and **Main** *controls and orchestrates the actions* of the entire system. This is how it ought to be and the design is as we intended.

It is possible, though, that we may need the other cogs to interact. Consider, for example, that we have a turret with a Ping))) mounted on it. The turret itself is a servomotor. It would be logical to have it controlled by the **Motors** cog. However, the Ping))) reading takes place in the **Others** cog. So here we have a slight *logistics* dilemma. We need two actions that in our system occur in different cogs that are not communicating but are both under the control of **Main**.

In the above example, what we want is to be able to command the turret servomotor to move to a particular position (it is a standard servo with fixed travel). Once the motor reaches the commanded position, we acquire a reading from the Ping))). There are four alternatives to achieve this:
1. We can issue two separate commands from within the RB program to rotate the servo then issue another command to read the Ping))). But this is not efficient.
2. We can send one command to the firmware from the RB program with the parameter of the command indicating the angle the servomotor needs to be at before taking a Ping))) reading. **Main** will automatically issue a command to the **Motors** cog to control the servomotor to the appropriate position. Once that is done **Main** will issue a command to the **Others** cog to read the Ping))) and return the results. This method is perfectly fine and in fact is how the task ought to be implemented since it is effective and simple.
3. We can send one command to the firmware from the RB program with the parameter of the command indicating the angle the servomotor needs to be at before taking a Ping))) reading. **Main** will then issue the command to the **Others** cog. The **Others** cog will do the whole process. If you remember in Chapter 7.2.1 we

had a simple way to drive a servomotor. This would be sufficient and we can include it in the **Others** cog as a method. The cog uses that to drive the turret and then read the Ping))). This is fine too. However, the 2nd method is more logically apt. Furthermore, the simple method of driving the turret's servomotor is fine but not strictly speaking correct. This is because with the simple method there will not be a continuous signal maintained after the motor reaches its commanded position. This is not so bad if there is no load on the motor. But if the robot is at an incline then the turret may slip because a servomotor without a continuous signal to keep it at the commanded position will lose torque.

4. We can send one command to the firmware from the RB program with the parameter of the command indicating the servomotor angle needed for the Ping))) reading. **Main** will then issue the command to the **Others** cog. The **Others** cog will do the whole process with the help of the **Motors** cog. That is, the **Others** cog will command the **Motors** cog to move the turret, read the Ping))), and return the results.

The fourth option is a complex, but viable one. For the particular case of the turret we advice using option 2 above (see Section 8.2.4). For the case of the automatic compass calibration though, option 4 will be used since it is the only viable one because we are going to provide two methods for calibrating the compass. One method will use the wheel servomotors to automatically turn the robot during the calibration process. The other method is a manual one where the operator will have to turn the motor by hand.

> ⚠ The discussion above about the turret was used as an example and will be of relevance in Section 8.2.4. The compass is mounted on the PPDB breadboard and is not on a turret. There will be a need to turn the compass around during the calibration process. This will be done in two ways. Manually by turning the PPDB board by hand since the compass is mounted on it, or automatically (if the board is mounted on a robot) by turning the wheels (servomotors).

The complexity of option 4 is in the requirement that the **Others** cog to be able to command the **Motors** cog to move the turret's servomotor. How should this be achieved? Well, if you have understood how **Main** signals **Motors** (and **Others**) to do their work you already know how to allow **Others** to control **Motors** or vice versa.

Just as **Main** flags **Motors** and puts the command and parameter in the Command buffer, so can **Others**. Remember the flags buffer is also accessible to both cogs. So all **Others** has to do is pretend that it is **Main** and put the command it requires in the command buffer and then raise the flag for **Motors**. **Motors** does not care who raised the flag. As soon as it sees the flag it will execute the command that is in the command buffer. **Others** is in fact acting just like **Main**.

This is a complex interaction and is tricky to program. Firmware_Others.Spin accomplishes exactly this strategy. Look at the **Calibrate_Compass** method to see how it is implemented.

> ⓘ Another way we can also achieve the above is to provide a method in the **Motors** object that the **Others** object can call. But then we would have to also instantiate the **Motors** object in the **Others** object. Also calling methods requires more overhead and execution time than just setting the value of a bit in a shared memory variable; method 4 is a better way.

8.1.3 Using the Compass Calibration

The HMC6352 compass module has a very good resolution. It is accurate to 1°, which is as accurate as any robot may need. However, the readings can be affected by surrounding magnetic fields. One way to minimize this error is to calibrate the module in the environment it is to be used in.

The compass has a very easy and effective inbuilt calibration. All you have to do is invoke the calibration process, which lasts 20 seconds. It is important to keep the module level and to turn it slowly through two complete turns. We have provided a method in our protocol to perform this calibration. There are two ways you can perform this; a *manual calibration* and an *automatic calibration*.

Manual Compass Calibration

In this method sending a command of 24 with a parameter of 2 causes the firmware to start the calibration process but *in the background*. It will also immediately return the 5 bytes without delay, ***allowing the RB program to continue processing and to issue other commands as needed.***

This mode does ***not*** cause a timeout since it returns immediately. Also remember that the compass needs to be turned around slowly preferably twice and on a level surface. This can be accomplished manually by hand, or the RB program can issue the turn command (12 or 13) in a loop for 20 seconds. Just do not try to issue further compass commands before 20 seconds are out; you will get 0 if you do.

Automatic Compass Calibration

In this mode you will issue command 24 with a parameter other than 2. The firmware will then start the calibration process but it will automatically cause the motors to keep turning for a period of 20 seconds.

This mode ***will*** cause a timeout, unless you have modified the timeout parameters in both the firmware and RB using the commands to do so before performing the calibration. However, you do not really need to do so. Just take appropriate measures in your RB code to handle the time out. The best way to do that is to use a delay of 20 seconds in the code right after issuing the command.

Do note that even though the firmware will time out and so will RB you still won't be able to do any further actions for 20 seconds. During those 20 seconds the motors will be turning (i.e. rotating the robot).

The manual method is better because you have more control and it does not cause timeouts. However, the automatic option is useful in that turning the motors is performed automatically. Also since you cannot issue any further commands until the 20 seconds are over it means you are not likely to try to use the compass before the calibration is completed.

Complexity of Programming the Automatic Calibration:

How does the automatic calibration achieve turning the motors? The way described in Section 8.1.2 (option4). The **Others** cog flags the **Motors** cog after specifying the command 12 in the command buffer with a parameter of 1. It then waits for 20 seconds repeating the flagging and commanding to keep turning the motors. When the 20 seconds are over it returns to **Main**. This is why the time out occurs. Because both **Motors** and **Others** are busy for the duration, you must not issue any more commands that require either of these two cogs.

> This procedure is a very good illustration of how the ***inter-cog interactions*** can be achieved. If you require this kind of control you now have an effective ***template*** to follow.

8.1.4 A Simulated Compass Instrument

We will now develop a program that displays the compass heading in a more interesting manner than just numbers on the screen. Compass_Animation.Bas is similar to Compass_Tester.Bas above but instead of printing out the heading as a text number it calls to subroutine called **DisplayCompass()**. However, you will notice that the subroutine is not listed in the program. It is part of a library of subroutines called Instruments.Bas. The Compass_Animation.Bas program knows how to use the subroutine because the Instruments.Bas library has been ***included*** in the program. This is the purpose of the line:

```
#include "..\Utilities&IncludeFiles\Instruments.Bas"
```

This line tells the program where to find the file that has the subroutine. When Compass_Animation.Bas runs it will look for the file Instruments.Bas in the directory called Utilities&IncludeFiles that is in the parent directory of the one in which Compass_Animation.Bas resides. That is the reason we had the "..\Utilities&IncludeFiles\" before the name of the file. When Compass_Animation.Bas finds the library file, it incorporates it as if it were part of the program and when a call to **DisplayCompass()** is made it works.

ⓘ The advantage of placing subroutines in a library is that many programs can use the subroutines. We will do precisely this with many programs to come. You will notice that Instruments.Bas has another subroutine that we will use later, so ignore it for now.

The **DisplayCompass()** subroutine implements an authentic looking Compass Instrument like ones found on boats or airplanes and it will behave very much like a real instrument. The subroutine is designed to be versatile and generic. You can pass optional parameters to it to configure where to place the instrument on the screen and how many gradations it will display. Additionally it will display the numeric value of the heading (not available on a real device). All the parameters are optional and if you do not specify any they will have default values. In the main program the subroutine is used in its default mode. We will use the same subroutine in Section 8.4.3 (see Figure 8.11), but by passing it different parameters, the instrument will be different in size and position.

If you are not a pilot or navigator, the heading markings might look to you as if they are the wrong way around. We will not go into the details of this here since this is not a book on navigation – but this is in fact how it is on a real compass instrument in real life.

ⓘ The subroutine allows for a way to make the instrument display the markings in a more intuitive manner. The main program will provide a checkbox that you can uncheck to make the instrument have the graduations increase to the right. This illustrates how using a programming language like RobotBASIC can be a major advantage when creating GUI instrumentation. You can simulate authentic looking and behaving instruments or you can improve on the old mechanisms and increase the *ergonomic* effectiveness and create a more amenable *human interface*.

The HMC6352 is in fact just like a real compass. It has to be level to read accurate headings. If you pitch and roll the heading will change even if you did not turn. Again, we will not discuss the reasons for this, but notice how the compass heading changes when you do any roll or pitch. Pickup the PPDB and keep the reference axis pointing in the same direction and keep it straight and level. Note the heading. Now tilt the PPDB to the right or left or downward and upward. Notice how the heading changes. The change is in fact a predictable value depending on the bank angle and direction as well as what latitude you are at and what heading you are facing. A gyroscopic device[29] does not give different heading readings when you pitch and roll.

In order to make the display flicker free, the subroutine uses RobotBASIC's back-buffered screen graphics (**Flip on**). Comment out the line in the main program that says **Flip On** and observe what happens.

ⓘ The HMC6352 compass module is just like a real compass and is subject to all compass errors: Variation, Deviation, Dip, Acceleration/Deceleration and Pitch and Roll.

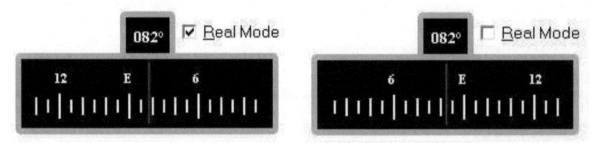

Figure 8.4: Screenshot of Compass_Animation.BAS simulating an authentic looking GUI Compass Instrument. Notice the difference between the real mode (left) and enhanced mode (right).

Compass_Animation.Bas

```
//Compass_Animation.Bas
//works with Firmware_Main.Spin
Port = 8 //change this as per your system
#include "..\Utilities&IncludeFiles\Instruments.Bas"
Main:
   setcommport Port,br115200
   flip on
   call SendCommand(24,1,s)  //see if there is a compass
   if SendCommand__Result
      if !getstrbyte(s,5) then print "no compass available" \Terminate
   endif
   //uncomment the following three lines to invoke a manual calibration
   //print "Calibration in progress...rotate two turns while level"
   //call SendCommand(24,2)
   //delay 20000
   AddCheckBox "Mode",430,230,"&Real Mode",1,0
   while true
      call SendCommand(24,0,s)  //read the compass
      if !SendCommand__Result then continue
      x = (getstrbyte(s,4)<<8)+getstrbyte(s,5)
      call DisplayCompass(!GetCheckBox("Mode"),x)
      Flip
   wend
end
//----------------------------------------
sub SendCommand(C,P,&s)
  m = ""
  serialout C,P
  serbytesin 5,s,x
  if x < 5 then m= "Comms Error"
  xystring 500,20,m,spaces(30)
return (x == 5)
```

Instruments.Bas (a library of reusable subroutines)

```
//Instruments.Bas
//to be used as an #include file in all programs
//that need to display the instruments
//------------------------------------------------------
sub DisplayCompass(Mode,H,x,y,f,t)
   fnt = "Times New Roman"
   if !vType(Mode) then Mode = 0
   Mode = Limit(Mode,0,1)*2-1
   if !vType(H) then H = 0
   if !vType(x) then x = 400
   if !vType(y) then y = 300
   if !vType(f) then f = 2
   if !vType(t) then t = 10
   dim xx[2,t*2]
   erectanglewh x-20,y-75,40,35,9,gray
   rectanglewh x-20,y-75,40,35,gray,black
   xyText x-12,y-65,Format(H,"000°"),fnt,10,fs_Bold,white,black
   erectanglewh x-t*f*5-t,y-40,2*(t*f*5+t),60,9,gray
   rectanglewh x-t*f*5-t,y-40,2*(t*f*5+t),60,gray,black
   n= H # 5
   for i=0 to t-1
```

```
      xx[0,i] = H-n-5*i \ if xx[0,i] < 0 then xx[0,i] += 360
      if xx[0,i] == 360 then xx[0,i] = 0
      xx[1,i] = Mode*f*(n+i*5)
      xx[0,i+t] = H+5-n+5*i \ if xx[0,i+t] == 360 then xx[0,i+t] = 0
      xx[1,i+t] = -Mode*f*(5-n+i*5)
   next
   for i=0 to t*2-1
      l = 5 \ hh = xx[0,i]
      if !(hh#10) then l = 7
      if !(hh #30)
         hh /= 10
         if hh == 0
            hh = "N"
         elseif hh == 9
            hh = "E"
         elseif hh == 27
            hh = "W"
         elseif hh == 18
            hh = "S"
         endif
         xytext x-xx[1,i]-5,y-30,hh,fnt,8,fs_Bold,white,black
         l = 10
      endif
      line x-xx[1,i],y-l,x-xx[1,i],y+l,2,white
   next
   line x,y-36,x,y+15,1,red
return
//---------------------------------------------------
sub DisplayAttitude(Pitch,Roll,Cx,Cy,r,LW,CW)
   if !vType(Pitch) then Pitch = 0
   if !vType(Roll) then Roll = 0
   if !vType(r) then r = 100
   if !vType(Cx) then Cx = 400
   if !vType(Cy) then Cy = 300
   if !vType(LW) then LW = 2
   if !vType(CW) then CW = 10
   //horizon
   T = -Roll-Pitch \ TT = -Roll+Pitch+pi()
   x1 = cartx(r,T) \ y1 = carty(r,T)
   x2 = cartx(r,TT) \ y2 = carty(r,TT)
   x3 = (x2+x1)/2 \ y3 = (y2+y1)/2
   Circle Cx-r,Cy-r,Cx+r, Cy+r
   line x1+Cx,y1+Cy,x2+Cx,y2+Cy,LW,red
   //ground and sky
   for i=-3 to 3 step 6
      T1 = -Roll-Pitch+dtor(i) \ TT1 = -Roll+Pitch+pi()-dtor(i)
      x1 = cartx(r,T1) \ y1 = carty(r,T1)
      x2 = cartx(r,TT1) \ y2 = carty(r,TT1)
      x4 = (x2+x1)/2 \ y4 = (y2+y1)/2
      j = brown
      if i < 0 then j= lightcyan
      floodfill Cx+x4,Cy+y4,j
   next
   //ground texture arrays
   if !vType(_DAI_Flag)
      dim DAI_b[0]
```

```
   data DAI_b;5,10,20,40,60
   dim DAI_a[0]
   data DAI_a;0,dtor(30),-dtor(180),-dtor(40),dtor(10),-dtor(140)
   _DAI_Flag = true
endif
//horizontal ground texture
for i=0 to 4
  T1 = -Roll-Pitch+dtor(DAI_b[i]) \ TT1 = -Roll+Pitch+pi()-dtor(DAI_b[i])
  x1 = cartx(r,T1) \ y1 = carty(r,T1)
  x2 = cartx(r,TT1) \ y2 = carty(r,TT1)
  line x1+Cx,y1+Cy,x2+Cx,y2+Cy
next
//diagonal ground texture
j=dtor(20) \ i=T+j
repeat
  x1 = cartx(r,i) \ y1 = carty(r,i)
  line Cx+x3,Cy+y3,Cx+x1,Cy+y1
  i += j
until abs(i) > abs(TT-j+.2)
Arc Cx-r,Cy-r,Cx+r, Cy+r,,,CW,gray  //instrument rim
//roll gradations
for k=0 to maxdim(DAI_a)-1 step 3
  i = -Roll+DAI_a[k] \ j=DAI_a[k+1]
  TW = CW/2
  if k >=3 then TW = 2
  rr1 = r+TW \ rr2 = r-TW
  repeat
    x1 = cartx(rr1,i) \ y1 = carty(rr1,i)
    x2 = cartx(rr2,i) \ y2 = carty(rr2,i)
    line Cx+x1,Cy+y1,Cx+x2,Cy+y2,2,white
    i -= j
  until i < -Roll+DAI_a[k+2]-.2
next
//roll or bank indicator
for j=-2 to 2 step 4
  i = -dtor(90-j)
  x1 = cartx(r+CW/2,i) \ y1 = carty(r+CW/2,i)
  x2 = cartx(r-CW/2,i) \ y2 = carty(r-CW/2,i)
  line Cx+x1,Cy+y1,Cx+x2,Cy+y2,3,red
next
//small airplane
rr = r/10
circlewh Cx-2,Cy-2,4,4,white
line Cx,Cy,Cx,Cy+rr-1,2,white
Arc Cx-rr,Cy-rr,Cx+rr,Cy+rr,pi(),pi(),2,white
Line Cx-rr,Cy,Cx-4*rr,Cy,2,white
Line Cx+rr,Cy,Cx+4*rr,Cy,2,white
Return
```

8.2 A Procedural Strategy for Adding Other Hardware

As you have seen so far, because of the way the system is designed, adding hardware is extremely simple and routine. As a matter of fact, the hardware we added covers almost every category of hardware that you are likely to want to incorporate into your system.

List 1: Categories of Hardware

a) Digital hardware with On/Off type I/O (Pushbuttons, LEDs)
b) Digital to Analog output (Dimmer LED)
c) Pulsating Frequency output (Blinking LEDs and Speaker)
d) Analog To Digital input with RC-Time (Pots)
e) Controlling Servomotors (Servomotors)
f) Counting Time Intervals (Ping and RC-Time)
g) I^2C I/O (Compass)
h) RS232 I/O (FDS, SM)
i) Using Counters (in Duty, NCO, and Edge Detector modes)

List 2: Programming Techniques Required to Develop the Firmware

j) Using Semaphores and Flags
k) Using Parallelism
l) Using Polling
m) Sharing RAM
n) Inter-Cog communications and control
o) Creating objects and methods

Just about any hardware that you are likely to want to add as well as the programming techniques required to add them to the firmware are most likely to belong to one of the above categories. Let's have a look at some hardware that we may wish to add to a project:

Table 8.1: Possible Hardware and its Category

Hardware	Category
Bumper Switch[30]	a
Infrared Proximity Sensors[31]	a or c
QTI Line Sensors[14]	a or d
PIR Movement Sensor[32]	a
Turret[33]	e
Accelerometer[34]	g
GPS[35]	h or g
DC motors[36]	e
Thermometer[37]	G
2-Axis Joystick[38]	D
Sound Impact Sensor[39]	A
5-Way button[40]	A
Piezoelectric Speaker[27]	I
Quadrature System[41]	H

8.2.1 Commands in the Protocol So Far

In our protocol so far we have allowed for many possible commands and Table 8.2 below is a good overview.

Table 8.2: List of protocol command codes at this stage.

Command	Code	Parameter	Updates Critical Sensors	Data Returned
Stop Motors	0	0	Yes	None
Forward	6	Amount	Yes	None
Backwards	7	Amount	Yes	None
Turn right	12	Amount	Yes	None
Turn Left	13	Amount	Yes	None
Read the Compass	24	0	Yes	Last two bytes
Check if the compass is available	24	1	Yes	4th byte 0, 5th byte is 1 for yes or 0 for no
Calibrate the Compass	24	2=Manual 3=Automatic	Yes No	None
Read the Pots	66	0	No	First 4 bytes
Read the Ping)))	192	0	Yes	Last two bytes
Set P20..P18 LEDs	1	LED States	Yes	None
Set P21 Frequency	2	Hz Value	Yes	None
Reset the Propeller	255	0	No	None
Set P23 LED brightness	200	Level	Yes	None
P22 LED Blink duration	201	Level	Yes	None
Set 2nd byte receive Timeout1	202	N x 10ms	Yes	None
Set operations Timeout2	203	N x 10ms	Yes	None
Set L_Speed	240	Speed	Yes	None
Set T_Speed	244	Speed	Yes	None
Set L_Timeout	241	N X 10 ms	Yes	None
Set T_Timeout	245	N X 10 ms	Yes	None
Set StepTime	242	N X 10 ms	Yes	None
Set TurnTime	243	N X 10 ms	Yes	None

8.2.2 A Procedural Strategy For Extending the Hardware

Much of the hardware you may wish to add is likely to be just a matter of deciding what category it is under (List 1 and List 2 and Table 8.1) and then looking at the commands in Table 8.2 to decide which command resembles it best. Once you have decided on this, use the command from Table 8.2 as a template for adding the new hardware. It is not just hardware that we might want to add. We may also want to add more housekeeping commands.

List 3: There are three types of commands:

1. Ones that set/change system parameters (**Main** object but can be any of the objects)
2. Ones that do something in the background and do not need to be commanded (**Reader** object)
3. Ones that carry out a task and then
   a. Do not return data (**Motors** object but can be **Others** too)
   b. Return data in the last two bytes of the primary send buffer (**Others** object)
   c. Return data in all or some bytes of the secondary send buffer (**Others** object)

Procedure For Adding a New Hardware or Command

To add a new command you need to

     i.   Decide which category of hardware it is from Lists 1 and 2 and Table 8.1.
    ii.   Decide what type of command it will be from List 3.
   iii.   Select a template command from Table 8.2.
   iv.   Modify the appropriate object to incorporate the methods needed to interact with the hardware and fill the send buffer if required. If you decide that you need a new object then use one of the existing objects as a template and modify it as needed.
    v.   Add any constants in the **CON** section.
   vi.   Add any variables in the **Var** or **Dat** section.
  vii.   Instantiate any required supporting objects in the **Obj** section and invoke their **Start()** methods in the **Initialization** method.
 viii.   Decide on a code for the command (make sure there is no clashing) and what parameters it has to be passed.
   ix.   Add the Case statement in the Case block to call the method. This should follow the template command.
    x.   Add the Case Statement in the **Main** object to allow for the new case statement in the subordinate object. This should follow the template command.

To illustrate the process we will now add new commands to:

- ❑ Allow for actuating the motors separately in any direction for a certain number of steps or to keep them on (Section 8.2.3).
- ❑ Allow the Ping))) mounted on a turret to be turned by 90 degrees right and left before measuring the distance (Section 8.2.4).
- ❑ Save all the system parameters to the EEPROM. We will also extend the system to read them from the EEPROM upon boot up if there are any valid saved ones (Section 8.3) and also allow for resetting them to factory settings.
- ❑ Add an Accelerometer (Section 8.4).
- ❑ Add three QTI infrared line sensors (Section 8.5).
- ❑ Add a speaker similar to Chapter 5.8 (Section 8.6).

8.2.3 Controlling Motors Separately

If you have noticed with our commands for controlling the motors they can only be rotated together. This is what we need on a robot for example. However, it may be desirable to control the motors separately in certain occasions, such as if you wish to effect curved turns where the center of turning is not the center of the robot's wheel axis. Also, if the motors are used in a process other than robotics, we may want to be able to control the motors as separate entities.

In the process of implementing independent control, we want to illustrate how following the procedure outlined in Section 8.2.2 makes the process simple and quick.

Step i:	It is still a servomotor.
Step ii:	It is like commands 6,7 in Table 8.2.
Step iii:	Commands 6 and 7, but allowance has to be made for different processing.
Step iv:	We will do them in the **Motors** object (see bold lines in the listing).
Step v:	Not required.
Step vi:	See Listings (added variables in **Motors** object).
Step vii:	Not required; but for **Main** we changed the name of the **Motors** object to allow for the new version.
Step viii:	Codes 8/9 move the right motor forward/backward and Codes 10/11 for the left motor. We will have it so that parameter 0 means stop, parameter 255 means stay on. Any other number is for n-steps. But the command will not wait for the steps to be completed, it will always return immediately. Therefore, We will need to allow for timing and switching the motors off in the **Process0** method.
Step ix,x:	See bold lines in the listings.

Here are the listings of the new Firmware_Motors_B.Spin and Firmware_Main_B.Spin. Notice the bold code performs the steps above. We will only list areas where there are changes. The rest of the code is as before. The **Others** and **Reader** objects are not changed and we will use the same ones as before.

Firmware_Main_B.Spin (only changes)

```
OBJ
  RB      : "FullDuplexSerial"
  D       : "SerialMirror"
  Others  : "Firmware_Others"
  Reader  : "Firmware_Reader"
  Motors  : "Firmware_Motors_B"

Pri ExecuteTheCommand
  case Command[0]
    255: 'reset the propeller
      Reboot

    200:'set the Dimmer level on P23
      frqA := Command[1] *DimmerScale

    201:'set blinker duration for Reader cog(P22)
        '256 levels between 0 to 2 secs (0=off)
      Settings[0] := Command[1]*(2_000/256)*(ClkFreq/1_000)

    202: 'set the TimeOut1 for waiting for parameter byte (second command byte)
         'in seconds
         TimeOut1 := (clkfreq/1000)*Command[1]*500
    203: 'set the TimeOut2 for waiting for a command to finish its actions
         'it should reflect and be related to the PC system's timeout (secs)
         TimeOut2 := (clkfreq/1000)*Command[1]*500

    1,2, 24,192:
      'commands in the Others cog that may fill the
      'the last two bytes in the primary send buffer
      Sems_Flags[1] |= OthersFlagMask    'set flag
      WaitForFlagResetWithTimeOut(OthersFlagMask)

    66:'commands in the Others cog that fill the secondary send buffer
      SendBufferOffset := 5             'command uses the secondary buffer
      Sems_Flags[1] |= OthersFlagMask 'set flag to signal the cog
      WaitForFlagResetWithTimeOut(OthersFlagMask)

    0,6,7,12,13,240,241,242,243,244,245,8,9,10,11:'commands in the Motors cog
      Sems_Flags[1] |= MotorsFlagMask    'set flag
      WaitForFlagResetWithTimeOut(MotorsFlagMask)
```

Firmware_Motors_B.Spin (Only changes)

```
CON
  FlagMask  = %0000_0010   'mask for flag for this cog
  Offset_1  = 5   'offset for location of 2 byte data buffer
  Offset_2  = 7   'offset for location of 5 byte data buffer
  MidVal    = 1500
  MinVal    = 1000
  MaxVal    = 2000
  Servo1    = 16
```

```
  Servo2      = 17

Var
  long CogN,Stacks[50], t, onTimer, MotorsOn, MotorsTimeOut
  Long Command,Settings,Sems_Flags
  Long LMotorOn,LMotorTimer,LMotorDuration,RMotorOn,RMotorTimer,RMotorDuration

Dat
  L_Speed      long 255    'speed factor for moving forward/backward
  T_Speed      long 255    'speed factor for turning
  StepTime     long 30
  TurnTime     long 20
  L_TimeOut    long 100    'motor keep on time after forward/backward
  T_TimeOut    long 0      'motor keep on time after turning

Obj
  D      : "SerialMirror"
  Servo  : "Servo32V7"

PUB Start(CommandAddr,SettingsAddr,Sems_FlagsAddr)
  Command    :=    CommandAddr    'save all passed addresses as
  Settings   :=    SettingsAddr   'local variables to be used
  Sems_Flags :=    Sems_FlagsAddr 'by all processes
  CogN := Result :=cogNew(Motors,@Stacks[0])+1      'start the cog

Pub Stop
  If CogN
    CogStop(CogN~ -1)

Pri Motors
  Initialization
  repeat
    Process0
    if Not(byte[Sems_Flags][1] & FlagMask) 'if flag not set then no action
      Next                                  'required, just loop back
    case byte[Command][0]                   'execute the command
       00:  StopMotors(0)
       06:  MoveMotors(1)  'forward
       07:  MoveMotors(-1) 'back
       12:  TurnMotors(1)   'right
       13:  TurnMotors(-1)  'left
       08:  RightMotor(1)    'move Right motor separately forward
       09:  RightMotor(-1)   'move Right motor separately backward
       10:  LeftMotor(1)     'move Left  motor separately forward
       11:  LeftMotor(-1)    'move Left  motor separately backward
      240:  L_Speed   := byte[Command][1]    'set speed
      241:  L_TimeOut := byte[Command][1]*10 'set timeout in steps of 10ms
      242:  StepTime  := byte[Command][1]*10 'set step time in steps of 10ms
      243:  TurnTime  := byte[Command][1]*10 'set turn time in steps of 10ms
      244:  T_Speed   := byte[Command][1]    'set speed
      245:  T_TimeOut := byte[Command][1]*10 'set timeout in steps of 10ms

    OutputToPST                             'output some info to the PST
    byte[Sems_Flags][1] &= !FlagMask  'clear flag to signal Main to proceed
```

```
Pri Initialization
  'initialize variables I/O direction etc.
  'none needed here
  t := cnt                           'initialize timer
  Servo.Start
  MotorsOn~

Pri Process0
  'can do anything here that requires polling or updating etc.
  'We will use this to turn motors off after a certain timeout
  if MotorsOn And cnt-onTimer > MotorsTimeOut*(clkfreq/1000)
     StopMotors(0)   'stop motors after timeout
  if LMotorOn And cnt-LMotorTimer > LMotorDuration
     StopIndividualMotor(2) 'Left motor stop after steps run out
  if RMotorOn And cnt-RMotorTimer > RMotorDuration
     StopIndividualMotor(1) 'right motor stop after steps run out


Pri LeftMotor(Dir)|x
  StopIndividualMotor(2)
  x := byte[Command][1]
  if x
     Servo.Set(Servo2,MidVal+Dir*1000*L_Speed/255)
     if x <> 255 'on for distance
       LMotorOn~~
       LMotorTimer := cnt
       LMotorDuration :=StepTime*x*(clkfreq/1000)  'set time out

Pri RightMotor(Dir)|x
  StopIndividualMotor(1)
  x := byte[Command][1]
  if x
     Servo.Set(Servo1,MidVal+Dir*1000*L_Speed/255)
     if x <> 255 'on for distance
       RMotorOn~~
       RMotorTimer := cnt
       RMotorDuration :=StepTime*x*(clkfreq/1000)  'set time out

Pri StopIndividualMotor(which)
  if which==2   'right
     Servo.Set(Servo2,MidVal)
     LMotorOn~
  else  'left
     Servo.Set(Servo1,MidVal)
     RMotorOn~

Pri StopMotors(wait)
  LMotorOn := RMotorOn := 0    'make sure separate movement is canceled
  Servo.Set(Servo1,MidVal)
  Servo.Set(Servo2,MidVal)
  MotorsOn~
  if wait
    waitcnt(cnt+(clkfreq/1_000_000)*50)   'wait 50 microsecs
```

Testing the New Commands

Firmware_Motors_B.Bas tests the new commands. But, before reading further, see if you can devise a test on your own before looking over the listing below.

Note how simple the changes were, yet, they were not trivial. We did have to do some intricate work with timing. You can now appreciate the design we did for our protocol. See how **Process0** has even more work to do. It now is vital in implementing the number of steps the motor will move. Since the moving is occurring in the background, **Process0** is the only way we can stop the motor when the number of steps are over.

⚠ Note the difference between commands 6,7,12,13 and 8,9,10,11:

With Commands 6/7 and 12/13:
- The motors are always activated *together*.
- **Main** has to wait for the number of steps to be completed before returning to RB and therefore RB too has to wait. *This means that the RB program flow does not proceed to the next statement until the steps are completed.*
- Only on-the-spot turns can be made.

With Commands 8/9 and 10/11
- By moving the motors *separately* you can effect curved turns.
- Since **Main** returns to RB immediately and does not wait for the steps to complete (they are done in the background), the RB program flow is not paused until the command completes. *The RB program can do other things while the steps are completing or if the motors are turned on indefinitely the program logic can decide when to turn them off.*
- The motors can be used as two independent motors for purposes other than wheel turning.

We hope you now can see how simple it is to follow the procedural strategy in Section 8.2.2.

Firmware_Motors_B.Bas

```
//Firmware_Motors_B.Bas
//works with Firmware_Main_B.Spin
Port = 8 //change this as per your system
setcommport Port,br115200
serialout 8,255 //turn right motor forward forever
delay 3000
serialout 7,20  //backward both motors 20 steps
delay 2000
serialout 11,100 //left motor backward 100 steps
delay 3000
serialout 9,255  //right motor backward forever
serialout 10,255 //left motor forward forever
delay 5000
serialout 12,50 //both motors right turn 50 steps
```

8.2.4 Controlling a Ping))) on a Turret

If we mount the Ping))) on a <u>Servomotor turret</u>[33] like the one sold by Parallax, we can extend the utility of the ranger because we can then turn it left and right. The way we have previously implemented the ranger command (#192) the parameter is ignored. If we allow the parameter to specify the angle right of the straight ahead and if we add another command (#193) and allow the parameter to define left of the straight ahead then we would have full control over the turret and once the turret finishes the turn, a reading of the Ping can be taken and returned as before.

> ⓘ Since now the Ping))) would be mounted on a turret the connection to it should now be made using a 3-wire cable (just like the one for the servomotors) to one of the 8 servomotor headers on the PPDB (see Figure B.3 in Appendix B). The - pin (black) on the header goes to the Ping's Ground pin. The + (red line) goes to the 5V pin on the Ping))) and the S pin (white) goes to the Sig pin on the Ping. There is no longer a need for the 1KΩ since the servos header has a 150Ω resistor already and that should suffice. See Figure B.3 in Appendix B.

As discussed in the strategy outlined in Section 8.1.2, we will have the **Main** cog control the *division of labor*. **Main** will receive the command 192 or 193. It will then flag the **Motors** cog to turn the Servomotor of the turret (we will use a standard servomotor[42] on P15) to move to the correct position. When the **Motors** flag is lowered **Main** will then flag the **Others** cog as before to read the Ping))).

To implement the required changes we will follow the steps in Section 8.2.2. The changes are only to **Main** and **Motors**. Another thing to note here is that due to the division of labor aspect the **Others** object needed no changes at all despite the new commands being all to do with the Ping))) which is read by the **Others** cog. We also added a constant in the **Motors** object so that we can data-map the value 0-90 into in a number that causes the turret to be truly turned 0 to 90 degrees, where 0 is straight ahead. Remember that servomotors have the 1500 microseconds pulse as the center. We want to limit the Max and Min values so that the motor will turn 90 degrees either way. Thus we can use the number 0 to 90 as

ServoSignal := 1500+n*Max/90 'for the left turns
ServoSignal := 1500-n*Min/90 'for the right turns

We need to experiment to determine what Max and Min have to be. We can always of course add two more commands to set these values at run-time from RB. But we will leave this up to you. Use Servo_01.Spin to experiment with the servomotor to see what values set it to about 90 degrees either way and use these values. Remember we are using P15 as the motor's signal pin so change the Pin number to 15. We did this and for our motor the Max and Min are both 800 (2300-1500 = 800 and 1500-700 = 800)

See the Listings of Firmware_XXXX_C.Bas, where XXXX are Main and Motors; the bold lines are the new code. Only changed areas are listed.

Firmware_Main_C.Spin (only changes)

```
OBJ
  RB      : "FullDuplexSerial"
  D       : "SerialMirror"
  Others  : "Firmware_Others"
  Reader  : "Firmware_Reader"
  Motors  : "Firmware_Motors_C"

Pri ExecuteTheCommand
  case Command[0]
    255: 'reset the propeller
      Reboot

    200:'set the Dimmer level on P23
      frqA := Command[1] *DimmerScale

    201:'set blinker duration for Reader cog(P22)
        '256 levels between 0 to 2 secs (0=off)
      Settings[0] := Command[1]*(2_000/256)*(ClkFreq/1_000)

    202: 'set the TimeOut1 for waiting for parameter byte (second command byte)
         'in seconds
         TimeOut1 := (clkfreq/1000)*Command[1]*500
    203: 'set the TimeOut2 for waiting for a command to finish its actions
         'it should reflect and be related to the PC system's timeout (secs)
```

```
        TimeOut2 := (clkfreq/1000)*Command[1]*500

  1,2,24:
    'commands in the Others cog that may fill the
    'the last two bytes in the primary send buffer
    Sems_Flags[1] |= OthersFlagMask    'set flag
    WaitForFlagResetWithTimeOut(OthersFlagMask)

  66:'commands in the Others cog that fill the secondary send buffer
    SendBufferOffset := 5              'command uses the secondary buffer
    Sems_Flags[1] |= OthersFlagMask  'set flag to signal the cog
    WaitForFlagResetWithTimeOut(OthersFlagMask)

  0,6,7,12,13,240,241,242,243,244,245,8,9,10,11:'commands in the Motors cog
    Sems_Flags[1] |= MotorsFlagMask      'set flag
    WaitForFlagResetWithTimeOut(MotorsFlagMask)

  192,193:'turret and ping commands in Motors and Others cogs
    Sems_Flags[1] |= MotorsFlagMask      'set flag for Motors
    WaitForFlagResetWithTimeOut(MotorsFlagMask)
    Command[0] := 192  'force the command code to 192, this way we do not
                      ' need to change the Others object
    Sems_Flags[1] |= OthersFlagMask      'set flag for Others
    WaitForFlagResetWithTimeOut(OthersFlagMask)
```

Firmware_Motors_C.Spin (only changes)

```
CON
  FlagMask  = %0000_0010   'mask for flag for this cog
  Offset_1  = 5    'offset for location of 2 byte data buffer
  Offset_2  = 7    'offset for location of 5 byte data buffer
  MidVal    = 1500
  MinVal    = 1000
  MaxVal    = 2000
  Servo1    = 16
  Servo2    = 17
  Servo3    = 15   'standard servo for turret
  TS_MaxVal = 800
  TS_MinVal = 800

Var
  long CogN,Stacks[50], t, onTimer, MotorsOn, MotorsTimeOut
  Long Command,Settings,Sems_Flags
  Long LMotorOn,LMotorTimer,LMotorDuration,RMotorOn,RMotorTimer,RMotorDuration
  Long TurretPosition

Pri Motors
  Initialization
  repeat
    Process0
    if Not(byte[Sems_Flags][1] & FlagMask) 'if flag not set then no action
      Next                                 'required, just loop back
    case byte[Command][0]                  'execute the command
      00:  StopMotors(0)
      06:  MoveMotors(1)  'forward
      07:  MoveMotors(-1) 'back
      12:  TurnMotors(1)  'right
```

```
    13:  TurnMotors(-1)  'left
    08:  RightMotor(1)   'move Right motor separately forward
    09:  RightMotor(-1)  'move Right motor separately backward
    10:  LeftMotor(1)    'move Left  motor separately forward
    11:  LeftMotor(-1)   'move Left  motor separately backward
   192:  TurretSet(1)    'move the turret right
   193:  TurretSet(-1)   'move the turret left
   240:  L_Speed    := byte[Command][1]     'set speed
   241:  L_TimeOut  := byte[Command][1]*10 'set timeout in steps of 10ms
   242:  StepTime   := byte[Command][1]*10 'set step time in steps of 10ms
   243:  TurnTime   := byte[Command][1]*10 'set turn time in steps of 10ms
   244:  T_Speed    := byte[Command][1]     'set speed
   245:  T_TimeOut  := byte[Command][1]*10 'set timeout in steps of 10ms


    OutputToPST                            'output some info to the PST
    byte[Sems_Flags][1] &= !FlagMask    'clear flag to signal Main to proceed

Pri Initialization
  'initialize variables I/O direction etc.
  'none needed here
  t := cnt                     'initialize timer
  Servo.Start
  Servo.Set(Servo3,1500)       'make sure the turret is at center
  TurretPosition := 1500
  MotorsOn~

Pri TurretSet(Dir)|x,xx
  if Dir < 0
    x := MidVal+TS_MaxVal*byte[Command][1]/90
  else
    x := MidVal-TS_MinVal*byte[Command][1]/90
  Servo.Set(Servo3,x)
  xx := ||(TurretPosition-x) 'abs(difference)
  TurretPosition :=x
  if xx > 20 'only delay if more than 20ms
    waitcnt(clkfreq/1600*xx+cnt)
  'assuming it takes 1 sec to travel from 700 to 2300 then we delay
  ' a multiple 1/1600 secs depending how far it has to travel.
```

Adding the turret proved again how well designed our system is. Just a few changes to the firmware and now we have a way to control a Ping))) on a turret.

One complication we had with this improvement is in the timing. Moving the servomotor an appreciable angle can take a hundred milliseconds or more. In fact it might take about a second to move the full 180 degrees range of travel. So we had to do some delaying after setting the motor to allow for this time delay before lowering the flag. This is because if the flag is reset before the turret is at its commanded position the **Others** cog will read the Ping))) while still at the wrong place. Some testing enabled the refinement that allowed for smoother movement since for small distances there is no need for a delay.

A Radar Application

To test the new firmware we made the interesting program Turret_Radar.Bas. What you should pay most attention to is the **Ranger()** subroutine. Notice in this subroutine how we check if the angle is negative or positive and send the appropriate command accordingly (192 or 193) with the angle made positive. The other two subroutines are what implements the RADAR simulation. Notice the **SaveScr** and **RestoreScr** commands and also the usage of **cartx()** and **carty()**. In Chapter 10 we will see a slightly different version of this program.

Turret_Radar.Bas

```
//Turret_Radar.Bas
//works with Protocol_Main_C.Bas
Port = 8  //set this as per your system
Main:
  setcommport Port,br115200
  call RadarScreen()
  call Radar()
End
//-----------------------------------------
sub Ranger(Angle,&Value)
  C = 192 \ Value=-1 \ m= "Comms Error"
  if Angle < 0 then C = 193
  Angle = Limit(Abs(Angle),0,90)
  serialout C,Angle
  serbytesin 5,s,x
  if x == 5
    Value = (getstrbyte(s,4)<<8)+getstrbyte(s,5)
    m = spaces(40)
  endif
  xyText 600,10,m,,10,,red
return (x==5)
//-----------------------------------------
sub RadarScreen()
  for i=1 to 400 step 50
    arc i,i,800-i,800-i,0,pi(),2,gray
  next
  for i=0 to 180 step 20
    th = dtor(i) \ r = 400
    line r,r,r+cartx(r,th),r-carty(r,th),1,gray
  next
  savescr
return
//-----------------------------------------
sub Radar()
  j=-90 \ i=1
  while true
    call Ranger(j,V)
    if V < 0 then continue
    V *= 400/23000.  \ th = dtor(j-90)
    x = cartx(V,th) \ y = carty(V,th)
    circlewh 400+x-5,400+y-5,10,10,red,red
    j += i \ if abs(j)==90 then i= -i \ restorescr
  wend
return
```

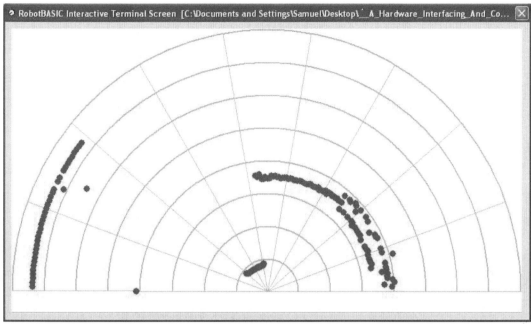

Figure 8.5: Screenshot of Turret_Radar.Bas in action.

8.3 Saving The System Parameters to EEPROM

As you have seen so far and as detailed in Table 8.3 below, we are able to change the values of the parameters shown in the table. As the system stands you can set the values but whenever the Propeller is rebooted the values will always revert to the ones assigned to them in the programs as shown in the listings. Some are operational, but most would be nice to retain so that whatever value you assigned to them last would be the value upon reboot.

Table 8.3: List of changeable system parameters

Parameter	Purpose	Cog
L_Speed	The speed for the motors in forward/backward travel	Motors
T_Speed	The speed of the motors while turning	Motors
StepTime	The time needed to accomplish a step of forward/backward travel	Motors
TurnTime	The time needed to accomplish a degree of turning	Motors
L_TimeOut	The time to leave motors on until a new command arrives in linear tavel	Motors
T_TimeOut	The time to leave motors on until a new command arrives in turning	Motors
P22 Duration	The on/off duration for the P22 LED in the **Reader** cog	Main
TimeOut1	The timeout period to wait for the parameter to arrive	Main
TimeOut2	The timeout period to wait for a command to finish	Main
P21 frequency	The blinking frequency for the P21 pin in the **Others** cog	
P23 Level	The voltage level for the dimmer LED in the **Main** cog.	

8.3.1 EEPROM Limitations

The PPDB has 32KB EEPROM used for the purpose of storing programs. Some boards have a larger EEPROM, which would be a more convenient setup. Nevertheless, 32KB is more than we need for our system and we can use the remaining space to store the system parameters and since it is an EEPROM the values can be retrieved every time the Propeller boots up.

There is a problem, however, in that when you compile and upload a program to the Propeller it will erase the entire 32KB. That is why a 64KB EEPROM would be more useful and many of the Propeller boards actually have that. The neat thing about the PPDB is that you can substitute the onboard 24LC256 chip with its larger capacity equivalents the 24LC512 (64KB) or 24LC1024 (128KB).

Notwithstanding this limitation, the EEPROM on the PPDB is useful for storing parameters that need to be retained between boots. Since the firmware is going to be compiled and then left alone, saving the various parameters in the EEPROM will be very useful and practical. The values will be lost if you re-compile the firmware but you can always reassign the parameters the values you require and save them before starting to use the system.

When in the Propeller Tool IDE instead of compiling the top-level-object using F10 use F8. This will give you a map of the memory requirements of the system and how much space remains to be free after the system is loaded. As shown in Figure 8.6 our system so far, including the generous allotment for the stacks and all the complexity, requires only 2279 Longs, which is 9116 Bytes so we have 23652 bytes or just over 23KB of free space.

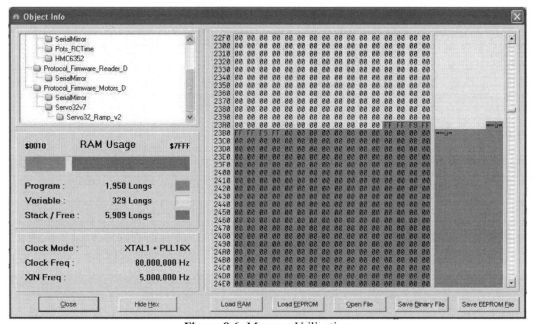

Figure 8.6: Memory Utilization

In Table 8.3 above we have 11 parameters and if we use a Long for each, we will need 11 Longs to store our data. In fact we will use 2 more Longs as explained later. We will use the memory area $7000 onwards to store our data. For now there are only 44 bytes but we can grow down to $7FFF which is 4096 bytes worth and is more than ample for what we may ever need for parameter storage.

If you are using the larger EEPROM then change the $7000 to &8000 since that will be the start of the lower 32KB which will not be erased whenever you reprogram the EEPROM with a new version of the firmware.

The system developed shortly can be easily extended to do data logging if you ever require this facility. With the methodology of our system and our protocol you can use the RB program to do all the logging you need. If you do need to log data in the firmware, using an SD card reader[43] with a FAT file system to store historical data is a useful option and can be very easily incorporated into our system using the right object like the FSRW26[44] driver. The advantage of this is that the SD card can be carried over to a PC and files can be read/created on a PC. Nonetheless, this requires extra hardware, wiring, I/O pins and expense. The EEPROM is already available for us without any wiring or loss of I/O pins or extra expense. Therefore we will use the EEPROM and we will develop our protocol to allow for saving the parameters and for restoring them and for printing them on the PST screen and for downloading them through RobotBASIC.

8.3.2 Required Changes to The Firmware

If you study Table 8.3 above you will notice that the last two parameters are not currently in a format that is useful for storing. All the others are in a contiguous area (buffer) where we can easily index into it and obtain the parameters for storing or for restoring.

We will need to reorganize these two parameters to be stored in the correct place. Currently they are variables in their respective objects. We will make them part of the **Dat** section in **Main**. The first 6 parameters in Table 8.3 are in the **Dat** section of the **Motors** object and we will need a method to acquire a pointer (address) to that buffer.

We will need additional command codes to allow for
  ➢ Storing the parameters to the EEPROM.
  ➢ Reading the parameters through RB as they are in the RAM.
  ➢ Restoring the parameters to factory settings.
  ➢ Listing the parameters on the PST screen as they are in the EEPROM or RAM.

You may wonder why we do not have a command for restoring the parameters from the EEPROM. Restoring the parameters from the EEPROM will be automatically performed upon boot up, so there is no need for a command to do it; but *there will be a method added to do it internally*.

All the system parameters will be divided into two buffers. One buffer is in the **Main** object and the other is in the **Motors** object. Within each buffer the parameters will be Longs (4 bytes) and will be contiguous. Table 8.4 below shows what parameter is in which buffer and in what order.

Table 8.4: Buffer Details

Main Buffer	Motors Buffer
P22 Duration	L_Speed
P21 frequency	T_Speed
P23 Level	StepTime
TimeOut1	TurnTime
TimeOut2	L_TimeOut
	T_TimeOut

8.3.3 CRC and Validity Check

The parameters may not have been stored in the EEPROM especially if you have compiled the firmware recently and uploaded to the EEPROM. Also reading the parameters process itself may fail or the storing process may go bad. Therefore, we will need a mechanism to assure that the EEPROM has been read correctly and that the data is indeed a valid data. If you have noticed we need 11 Longs (44 bytes) but we will also need two more longs to store two pieces of information that will assure us, with a very high probability, that the data in the EEPROM is valid.

We will use a 12th Long to store the count of parameters stored in the buffer in the EEPROM (11 now). The next long will be the sum of all the values in the 11 parameters. This may of course overflow but that does not matter. We will use this simple CRC mechanism to verify the validity of the data. After storing the parameters we will also store the count (11 now) in the 12th long and then also the 32-bit sum of all the 11 parameters' values (no matter if there is an overflow we always store the 4 bytes Long result of the sum).

Upon reading the buffer we will read the additional 2 longs and verify that the first one is set to the right count (11) and that the second one corresponds to the sum of all the already read parameters. If either of these two checks fails then we abandon the restoring process. Also the action of writing the EEPROM itself may fail which will cause the CRC check to fail later upon restoration.

> ⓘ Writing to and reading from the EEPROM is done in chunks of bytes at a time (64 in our case). We will use a temporary buffer to transfer to and from the Propeller RAM to the EEPROM.

8.3.4 The New Commands & Firmware

In addition to rearranging things so that the two parameters that are not already in the contiguous buffer are moved over to the buffer in **Main**, we will also use the Basic_I2C_Driver.Spin[68] as the object that has all the necessary I²C protocols to communicate with the 24LC256 EEPROM and store/read data from it (included in the downloadable zip file too).

We will provide two new commands

Command code 5:

If the parameter is 0 it will store the current system parameters as they are in RAM to the EEPROM. It will return in the 4th and 5th bytes of the primary send buffer a $01 if the operation succeeds or a $00 if not.

If the parameter is 1 the system parameters will be restored *in RAM only* to the factory settings. This does *not* affect the EEPROM. If you want the factory settings to be in effect on the next boot up you must also issue another command 5 with parameter 0 to save the RAM parameters to the EEPORM.

If the parameter is 2 the system parameters as they are in the EEPROM will be sent out to the PST as text numbers. The PST screen will then display the values.

If the parameter is greater than 2 the system parameters that are in the RAM will be sent to the PST as text numbers.

Command code 4:

The system parameter (from RAM) is sent to RB using the secondary send buffer with the first 4 bytes being the system parameter in Little-Endian format. That is the 1st byte (byte 0) is the LSByte and the 2nd byte is the next byte and so on. The fifth byte is set to 0 to indicate that the requested parameter is a valid one.

Which system parameter is sent depends on the parameter of the command. If the requested parameter number is too large then all the returned 5 bytes will be 0xFF to indicate a wrong requested parameter number (i.e. -1). The order is from 0 to N (N=10 for now). See Table B.2 for the order and description of the parameters (or Table 8.4).

Modifications are mostly to the **Main** object, with two new methods in **Motors** to return a pointer to the buffer and to restore the factory settings. Rearrangement of **Others** implements the new setup for the parameters that are now stored as part of the buffer in **Main** instead of as variables in **Others**.

The new firmware suite is called Firmware_XXXX_D.Spin where XXXX is Main, Others, and Motors. **Reader** is not changed and is not renamed. All the changes are bold lines in the listings. Only changed areas are listed.

> ⚠ Remember that command 5 with parameter 1 will restore the factory settings but *only in RAM*. If you wish to also reset the EEPROM so that the settings will be factory settings on the next reboot, you must also save the restored factory settings to the EEPROM (command 5 parameter 0).

Firmware_Main_D.Spin (only changes)

```
CON
  _clkmode = xtal1 + pll16x
  _xinfreq = 5_000_000
  RB_TX          = 1
  RB_RX          = 0
  RB_BAUD        = 115200
  D_TX           = 30
  D_RX           = 31
  D_BAUD         = 115200
```

```
  DimmerPin         = 23
  OthersFlagMask = %0000_0001 'flag mask for flagging the Others Cog
  MotorsFlagMask = %0000_0010 'flag mask for flagging the Motors Cog
  DimmerScale       = 16_777_216 ' 2³²÷ 256   for DAC counter
                                 ' to make dimming to be 0 to 255
  eepromAddress     = $7000      'address in EEProm to write data buffer
  BufferSize        = 64         'has to be multiples of 32
  MainLongsToSave   = 5          'number of longs to store in EEPROM from Main
  MotorsLongsToSave = 6          'number of longs to store in EEPROM from Motors


  'factory settings
  F_P22_Blinker = 80_000_000   'is Reeader blinker duration
  F_P21_Blinker = 10           'is Others blinker freq
  F_P23_Dimmer  = 127          'is Main dimmer level
  F_TimeOut1    = 240_000_000  '3 secs time out for receiving second byte
  F_TimeOut2    = 320_000_000  '4 secs time out for being allowed to send data

Var
  byte SendBufferOffset
  Long Buffer[BufferSize/4]   'read/write buffer for the EEPROM
OBJ
  RB      : "FullDuplexSerial"
  D       : "SerialMirror"
  I2C     : "Basic_I2C_Driver"
  Others  : "Firmware_Others_D"
  Reader  : "Firmware_Reader"
  Motors  : "Firmware_Motors_D"


Dat
  Command         Byte 0,0            'command and parameter from RB
  PrimaryBuffer   Byte 0,0,0,0,0      'primary 5 bytes to send to RB
  SecondaryBuffer Byte 0,0,0,0,0      'secondary 5 bytes to send to RB
  Sems_Flags      byte 0,0,0          'semaphore1,flags,semaphore2
  Settings   Long F_P22_Blinker 'various settings buffer
                                 '[0] is Reader blinker duration
             Long F_P21_Blinker '[1] is Others blinker freq
             Long F_P23_Dimmer  '[2] is Main dimmer level
  TimeOut1   Long F_TimeOut1     '3 secs timeout for receiving second byte
  TimeOut2   Long F_TimeOut2     '4 secs timeout for being allowed to send data

Pri Initialization
  RB.Start(RB_RX,RB_TX,0,RB_BAUD) 'start FDS serial driver
  D.Start(D_RX,D_TX,0,D_BAUD)    'start SM serial driver (only need to do once)
  Sems_Flags[0] := LockNew        'create Semaphore for SendBuffer
  Sems_Flags[2] := LockNew        'create Semaphore for PST output

  RestoreSettings       'read settings from EEPROM if any available

  Others.Start(@Command,@Settings,@Sems_Flags)          'start Others Cog
  Reader.Start(@PrimaryBuffer,@Settings,@Sems_Flags)   'Start Reader Cog
  Motors.Start(@Command,@Settings,@Sems_Flags)          'Start Motors Cog
  'create a dimmer LED on P23
  ctra[30..26] := %00110             'Set ctra to DUTY mode
  ctra[5..0]   := DimmerPin          'Set ctra's APIN
  frqA := Settings[2] *DimmerScale 'Set frqa register to mid level initially
  dirA[DimmerPin]~~                   'make output pin
```

```
Pri ExecuteTheCommand|x ,a
  case Command[0]
      4: SendSystemParameter  'send requested parameter to RB
      5: StorePrintSystemParameters 'store parameters to EEPROM or print on PST

    255: Reboot 'reset the propeller

    200:'set the Dimmer level on P23
        frqA := Command[1] *DimmerScale
        Settings[2] := Command[1]

    201:'set blinker duration for Reader cog(P22)
        '256 levels between 0 to 2 secs (0=off)
        Settings[0] := Command[1]*(2_000/256)*(ClkFreq/1_000)

    202: 'set the TimeOut1 for waiting for parameter byte (second command byte)
         'in seconds
         TimeOut1 := (clkfreq/1000)*Command[1]*500

    203: 'set the TimeOut2 for waiting for a command to finish its actions
         'it should reflect and be related to the PC system's timeout (secs)
         TimeOut2 := (clkfreq/1000)*Command[1]*500

    1,2,24:
      'commands in the Others cog that may fill the
      'the last two bytes in the primary send buffer
      Sems_Flags[1] |= OthersFlagMask    'set flag
      WaitForFlagResetWithTimeOut(OthersFlagMask)

    66:'commands in the Others cog that fill the secondary send buffer
      SendBufferOffset := 5            'command uses the secondary buffer
      Sems_Flags[1] |= OthersFlagMask  'set flag to signal the cog
      WaitForFlagResetWithTimeOut(OthersFlagMask)

    0,6,7,12,13,240,241,242,243,244,245,8,9,10,11:'commands in the Motors cog
      Sems_Flags[1] |= MotorsFlagMask    'set flag
      WaitForFlagResetWithTimeOut(MotorsFlagMask)

    192,193: 'turret and ping commands in Motors and Others cogs
      Sems_Flags[1] |= MotorsFlagMask    'set flag for Motors
      WaitForFlagResetWithTimeOut(MotorsFlagMask)
      Command[0] := 192  'force the command code to 192, this way we do not
                         'need to change the Others object
      Sems_Flags[1] |= OthersFlagMask    'set flag for Others
      WaitForFlagResetWithTimeOut(OthersFlagMask)


Pri WaitForFlagResetWithTimeOut(Flag)|t
  t:=cnt
  repeat until cnt-t > TimeOut2       'wait for flag to clear with time out
    Process0
    if Not(Sems_Flags[1] & Flag)
      quit
```

```
Pri RestoreSettings|x,crc,a
  if i2c.ReadPage(i2c#BootPin, i2c#EEPROM, eepromAddress, @Buffer, BufferSize)
    return 'could not write
  a := MainLongsToSave+MotorsLongsToSave
  if Buffer[a] <> a 'bad count
    return
  crc~
  repeat x from 0 to a-1 'create crc
    crc += Buffer[x]
  if crc <> Buffer[a+1]    'bad crc
    return
  repeat x from 0 to MainLongsToSave-1    'copy buffer to Main data
    Settings[x] := Buffer[x]
  a := Motors.GetDataAddress
  repeat x from 0 to MotorsLongsToSave-1  'copy buffer to Motors Data
    Long[a][x] := Buffer[x+MainLongsToSave]

Pri StoreSettings|x,a,crc
  crc~
  PrimaryBuffer[3] := PrimarBuffer[4] :=0  'assume failure
  repeat x from 0 to MainLongsToSave-1    'copy Main data to buffer
    Buffer[x] := Settings[x]
    crc += Settings[x]                    'calc crc
  a := Motors.GetDataAddress
  repeat x from 0 to MotorsLongsToSave-1  'copy Motors Data to buffer
    Buffer[x+MainLongsToSave] := Long[a][x]
    crc += Long[a][x]                     'calc crc
  x := MainLongsToSave+MotorsLongsToSave
  Buffer[x] := x 'store count
  Buffer[x+1] := crc 'store crc
  if i2c.WritePage(i2c#BootPin, i2c#EEPROM, eepromAddress, @Buffer, BufferSize)
    return ' an error occured during the write
  x := cnt ' prepare to check for a timeout
  repeat while i2c.WriteWait(i2c#BootPin, i2c#EEPROM, eepromAddress)
    if cnt - x > clkfreq / 10
      return ' waited more than a 1/10 second for the write to finish
  PrimaryBuffer[4] :=1  'indicate success

Pri OutputToPST_1
  if Not LockSet(Sems_Flags[2]) 'output some info to PST if semaphore acquired
    D.Str(string(13,"Main Received:"))
    D.Dec(Command[0])
    D.Str(string(","))
    D.Dec(Command[1])
    LockClr(Sems_Flags[2])

Pri OutputToPST_2|x
  if Not LockSet(Sems_Flags[2]) 'output some info to PST if semaphore acquired
    D.Str(string(13,"Main Sending:"))
    repeat x from 0 to 4        'show the bytes sent
      D.Dec(PrimaryBuffer[x+SendBufferOffset])
      D.Str(string(","))
    LockClr(Sems_Flags[2])
```

```
Pri SendSystemParameter|x,a,fifth
    'send RAM parameter to RB if not valid then all bytes are $FF
    'if valid then Little Endian for the first 4 bytes and $00 for fifth
    fifth := x := $FFFFFFFF
    if Command[1] < MainLongsToSave  'if parameter request is in Main
        x := Settings[Command[1]]
        fifth := 0
    elseif Command[1] < MotorsLongsToSave+MainLongsToSave    'if in Motors
        a := Motors.GetDataAddress
        x:= Long[a][Command[1]-MainLongsToSave]
        fifth := 0
    SendBufferOffset := 5  'signal that it is secondary send buffer
    SecondaryBuffer[4] := fifth & $FF    'set the last byte
    repeat a from 0 to 3                 'set the 4 bytes Little Endian
        SecondaryBuffer[a] := x.byte[a]

Pri Restore_Factory
  Settings[0] := F_P22_Blinker
  Settings[1] := F_P21_Blinker
  Settings[2] := F_P23_Dimmer
  Settings[3] := F_TimeOut1
  Settings[4] := F_TimeOut2

Pri StorePrintSystemParameters|x,a
  case Command[1]
    0:StoreSettings  'write the setting to the eeprom
    1:Restore_Factory
      Motors.Restore_Factory
    2:'output EEPOROM parameter to PST
      D.Tx(0)
      D.Str(string("Reading the EEPROM",13))
      ifnot i2c.ReadPage(i2c#BootPin,i2c#EEPROM,eepromAddress,@Buffer,BufferSize)
        repeat x from 0 to MotorsLongsToSave+MainLongsToSave-1
          D.Dec(Buffer[x])
          D.Tx(32)
        D.Tx(13)
      else
        D.Str(string("Operation Failed",13))
    other: 'output RAM parameters to PST
      D.Tx(0)
      D.Str(string("RAM parameters",13))
      a := Motors.GetDataAddress
      repeat x from 0 to MainLongsToSave-1
        D.Dec(Settings[x])
        D.Tx(32)
      repeat x from 0 to MotorsLongsToSave-1
        D.Dec(Long[a][x])
        D.Tx(32)
      D.Tx(13)
```

Firmware_Motors_D.Spin (only changes)

```
Pub GetDataAddress    'return the address of the parameters buffer
   return @L_Speed


Pub Restore_Factory
   L_Speed    := F_L_Speed    'speed factor for moving forward/backward
   T_Speed    := F_T_Speed    'speed factor for turning
   StepTime   := F_StepTime
   TurnTime   := F_TurnTime
   L_TimeOut  := F_L_TimeOut  'motor keep on time after forward/backward
   T_TimeOut  := F_T_TimeOut  'motor keep on time after turning
```

Firmware_Others_D.Spin (changes only)

```
Pri Initialization
   'initialize variables I/O direction etc.
   ctrA[30..26] := %00100            'Set ctrA for "NCO single-ended"
   ctrA[5..0]   := Blinker           'Set ctrA's APIN
   frqA         := Long[Settings][1]*BlinkerScale 'set rate
   dirA[20..18]~~
   dirA[Blinker]~~
   t := cnt                          'initialize timer

Pri Set_BlinkRate
   'set the blink rate  for P21
   frqA := byte[Command][1] * BlinkerScale 'set rate
   Long[Settings][1] := byte[Command][1]
   if frqA == 0
      phsA~   'make sure the pin is low if it to be off
```

8.3.5 Testing the EEPROM Commands

EEPROM_Tester.Bas exercises all the new commands. Compile the new Firmware_Main_D.Spin and save to EEPROM (F11) then run the RB program. You may want to also run the PST and have it so that it does not disable when it loses focus because we want to go to the RB program and interact with it.

The program will
- ❏ Print all the EEPROM parameters (none to start with and they all should be 0) on the PST screen.
- ❏ Print all the RAM parameters (should be as the constants in the program code) on the PST screen.
- ❏ Print on the RB screen all the RAM parameters (same as 2).
- ❏ Modify some of the parameters.
- ❏ Save the parameters to the EEPROM and check if successful.
- ❏ Reset the Propeller and wait for it to reboot.
- ❏ Print all the EEPROM parameters (now they should be the same as set in 4) on the PST screen.
- ❏ Print all the RAM parameters (should be the same as 7) on the PST screen.
- ❏ Print all the RAM parameters (same as 8) on the RB screen.
- ❏ Restore Factory Settings.
- ❏ Save the parameters to the EEPROM.
- ❏ Print all the RAM parameters (should be as the constants in the program code) on the PST screen.
- ❏ Print all the EEPROM parameters (should be as in 12) on the PST screen.

> ⓘ In the program when printing the parameters to the RB screen we will use an extra count (12 instead of just 11) to see how reading an invalid parameter returns -1 (0xFFFFFFFF).

EEPROM_Tester.Bas

```
//EEPROM_Tester.Bas
//works with Firmware_Main_D.Spin
Port = 8 //change this is as per your system
Main:
  setcommport Port,br115200
  call SendCommand(5,2) 'print EEPROM params to PST
  call SendCommand(5,3)  'print out RAM params to PST
  for i=0 to 11  //using an extra to demo how it returns -1
    call SendCommand(4,i,s)
    print BuffreadI(s,0)," "
  next
  call SendCommand(200,250) 'set the P23 brightness
  call SendCommand(201,0)   'no blinking on P22
  call SendCommand(2,0)     'no blinking on P21
  call SendCommand(5,0,s)   'save to EEPROM
  m = "Saving to the EEPROM failed"
  if SendCommand_Result
    if getstrbyte(s,5) then m = "Saving to the EEPROM succeeded"
  endif
  print m
  print "resetting the propeller . . . wait 3 secs"
  call SendCommand(255,0) 'reset the Propeller
  delay 3000              'wait for Prop to finish reboot
  print
  call SendCommand(5,2) 'print EEPROM params to PST
  call SendCommand(5,3) 'print out RAM params to PST
  for i=0 to 11
    call SendCommand(4,i,s)
    print BuffreadI(s,0)," "
  next
  print "Resetting factory settings and saving to the EEPROM"
  call SendCommand(5,1) 'restore factory settings
  call SendCommand(5,0) 'save to EEPROM
  call SendCommand(5,1) 'print RAM params to PST
  call SendCommand(5,2) 'print EEPROM params to PST
  print "all done"
end
//---------------------------------------------
sub SendCommand(C,P,&s)
   serialout C,P
   serbytesin 5,s,x
   if x != 5 then return false
return (x==5)
```

8.4 Adding an Accelerometer

An accelerometer module is a very useful device in many robotic projects. To that end we will incorporate the H48C Tri-Axis Accelerometer module[34] (see Figure 2.10). The connection schematic is shown in Figure 8.7 below.

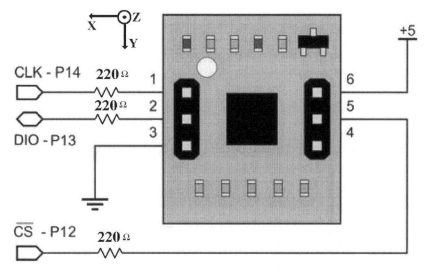

Figure 8.7: H48C Connection Schematic

8.4.1 Adding the Accelerometer Commands to the Protocol

The accelerometer provides acceleration values for the threes axes (x,y,z). From these values we can also ***calculate*** the tilts of these axes using math functions in RB. We need to obtain 3 parameters from the device; all will be 16 bit numbers (actually 12 see later). We can make our protocol return these values in the 4th and 5th bytes of the primary send buffer. This would then require RB to send a command to request each axis one at a time. This might not be quite good enough especially if you consider that the acceleration values are usually needed to control a robot in a very dynamic situation where we would need these values as quickly as possible. Algorithms that need acceleration values are for controlling a walking robot or a balancing robot for instance. In such situations any delay in obtaining the readings may cause control algorithms to be sluggish or even fail altogether.

A better alternative is to use the secondary buffer. However, there is a snag. Since the data is 16 bits we need 2 bytes for each value and since there are 3 we would need 6 bytes. However, our protocol only allows 5 bytes making it impossible to return all three values in one go and we would require two commands to get all three values. This may be acceptable if we are working in two dimensions and we mount the device to give us the most advantageous orientation of the x-y-plane. After all many robots have been designed with only 2-axis accelerometers and the algorithms work quite well. If we want to use all three axes then the application must not be very dynamic where acceleration values change too rapidly for the software's sampling rate since reading the z-axis as a separate command requires another command cycle.

There is a way to return all three readings in 5 bytes; all three values can be obtained with one command and one communications cycle and therefore as fast as our protocol allows. The data from the H48C does not quite need 16 bits since the maximum value can only be 4095 (0xFFF). So the maximum value is 3 nibbles. To transmit all three values we need 9 nibbles, which fit quite easily within our 5 bytes (10 nibbles) with 1 nibble to spare.

The 48HC values for the axes are actually voltage DAC values in reference to a reference voltage value. We will need to read this value for maximum accuracy. However this needs to be performed once upon startup since it is not going to vary during the operations of the device. It should be (4095/2) ± 2, which is between 2045 and 2049 with it almost always being 2047. Of course you can read the reference voltage every time before reading the axes' values but this will slow the whole operation a little and for a very dynamic system you can dispense with reading the reference voltage except for the first time. The gained accuracy is inconsequential as compared to the loss in speed.

The command to interrogate the H48C will have two modes depending on the parameter passed to it. If the parameter is other than 1 then the values of the axes' acceleration are returned in the secondary send buffer as 5 bytes. If the parameter is 1 the command will return the value of the reference voltage in the 4th and 5th bytes of the primary send buffer.

The procedure is as follows:
- ❑ Before using the H48C commands for the first time issue command 70 with parameter 1 and reconstitute the reference voltage value from the 4th and 5th bytes (MSByte first) and store the value (vRef).
- ❑ Whenever you need the acceleration value issue command 70 with a parameter of 0 (or any number other than 1) and reconstitute the values for the x-axis from the first three nibbles (xRef), the y-axis from the next three nibbles (yRef) and the z-axis from the last three nibbles (zRef).
- ❑ Once you have the raw values for the axis readings you can calculate the actual acceleration in reference to 1g using the formula (replace x with y and z for the other axis):
  $$xG = (xRef-vRef) * 0.0022$$
- ❑ To obtain tilt angles you can either calculate them from the raw data after subtracting vRef or from the calculated g values (xG above) using the **aTan2()** function in RB. So for example to get the tilt of the x-Axis you would do
  aTan2(xRef-vRef , zRef-vRef)
  to get the angle in radians or
  rTod(aTan(xRef-vRef , zRef-vRef)
  to get the angle in degrees.

To reconstitute the axes' values from the 5 bytes (see Figure 8.8):
- ❑ First byte and the MS-Nibble of the second byte constitute the xRef value.
- ❑ LS-Nibble of the second byte and the third byte constitute the yRef value.
- ❑ The fourth byte and the MS-Nibble of the fifth byte constitute the zRef value.

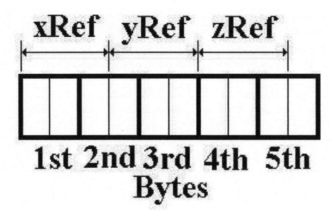

Figure 8.8: Order of the Acceleration Reference Values In the buffer.

You will see all this in the code listings in the Spin program and in the RB program.

ⓘ The orientation of the device on the PPDB itself has to be taken in consideration if you need the readings to be in reference to the PPDB axes. See Figure 8.7 for how the positive x-axis and y-axis are oriented and also the z-axis is pointing upwards from the plane of the figure. Also see Figure 8.10.

8.4.2 Incorporating the H48C in the Protocol

To communicate with the H48C we need to use SPI serial comms. There is a driver for the H48C that is very easy and convenient to use. However, this driver requires a dedicated cog. We do have a cog to spare and we definitely could use the H48C_Tri-Axis_Accelerometer.spin[45] driver to do continuous reading of the accelerometer in the background. Thus obtaining the readings would be very fast and up to date all the time. This might be a necessary quality for a driver of an accelerometer if the application is going to experience rapid and short accelerations and it is necessary to be able to track these accelerations as quickly as possible. For example if we were to implement an Inertial Navigation System (INS) we would need a way to track accelerations in all axes as quickly as possible. Using this driver object is simple if you need to use it. All you have to do is instantiate it and then **Start()** it and then use its methods to get the values.

We will not use this object. We will use a function that we developed that does not require a cog but still enables us to perform the necessary bit-banging to perform SPI serial communications. **ReadFromH48C()** sends the command to the H48C to tell it which reading is required and then obtains the readings. This is accomplished by sending out the bits of the command (5 bits) and then reading the bits of the result (13 bits). The bits are sent out MSBit First and received MSBit First. The function performs all the necessary Chip Select and Clocking actions.

Since this function is implemented in Spin it is not as fast as the previous object, which does its work in PASM. Nevertheless, it is sufficiently fast for most work with which you are likely to require the H48C. If you need a faster response, you can always use the other object. The new Firmware_Main_E.Spin and Firmware_Others_E.Spin implement all the required changes. The other objects (**Motors**, **Reader**) are unchanged. For Firmware_Main_E.Spin the changes are only a few lines from the _D version; they are just a new Case statement in the **ExecuteTheCommand** method and instantiation of the new _E object in the **Obj** section. For Firmware_Others_E.Spin there are a few changes. We will list only the changed areas.

Firmware_Main_E.Spin (Just the changes)

```
OBJ
  RB      : "FullDuplexSerial"
  D       : "SerialMirror"
  I2C     : "Basic_I2C_Driver"
  Others  : "Firmware_Others_E"
  Reader  : "Firmware_Reader"
  Motors  : "Firmware_Motors_D"


Pri ExecuteTheCommand|x ,a
  case Command[0]
      4: SendSystemParameter  'send requested parameter to RB
      5: StorePrintSystemParameters  'store params to EEPROM or print to PST
    255: Reboot 'reset the propeller

    200:'set the Dimmer level on P23
        frqA := Command[1] *DimmerScale
        Settings[2] := Command[1]

    201:'set blinker duration for Reader cog(P22)
        '256 levels between 0 to 2 secs (0=off)
       Settings[0] := Command[1]*(2_000/256)*(ClkFreq/1_000)

    202: 'set the TimeOut1 for waiting for parameter byte (second command byte)
         'in seconds
         TimeOut1 := (clkfreq/1000)*Command[1]*500
    203: 'set the TimeOut2 for waiting for a command to finish its actions
         'it should reflect and be related to the PC system's timeout (secs)
         TimeOut2 := (clkfreq/1000)*Command[1]*500
```

```
  1,2,24:
    'commands in the Others cog that may fill the
    'the last two bytes in the primary send buffer
    Sems_Flags[1] |= OthersFlagMask     'set flag
    WaitForFlagResetWithTimeOut(OthersFlagMask)

  66:'commands in the Others cog that fill the secondary send buffer
    SendBufferOffset := 5              'command uses the secondary buffer
    Sems_Flags[1] |= OthersFlagMask   'set flag to signal the cog
    WaitForFlagResetWithTimeOut(OthersFlagMask)

  0,6,7,12,13,240,241,242,243,244,245,8,9,10,11:'commands in the Motors cog
    Sems_Flags[1] |= MotorsFlagMask     'set flag
    WaitForFlagResetWithTimeOut(MotorsFlagMask)

  192,193: 'turret and ping commands in Motors and Others cogs
    Sems_Flags[1] |= MotorsFlagMask     'set flag for Motors
    WaitForFlagResetWithTimeOut(MotorsFlagMask)
    Command[0] := 192  'force the command code to 192, this way we do not
                       'need to change the Others object
    Sems_Flags[1] |= OthersFlagMask     'set flag for Others
    WaitForFlagResetWithTimeOut(OthersFlagMask)

  70:'read the H48C if parameter is 1=>read vref
     'and any other value means read the axes
     if Command[1] <> 1
        SendBufferOffset := 5                'command uses the secondary buffer
     Sems_Flags[1] |= OthersFlagMask  'set flag to signal the cog
     WaitForFlagResetWithTimeOut(OthersFlagMask)
```

Firmware_Others_E.Spim (only changes)

```
CON
  Blinker        = 21
  RCPin1         = 2
  RCPin2         = 3
  PingPin        = 4
  FlagMask       = %0000_0001    'mask for flag for this cog
  MotorsFlagMask = %0000_0010    'Mask For Motors Flag
  BlinkerScale   = 54            ' 2³² ÷ 80_000_000 for NCO counter
  Offset_1       = 5   'offset for location of 2 byte data buffer
  Offset_2       = 7   'offset for location of 5 byte data buffer
  Compass_SDA    = 26
  Compass_SCL    = 27
  Compass_On     = 1   'if there is no compass make this 0
  Accel_CS       = 12
  Accel_DIO      = 13
  Accel_Clk      = 14
  Accel_Pause    = 200_000   '5 us

Pri Others
  Initialization
  repeat
    Process0
    if Not(byte[Sems_Flags][1] & FlagMask) 'if flag not set then no action
      Next                                 'required, just loop back
```

```
      case byte[Command][0]                    'execute the command
         1: Set_LEDS
         2: Set_BlinkRate
        24: 'compass commands
            case byte[Command][1]
                1: Is_Compass_Enabled 'return if compass is available or not
                2: Calibrate_Compass(0)
                3: Calibrate_Compass(1)
                other: Read_Compass
        66: Read_Pots
        70: if byte[Command][1] == 1
                H48C_vRef
            else
                H48C_AxisRef
       192: Read_Ping
    OutputToPST                                'output some info to the PST
    byte[Sems_Flags][1] &= !FlagMask    'clear flag to signal Main to proceed

Pri Initialization
  'initialize variables I/O direction etc.
  ctrA[30..26] := %00100             'Set ctrA for "NCO single-ended"
  ctrA[5..0]   := Blinker            'Set ctrA's APIN
  frqA         := Long[Settings][1]*BlinkerScale 'set rate
  dirA[20..18]~~
  dirA[Blinker]~~
  outA[Accel_CS]~~      'Make Chip select high since it is active low
  dirA[Accel_CS]~~      'Make Chip Select pin an output
  dirA[Accel_Clk]~~     'Make Clock an output pin
  t := cnt              'initialize timer

PPri H48C_AxisRef|x,y,z
  x := ReadFromH48C(%11_000)
  y := ReadFromH48C(%11_001)
  z := ReadFromH48C(%11_010)
  byte[Command][Offset_2]    := (x & $FF0) >> 4
  byte[Command][Offset_2+1] := ((x & $0F) << 4) + ((y & $F00) >> 8)
  byte[Command][Offset_2+2] := y & $0FF
  byte[Command][Offset_2+3] :=  (z & $FF0) >> 4
  byte[Command][Offset_2+4] := (z & $00F) << 4

Pri H48C_vRef|v
  v := ReadFromH48C(%11_011)
  byte[Command][Offset_1]    := (v >> 8) & $FF
  byte[Command][Offset_1+1] := v & $FF

Pri ReadFromH48C(which):Value
  Value~                        'clear value
  outA[Accel_Clk]~             'clear clk pin
  outA[Accel_Cs]~              'select the chip
  outA[Accel_Dio]~            'clear data pin
  dirA[Accel_Dio]~~           'make data pin as output
  'shift out the command 5 bits as MSFBit First
  REPEAT 5
    outA[Accel_Dio] := which >> 4 'send out bit from command
    which := which << 1          'Shift the command right
    !outA[Accel_Clk]            'cycle clock high-low
```

```
    !outA[Accel_Clk]
  dirA[Accel_Dio]~                    'Set data pin to input
  outA[Accel_Clk]~                    'Set clock low
  'shift in 13 bits value MSBit First
  REPEAT 13
    !outA[Accel_Clk]                  'cycle clock high-low
    !outA[Accel_Clk]
    Value:=(Value<<1)|inA[Accel_Dio]  'add the read bit to value
  outA[Accel_CS]~~                    'deselect chip
  outA[Accel_Clk]~                    'clk low
  waitcnt(clkfreq/Accel_Pause+cnt)    'delay 5 us
```

8.4.3 Testing the New Command

In the previous section you saw how the values of the three axes were placed in the 5-byte buffer. On the RB side the 5 bytes have to be broken up and the nibbles extracted to reconstitute the numbers. You can see all this in the listing of H48C_Tester.Bas in the **Read_H48c()** user defined subroutine. The subroutine will read the **vRef** and the axes values if the passed parameter **vRef** is 0 and if it is not 0 then only the axes' values will be read. The subroutine is a useful one you can use in other programs to read the H48C values.

Also notice in the main program how the tilt angles are calculated using the **aTan2()** and **rToD()** functions to get the angle in degrees.

> For later programs that require the use of the H48C we will put the subroutine **Read_H48C()** in the Instruments.Bas include file we used previously in Section 8.1.4.

H48C_Tester.Bas

```
//H48C_Tester.Bas
//Works with Firmware_E.Spin
Port =8  //change as per your system
Main:
  fmta = "#0.0000   " \ fmtb = "  #00     "
  setcommport Port,br115200
  v=0
  while true
    call Read_H48C(v,x,y,z,gX,gY,gZ)
    xystring 10,10,v;x-v;y-v;z-v;spaces(20)
    xystring 50,30,Format(gX,fmta),Format(gY,fmta),Format(gZ,fmta)
    xystring 50,50,Format(rtod(atan2(gX,gZ))-90,fmtb)
    xystring -1,-1,Format(rtod(atan2(gY,gZ))-90,fmtb)
    xystring -1,-1,Format(rtod(atan2(gZ,gY)),fmtb)
    //v = 0    //uncomment this to refresh the vRef all the time
  wend
End
//================================
sub SendCommand(C,P,&s)
  m = ""
  serialout C,P
  serbytesin 5,s,x
  if x < 5 then m= "Comms Error"
  xystring 500,20,m,spaces(30)
return (x == 5)
//================================
```

```
sub Read_H48C(&vRef,&xRef,&yRef,&zRef,&xG,&yG,&zG)
  xRef = 0 \ yRef = 0 \ zRef = 0
  xG =0 \ yG = 0 \ zG = 0
  if vRef == 0
     call SendCommand(70,1,s) //read vRef
     if !SendCommand__Result then return false
     vRef = (getstrbyte(s,4)<<8)+getstrbyte(s,5)
  endif
  call SendCommand(70,0,s) //read the axes
  if !SendCommand__Result then return false
  xRef = (getstrbyte(s,1) << 4) + (getstrbyte(s,2) >>4)
  yRef = ((getstrbyte(s,2)&0x0F) << 8) + getstrbyte(s,3)
  zRef = (getstrbyte(s,4) << 4) + (getstrbyte(s,5) >> 4)
  xG = (xRef-vRef)*.0022   //convert to g-forces
  yG = (yRef-vRef)*.0022
  zG = (zRef-vRef)*.0022
return true
```

8.4.4 Three Dimensional Animation of Airplane Pitch, Roll & Heading

Using acceleration data has numerous uses in the field of engineering. Combined with heading data from a compass you can control cars, airplanes, ships, submarines and robots. You can create balancing and walking robots. You can control a robot arm with accurate positioning.

Using acceleration data (with a gyroscopic unit) you can create a very viable Inertial Navigation System. An INS uses acceleration data to calculate speeds and translations (distances) from a start point. With an INS you do not even need a compass to know where you are. Using the translations in the three axes you can calculate how high and where you are quite accurately. The math is quite complex; it is not just straightforward integration. There are nuances to things like using filtering to filter out noisy data and combining data from other sources like gyroscopes and compasses. See Chapter 10 for an implementation of a ***very simplistic*** but entertaining INS of sorts.

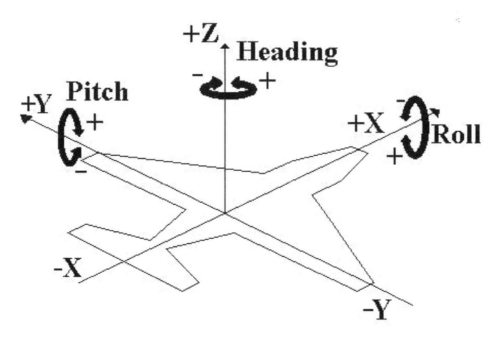

Figure 8.9: Pitch, Roll and Heading

Another use for acceleration data is calculation of Pitch and Roll. Pitch is the angle between the longitudinal axis (body) of an airplane (for instance) and the horizontal. Roll is the angle between the lateral axis (wings) and the horizontal. For full control of an airplane one also needs the Heading, which is the angle between the x-axis and the magnetic north pole. This is obtained from a compass.

If our PPDB were to be placed on an airplane with the HMC6352 and H48C we would be able to acquire information on the attitude of the airplane in 3D-Space. To calculate the pitch and roll we assign the longitudinal axis as the x-axis and the lateral axis as the y-axis. Heading will be a rotation around the z-axis.

To calculate pitch we will need to find the tilt angle the longitudinal (x-axis) is making with the vertical (z-axis). This is **aTan(gX , gZ)**. Likewise the roll is the angle of the y-axis with the vertical. This is **aTan(gY,gZ)**. For the heading we will use the compass reading.

> (i) When we calculate the tilt of the x-axis or y-axis we are actually calculating the angle it makes with the vertical using **aTan2(gX,gZ)**. If the plane is level this angle will be 90º ($\pi/2$). We need to subtract $\pi/2$ from the calculated tilts to have the correct pitch and roll values.

> ⚠ In RobotBASIC the **aTan(x,y)** function requires the first parameter to be the x-value ($\cos\theta$) and the second the y-value ($\sin\theta$). In other languages (e.g. C++) it might be the other way round.

> ⚠ The tilt calculations require that the device **not** be experiencing any forces other than gravity. Any additional forces would introduce additional acceleration, which would render the tilt calculations incorrect due to the additional component accelerations. A better way to obtain pitch and roll is to use a gyroscopic device.

The program H48C_Plane.Bas will use the power of RB and the power of our protocol and firmware to display a 3D-Animation of the orientation in 3D space of a simple airplane representation. We will keep the program as simple as possible so not to cloud the issues with too much detail. Nevertheless, you will be quite impressed. You will be able to pitch and roll and turn the PPDB and you will see the airplane figure respond according to your movements. Moreover, there will also be a Compass instrument and Attitude Indicator (AI) instrument. The response is instantaneous. When you consider what is going on you will be quite surprised at how responsive and dynamic the display is. The system will:
- Send a command over the serial link to ask for the H48C data.
- Receive the 5 bytes.
- Reconstitute the 3-axis raw data.
- Calculate the g-forces.
- Calculate the tilt angles of the x and y axes.
- Send a command to get the HMC6352 heading.
- Reconstitute the heading.
- Use these angles to calculate the transformation of the airplane's body coordinates.
- Use RB's graphics engine to transform the body coordinates using matrix transformations.
- Use RB's graphics engine to transform the 3D body coordinates into 2D coordinates.
- Draw the airplane representation on the 2D screen.
- Draw the Compass instrument including its required calculations.
- Draw the Attitude Indicator (Artificial Horizon Indicator) and its required calculations.

All the above has to be performed continuously and rapidly enough to be able to display a faithful representation of the plane and the two instruments in response to moving the PPDB in 3D-space in a convincing animation.

H48C_Plane.Bas uses RB's 3D graphics engine to transform the airplane's body coordinates (3D) and to calculate the screen coordinates (2D) of these transformed points so as to draw the plane on the screen. The program also uses some of the math functions in RB to calculate geometric properties of the AI instrument and to plot it and the compass instrument in 2D.

The transformations are rotations around the x,y and z axes. Heading is a rotation around the z-axis. Pitch is a rotation around the y-axis. Notice, it is the y-axis since pitch is a tilt of the x-axis as if the plane is hinged by its lateral (y) axis. Likewise Roll is a rotation around the x-axis. See Figure 8.9. The origin of the axes is at the center of gravity of the plane.

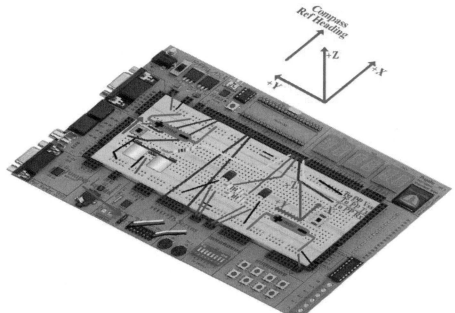

Figure 8.10: Compass and Accelerometer orientation and axes setup.

In the program we use the **Read_48HC()** subroutine that we used in the H48C_Tester.Bas program. Also notice the **PlotPlane()** subroutine. You are of course already familiar with the **SendCommand()** routine. Additionally, notice how the **Initialization** routine creates the body coordinates of the airplane. The airplane is not an elaborate image, all we want is to see the principle in action and complicating the program would not serve that purpose.

The H48C was placed on the PPDB so that the positive x-axis is pointing in the same direction as the heading reference on the HMC6352 compass (Figure 8.10).

The RobotBASIC 3D-graphics engine follows the right-handed coordinate system standard. The H48C Axis system obeys the right-handed standard too (see Figure 8.10). However, when tilt angles are calculated the positive Y-axis tilting down to the left (Figure 8.10) is a positive angle. This is opposite to the right-handed standard where a rotation around the x-axis as shown in Figure 8.10 is to the right. Thus we will need to make the tilt angle negative before we use it to calculate the rotation transformation around the x-axis (see bold lines in the listing below). The same for the Heading; the right-handed standard dictates that a turn to the left (Figure 8.10) is positive while compass turns are positive to the right. Therefore we also need to negate the compass heading before using it in the rotation transformation around the Z-axis (see highlighted lines in the listing below).

In the listing you will notice that the line of code to transform the body coordinate points for the heading is commented out. This is because to control the plane you want the picture to be oriented as if you are looking at the plane from behind. If the line is uncommented the plane will be rotated in 3D-space and you will not be able to orientate yourself for the picture correctly. Try to uncomment the line and see how this affects your *perspective*.

Notice the use of the *include* file Instruments.Bas we used in Section 8.1.4. You already saw how we used the **DisplayCompass ()** subroutine. We will use the routine in this program too, with some parameters to force the instrument to be of a certain size and position on the screen. The subroutine **DisplayAttitude()** is a similarly versatile and generic subroutine to draw an Attitude Indicator (AI) instrument for pitch and roll. The AI is a simple one but quite functional and gives an excellent feedback in addition to the 3D airplane representation of the roll (bank) and pitch. The subroutine **PlotPlane()** takes care of all the calculations and plotting of the 3D plane on the 2D computer screen.

Also now the subroutine **Read_H48C()** from the program H48C_Tester.Bas in Section 8.4.3 has been moved to the include file, so there is no listing of it in the program below.

The 3D airplane and both the Compass and AI instruments are animations using RB's easy and intuitive graphics commands with a few mathematical functions. We will not explain the details. You should find it easy to figure out the program by just reading the code (also read the code of Instruments.Bas in Section 8.1.4). If there are commands and functions in the program with which you are not familiar, look them up in the RobotBASIC Help file. All the commands that start with **ge** are the graphics engine commands. RB's matrix manipulation commands are another powerful feature that enables the program to be so small yet so powerful.

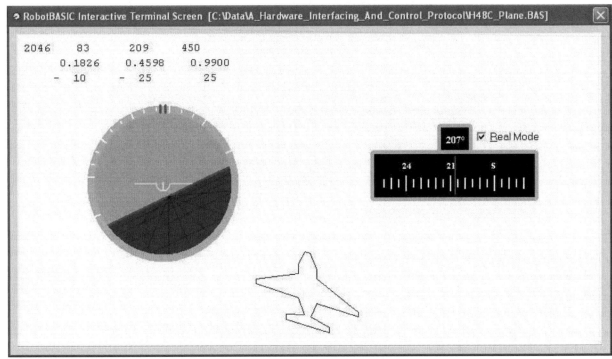

Figure 8.11: Screenshot of H48C_Plane.Bas

H48C_Plane.Bas

```
//H48C_Plane.Bas
//works with Firmware_Main_E.Spin
Port = 8 //change this as per your system
#include "..\Utilities&IncludeFiles\Instruments.Bas"
Main:
  gosub Initialization
  while true
    call Read_H48C(v,x,y,z,gX,gY,gZ)
    xystring 10,10,v;x-v;y-v;z-v;spaces(20)
    xystring 50,30,Format(gX,fmta),Format(gY,fmta),Format(gZ,fmta)
    xystring 50,50,Format(rtod(atan2(gX,gZ))-90,fmtb)
    xystring -1,-1,Format(rtod(atan2(gY,gZ))-90,fmtb)
    xystring -1,-1,Format(rtod(atan2(gZ,gY)),fmtb)
    //v = 0    //uncomment this to refresh the vRef all the time
    call SendCommand(24,0,s)
    H = 0
    if SendCommand__Result then H = (getstrbyte(s,4)<<8)+getstrbyte(s,5)
    call PlotPlane(gX,gY,gZ,H)
  wend
End
```

```
//==================================
Initialization:
  fmta = "#0.0000   " \ fmtb = "  #00       "
  setcommport Port,br115200
  v = 0
  data plane;9,.5,6,1.5,4,1.5
  data plane;0,8.5,-1,8.5,-1,1.5,-4,.5,-5,3.5,-6,3.5
  data plane;-6,-3.5,-5,-3.5,-4,-0.5,-1,-1.5,-1,-8.5,0,-8.5
  data plane;4,-1.5,6,-1.5,9,-0.5,9,.5

  data Eye;170,pi(),pi(.30),1550,400,350 //rho,theta,phi,d,Cx,Cy
  dim Plane[maxdim(plane)/2,5]
  mconstant Plane,0
  for i=0 to maxdim(plane)/2 -1
    Plane[i,0] = plane[i*2]
    Plane[i,1] = plane[i*2+1]
  next
  flip on
  AddCheckBox "Mode",630,130,"&Real Mode",1,0
return
//==================================
sub SendCommand(C,P,&s)
  m = ""
  serialout C,P
  serbytesin 5,s,x
  if x < 5 then m= "Comms Error"
  xystring 500,20,m,spaces(30)
return (x == 5)
//==================================
sub PlotPlane(gX,gY,gZ,H)
  thX = atan2(gX,gZ)-pi(.5) //x-tilt
  thY = atan2(gY,gZ)-Pi(.5) //y-tilt
  mcopy Plane,K  //refresh body coordinates array
  geRotateA K,-thY,1 //rotate around x-axis i.e. Roll
                     //negative to orientate for Right-Handed Standard
  geRotateA K,thX,2  //rotate around y-axis i.e. Pitch
  //geRotateA K,dtor(-H),3  //rotate around z-axis i.e. Heading
                     //negative to orientate for Right-Handed Standard
  ge3dto2da K,Eye    //calculated screen coordinates
  for i=1 to maxdim(K)-1  //plot the plane
    line K[i-1,3],K[i-1,4],K[i,3],K[i,4]
  next
  call DisplayCompass(!GetCheckBox("Mode"),H,600,200)
  call DisplayAttitude(thX,-thY,200,200)
  flip
  clearscr
return
```

8.5 Using the QTI Infrared Line Sensors

This penultimate improvement to the system aims at adding a piece of hardware that can be used in robotics projects. We will add three QTI Infrared Line Sensors (Part#555-27401) [14] (See Figure 2.11). The Connection diagram is as shown in Figure 8.12

Figure 8.12: Connection For the QTI Sensors

There is a most excellent tutorial on how to use the QTI[46] on the Parallax Forum. The discussion shows how to use the QTI with the Basic Stamp 2. The only difference for the Propeller is that we would need a 1KΩ resistor between the red pin on the QTI and the pin on the Propeller.

With the setup suggested in the tutorial the red pin would go high (1) when the QTI is not sensing a return on the infrared and low (0) if it is. The QTI can be used as a sensor to sense a Black line on a white background or as a drop-off sensor. On a normal reflective surface it would see the reflected infrared and output a low. If the sensor is raised too high above the surface or the surface drops off there would be no reflected infrared and the sensor outputs a high. The same happens when there is a black absorbent line since it will stop the infrared from being reflected. The sensor can be used as a line follower sensor or as a drop-off sensor. We will put the three sensors on pins P10..P8.

8.5.1 The New Firmware

To read the sensors we would set the pins on the Propeller (P8..10) high *but leave them as inputs* to prevent the high from showing on the pins. When we are ready to read the state of the sensors we turn the pins to output thus reflecting the highs. We then wait for 230 μs and then turn the pins to inputs and wait another 230 μs then read the pins. The status of the pins will reflect the status of the QTIs (1 there is a line or the surface is too far, 0 there is no line or the surface is close).

We will incorporate the process in the **Reader** object. The value will be placed in the 3rd byte of the primary send buffer and the sensors will be read continuously by the object. There is no new command needed since the values are always returned in the third byte in the primary send buffer which is always returned with most commands as we have been doing all along. The byte will have bits 0,1 and 2 set according to the line sensors instead of one bit reflecting the status of the P7 pushbutton. We will put the P7 pushbutton along with P6 in the second byte. The pushbutton on P5 will be just as before in the first byte. The second byte will now have P6 as the 1st bit and P7 as the 2nd bit of the byte. The new QTI sensors (three) will be in the third byte (three bits).

The only new objects are the **Reader** and **Main**. The change in **Main** is just to instantiate the object's new name. So we will only list the changes in **Reader**. The changes are minor and are in bold.

Firmware_Reader_F.Spin (just changes)

```
CON
  Blinker     = 22
  QTI_Top     = 10
  QTI_Bottom = 8

Pri ReadByte1
  'could do all sorts of actions here that are needed
  'to read the byte from any source eg. Bumpers
  'for now just read the pushbutton on P6 invert it
  'and mask it to make sure it is and active high not low
  'and in the LSbit
  LocalBytes[1]:= !inA[7..6] & %11

Pri ReadByte2
  'could do all sorts of actions here that are needed
  'to read the byte from any source eg. Bumpers
  'for now just read the pushbutton on P7 invert it
  'and mask it to make sure it is and active high not low
  'and in the LSbit
  dirA[QTI_Top..QTI_Bottom]~~         'turn pins to output
  waitcnt(clkfreq/100_000*23+cnt)     'wait 230 us
  dirA[QTI_Top..QTI_Bottom]~          'make the pins input
  waitcnt(clkfreq/100_000*23+cnt)     'wait 230 us
  LocalBytes[2]:=inA[QTI_Top..QTI_Bottom] 'read the states and store in byte
```

8.5.2 Testing the QTI

The program QTI_Tester.Bas uses the new Firmware_Main_F.Spin to read the three line sensors' states and continuously display them on the screen. Either use a table and experiment with them as drop-off sensors or fashion a white cardboard and place some matte (non-glossy) black electric tape on it to test how the sensors work. You may want to hold them together as if they were fixed to the bottom front of a robot and see how they will respond when you scan them across the line or slowly off the table.

The program is extremely simple to demonstrate the new devices. You may want to improve on the program by making the motors go forward when the middle sensor sees the line and turn when the sensors on the left or right see the line. We will leave this as an exercise for you. In Chapter 10.3.3 there is another version of this program that will interest you.

QTI_Tester.Bas

```
//QTI_Tester.Bas
//Works with Firmware_Main_F.Spin
Port = 8  //set this as per your system
Main:
  setcommport Port,br115200
  xystring 10,10," P5    P7,P6   QTIs"
  while true
   call SendCommand(0,0,,A,B,C)
   if SendCommand_Result
     xystring 10,30," ",A;"   ",Bin(B,2);Bin(C,3)
     xyText 100,100,Bin(C,3),"",70,fs_Bold,White,Blue //for fun
   endif
  wend
```

```
End
sub SendCommand(C,P,&s,&B1,&B2,&B3)
    serialout C,P
    clearserbuffer \ serbytesin 5,s,x
    if x != 5 then xystring 500,10,"Comms error" \ return false
    B1 = getstrbyte(s,1) \ B2 = getstrbyte(s,2) \ B3 = getstrbyte(s,3)
return true
```

8.6 Adding Sound

In the early stages (Chapter 5.8) of developing the hardware and firmware we had a system that used a Piezoelectric speaker and we had it play musical tones. The system was then still in a primitive state and we had no protocol to follow so we had RB send the desired frequency as a 32-bit frequency value to be inserted directly into the **frqB** register. We cannot use this in our system as we have it now. The protocol only allows a command bye and one parameter byte. Therefore there is no way we can tell our protocol to play a tone by giving the 32-bit frequency value of the tone.

What can we do? Before you consider that the protocol might be short sighted and that it needs to be altered, think about what can be done. Do we really need to send the frequency itself? A musical scale is really just about 84 notes. So can't we send the note number instead of its frequency and the firmware would then decide what the frequency should be? As far as playing the note, the new system will have a look-up table for notes' frequency values and use that to determine the 32-bit frequency from the 8-bit note number. The rest of the methodology is the same as before.

As a final improvement to our firmware (but see Chapter 11) we will add the speaker and a command (code 73) to allow for playing one out of 84 musical notes (0 being stop playing). Previously we used the speaker on P4 because we were using the PDB and there were not that many available I/O pins. In our firmware as we have it now we are using P4 for the Ping))) so instead we will use P11 for the speaker.

Previously when we pulsed the Piezoelectric Speaker we did so directly from the Propeller pin and the voltage level was 3.3V. This meant that the volume on the speaker was sorely lacking. The L293 on the PPDB provides a means of driving the speaker with a 5V signal instead of 3.3V (Figure 8.13). However, the best method is to use a filtering audio amplifier to boost the volume and to filter out the harmonics from the square-wave TTL signal and make it into a proper sine-wave signal (Figure 8.14). The PPDB has an audio amplifier/filter already built in but it is only for a headphone jack (see Figure 8.2 just to the right of the DB-9; bottom left). So the options are:
1. Piezoelectric speaker driven from P11 directly.
2. Piezoelectric but with the 5V supply through the L293 drive chip driven by the P11 signal (Figure 8.13).
3. 8 Ω standard magnetic coil speaker with P11 signal going through a filter and audio amplifier (Figure 8.14).
4. The PPDB headphones jack header directly connected to P11. You can use headphones to listen to the sound or you can connect the output to amplified speakers with their own external power supply.

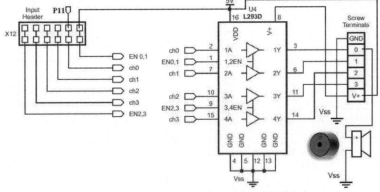

Figure 8.13: Piezoelectric Speaker with an L293 Driver

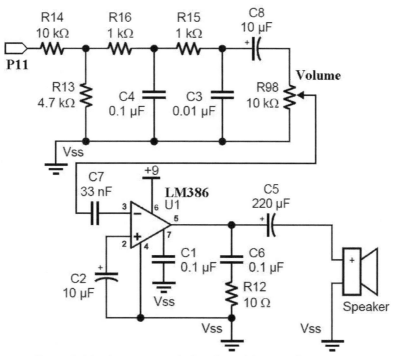

Figure 8.14: Electromagnetic Speaker with an Audio Amplifier

8.6.1 The New Firmware

We will incorporate the speaker code in the **Reader** object. The methodology is not different from what we did back in Chapter 5.8. **Main** will also be changed to incorporate the new command and instantiate the new **Reader** object. The changes in Firmware_Reader_G.Spin object are shown (bold lines) in the partial listing below (code not listed is the same as before). For Firmware_Main_G.Spin we will only list the changes too. The **Others** and **Motors** objects are not changed.

The new command code will be 73. The parameter will be 0 to stop any notes playing and 1 to 84 to play one of the musical notes. The **frqB** value required to play the note will be obtained from a table with the values for each note. The table was created with the help of RB. In the zip file with all the source code find a program called Create_Notes.Bas, which will create a table for you that you can then cut and paste into the Spin program in the **Dat** section.

You should recognize most of the code in the new **Reader** object from Chapter 5.8.

> If you want to save memory usage in the program you can use only 13 frequencies (1st 12 and the 0) instead of 85. Since the other frequencies are scales of the first octave. Every octave is a multiple of two of the previous. But then you will have to also change the way the **frqB** value is obtained from the note number. We will leave this as an exercise for you.

Firmware_Main_G.Spin (only changes)

```
OBJ
  RB      : "FullDuplexSerial"
  D       : "SerialMirror"
  I2C     : "Basic_I2C_Driver"
  Others  : "Firmware_Others_E"
  Reader  : "Firmware_Reader_G"
  Motors  : "Firmware_Motors_D"
```

```
Pri ExecuteTheCommand|x ,a
  case Command[0]
    'Other cases not listed
    73: 'Speaker
      Reader.Play_Note(Command[1])
```

Firmware_Reader_G.Spin (Only changes)

```
CON
  Blinker    = 22
  QTI_Top    = 10
  QTI_Bottom = 8
  Speaker    = 11

Var
  long CogN,Stacks[50]
  long t, SendBuffer,Settings,Sems_Flags ,tt,Frequency
  byte LocalBytes[3]

Obj
  D      : "SerialMirror"


Dat
  Notes    Long 0
           Long 1756,1860,1971,2088,2212,2344
           Long 2483,2631,2787,2953,3128,3314
           Long 3511,3720,3941,4176,4424,4687
           Long 4966,5261,5574,5906,6257,6629
           Long 7023,7440,7883,8352,8810,9374
           Long 9932,10523,11148,11811,12513,13257
           Long 14046,14881,15766,16704,17697,18749
           Long 19864,21045,22297,23622,25027,26515
           Long 28092,29763,31532,33407,35394,37498
           Long 39728,42090,44593,47245,50054,53030
           Long 56184,59523,63066,66814,70786,74995
           Long 79457,84181,89185,94489,100110,106059
           Long 112367,119051,126127,133627,141573,149991
           Long 158914,168363,178370,188979,200215,212123

Pub Play_Note(Note)
  Frequency := Notes[(0 #> Note <# 84)] 'set frqB
  tt := cnt                             'set the timer

Pri Initialization
  'initialize variables I/O direction etc.
  outA[QTI_Top..QTI_Bottom]~~
  dirA[Blinker]~~
  t := cnt                 'initialize the timer
  ctrB[30..26] := %00100   'set ctrb to NCO
  ctrb[5..0]   := Speaker  'Set ctrb's APIN
  frqB~                    'clear freqB
  dirA[Speaker]~           'speaker off for now
  tt := cnt                'init speaker timer
```

```
Pri Process0
  'can do anything here. That require polling or regular updating
  'For example we are blinking an LED on P22 using a stop watch
  'action with the variable t that hast to be initialized before
  'calling this process for the first time.
  if Long[Settings][0] == 0          'if duration is 0 then off
    outA[Blinker]~
  elseif (cnt-t) => Long[Settings][0]  'blinker time out
    !outA[Blinker]                      'toggle the LED
    t :=cnt                            'reset the timer
  if Frequency <> -1
    frqB := Frequency     'set frqB
    'phsB~                 'clear phsB will cause clicking if uncommented
    dirA[Speaker] := (frqB <> 0) 'make the pin output allowing sound
    Frequency~~                  'set Frequency to -1 to prevent re-playing
  if (cnt-tt) > 400_000_000     'if no new frequency in 5 secs
    dirA[Speaker]~             'set pin as input to turn sound off
    tt := cnt
```

8.6.2 Testing the Speaker

To test the new firmware we will use Speaker_Tester_2.Bas, which is a modification from Speaker_Tester.Bas back in Chapter 5.8.3. Before you look at it, go back to the original one and see if you can figure out what changes are required to make it work with the new firmware. Remember in the old one we had to send the 4 bytes of the 32-bit frequency value after multiplying with a factor to convert it to a value needed by the **frqB** register. Now, we want to send a command byte (73) and a note number (0 to 84). Also, remember, previously we received back only one byte, now we receive back 5 bytes.

Speaker_Tester_2.Bas

```
//Speaker_Tester_2.Bas
//works with Firmware_Main_G.Spin
Port = 8 //change this as per your system
Main:
   setcommport Port,br115200
   while true
     call PlayNote(random(85),600) //now we use a random note # not frequency
   wend
End
//-----------------------------------
sub PlayNote(N,D,&s)
   xystring 1,1,"Note = ",N;"Duration = ",D,spaces(10) //display data
   B = 0 \ c = 5
   if _Port == 0       //if not serial
     //sound F,D        //play on PC speaker...only XP machines
   else
     serialout 73,N     //command code 73 and note #
     delay D            //delay
     serbytesin 5,s,c //get the confirmation bytes
   endif
Return (c==5) //return true or false if 5 bytes received
```

8.6.3 An Exercise

Based on the changes you can see in Speaker_Tester_2.Bas rewrite Piano.Bas (Chapter 5.8.4) so that it would now work with the new firmware. The changes should be simple. Try to do it by yourself. If you need help read the hints below. The solution is Piano_2.Bas in the zip file with all the source code.

Hint: In the previous program we determined the frequency to send to the firmware with this line

```
Frequency = Notes[Song[i]+12*Scale]   //determine freq from scale and note
```

Since now we do not need the frequency we would do this instead

```
Note = Song[i]+12*Scale+1   //determine note number from scale and note
```

Why the +1? Look at the table in the Spin code; remember there is now the 0 note.

Hint: Now the firmware sends back 5 bytes not 1. Also the 1st byte is the status of the P5 pushbutton.

8.7 The Final System Firmware

Our firmware is now complete. We will change the hardware to be wireless in the next chapter, but that requires no firmware changes and just a minor hardware change (also see Chapter 11). In the zip file with all the source code there is a folder called Final_Protocol. In it you will find all the files needed to compile and upload the firmware to the Propeller's EEPROM (F11). Now that the firmware is complete you should write it to the EEPROM so you can use the PPDB with any programs you develop. You would not have to change the firmware again – unless you want to add new hardware. We have renamed all the four objects to Protocol_XXXX.Spin where the XXXX is Main, Reader, Others, or Motors. The *top-level* object is Protocol_Main.Spin.

In the subfolder are also copies of all the third-party objects that we used. You will also find all the RB programs that work with the new firmware. They are mostly copies of the programs we have seen so far placed there for your convenience. There is *one new program* called Complete_System_Tester.Bas (See Figure 8.15 below). This program incorporates all the generic and versatile subroutines from all the other programs that we developed during the progression through Chapters 7 and 8. The program performs a dazzling number of tasks all going on simultaneously and yet in real time. It is a testament to the power of our protocol, the Propeller Chip and RobotBASIC.

See Appendix B for the following:
  ➤ A tree of objects hierarchy for the Final Protocol.
  ➤ A tree of objects hierarchy for the Extended Protocol (from Chapter 11).
  ➤ Figure B.1: The System's Conceptual Schematic.
  ➤ Figure B.2: Propeller Pin Utilization.
  ➤ Figure B.3: Hardware Connections Schematics.
  ➤ Figure B.4: Picture of the final PPDB setup.
  ➤ Table B.1: List of Protocol Command Codes for the Final Protocol.
  ➤ Table B.2: System Parameters Value Mapping when using the Final Protocol.
  ➤ Table B.3: List of Extended Protocol Command Codes (as in Chapter 11), in addition to Table B.1.
  ➤ Figure B.5: Protocol State Diagrams.

Here is a list of all programs that work with the Final or Extended Protocols
  ➤ Complete_System_Tester.Bas (a new program for the final firmware)
  ➤ Compass_Tester.Bas
  ➤ Compass_Animation.Bas
  ➤ EEPROM_Tester.Bas
  ➤ H48C_Plane.Bas
  ➤ H48C_Tester.Bas
  ➤ Individual_Motors.Bas
  ➤ Piano_2.Bas
  ➤ Ping_03.Bas
  ➤ Pots_03.Bas
  ➤ Program_12_ReallySimple.Bas
  ➤ QTI_Tester.Bas
  ➤ RobotMoves_12.Bas
  ➤ Servomotor_12.Bas
  ➤ Speaker_Tester_2.Bas
  ➤ Turret_Tester.Bas

Complete_System_Tester.Bas (Figure 8.15) is a variation on Program_12_Advanced.Bas to incorporate all the new hardware from Chapter 8. It is an interesting and comprehensive GUI system for testing the firmware and hardware. Also, it has numerous reusable and versatile subroutines that you may want to use or emulate in your software. Notice how the Compass and AI instruments are now smaller and repositioned. The same include file was used to draw them as before. You may want to migrate some of the subroutines in the program to another include file so that you can use them in your own programs. **Read_48HC()** for example and **mmDistance()** have already been moved to the Instruments.Bas include file.

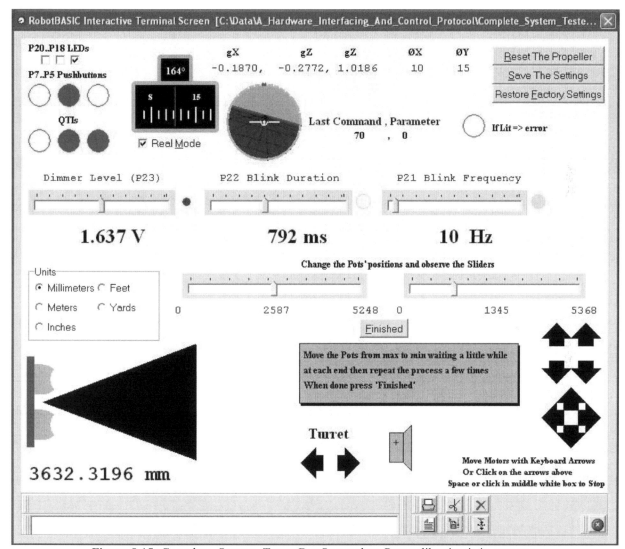

Figure 8.15: Complete_System_Tester.Bas Screenshot. Pots calibration is in progress.

8.8 Summary

In this chapter we:

- Added an HMC6352 compass unit.
- Learnt about inter-cog interactions.
- Learnt about a procedural strategy for adding other hardware in a systematic manner.
- Added a turret for the Ping))).
- Added the ability to control the motors individually.
- Added the mechanisms to save/retrieve the system parameters to/from EEPROM.
- Added an H48C accelerometer unit.
- Developed authentic looking simulated Compass and Attitude Indicator instruments.
- Utilized the **#Include** command in RB to include a library of routines into our program so that we won't have to rewrite these useful subroutines.
- Utilized RB's 3D graphics engine.
- Added 3 QTIs.
- Added a Piezoelectric Speaker with the ability to play RTTTL like musical tunes.

Chapter 9

Severing the Tether

Our system so far has a direct connection with a serial wire between the hardware and the PC. This is an acceptable option if the hardware and environment allow for it. For instance you can have a Notebook on top of a robot. However, more often, we would prefer the hardware to be remote from the control system.

Imagine you have multiple hardware systems distributed throughout an area. You can have one PC with multiple control programs each controlling one of the distributed systems. The user can then interact with each system and have an overall picture of the entire area and can interact with the various remote hardware all being controlled simultaneously and in parallel. Alternatively you can have one program controlling all the remote systems where each is a sub-process of a multifaceted and distributed overall process.

The strategies and methodologies we developed into our system facilitate the implementation of a remote control system effortlessly. There are two ways to implement remote control:
 - Using a Radio Frequency transceiver with or without an inbuilt advanced protocol such as Bluetooth or XBee.
 - Using the Internet or Local Area Network with a TCP or UDP protocol using a wired Ethernet connection or wireless Wi-Fi.

9.1 Wireless With RF, Bluetooth or XBee

The system can be made into a wireless one with surprising ease. In fact, as far as programming the firmware and software is concerned we would need almost no changes. Even the hardware will hardly need any change. If we ignore the debugging connection to the PST (only needed during the development stage) then the system we have now is as depicted in Figure 9.1(A). Of course, you can also hook up the PST along with the wireless for further debugging when required.

All we have to do to achieve a remote system as depicted in Figure 9.1(B) is:
 - On the hardware side replace the Propeller Plug with a suitable wireless transceiver.
 - On the PC add a compatible wireless transceiver.

The best system for our purposes is the XBee transceiver. Another very good alternative is to use the Bluetooth system. A third choice is to use normal Radio Frequency digital transceivers, but it is not simple to make this option work well.

Both the Bluetooth and XBee transceivers can be configured to act in a mode called "transparent" mode. This mode is basically a wireless replacement for the serial cable, and in both systems we can use them in exactly the same way we have been using the Propeller Plug with a USB cable; except there is no cable. Just as the PP was plugged to our hardware using the TX and RX pins so would be the Bluetooth or XBee device.

The only difference is that on the PC end we need a BT or XBee device too. However, in both cases the device plugs in the USB port giving us practically the same logical setup as we had with the PP. The protocol used by these systems provides us with a seamless and error-resilient link to make it appear as if they were connected with a wire.

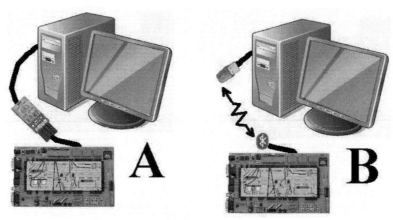

Figure 9.1: Wired and Wireless Systems

9.1.1 XBee

The best system for achieving wireless control is the XBee[47] transceiver (Figure 9.2). For the PC side, an XBee module is used with an XBee USB adapter[48] (Figure 9.2 Right) that allows it to be used with a USB port which, as far as RB is concerned, is a com port just like the PP.

On the Hardware side another Xbee is used with an SIP adapter[49] with its DOUT pin connected to P0 on the Propeller and DIN pin connected to P1. We also need to connect the Gnd to the Vss on the PPDB and the +5V line to the 5V bus on the PPDB. For all intents and purposes it is just a replacement for the PP with DOUT being the equivalent of the TX on the PP and the DIN the equivalent of the RX on the PP. We will not use the CTS pin.

Figure 9.2: XBee wireless transceiver with SIP adapter for hardware side and USB adapter for the PC side.

The XBee as configured out of the box is a direct replacement for the PP with a slightly larger footprint on the breadboard. The XBee module can also be configured to work as peer-to-peer or point-to-point or even as a mesh net. All these options are advantageous but may need some more firmware programming to activate and utilize them. An example is that an XBee can send to a specific other XBee using addressed transmissions, but this requires the software and firmware to configure the address prior to sending if address changes are to be effected on the fly.

The firmware needs absolutely no change. In the RB programs (software) the only change we would need to do is to set the value of the variable **Port** to be the port that the USB adapter will establish when it is connected to the PC, just like we did for the PP.

There is one small configuration change that will need to be performed to both transceiver units. Out of the box the units are configured to work at 9600 Baud. We will need to change this configuration to 115200 baud. The best way to do this is to use the XBee X-CTU software[50]. Plug the transceivers into the USB unit one at a time and then use the X-CTU software to change the baud rate. You can also use the program XB_Baud_Changer.Bas below to do the job. It assumes that the units are already at 9600 baud. If you need to find out what port numbers are active use the AvailablePorts.Bas program we used in Chapter 3.6. There is an excellent tutorial[51] on how to setup and use the XBee at the Parallax forum.

XB_Baud_Change.Bas

```
//XB_Baud_Change.Bas
//To change the baud of an XBee transceiver from 9600 to 115200
Port = 16   //change this as per your system
Setcommport Port,br9600
Print "Changing the Baud to 115200"
Delay 1000 \ Serout "+++"   \ Delay 2000
Serout "ATBD 7"   +char(13) \ delay 200
Serout "ATWR"+char(13)      \ delay 200
SerOut "ATCN"+char(13)      \ delay 200
setcommport 0 \ delay 300
SetCommport Port,br115200
clearserbuffer
Delay 2000 \ Serout "+++" \ Delay 2000
clearserbuffer
SerOut "ATBD"+char(13)      \ Delay 1000
SerIn s
Print "The new baud should now be (7) it is:",s
SerOut "ATCN"+char(13)
clearserbuffer
setcommport 0
end
```

The XBee Advantage

Using XBee to achieve wireless control with our system has the following advantage:
1. It is well supported.
2. It is very simple but also is versatile with more advanced options.
3. The protocol itself provides error correction and packet resending all in the XBee hardware, so we do not need to create a system ourselves. This is a major advantage.
4. It can be configured as a ***mesh system***. That is you can create a network of XBees communicating and relaying signals and you can ***broadcast*** data.
5. Some XBee modules can have a range of over a mile.
6. The hardware is extremely simple to configure using AT modem commands. On the PC side there is very little configuration needed. It is no more complex than using the PP.
7. Supports high baud rates (115200 bps).
8. The XBee device has I/O pins that can be used as A/D or digital pins to provide additional I/O to a project.

The XBee Disadvantage

To use the XBee-USB adaptor you need to do some simple soldering of a few headers.

9.1.2 Bluetooth

A good choice for converting our system into a wireless one is the <u>Easy Bluetooth transceiver</u>[52] from Parallax shown in Figure 9.3. This device is very suitable because all we have to do is replace the TX and RX connections we had on the PP with the ones on the EBT's. Of course we also have to connect the EBT to a 5V (Vdd) and Gnd (Vss) connection. But that is all we have to do as far as the hardware is concerned. P0 on the Propeller is connected to the TX on the EBT and P1 to the RX.

Figure 9.3: Easy Bluetooth Transceiver Module

You can configure the EBT to be able to work at one of a variety of baud rates. In our firmware and software we use 115200 bps and you can configure the EBT to work at that rate but it comes out of the box configured at 9600 bps and therefore to make things easy we will use this baud rate in our software and firmware, especially because configuring the EBT is not straightforward.

All we have to do in our firmware is to change the line in the **Main** object:
```
RB_Baud = 115200
```
To
```
RB_Baud = 9600
```

Also in the RB programs, change the line:
```
SetCommport Port,br115200
```
To
```
SetCommport Port,br9600
```

In the RB program we will have to change the value of the **Port** variable to the Bluetooth's port once the PC makes a connection with the EBT (see below). That is all we need to do for the hardware, software and firmware. For the PC side you also need to use a Bluetooth dongle if your computer does not already have a built in Bluetooth. One most suitable option is the <u>D-Link DBT-120 dongle</u>[53] (Figure 9.4). From experience we have discovered that the more suitable dongles to operate with the EBT are the plug and play variety, which use the Windows Stack without additional drivers. Ones that need additional drivers may cause communications delays that will cause timeout errors.

Figure 9.4: Bluetooth Dongle for the PC

The procedure for establishing communications between the EBT and the PC is described in the Parallax documentation[54] and it is best to follow this procedure; it is very easy. Additionally, there is a superb tutorial about the EBT at the Parallax Forums[55]. When the PC makes a connection with the EBT it also creates a serial communications port that should be the value to which the **Port** variable in our RB programs must be assigned. To determine this value, use the Bluetooth management software as shown in Figure 9.5; as shown we would set **Port** to the value 11.

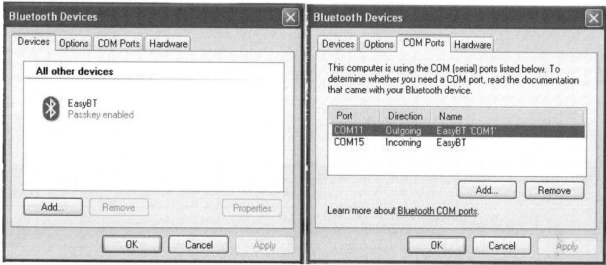

Figure 9.5: Bluetooth Port number. In this case it is Com11.

The Bluetooth Advantage

Using Bluetooth to achieve wireless control with our system has the following advantages:
1. It is relatively simple.
2. It is well supported.
3. The protocol itself provides error correction and packet resending all in the Bluetooth Stack (hardware + firmware) itself and we do not need to create a system ourselves. This is a major advantage.

The Bluetooth Disadvantage

1. Bluetooth links are one-to-one. If we would like to control multiple hardware systems, we need to use a separate com port for each system. This can be a disadvantage if we need to *broadcast* communicate. That is to send commands to many systems simultaneously. With BT we have to have different RB programs using different com ports to communicate with each hardware system. We can use the same RB program to communicate with multiple hardware systems, but we would have to set the com port every time we need to switch systems.
2. The BT range is not very extensive; less than 100 feet.
3. Configuring the EBT is not a simple undertaking and the manual is not helpful.

9.1.3 Pure Radio Frequency

In this method we would use an RF transceiver[56] (Figure 9.6) on the hardware as well as the PC side. The modules are not direct replacements for the PP due to the method they transmit and receive. So there has to be some hardware and firmware changes. Additionally, on the PC side we would have to use another Propeller hardware setup to control the PC-side transceiver.

Moreover, since the devices do not provide any error detection and elimination protocols, we have to create one in our firmware (but not the software). All this makes this option more cumbersome to realize. However, it is an attainable alternative if you wish to go with this method and the hardware and firmware modifications are not hard to do at all.

The PC side will need to use another Propeller with the appropriate programming to act as a USB adapter to communicate the PC with the transceiver and control it. So as far as the software is concerned there would be little change since the transceiver and propeller combination will act just like the XBee or Bluetooth USB adaptors.

To implement the error correction and so forth the PC-side Propeller would implement all the *packet wrapping* needed to send to the remote hardware + firmware. The firmware on the hardware side would need to have that extra *layer of packet wrapping* as well. However, if this is accomplished properly all our firmware that we have developed in this book would not be affected except in that we would need to use a replacement object for the FDS. The new object would provide the RX and TX methods that the FDS provided. As far as our firmware is concerned there would be very little change; only baud rates and replacement for the FDS.

The replacement for the FDS takes care of the packeting layer by adding some headers and trailers around the actual data bytes. These added bytes will be used on both sides to carry out all the CRC checks, Ack/Nack, addressing and packet resending aspects of a robust communications protocol over a noisy medium such as RF.

In fact this is exactly what the XBee and EBT devices do. So all we would be doing is to create our own equivalent of these two devices. Except it would be our own protocol and we would have flexibility. Nevertheless, it is more cumbersome, more expensive and the baud rate is low. Reinventing the wheel is only a good option if you really need an extra special wheel.

Figure 9.6: RF transceiver unit

The RF Advantage

Using RF transceivers to achieve wireless control with our system has the advantage of
1.   Long range. Especially if UHF is used.
2.   Ability to broadcast.
3.   More versatility since we have our own error correction protocol and it can be what we want.
4.   Opens up possibilities for control of space or submarine vehicles.

The RF Disadvantage

1.   The hardware and firmware have to be modified to accommodate this option.
2.   Too much hardware is needed to implement a PC-side transceiver.
3.   The baud rate is limited to a maximum of 9600.
4.   The transceiver is a Half-Duplex device. You can only transmit or receive one at a time not simultaneously. In fact this does not affect our protocol.
5.   There is no error correction or packet resending. We will have to create our own protocols on both the firmware and PC sides. You cannot really make do without this since all RF communications are noisy and bit loss or inversion is very likely to occur.

9.1.4 Summary of the Wireless Options

Regardless of which system you use, the end result is that:

- ❑ The hardware will now use the RX and TX pins on the transceiver hardware in place of the PropPlug.
- ❑ The baud rate may have to be changed on the firmware and software.
- ❑ If the transceiver requires a little more software control than was used with the PropPlug, like for instance an initialization sequence or some handshaking then the firmware will have to achieve that.
- ❑ The PC side will have to undergo some onetime setup procedure to install the dongle or other hardware required to actuate the PC-side transceiver and make it available as a com port.
- ❑ The software will have to use the new com port in place of the one that was used for the PP. Also the baud rate may have to be changed according to the new hardware.

All of the above is not complicated at all. More importantly, the protocol, firmware, software and system we have developed would not have to undergo any major alteration.

Converting our system to a wireless one imparts it with versatility and utility that makes it a powerful setup for many projects. On a robot it becomes a vastly viable robot that can be controlled with an easy to program and yet AI capable language (e.g. RB) enabling the robot to perform more interesting projects. But what is even more advantageous is that when we need to reprogram the robot to do different things we just change the software, not the robot's firmware. This makes it possible to use the robot in a less burdensome manner. Also (as you will see in Chapter 10) with RB's inbuilt simulator and simulator protocol you can try out the algorithms safely and effectively on the simulator, then with the addition of one line of code start controlling the real robot.

9.2 Wi-Fi & Internet

Another way we can provide remote control to our system is by using the TCP or UDP networking protocols. Moreover, this option provides limitless range. With the wireless system we are limited to line of sight and range of the device. With the TCP/UDP option the controller PC can be halfway around the world away from the hardware.

This is not an idea to take lightly. As you will see shortly, with **surprisingly few lines of code** we can give our system the ability to run software on one PC controlling hardware connected to another PC either directly or wirelessly (as in Section 9.1). The hardware-side PC can be within the same LAN or even in a LAN across the Internet. Moreover, either side may be connected directly to the LAN router or wirelessly using Wi-Fi.

Figure 9.7 illustrates the various possible combinations for effecting this amazingly versatile methodology. Our system as we have designed it so far will not require any change whatsoever in the firmware side. All the changes are to be implemented in the RobotBASIC software, and besides, these changes are completely simple thanks to the power RB provides.

9.2.1 TCP and UDP Networking Protocols

TCP is a networking protocol using the Client/Server model. UDP on the other hand utilizes the peer-to-peer model. UDP is an adequate protocol but is not as robust as TCP. It is sufficient if you are going to limit your connectivity to within a LAN but not across the Internet. Using a UDP connection over the Internet requires an additional protocol layers to assure communications reliability. A TCP connection already has all the reliability assurance needed.

Our system functions just as well with UDP or TCP due to our protocol. It provides an additional layer for data packet synchronization, which is one of the shortcomings of UDP. A UDP packet sent earlier may arrive at the destination later than one sent later. Our protocol provides a solution to the problem by sending out a few bytes and then waiting for a reply before sending the next packet. The outcome is that our protocol works equally with UDP or TCP.

We will not use UDP in this book. If you wish to do so, you can find out all about UDP and TCP in a document from our web site called RobotBASIC_Networking.Pdf[57]. The document has many projects and intricate details explaining how to implement control across the Internet and LAN using TCP and UDP. You should read it along with this chapter to assure maximum proficiency in all aspects of RB's networking facilities.

We will not go into the details of how to setup *Port-Forwarding* to enable across the Internet communication through firewalls and routers. This is all explained in the aforementioned PDF. Here we will assume that you have read it and are able to use RB to communicate between two computers either on the same LAN or across the Internet. We will only deal with how to use RB's Internet commands and functions to add to our system the ability to control hardware from a PC other than the one directly or wirelessly connected to the hardware.

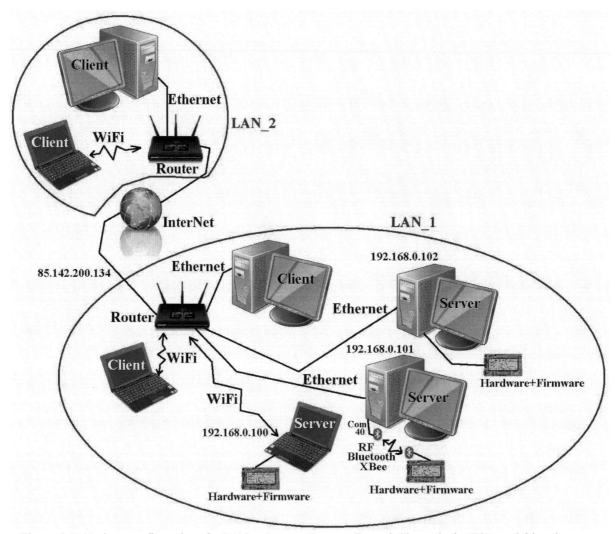

Figure 9.7: Various configurations for LAN or Internet Remote Control. Shown is the TCP model but the same topology would also apply to UDP.

9.2.2 The Topology

At the top of Figure 9.8 is a depiction of the system we have been using thus far in the book. The laptop controls the hardware + firmware through Link-A using an RB program (software). In Section 9.1 we showed how Link-A can be made wireless. In this section we want to transform our setup to be as depicted in the lower section of Figure 9.8. We will use TCP, so one computer has to be a *client* and the other has to be a *server*. The software application will be migrated over to a remote PC which is the *client*. Some modification of the software will be required to make it run over the TCP link in place of the serial link as before.

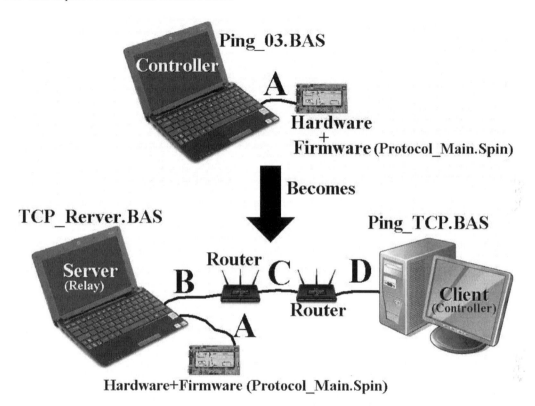

Figure 9.8: Converting our setup to work over a LAN or the Internet.

The PC controlling the hardware is now the *server*. It no longer runs the hardware control software. Instead it runs specialized software acting as a *relay* between the *client* PC and the firmware on the hardware. This specialized software is called TCP_Server.Bas and is the same regardless of the controller software running on the client and regardless of the hardware being controlled locally by the server. The server receives the command and parameter bytes from the *modified control software* running on the client PC and relays them to the *unmodified firmware* on the hardware. The server also receives the 5 bytes from the firmware and relays them to the client PC.

Notice that in the setups of Figure 9.8 there are the links:
> A: can be either a direct wired link (e.g. PP) or a wireless link (e.g. XBee).
> B: can be a directly wired Ethernet link to the router or a Wi-Fi wireless link.
> C: can be a non-link in that the two routers are actually the same router, or it can be a link across the Internet between two separate routers.
> D: can be a directly wired Ethernet link to the router or a Wi-Fi wireless link.

Each link can be one of two possibilities. There are 4 links. So there are 16 possible combinations of the setup.

As you can see we need to modify the controller software application for each application. However, the TCP_Server.BAS software is the same for all. We will develop this new software and you can use it to act as the relay software regardless of the firmware or the controller application as long as they both follow our protocol.

The Software Side

Remember that in our protocol the RB software sends two bytes to the firmware and then expects 5 bytes back. In the setup at the top of Figure 9.8 the RB software sends its two bytes on the USB port that is either directly connected to the hardware using the PropPlug or indirectly using the XBee. When it looks for the bytes to be received it also looks on the same com port.

When we separate the control program to a PC across the LAN or Internet there will be no com port to use for sending/receiving. Instead there will be an Ethernet link from the PC to a router. The link may be a direct Ethernet wired link or it can be a wireless Wi-Fi link. The final outcome is that the PC is linked to a router and is able to send TCP packets.

When the program wants to send its two bytes it will have to send them over the Ethernet link; likewise for receiving the 5 bytes. So in our RB control program such as Ping_03.Bas we will have to change the sending/receiving commands from serial commands to networking (TCP) commands.

The Hardware Side

As far as the hardware + firmware we used a connection to the PP or XBee to effect the communication with the PC running the RB control program. But now we cannot use that since the control program is now across the LAN/Internet.

What we need is a method for our firmware to receive/send across the LAN/Internet. There are many devices that provide an easy way to implement a TCP stack on a microcontroller such as the Propeller. One such device is the Spinneret Web Server[58]. However, this device does not provide Wi-Fi and the hardware would have to be wired directly to a router.

There is a very effective and amazingly simple to implement method for providing our hardware with a link to the LAN/Internet without any change to the hardware or firmware. *No change whatsoever*. Neither the hardware nor the firmware would have to be changed.

The method is to use a *relay* PC. The hardware communicates with the relay PC as if it were the controller PC. As far as the firmware is concerned it does not care at all what the controller PC does. As long as it receives the two bytes and is able to send the 5 bytes back, the firmware does not care what the controller PC does with the 5 bytes and neither does it care how the controller PC gets the two bytes the firmware receives. As far as the firmware is concerned the PC sending to it and receiving from it is the controller PC and it does not care what it does to effect the communications protocol. No changes at all are needed to the firmware and hardware to communicate with the *relay* PC whether it is directly or wirelessly linked.

This relay PC receives from the control program over the TCP link the two bytes and sends them to the firmware across the serial link. It then receives from the firmware the 5 bytes and sends them across the LAN/Internet to the RB program. This relay PC can be directly wired to the router or using a Wi-Fi link.

The relay PC runs a special RB program (TCP_Server.Bas) that effects all the serial communications as well as the TCP communications.

The Client and the Server

In our arrangement using the TCP protocol (bottom of Figure 9.8), the PC running the control software (e.g. Complete_System_Tester_TCP.Bas) will be the *Client* side. The PC that acts as the relay PC and connects to the hardware is the *Server* side.

The server PC will have to have a specialized program that sends/receives bytes to and from the client PC on the TCP link and then sends/receives those very same bytes to and from the hardware across the serial link (TCP_Server.BAS).

The control software will have to be changed so that instead of sending/receiving on a serial port it will do so on a TCP port.

The Required Modifications

The required changes to the Control Application Software (e.g. Ping_03.Bas) are:

❑ Change the send/receive commands to do so using TCP commands instead of serial commands.
❑ Add the relay program to run on the relay (server) PC.

The required changes to the firmware are:

❑ No changes are needed.

The required changes to the Hardware:

❑ No changes are needed.

The required changes to the link between the hardware and the PC:

❑ Since the relay PC is acting as a surrogate controller, no changes are required to the connection hardware.

Requirements to add the Networking ability:

❑ The client PC has to be linked to a *router* with a Wi-Fi or direct Ethernet link.
❑ The server PC has to be connected to a router with a Wi-Fi or direct Ethernet link.
❑ Two routers connected to the Internet if you want to effect across the Internet control. If you only need LAN control then only one router is needed and it does not need to be connected to the Internet.

An Example Topology

To illustrate the power of this option imagine you have a robot with the hardware and firmware similar to that developed in Chapters 7 and 8. You have done all the testing you need. You then made it wireless as we did in Section 9.1 then you tested again and all is working.

Now you move the control program to another PC and do the required changes to it as we will describe later. This PC is now called the Client PC. You also install on the old PC the new server software that will be described later. This PC is now called the Server PC.

After accomplishing the above you run the server program which will start listening on the TCP for incoming bytes. Then you run the control program (on the Client PC) which will start sending and receiving to and from the relay program (Server). The server will also send to and receive from the robot over the wireless serial link.

The outcome is that we have a robot that can be controlled from a PC either across the Internet half way around the world or in a different building. If the robot is big enough you can dispense with the RF link and have the Server PC onboard the robot with a Wi-Fi link to the router.

A Testing Topology

For the sake of testing and experimenting it would be inconvenient to keep moving between two PCs, also you may not have two PCs available. Can you still do all the required testing? Indeed you can. This is yet another testament to RB's versatility and power. Just as you can run two programs on the same PC simultaneously, you can run two versions of RB on the same PC, simultaneously. You can run two instances (or as many as you want) of RB's IDE on the same PC. You will have to do some rearrangement and organization of the windows to see all the output simultaneously but that is what you do anyway with other software.

> ⓘ Now you can dispense with the second PC. You can run the RB client software as well as the RB server software on the same PC. This way the Server and the Client PCs are the same PC running two instances of RB and each instance has the required RB program.

When the client software runs it will still be sending the two bytes through the router, but now the router will route the bytes back to the same PC and the server software will receive them just as if the two programs where running on different PCs. The server will then send the two bytes to the firmware on the serial com port.

When the hardware sends the 5 bytes they will be received by the server software on the serial com port. The server will then send the 5 bytes to the router. But now the router will send them back to the same PC and the client software will receive them, completing the protocol just as we need.

ⓘThe fact that the Client and Server software are running on the same PC makes no difference as far as the routing of the data through the router. The outcome is now we can view the actions of the Server and Client on the same screen on the same PC and we do not have to keep moving from one PC to another.

ⓘOnce development and testing are over, you ought to procure another PC and run the system on two PCs across the LAN. After that you ought to arrange with a colleague to run the Client software on his PC on his LAN across the Internet to a LAN with your PC acting as the Server and linked to the firmware + hardware.

⚠To accomplish across the Internet control you will need to know how to setup your router to carry out *port forwarding* to allow for Firewalls and IP address masking and so forth. All this is explained in detail in the document RobotBASIC_Networking.Pdf[57] which is requisite reading to appreciate the programming in the next section.

9.2.3 IP Address and Port

You are expected to have read RobotBASIC_Networking.Pdf[57] and therefore very little detail will be given about networking with RobotBASIC. We urge you to read this document since the information in it is vital for the proper understanding of what is to come.

An important thing to realize with networking is that for a client to be able to link to a server it has to know two things:
1. The Server PC's IP address.
2. The Port the Server Program is using.

The above data are straight forward if the client PC and the server PC are both on the same LAN (i.e. sharing the same router). However, if the two PCs are on separate LANs (i.e. different routers) then the above two pieces of information are much more complicated to obtain and arrange. How to do that is explained in the reference PDF document above.

ⓘFor the purpose of our programs it is immaterial how you obtain the IP/Port combination as long as you have the correct values. As you will see in the server program below, when it starts it will display the Local IP address and port number. But keep in mind that the Local IP address is the one to be used in the client program *only* when the client and server are local to each other (using the same router).

⚠Remember that you have to do more work to obtain the proper IP Address if the PCs are on different LANs and also that you have to set the router on the server side to perform *port forwarding* to forward the communication to the server.

We will not concern ourselves with the details of across the Internet communications; we will just use LAN addresses. The programs are not affected at all. All you have to do to make the same programs work with PCs on different LANS is to replace the IP address on the client software with the correct one instead of the one reported by the server program. All this is expounded upon in fine detail in the above PDF document.

9.2.4 The Server Program

The server program we develop here implements the strategies discussed in Section 9.2.2. The program is not GUI nor does it need to be so. In fact making it GUI would be counterproductive. The program is supposed to be a *relay* between the client PC and the firmware. Therefore we want it to be as fast as possible. This means that the program should in fact do the minimal possible processing to minimize the time between receiving a byte from the client and sending it out to the firmware and vice versa. Nevertheless, all you have to do to make it GUI is add the GUI programming elements; the functionality requirements for it to act as a relay between the client and the firmware remain the same regardless of the user interface.

The program establishes a serial link to the firmware then starts listening over the TCP port. It also displays the Port number and IP address it is using so that you can set them on the client side. Also it clears the serial as well as the TCP buffers just in case there were leftover data from previous operations.

The program then repeats the following tasks forever:
- ❑ Display the status of the TCP link for diagnosis purposes.
- ❑ Checks if there are any bytes in the TCP receive buffer. If there are any it reads them and sends them out through the serial port.
- ❑ Checks the serial receive buffer and if there are any bytes it reads them and sends them out through the TCP port.

> ℹ This simple short program running on the server is all that is needed to act as a relay between the Propeller hardware + firmware and the control application program running on the client (remote) PC. The program is the same regardless of the software application on the client and regardless of the hardware + firmware as long as they obey the protocol.

> ℹ Due to the design of TCP_Server.Bas it can act as a server (relay) for any protocol that you are likely to devise. See Chapter 11 for how the server still works with the quite different sending and receiving that occurs on some of the extended commands in the extended protocol of Chapter 11.

TCP_Server.Bas

```
//TCP_Server.Bas
SerialPort = 16        //change this per your system
SerialBaud = br115200  //and this
TCPS_Port = 50000      //change this if you need to do so
xystring 10,10,"IP:",TCP_LocalIP();"Port:",TCPS_Port  //show Local IP address
xystring 10,50, "Status    :"
Main:
  setcommport SerialPort,SerialBaud   //connect to the serial port
  tcps_serve(TCPS_Port)               //start the Server
  TCPS_Read() \ clearserbuffer        //clear both buffers
  while true
    xystring 100,50,TCPS_Status(),spaces(30)      //display status
    if TCPS_BuffCount() then  serout TCPS_Read() //if TCP bytes send to serial
    CheckSerBuffer n
    if n then Serin s \ TCPS_Send(s) //if serial bytes send them to TCP
  wend
end
```

9.2.5 The Client Program

To easily understand the changes required in a program that will run through the LAN/Internet and communicate with the firmware using our protocol, we will develop a simple program. Thus we can see the changes without the burden of complexity. We will develop a program that will turn the motors forward for one step in a continuous loop. We will first see what it looks like in the normal format using the serial port to perform normally as we have been doing all along. The program is later converted to function over the TCP. This way you can see what is required. Later we will modify a program we developed in a previous chapter to show that changing a complicated program is not much more work. The same steps taken to convert the simple program apply regardless of the complexity of the software application.

The Serial Link Program

TCP_Tester_Normal.Bas will cause the wheels to turn repeatedly for one step. Notice the **SendCommand()** subroutine. This subroutine performs the tasks of sending out the two bytes and then receiving the 5 bytes. It does so using the serial port as normal. Run the program as we have been doing all along using Protocol_Main.Spin for the firmware.

TCP_Tester_SerialLink.Bas

```
//TCP_Tester_SerialLink.Bas
//works with Protocol_Main.Spin
Port = 16 //change this as per your system
Main:
  setcommport Port,br115200
  while true
    call SendCommand(6,1)  //move the motors forward one step
  wend
End
//=====================================================
sub SendCommand(C,P,&s,&n)
  Serialout C,P   //send the two bytes
  serbytesin 5,s,n //receive the 5 bytes with timeout
return (n == 5) //return true or false depending on number of arrived bytes
```

The LAN Program

Before we run TCP_Tester_LAN.Bas let's discuss the code. Study the listing below and try to figure out what it accomplishes. It ought to be self-documenting since RB's syntax is very intuitive.

Compare it with TCP_Tester_Normal.Bas. The LAN program has a few more constants defined at the top. The **Main** section is almost the same except that it initializes a connection to the Server instead of the com port. To be more thorough here we ought to test for success and issue a message if the connection is not successful. We left this out for simplicity.

The primary difference between the two programs is the **TCP_SendCommand()** subroutine. The new subroutine will do the communications over the TCP. The first thing is to clear the TCP receive buffer to discard any bytes from a previous communication. Then the command code and parameter bytes are sent over the TCP link to the server.

The variable **s** is cleared and the receive count is zeroed, then the current serial communications timeout period is obtained and assigned to the variable **T** with an additional 150 ms to allow for the time to transfer the bytes from the server to the client. This value in **T** will be used to monitor a timeout in case the 5 bytes never arrive. Remember with the serial link we checked for the 5 bytes with a timeout. This mechanism will do the same for the TCP link and will keep to the same timeout duration as the serial link but with an additional 150 ms to allow for the extra relaying.

We then start a timer to act as a stopwatch and enter the **_polling_** loop where the buffer is checked for the correct number of bytes (5) to arrive. When they arrive they are extracted and put in the by-reference variable **s** to pass them back to the caller code. Also the number of bytes is stored into the other by-reference parameter **n** again to pass it back to the caller code. The subroutine returns true or false depending on if 5 bytes were received or not.

This subroutine is really all we need for other programs to convert them for LAN use. We need to change all calls to the **SendCommand()** subroutine to the **TCP_SendCommand()** subroutine. Of course we also need to connect to the correct server and remove any serial port related code. In Section 9.2.7 we will see how to do all this for a more complex program we developed in a previous chapter.

> We will add the subroutine **TCP_SendCommand()** to the Instruments.Bas include file from Chapter 8.1.4 so that many other programs can use it.

TCP_Tester_LAN.Bas

```
//TCP_Tester_LAN.Bas
//works through the LAN with the Protocol_Main.Spin
//Over the LAN or Internet
//Port = 16 //change this as per your system
TCPS_IP = "192.168.0.100" //change this to the correct server's IP address
TCPS_Port = 50000  //change this if you change the one in the server
Main:
  //setcommport Port,br115200
  TCPC_Connect(TCPS_IP,TCPS_Port) //connect to the server
  while true
    //call SendCommand(6,1)  //move the motors forward one step
    call TCP_SendCommand(6,1)  //move the motors forward one step
  wend
End
//=======================================================
sub SendCommand(C,P,&s,&n)
  Serialout C,P   //send the two bytes
  serbytesin 5,s,n
return (n == 5) //return true or false depending on number of arrived bytes
//=======================================================
sub TCP_SendCommand(C,P,&s,&n)
  TCPC_Read()                 //read the buffer to clear it
  TCPC_Send(char(C)+char(P))  //send the two bytes
  s = "" \ n=0
  GetTimeOut T \ T += 150     //get the actual timeout limit and add
                              //150 ms to allow for processing
  t=timer()                   //start a timer
  repeat                      //wait for the 5 bytes to arrive with timeout
    if TCPC_BuffCount() != 5 then continue  //if not arrive keep waiting
    s = TCPC_Read() \ n=5     //if arrived get them from the buffer
    break                     //since bytes have arrived then end the loop
  until timer()-t > T         //repeat until timeout
return (n == 5) //return true or false depending on number of arrived bytes
```

9.2.6 Running the LAN System

To run TCP_Tester_LAN.BAS do the following:
- ❑ Make sure Protocol_Main.Spin is compiled and uploaded to the hardware using F11. You can use F10 but we will be resetting the Propeller for a robustness test later. Besides, the firmware is now stable and you will not need to do any more changes, so it should be loaded in the EEPROM for all future work.
- ❑ Make sure that the hardware is connected to the Server PC either using the wired (PP) method or the wireless method.
- ❑ Make sure TCP_Server.Bas is running on the server. When it runs note its IP address and Port number as displayed. You need these to set them in TCP_Tester_LAN.Bas before running it.
- ❑ If you are going to use another PC then move to that one. If you are going to use the same PC as the client and server then start another instance of RB's IDE.
- ❑ Load TCP_Tester_LAN.Bas and edit the **TCPS_IP** and **TCPS_Port** variables to be the correct values as displayed by the Server program.
- ❑ Run the program.
- ❑ You should now see the motors on the hardware moving.

You may wish to swap over to the server's window and watch how the displayed messages reflect the status of the link. Also do one more thing that will impress you (we hope). Switch the PPDB off then wait a few seconds then switch it back on and note how control is resumed without having to reset either the server or the client programs.

⚠️That is all there is to it. You may not realize it but you have just accomplished an amazing feat. With just a few lines of code you managed to control hardware across a LAN (and wirelessly, if you did the wireless connection). This is not a small accomplishment, and it was all made possible because of a well-designed firmware and software system with the help of the great Propeller Chip and RobotBASIC's power and ease.

9.2.7 Converting a More Complex Program

To illustrate converting a more complex program we will do so for Ping_03.Bas. The new version is listed below and is called Ping_TCP.Bas. All the new and modified lines are in highlighted code. We have also converted the following files; they are not listed but you will find them in the downloadable Zip file. Study them to see how they are converted in a very similar manner to Ping_TCP.Bas. The subroutine **TCP_SendCommand()** is what makes it all very simple (it is now in the Instruments.Bas include file).

Command_Turnaround_TCP.Bas
Compass_Animation_TCP.Bas
Complete_System_Tester_TCP.Bas.
H48C_Plane_TCP.Bas
Piano_TCP.Bas
Ping_TCP.Bas
Pots_TCP.Bas
Servomotrs_TCP.Bas
Turret_Radar_TCP.Bas

ℹ️You may also be especially interested in Complete_System_Tester_TCP.Bas. When this program runs over the LAN/Internet you will be able to appreciate the power of combining RobotBASIC with the Propeller Chip, but above all the utility of a good well designed protocol.

ℹ️The program below uses the subroutine **TCP_SendCommand()** we saw in Section 9.2.5 which is now residing in the include file Instruments.Bas.

Ping_TCP.BAS

```
//Ping_TCP.Bas
//works with Protocol_Main.Spin
//but over the LAN or internet
Port = 0 //change this as per your system
#include "..\Utilities&IncludeFiles\Instruments.Bas"
TCPS_IP = "192.168.0.100" \ TCPS_Port = 50000
tcpc_Connect(TCPS_IP,TCPS_Port)
Main:
  gosub Initialization
  while true
    call ReadPing(t)                  //get the time value from the propeller
    if ! ReadPing__Result then continue  //if failed loop back
    call mmDistance(,t,D)             //convert to mm
    n=getrbgroup("Units")-1           //get desired units
    x=Format(D*factors[n],"0.0####")  //convert to units and format
    call DrawSignal(Px,Py,t,x+unitn[n]) //draw beam and display value in
units
  wend
end
//------------------------------------------
Initialization:
  setcommport Port,br115200
  data units;"Millimeters","Meters","Inches","Feet","Yards"
  data unitn; " mm"," m"," in"," ft"," Yrds"
  data factors;1.,.001,Convert(.001,cc_MTOIN)
  data factors;Convert(.001,cc_MTOIN)/12
  data factors;Convert(Convert(.001,cc_MTOIN)/12,cc_FTTOYRD)
  AddRBGroup "Units",10,10,200,100,2,mToString(units)
  SetRBGroup "Units",1
  Px = 10 \ Py = 300
  call DrawPing(Px,Py)
  savescr
  Flip on
Return
//------------------------------------------
sub ReadPing(&P)
  P = -1
  //serialout 192,0                    //signal the Propeller
  //serbytesin 5,s,n                   //receive the value bytes
  call TCP_SendCommand(192,0,s,n) //this routine is in the include file
  if n < 5 then return false    //if error just return false
  P = (getstrbyte(s,4)<<8)+getstrbyte(s,5) //reconstitute the value
Return true
//------------------------------------------
sub DrawPing(x,y)   //draw picture of Ping device
  s = 30
  for i=-1 to 1 step 2
    line x,y+s*i,x+20,y+s*i,40,gray
    circlewh x+30,y-20+s*i,40,40,white,white
  next
  rectanglewh x-20,y-2*s,25,s*4,white,white
  rectanglewh x-2,y-s*2,10,s*4,green,green
Return
//------------------------------------------
```

```
sub DrawSignal(x,y,d,str)
  d *= 500.0/22000        //scale value to screen coordinates
  restorescr
  xx1 = x+20+CartX(d,dtor(20))
  yy1 = y+CartY(d,dtor(20))
  Line x+20,y,xx1,yy1
  xx2 = x+20+CartX(d,dtor(-20))
  yy2 = y+CartY(d,dtor(-20))
  Line x+20,y,xx2,yy2
  Line xx1,yy1,xx2,yy2
  if d > 3 then floodfill x+20+d/2,y,black
  xytext x,y+80,str,,20,fs bold
  flip
return
//-------------------------------------------
```

9.3 Summary

In this chapter we:
- Examined various ways to make the hardware remote from the controller PC.
- Used XBee transceivers to make the link wireless.
- Considered the Easy Bluetooth and D-Link dongle as an alternative method for wireless links.
- Considered pure RF modules but saw that they are not as convenient as the above two alternatives.
- Examined various configurations to implement LAN or Internet connection between the hardware and the controller PC.
- Developed a Server program to act as the server/relay between the hardware and controller PC.
- Converted previously developed control programs to work over the LAN/WAN.

RobotBASIC's Inbuilt Protocol

The firmware as implemented by Protocol_Main.Spin represents a complex and quite interesting system, with hardware that typifies devices likely to be encountered in applications such as a robot. In fact the PPDB as it is now (Figure B.4 in Appendix B) can be mounted on the chassis of a robot (e.g. Boe-Bot[59]) and we would be able to control it quite adequately. Let's have a look at what we have:

- Ultrasound Ranger on a Turret.
- Compass.
- 3xQTI line or drop-off sensors.
- Accelerometer.
- Pushbutton that can be replaced by a Bumper Switch[30] (See Figure 10.1).
- 2xPushbuttons that can be replaced with Infrared Proximity Sensors[31] (see Figure 10.2).
- 2x Continuous Rotation Servomotors.
- Piezoelectric Speaker.
- 2xPotentiometers that can be replaced with Photo Resistors[60] with an appropriate value capacitor, or even better with Photo Diodes[61]. Although this requires a slight change in the circuit, it is still an RC circuit just with a slightly different setup. Another possible device is a thermistor for heat source detection instead of light.

This collection of hardware enables us to drive the robot and determine its heading while avoiding objects and even following a line. One bumper would not be sufficient but you can very easily add more. We can even control an airplane or a walking robot. You may wonder how can this be accomplished when there is no specific code in the *firmware* that implements object avoidance or heading tracking or line following. There is no code that is in anyway specific to a robot. How can we make the system achieve robot specific tasks when there is nothing in the firmware that would carry out any such tasks? The answer, as you have seen throughout the book, is the *software*. What gives the system versatility and ability is the partnership between:

- Hardware
- Firmware
- Software

Our system is very much like a PC, which is a collection of hardware with firmware (OS and BIOS) and software applications. All we need to make our system *multifaceted* is to add different software, as you have already seen in previous chapters. In this chapter, we will use the same system in an interesting and novel manner.

Figure 10.1: Snap-Action Bumper Switch **Figure 10.2:** A very handy Infrared Proximity Sensor.

Normally, while programming new features on a robot, we
- ❑ Place the robot on a pedestal to prevent it from moving when the wheels turn.
- ❑ Connect it to the programming IDE on the PC (usually).
- ❑ Download a program we think is a working one.
- ❑ Unplug it.
- ❑ Take it off the pedestal and place it in the environment in which it is supposed to function (assuming we have one).
- ❑ Normally things will probably not function quite as expected.
- ❑ We need to make sure the robot does not fall off edges or cause damage or be damaged.
- ❑ Stop the robot, pick it up.
- ❑ Repeat the whole process with what we think is a fix for the latest bug.
- ❑ Often it is not easy to determine why the robot is not acting as expected and may have to iterate the process numerous tedious times, usually guessing at what fixes might work since we did not have an adequate means of diagnosing the problem.

Imagine that you have a system that allows you to experiment with robotic algorithms using a simulator. Moreover, imagine that the very same program you developed and verified using the simulator can now be run on a real robot painlessly and without having to go through the above quite cumbersome and tiresome process. Furthermore, while the program is running and the real robot is carrying out its tasks, you can collect telemetry from it and even command it to change its actions in real time while it is in the field and may even be inaccessible (e.g. submarine rover). Telemetry serves two purposes:
- ➤ Data about the environment and the sensory status of the robot. This data is an integral part of the robot's mission.
- ➤ Diagnostics data for the internal integrity of the robot's mechanisms.

These two sources of information make it extremely easy to diagnose any shortcomings or bugs in the robot or the algorithms it is executing.

Well, stop imagining, because that is exactly what we can now do. By following the methodology we have outlined in Chapters 5 and 6 and demonstrated in Chapters 7, 8 and 9 we can build a robot with any combination of actuators and transducers and then fully control it from a PC. The PC can run any software you wish to make the hardware combination you created do anything within its capabilities.

Despite the limitations of the hardware we utilized in Chapters 7 and 8, a robot fitted with it and our firmware can be an adequate robot. In this chapter we will use our hardware as a robot *emulator* to illustrate the efficacy of our protocol. However, the book *Enhancing The Pololu 3pi With RobotBASIC*[69] decisively proves the power of the **principles** outlined here while creating a very real, amusing and capable robot. The book improves upon the stock Pololu 3pi robot by implementing our protocol on the 3pi's ATmega328 microcontroller programmed in C. This further verifies the versatility and adaptability of our protocol proving that the details of the microcontroller, hardware or programming languages are incidental.

10.1 The RobotBASIC Simulator

One of the distinguishing features of RB is its integrated robot simulator. There are four books that deal with the RB simulator[62] and teach how to use it. There are also many YouTube video tutorials[63] showing how to use the simulator and RB's other features. So we won't go into too much detail here; we will just deal with aspects of RB's simulator that pertain to our strategy throughout this book. We will show how programs developed in previous chapters can be made to work through the simulator's protocol and how simulation programs can work with our hardware by changing the value of a single variable and using some data mapping techniques as we have seen throughout.

Let's start with a very simple example. The following is ***pseudo code*** for an ***algorithm*** that ought to make a robot – if we had one aptly equipped and easily programmable – move around forever in a square pattern:

```
Repeat the following forever
   Repeat the following 4 times
      Move forward 70 steps
      Turn about 90 degree to the right
```

It looks simple enough! Go put on the kettle and while your cup of tea is brewing mull over this ***thought experiment***. You have a robot with a nice microcontroller and two wheels with two motors. What would it take to make it perform the above algorithm? How much programming would you have to do? How soon do you reckon it will be from the moment you thought about making a robot do the above action before you actually see one doing it?

Type the following distinctly simple program in RobotBASIC and run it:

```
rLocate 400,300
repeat
   for i=0 to 3
      rForward 70
      rTurn 90
   next
until false
```

First, notice the amazing similarity between the pseudo code above and the actual implementation in RB's language. Second, notice how ***quick*** and ***easy*** it was to see a robot actually performing the devised algorithm. But this is not a real robot, you say. It is never going to be as satisfying as a real robot, you say. Fine, let's make it a real robot. We have all that great hardware we developed in Chapters 7. What would it take to make the exact same program above drive the real servomotors so that if the PPDB were mounted on wheels driven by the servomotors it would have moved as the simulated robot did? Initially, you might think that you need to add code to take care of sending the command code 6 over the serial port and then receive the 5 bytes and so forth; also the same for turning.

Use the PPDB system as we have done in Chapter 8 or 9 (wireless). Now, add the following two lines of code ***to the top*** of the above program. Make sure the value of **Port** is set to what you have been using to communicate with the Propeller and then run the program,

```
Port = 16 //change this as per you system
rCommport Port,br115200
```

What just happened? The simulated robot did not move as before. In its place the servomotors on the PPDB started moving. Had the servos been connected to the chassis of a robot it would have actually moved in a similar manner to the simulated robot. It may not in reality circumscribe a perfect square, but if the system were calibrated correctly it could have actually made a pretty good square.

How was this achieved? There were no **SerialOut** commands as we had so far in all the previous chapters. Try again to run the program above with the additional lines but set **Port** to 0. What happens now? The simulated robot is now moving. Change the number back to what it was and run the program again. Again the PPDB is the one doing the actions. This is how simple it is to make the hardware and firmware we have developed behave as if it were a robot.

Consider the versatility and potential power of the actions above:
1. You experiment with the simulator to test an algorithm.
2. Change **Port** from 0 to a valid port where there is a robot programmed with a firmware that obeys our protocol.
3. Run the program and the real robot starts moving.
4. To stop the robot all you have to do is stop the program; you do not have to go to it and switch it off.
5. You want to change the behavior.
6. Switch **Port** to 0.
7. You implement any program changes to do whatever new thing you wanted.
8. Go back to step 1.

Change the statement **rTurn 90** to **rTurn –90** and make sure **Port** is 0. Run the program and watch the simulated robot. It is now going round in squares with left hand turns instead of right hand turns. That is how simple it is to change the behavior of the simulated robot. Just as easily, you can also change the behavior of the ***emulated robot*** (the PPDB). Change **Port** back to the port number for your system; now the hardware without ever touching it or reprogramming it or uploading to it anything is behaving in a different manner.

Compare the above to the development cycle on a real robot using the traditional methods. There are more advantages that we will discuss in Section 10.4. But first let's see how the RB simulator protocol functions. Also let's see how convenient it is to use this built in protocol as compared to using the raw serial commands we were using in the previous chapters.

> (i) This, purely and simply, is the power of what we have achieved. You can make your robot do different things by just changing a few lines of code on a PC screen and immediately have your robot change its behavior without ever connecting it to anything or even touching it (if using a wireless link).

10.2 How Does RB's Protocol Work?

In fact, you already know how the RB protocol works. You have been using it all along since Chapter 6. Many of the commands and functions relating to the simulated robot have ***two modes*** of operation. In the normal mode they make the simulated robot move around and sense objects in the simulated screen environment. With just one additional line of code (issuing an **rCommPort** command with a valid port number) the very same commands and functions will switch over to the second mode. In this alternate mode, the commands will send two bytes over a serial communications link. The two bytes are (as you already know) a command code and a parameter. The command will then wait for 5 bytes to be sent back over the serial link. When these bytes arrive the command will use the first three bytes (except in some cases) as follows:
- ❑ 1st byte is interpreted as the state of the bumpers.
- ❑ 2nd byte is interpreted as the state of the infrared proximity sensors.
- ❑ 3rd byte is interpreted as the state of the line sensors.

Additionally the 4th and 5th bytes are used in some commands to be data specific to the command itself. For instance the **rRange()** function will use the 4th and 5th bytes as the measurement of the ultrasound ranger (the 4th byte is the MSByte). Some commands (e.g. **rGPS**) will not set the bumpers and other bytes. Instead these commands will use all 5 bytes as needed to return their own data. For example the **rGps** command will use the 1st and 2nd bytes to be the Latitude and the 3rd and 4th bytes to be the Longitude.

For example the command **rForward 1**:
- ❑ Sends command 6 with a parameter of 1.
- ❑ Waits for 5 bytes to come back with a timeout.
- ❑ If no bytes come back an error is issued.
- ❑ If the bytes arrive then the first three are used as described above and the last two are ignored.

The latest status values of the bumpers and so on are now also updated due to the call to **rForward**. So we can use **rBumper()**, **rFeel()** and **rSense()**. These functions will return the status of their respective sensors since the last time they were updated by any of the commands that do not use the full five bytes as data. It is important that these three values are always returned with every command (except for the occasional one) because they are sensory data used to decide how to move the robot; moving a robot usually ought to depend upon the current status of these sensors. That is why we designed the protocol to return their values in the 5 bytes send buffer. They are *critical* data.

The function **rRange(±50)** in contrast to the **rForward** command will also need to return a value. So it:
- ❑ Sends command code 192/193 with parameter 50.
- ❑ The parameter is used by the firmware to move a Turret so as to angle the Ping))) to the right or left (+ is right and the command code is 192, - is left and the command code is 193).
- ❑ It then waits for the 5 bytes.
- ❑ If no bytes arrive the function returns -1instead of a valid value (no error is issued).
- ❑ When the bytes arrive the first three are used as before.
- ❑ The 4th and 5th bytes are deemed to be the value of the ultrasound ranger. They are then reconstituted into a 16-bit number (using MSBF) and then that value is returned as the function's return value.

In the RB help file in the Robot Simulator section there is a detailed description of the codes for each of the commands and functions that use the protocol and how they will send the command and parameter. There are commands that have *two codes* depending on the parameter. For instance **rForward 1** will use code 6 with parameter 1 while **rForward -1** will send code 7 with parameter 1. This is because **rForward -1** is in fact a command to move backwards and so it is sent through the protocol as command code 7 not 6 but now the parameter is 1 not -1.

Table 10.1: List of RobotBASIC Inbuilt Protocol Command Codes

Command/Function	Code	Parameter	Updates Three Critical Sensors	Data Returned	Error
rLocate ne_X,ne_Y	3	ne_X	Yes	None	None
rForward +ne_Amount	6	ne_Amount	Yes	None	Halts program
-ne_Amount	7	ne_Amount	Yes	None	Halts program
rTurn +ne_Amount	12	ne_Amount	Yes	None	Halts program
-ne_Amount	13	ne_Amount	Yes	None	Halts program
rCompass()	24	0	Yes	Last two bytes	-1
rSpeed ne_Speed	36	ne_Speed	Yes	None	None
rLook({+ne_Angle})	48	ne_Angle	Yes	Last two bytes	-1
({-ne_Angle})	49	ne_Angle	Yes	Last two bytes	-1
rGPS vn_X,vn_Y	66	0	No	First 4 bytes	-1,-1
rBeacon(ne_Color)	96	ne_Color	Yes	Last Two bytes	-1
rChargeLevel()	108	0	Yes	Last two bytes	-1
rPen ne_State	129	ne_State	Yes	None	None
rRange({+ne_Angle})	192	ne_Angle	Yes	Last two bytes	-1
(-ne_Angle)	193	ne_Angle	Yes	Last two bytes	-1
rCommand(ne_Command,ne_Data)	ne_Command	ne_Data	No	String with 5 bytes	Empty buffer

Compare Table 10.1 above with Table B.1 in Appendix B. You will notice that many of the commands are the same code and the same requirements. This, of course, is not by happenstance; it was by design. That is why we had the codes we did for some of the commands. There are commands in Table 10.1 that do not have a corresponding one in Table B.1 and vice versa. The reason the firmware does not implement a few of the RB commands, is of course because they are not implemented in the hardware. The firmware protocol will not execute any command code that it does not recognize. It will ignore it, but will still return the 5 bytes primary send buffer with the first three bytes filled as normal.

As you saw when we added the compass and other hardware, all you have to do to expand the firmware is to add the hardware and then implement the few changes as you saw in Chapter 8 and then assure the same command code as in RB's protocol. Once this is accomplished, RB can then use the command through the inbuilt protocol.

The simulator protocol is made more versatile with the function **rCommand(Command,Parameter).** It sends the specified command and parameter and will return the received 5 bytes as a string buffer. If no bytes are received within the timeout then the string buffer is empty; no error is issued. It is up to you to check if the buffer is empty and handle the situation as needed. With **rCommand()** you can extend the simulator protocol beyond the commands in Table 10.1. So any commands in Table B.1 can still be executed. For instance the commands for setting the blinking rate of blinker LEDs, the on/off LEDs on P20..P18, the **L_StepTime**, and so forth, have no corresponding simulator commands. However, you can still execute them using the **rCommand()** function and extend the simulator's inbuilt protocol to do more tasks than just controlling the robot. As an example we can set the wheels' speed in the forward/backward movement to a mid-level speed using **rCommand(240,127).**

Of course you can still use the **SerialOut** and **SerBytesIn** methods to accomplish any interaction you wish. The function **rCommand()** in fact performs the sending and receiving for you implicitly. It is not unlike the **SendCommand()** subroutine we have seen in many programs in the previous chapters, but without you having to write the code yourself. You do not need to issue a **SetCommPort** statement since **rCommport** does the same thing.

10.3 The PPDB Hardware as a Robot Emulator

As you can see from Table 10.1 in Section 10.2, the RobotBASIC simulated robot has quite an array of devices that allow for building a variety of complex and fascinating projects:
   a)   Wheel motors that let it go forward backwards or turn right or left §
   b)   4x Bumpers †
   c)   5x Infrared proximity sensors †
   d)   3x Line Sensors (or 5 if you configure it to do so) §
   e)   Ranger on a turret §
   f)   Compass §
   g)   GPS ‡
   h)   Color Sensor on a turret
   i)   Beacon Detector
   j)   Battery Charge Level Detector

Let's look at what actual hardware we have on the PPDB as we have finalized it in Chapter 8:
   a)   Servomotors that can be commanded to go backward or forward or turn right or left §
   b)   Pushbutton on P5 †
   c)   2xPushbuttons on P7 and P6 †
   d)   3xQTI line sensors §
   e)   Ping))) on a turret §
   f)   Compass §
   g)   2xPots ‡
   h)   Accelerometer
   i)   Piezoelectric Speaker
   j)   Ability to move the motors forward or backward individually

Notice that items a, d, e and f on the simulator are directly supported on the hardware (items marked § in both lists). Also we can use items b and c on the hardware to **emulate** (in a limited manner and with some remapping) the simulator's corresponding items b and c (items marked † in both lists). We do not have a GPS on the hardware but we can use the pots to emulate the latitude(y) and longitude (x) values returned by the GPS (item marked ‡ in both lists). Even though of course they are not real GPS values we can pretend they are. Alternatively, if they are photo resistors or photo diodes, or thermistors you can use the **rGps** command to read them and use that in your algorithms to, say, follow a light source in a similar manner to line following. If you do add an actual GPS unit one day, then you would change the firmware to return the GPS readings in the command code 66. But then you would have to also add a new command to read the Pots.

Items h, i and j on the simulator do not have a possible candidate emulator on the hardware. Also items h, i and j on the hardware do not have an equivalent on the simulator.

Our PPDB is not exactly a real robot. However, it is real hardware and if it were on a real robot it would be able to work just like a real robot with quite a few capabilities. So what we will do is use the hardware we have as if it were a robot. We will use it as an **emulated robot**.

> This should not be a strange concept. If you wanted to experiment with controlling a Space Station for example you have three levels of design. You can start with a simulator to test all the control algorithms. Then move on to hardware that emulates a space station but it would be hardware here on earth that you can tweak and manipulate with ease and minimal costs. This will then be controlled using the simulator. Finally when the simulator is working and can control the emulator as equally well as the simulator you can go on to the real space station and most likely with minor changes the simulator's interface will work with the actual station as it did with the emulator and the simulator stages. In fact that is what engineers do all the time. Simulate – control using the proven simulator an emulation (prototype) – use the simulator user interface and algorithms to control the deployment system (functional hardware).

The motors will move and you will be able to observe their direction. The Ping))) will be the sonar, but since the PPDB is not moving you will need to bring objects up to it to see any reading changes. Alternatively, since it is on a turret, the readings will vary as the turret rotates. Additionally, the compass will be used but of course you will have to turn the PPDB by hand to see any heading changes since the PPDB is not actually a real robot able to turn and move (unless you did put it on a real robot). The accelerometer readings will change if you pitch and roll the PPDB board.

For the Bumpers we will use the button on the P5 pin and for Infrared Proximity Sensors we will use the P6 and P7 buttons. With this arrangement we would have only **one** bumper and with the way it is reported in the byte sent by the firmware it is in the first bit of the 8-bit (byte) value returned to RB. This is a slight problem. The simulator's protocol expects that there should be 4 bumper sensors and the 1st bit (LSBit) is the rear bumper, the 2nd bit is the right bumper, the 3rd bit the front bumper and the 4th bit the left bumper. So if we get back a byte with the 1st bit representing the button on P5 then it would be interpreted by RB as the rear bumper. Since with our limited hardware we want the pushbutton to represent the front bumper we need to **left-shift** (<<) the byte by 2 bits to make it become the 3rd bit; i.e. the front bumper.

This is an example of **data-remapping** and we could do this either in the firmware or in RB. So in the firmware' object Protocol_Reader.Spin we can modify the method **ReadByte0** to shift the **!inA[5]**. This is certainly possible. But for the purposes of generality and as a demonstration we will not do so. We will instead do the remapping in RB (see Section 10.4.2). The same would also have to be performed for the P6 and P7 pushbuttons because the simulator has 5 IR proximity sensors (see RB's help file for details). The two bits will again have to be shifted to correspond better to the arrangement on the simulated robot. However, we will not use the IR sensors and will not show this. But it is a similar process of data remapping as we do for the bumper above.

Do keep in mind that Protocol_Main.Spin and its sub-objects are the firmware for the hardware we have so far. We have seen how we can change the RB programs to make the hardware do different things. Similarly, we can also change the RB program to make the hardware behave as if it is a robot. Of course since the hardware is **not** a robot then it is in a way an **emulation**. We are using the pushbuttons to emulate a bumper and infrared sensor. So when we want to make the *emulated robot* think it is bumped into something we push the pushbutton on the PPDB or if we want to make the emulated robot think it has detected an object with the infrared sensor we will push the other button and so forth.

For the Sonar we will use the Ping))) but there is an additional detail to consider which will again entail data remapping. As we have it, the hardware reports the raw reading of the Ping))). Remember that to convert the reading to millimeters (or any other units) we need to apply a formula to the value (**mmDistance()** in programs of the previous chapters). Again we could have done this in the firmware. But for the sake of maximum flexibility and adaptability we have opted to do the mapping in RB and have the firmware always return raw data. In the simulated robot the **rRange()** function returns the distance to a simulated object as a number of pixels on the screen. If we are to use the **rRange()** for a real robot then some *scaling* (i.e. data remapping) will have to be performed to make the values have a meaningful relationship to each other as far as the algorithms are concerned (see Section 10.4.2).

We will use the Pots to simulate a GPS system. Therefore, their values will be returned in RB's **rGPS** command. Of course, you can also use them as actual reading of the pots in your programs if they were for instance photo resistors you can use the values to make the robot follow some light source. The compass will be returned by the **rCompass()** command.

We will use the **rCommand()** function to interact with the accelerometer and the speaker and other processes that do not have a corresponding simulator command.

To summarize:
- The Servomotors are driven with the RB's **rForward/rTurn** commands.
- The Ping))) is read using the **rRange(Angle)** function. *Data remapping* is needed. Also the turret is moved by the **Angle** parameter.
- The Pots are read using the **rGPS** command.
- **rBumper()** is one bit which is the pushbutton P5 but *data remapping* is needed to shift it to be the front sensor.
- **rFeel()** is 2-bits which are the pushbuttons P6 and P7 but *data remapping* is needed to shift them to be the front sensors.
- **rSense()** will read the QTI sensors.
- **rCompass()** will read the compass value.
- **rCommand()** will be used to read the accelerometer.
- **rCommand()** will be used to play notes on the speaker.
- **rCommand()** will be used to send additional commands to change parameters or light up LEDs.

You already saw in Section 10.1 how the **rForward** and **rTurn** commands on the simulator are also able to control the real hardware motors. In the next three sections we will see how programs from Chapter 8 that we used to test the Ping and turret and the compass as well as the QTIs can also be run directly from the simulator. The programs will also show how the simulator can be used to read the *emulated* bumpers and infrared sensors. After that we will show how the simulator can read devices on the hardware that do not have a corresponding simulator command and we will use the **rGPS** command to read the pots.

10.3.1 Ranger and Turret

Remember the program Turret_Radar.Bas back in Chapter 8.2.4? The program Turret_Radar_RB.Bas listed below shows how simple it is to do the same program using the simulator. Keep **Port** set to 0 for now. The only changes are the highlighted lines.

Turret_Radar_RB.Bas

```
//Turret_Radar_RB.Bas
//works with Protocol_Main.Bas
Port = 0  //set this as per your system
Main:
  rcommport Port,br115200
  rLocate 400,400
```

```
 rinvisible gray,red
  call RadarScreen()
  call Radar()
End
//-------------------------------------------
sub Ranger(Angle,&Value)
  m= "Comms Error"
  Value = rRange(Angle)
  if Value >= 0 then m = spaces(40)
  xyText 600,10,m,,10,,red
return (Value >= 0)
//-------------------------------------------
sub RadarScreen()
  for i=1 to 400 step 50
    arc i,i,800-i,800-i,0,pi(),2,gray
  next
  for i=0 to 180 step 20
    th = dtor(i) \ r = 400
    line r,r,r+cartx(r,th),r-carty(r,th),1,gray
  next
  savescr
return
//-------------------------------------------
sub Radar()
  j=-90 \ i=1
  while true
    call Ranger(j,V)
    if V < 0 then continue
    f = 1/sqrt(2)  \ if _Port then f = 400/23000.0
    V *= f \th = dtor(j-90)
    x = cartx(V,th) \ y = carty(V,th)
    circlewh 400+x-5,400+y-5,10,10,red,red
    j += i \ if abs(j)==90 then i= -i \ restorescr
  wend
return
```

Notice the **rInvisible** command. This command tells the simulator to ignore the colors gray and red. This is because we are drawing the radar screen markings and return spots using these colors. Without the command the simulator's ranger would see them as objects. To avoid this, we use the command to tell the simulator that these colors are not to be considered as objects.

The main change is in the **Ranger** subroutine. It now uses the **rRange()** function to read the distance instead of sending an explicit command over the serial port. If the simulator is active (**Pot = 0**) then the function will read the simulated distances. If the variable **Port** is set to other than 0 then **rRange()** would use the real Ping))) and the real turret and return real distances (actually the raw data is time in microseconds).

Notice in the **Radar()** subroutine how we now multiply the value returned from the ranger by a different factor when the simulator is active than when the real robot is active. To decide whether it is the real robot or the simulator the variable **_Port** is checked. Since we are inside a **call/sub** subroutine we need to specify that we need the global variable. So we use **_Port** instead of **Port** to indicate that the global variable is the desired one.

> ⚠️Call/Sub subroutines use *local-scoping* of variables. To access a *global variable* you have to prefix the variable's name with the operator _ to indicate a global variable not a local variable with the same name. See RobotBASIC_Subroutines.PDF[72] for a tutorial on the powerful features of Call/Sub subroutines in RB.

In order to draw the sonar data on the screen we need to scale the measured distance so as to make it fit within the allotted screen scale. Since the simulated ranger returns the range in pixels while the real ranger returns the reading in microseconds, we will need to scale these readings using different scale factors. The real ranger will return a value with a maximum of 2300; we know this from experience we gained using it in Chapter 7. What is the maximum return on the simulated ranger? In the Radar program we placed the robot at coordinates 400,400. So the maximum reading the simulated sonar can return is the distance to the corner of the screen. This would of course be **Sqrt(2)*400** (Pythagorean Theorem).

To scale a reading X ranging from 0 to N to a reading Y ranging from 0 to 400 we use the formula
$$Y = X * 400/N$$

So we need to multiply the ranger value by a factor F where F is 400/(sqrt(2)*400) in the simulated case (i.e. F = 1/sqrt(2)). In the real ranger case you might be tempted to use **mmDistance()** to convert it first to millimeters or inches before scaling. But that is entirely unnecessary. The scaling factor can be calculated for the pure raw return value without having to convert it to distance units. Since we know the maximum is 2300 then F = 400/2300.0. Notice that we use the floating point 2300.0 not just the integer 2300. This is to force a floating-point division rather than integer division which would not be correct. Look at the bolded lines in the **Radar()** subroutine.

Run the program with **Port** set to 0 and see how the simulated return is rectangular as expected since the room is rectangular. Now set **Port** to the value corresponding to the PPDB communications port you have been using and see that the same program is working with the real turret and Ping))) and that the plotted sonar returns are real objects.

> ⓘ This mechanism of using a different factor for the simulator than for the real robot is to do with the *data remapping* concept. It is necessary since the simulator's world coordinates and measurements are not the same as ones of the real world. To make the real robot's values correspond to the simulated values we need to data remap (*transform*) the values to keep them both to a *related reference scale*. We will see more of this later.

> ⚠ The program Turret_Radar_RB.BAS is not something to be taken lightly. You need to read this program carefully and make sure you understand its action well.
> - It demonstrates almost all the strategies, methodologies and procedures we have outlined in this book.
> - It decidedly demonstrates how you can relate a simulated environment to a real one and how *the same program* works with either environment by flipping a switch (**Port** value in this case).
> - It demonstrates how the PC can be a crucial and integral component in a sophisticated engineering project.
> - In short, *this program is the embodiment of what we are trying to achieve*.

10.3.2 Reading the Compass

The program Compass_Animation.Bas in Chapter 8.1.4 was used to test the hardware compass. The program below will do the exact same thing but using the simulator's commands. Run the program; make sure the variable **Port** is set to the port number for talking to the firmware.

Compass_Animation_RB.Bas

```
//Compass_Animation_RB.Bas
//works with Protocol_Firmware_Main.Spin
Port = 16 //change this as per your system
#include "..\Utilities&IncludeFiles\Instruments.Bas"
Main:
    rcommport Port,br115200
    rLocate 10,10
    flip on
    s = rCommand(24,1)  //see if there is a compass
    if length(s)==5
        if !getstrbyte(s,5) then print "no compass available" \Terminate
    endif
```

```
    //uncomment the following three lines to invoke a manual calibration
    //print "Calibration in progress...rotate two turns while level"
    //rCommand(24,2)
    //delay 20000
    AddCheckBox "Mode",430,230,"&Real Mode",1,0
    while true
        call DisplayCompass(!GetCheckBox("Mode"),rCompass())
      Flip
    wend
end
```

Now switch on the PPDB, move it about and watch how the heading changes. The above program is able to detect if there is a compass using the **rCommand()** function and then reads the real compass using the Simulator's **rCompass()** function.

Notice how we had to use **rCommand()** function to send the hardware the specific code #24 with a parameter of 1. Remember that this was the command code to check if there is a compass and the 5th byte retuned indicates 0 or 1 (see Table B.1 in Appendix B). However, when it came to reading the compass we used the simulator function **rCompass()**. No specific command code was needed since **rCompass()** took care of all that. But, since the RB inbuilt protocol commands do not have one for detecting if a compass is available (it is assumed to be available), we had to use the versatile **rCommand()** function that allows the RB protocol to be extendable.

Notice how simple it is to work with our firmware using the RB protocol. The program in Chapter 8.1.4 is not much harder than the above program, but not withstanding, RB's inbuilt protocol makes it extremely simple and seamless.

10.3.3 Reading the QTI Line Sensors

In Chapter 8.5.2 we developed QTI_Tester.Bas to test the QTI sensors. The program below will do the exact same thing using the simulator.

QTI_Tester_RB.Bas

```
//QTI_Tester_RB.Bas
//Works with Protocol_Main.Spin
Port = 16  //set this as per your system
Main:
  rcommport Port,br115200
  rLocate 400,100
  xystring 10,10," P5     P7,P6   QTIs"
  while true
   rForward 0
   xystring 10,30," ",rBumper();"  ",Bin(rFeel(),2);Bin(rSense(),3)
   xyText 100,100,Bin(rSense(),3),"",70,fs_Bold,White,Blue //for fun
  wend
end
```

Notice how the **rSense()** function is used to read the QTIs. But also notice how **rBumper()** is used to read the P5 pushbutton and **rFeel()** is used to read the buttons on P6 and P7.

From Section 10.1.1 above we saw that the QTIs on the hardware correspond to the line sensors on the simulator. This is why the **rSense()** function on the simulator will read the QTIs on the hardware when the simulator is switched over to the real robot mode. However, when it came to the bumpers and infrared proximity sensors we did not have real sensors on the real hardware that correspond to the ones on the simulator. We decided to make the P5 button emulate one bumper and to make the P7 and P6 emulate two infrared sensors. So that is why the **rBumper()** and **rFeel()** functions will now read the P5 and P7,P6 buttons.

Notice that in the original version of the program we did

```
call SendCommand(0,0,,A,B,C)
```

to send a null command that did nothing, but still caused the 5 bytes to be sent back. Then the bytes where used to display the QTIs and the buttons.

In the simulator version of the program we used

```
rForward 0
```

to be the null command. Forwarding 0 steps stops the motors if they are running and does nothing if they are not running. But this action causes the 5 bytes to be returned. We then use **rSense()**, **rBumper()** and **rFeel()** to read the bytes.

10.3.4 Other Devices

From the list in Section 10.1.1 all that is left on the hardware that we want to be able to use with the simulator protocol are the Pots, Accelerometer, Speaker and finally, turning the motors separately.

> (i) Even though pot readings have nothing to do with a GPS we designed it so that the **rGPS** command is used to read the pots as if they were GPS coordinates. The two numbers returned are the Pots' values but since we do not have a GPS we might as well use the **rGPS** command to read the pots for convenience. If you do add a GPS to your hardware you may want to add a new command for the Pots and of course do the real GPS with the **rGPS** command (66).

The accelerometer and Speaker have no convenient simulator commands that we can use to interact with them. So we will use the general simulator function **rCommand()**. This function will do the work of sending the command and parameter and receiving the 5 bytes back. The 5 bytes are returned as a string (buffer) where we can extract the individual bytes using the **GetStrByte()** function as we have been doing all along. But now, we do not have to do any explicit sending and receiving; it is all done for us.

Other_Devices.Bas will use the **rGPS** command to read the pots and the **rCommand()** function to read the Accelerometer and reconstitute the values and calculate the three axes g-forces. Furthermore, the program will turn the motors individually and play notes on the speaker.

Notice the subroutine **Read_H48C()**. Compare it to the same subroutine listed in H48C_Tester.Bas in Chapter 8.4.3. See how **rCommand()** is used instead of **SendCommand()**.

Use Table B.1 in Appendix B for the codes of the commands.

Other_Devices.Bas

```
//Other_Devices.Bas
//Works with Protocol_Main.Spin
Port = 16 //set this as per your system
Main:
  rcommport Port,br115200
  rLocate 400,100
  xystring 10,10,"Pot1     Pot2     gX          gY          gZ "
  j = 0
  while true
   rCommand(8+j,100)  //turn right/left motor forward
   for i=0 to 10
      call DisplayData()   //read and display Accel and Gps
      rCommand(73,i+74)    //play a note on the speaker
      delay 100
   next
   rCommand(8,0)          //stop
```

```
      rCommand(11-j,100)   //turn left/right motor backwards
      for i=0 to 10
         call DisplayData()   //read and display Accel and Gps
         rCommand(73,84-i)    //play a note on the speaker
         delay 100
      next
      rCommand(11,0)      //stop
      j = !j
   wend
End
//========================================================
sub DisplayData()
   rGps x,y
   call Read_H48C(0,,,,,xg,yg,zg)   //get and calculate the g-forces
   xystring 1,30,Format(x,"####0");Format(y,"####0")
   fmt = "#0.0000"
   xystring -1,-1,"   ",Format(xg,fmt);Format(yg,fmt);Format(zg,fmt)
Return
//========================================================
sub Read_H48C(&vRef,&xRef,&yRef,&zRef,&xG,&yG,&zG)
   xRef = 0 \ yRef = 0 \ zRef = 0
   xG =0 \ yG = 0 \ zG = 0
   if vRef == 0
      s = rCommand(70,1) //read vRef
      if Length(s)!= 5 then return false
      vRef = (getstrbyte(s,4)<<8)+getstrbyte(s,5)
   endif
   s = rCommand(70,0) //read the axes
   if Length(s) != 5 then return false
   xRef = (getstrbyte(s,1) << 4) + (getstrbyte(s,2) >>4)
   yRef = ((getstrbyte(s,2)&0x0F) << 8) + getstrbyte(s,3)
   zRef = (getstrbyte(s,4) << 4) + (getstrbyte(s,5) >> 4)
   xG = (xRef-vRef)*.0022   //convert to g-forces
   yG = (yRef-vRef)*.0022
   zG = (zRef-vRef)*.0022
return true
```

10.3.5 Handling Errors With the RB Simulator Protocol

When we used the **SerialOut** and **SerBytesIn** commands to send and receive data a timeout condition did not cause an *explicit error*. There was no halting of the program and an RB error message display. We handled the timeout by doing our own checking and handling of the situation by using a *controlled* form of displaying some kind of error indicator. For example in the Complete_System_Tester.Bas (and its earlier equivalents) we had a simulated LED light up.

When using the RB Simulator Protocol there is a slight problem. If there is a timeout during the execution of the **rForward** and **rTurn** commands there will be a *system error* issued by RB and *the program will be halted* (Figure 10.3). All the other commands and functions will not cause an error but will return a value that is inappropriate as the value of the function (see Table 10.1 above or Table B.4 in Appendix B). Of course the program will also slow down considerably since the timeout period has to elapse before the next statement is executed.

For the commands and functions that do not cause a system error you need to check the value returned and act accordingly. However, for the ones that cause a system error you may not want the program to stop. You may want to handle the error and keep on running. You can do this easily with the **OnError** command to divert any run time errors to an error handling subroutine where you can do whatever is necessary to handle the error.

Error_Handling.Bas illustrates how this works. Make sure the PPDB is on and loaded with the Protocol_Main.Spin firmware. Then run the program. It should start the motors running. Now turn the PPDB off. Within 5 seconds you should see a message as in Figure 10.3.

Now turn the PPDB back on again and uncomment the first highlighted line and then run the program again. Turn the PPDB off and see how the error is now handled. Repeat the process after having changed the **ErrorHandlingMode** variable to be 1. See how the error is handled differently.

Repeat the process but after having uncommented the third highlighted line. See how a normal programming error is now handled.

> ⚠️Beware that using **OnError** will cause *all* errors to be diverted to the handler routine, not just the simulator protocol timeouts. You must use **GetError** to check what error has caused the jump to the error handler and handle the ones you need to handle and then return. For the others you may need to display a message and halt the program since they would be programming errors rather than communications timeout error.

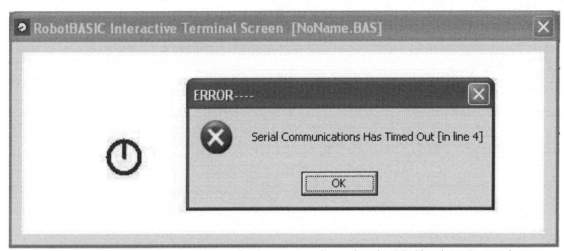

Figure 10.3: Example of a communications error when using the RB Simulator Protocol.

Error_Handling.Bas

```
//Error_Handling.Bas
//Works with Protocol_Main.Spin
Port = 16 //change this as per your system
Main:
  rcommport Port,br115200
  //onError ErrorHandler  //uncomment this line to handle errors
  ErrorHandlingMode = 0 //change this to 1 to change the method of handling
  rlocate 100,100
  while true
    rForward 1
    //print x  //uncomment this to cause a programming error
  wend
end
//------------------------------------------------------------
ErrorHandler:
  GetError E,M,LN,CN
  if E == 82 //comms error
    if ErrorHandlingMode
      xystring 500,10,"There is a comms error"
```

```
      else
        er = ErrMsg(M+Crlf()+"Check your system and press Retry to continue"+\
               crlf()+"Or press Cancel to quit the program","Error Handler...",\
                 MB_RETRYCANCEL|MB_ERROR)
        if er == MB_Cancel then Terminate
      endif
    else
      ErrMsg(M+" In line:"+LN+" Charater:"+CN,"ERROR Handler...",MB_OK|MB_ERROR)
      Terminate
    endif
    onError ErrorHandler
Return
```

10.3.6 Your Turn to Have a Go

You saw in Sections 10.3.1 to 10.3.4 how we converted previous programs to work with the RB Simulator Protocol (RBSP). It is now your turn to try doing the same. If you remember back in Chapter 7.8.8 we developed RobotMoves_12.Bas to exercise the movement of the motors and at the same time to read the Pots, Ping and the pushbuttons. At the time we did not have the QTIs but the very same program should work still with the new firmware and will read the QTIs.

Notice that without any change whatsoever, the program written for the old firmware still works with the new firmware. Also despite having a different arrangement of hardware, utilizing the same protocol enables us to read the new hardware even though we are using old software. Go back to RobotMoves_12.Bas and run it with the Protocol_Main.Spin firmware and see how it works.

Can you convert this program to work through the RBSP instead of raw serial commands? Try your best to convert the program. If you need any help, we have done the conversion for you; see RobotMoves_RB.Bas in the zip file.

Hint: Use Table B.1 in appendix B for the command codes.
Hint: To make the robot move we now use **rForward** and **rTurn**.
Hint: To read the 1st byte we now use **rBumper()** and the 2nd with **rFeel()** and the 3rd with **rSense()**.
Hint: In the old program the subroutine **SendCommand()** took care of reconstituting the required values. With the RBSP the commands of the protocol take care of the sending and receiving as well as reconstituting the values. You may no longer need to use the subroutine.

Another program you may enjoy converting to using the RBSP is the H48C_Plane.Bas from Chapter 8.4.3. It should be very similar to the above. However, for the H48C commands there are no equivalent RBSP commands and you need to use **rCommand()**. We have converted the program for you (H48C_Pane_RB.Bas) and it is in the zip file. Do not look at it until you have attempted to convert the original program.

10.4 The RobotBASIC Simulator Protocol Advantage

Three engineering disciplines are required in the design of a robot:
  ➢ Mechanical
  ➢ Electronic
  ➢ Software

The first two are of vital importance but limited duration. Once the robot's mechanical and electronic hardware is designed and manufactured the involvement of these two engineering disciplines comes to an end.

The software aspect is at two levels
  ➢ Firmware
  ➢ Artificial Intelligence

The firmware aspect of the software is also of limited duration. Once the firmware is designed and is working well with the electronics and the mechanics then there is nothing more to be done.

This leaves the AI level of software. This aspect of the software engineering of a robot should in reality never be over, as with a human being. Once a human is grown up there is nothing more in the biomechanical and bioelectrical aspects of the human body that change (except for the insidious deterioration due to aging and diseases – c'est la vie). However, mental development never stops (with some people at least ☺).

A closer analogy is to the PC. When you buy a PC the hardware is pretty much fixed and the OS is also mostly fixed (?). However, you are constantly installing new software to make it do new things. Using your computer is fun because you can change software. No one really enjoys changing the hardware or the OS. It is most probable that you don't much enjoy the interminable upgrading of the OS and you do not really relish forking out dollars for hardware. We bet that what you enjoy while using your computer is using new software that makes it do new things – a Flight simulator, a photo editor and of course, RobotBASIC.

So the same hardware + firmware become a new device by changing the software. It is not the aim to keep changing the hardware and the firmware. The aim is to change the software.

The same thing applies to robots. The fun is not to keep tinkering with the hardware and programming of the microcontroller on board (well, some may enjoy that as a goal in itself). Rather the aim is to make the robot do useful and interesting things. The enjoyment would be enhanced and the efficiency would be increased if we could achieve this goal with minimal tinkering with the hardware and minimal plugging and unplugging of the robot to keep changing its firmware.

That is exactly where RB comes into the picture. If we have a robot that has the right hardware and the right OS (firmware) we can then interact with it through RB programs to make it do new and interesting things. RB software makes the robot behave in different manners to do different and interesting things and all without having to modify the robot.

But the RobotBASIC advantage goes even further. The RB simulator provides another layer of enjoyment and effectiveness. With the simulated robot you can develop the software and try out its algorithms and nuances without the associated dangers to a physical robot that might be damaged when it does not behave correctly.

Furthermore, robots are expensive and you are more likely to be sharing the robot with others (perhaps in an educational environment). If you had to wait for your turn before you could develop your ideas you would be wasting much valuable time. With the simulator you can try out ideas, strategies and algorithms and when you do get a turn on the robot you can *immediately* try them out without having to translate to another language or reprogram the hardware.

As you have seen in Section 10.1, the ability of the RB simulator to transfer control to a real robot with the exact same software that was developed with the simulator is a major advantage.

As a teacher or club organizer you can develop a robot with all the hardware you need and then program the microcontroller with the firmware required to implement the protocol outlined in the previous chapters. Once this is achieved, you won't need to reprogram or reengineer the hardware on the robot again. You now have a platform that can be used to do interesting projects and to teach students all about robotics. This is easily accomplished with a PC running RB (or any other language you want).

You can use the simulator to *introduce* beginners to the whole concept of sensors and feedback control. Use the simulator to introduce *algorithmic development* principles. Then when the students/members are at a more advanced level you can *port* them over ☺ to the real robot. They can now use the real robot to do things without having to spend an inordinate time trying to build a robot. They do not have to be electronics engineers or mechanical engineers or experts in C and Assembly and microcontrollers. They can just concentrate on the software aspects in the convenient environment of the PC with all its advantages (keyboard, mouse, GUI, etc.).

Imagine if every time you wanted to teach a computer programming class, the participants had to build a computer from scratch first. How much time would be left over to teaching programming?

The day that *programming* robots becomes the focus, rather than *building* them, is the day more people will be interested in robotics. Once you reach the critical mass of innovators working on the Artificial intelligence aspects of the robot project and not only its low level engineering, we think an explosion in the robotics field will occur that will bring about future applications to rival the software engineering field.

> There are programmers today creating applications of paramount importance and utility who cannot distinguish a transistor from a resistor or a servomotor from a stepper motor. They are not electronic or mechanical engineers; yet, they make computers do amazing feats. We need the same level of expertise to be applied to robots. Give people a robot platform equivalent to a PC and let's see what innovations will result. With our proposed strategy and the methodology outlined in this book you can do precisely that. You can give robots that can be programmed just like a PC. The more we do this the closer we will be to that Robot-Lotus 123, or Robot-dBase, or Robot-Linux. And, once that occurs, robotic applications will boom onto the new frontier.

10.4.1 A Case Study

Let's illustrate the advantages of our strategy with a small project. Let's assume that we have a robot that has a sonar sensor and a bumper sensor both in the front of the robot. We want the robot to move around a room avoiding obstacles. We do not want it to get stuck and it would be nice if it managed to cover the whole room eventually.

The Design Advantage

We think about it and we come up with the following algorithm:

```
Repeat the following forever
  While there is nothing in front of the robot
    Move forward 1 step
  Decide to turn left or right randomly
  While there is something in front of the robot
    turn 1 degree in the decided direction
  Turn an additional random value between 20° and 50° in the same direction
```

To test the validity of the above algorithm, we will implement it using the RobotBASIC simulator with a simulated environment of a few obstacles. The program below is the first attempt:

Simulator_1.Bas

```
//Simulator_1.Bas
Main:
  GoSub Initialization
  repeat
    while rRange() > RangeLimit  //while path is not blocked
      rForward 1
    wend
    T = (random(1000)>500)*2 -1    //determine a random turn direction
    while rRange() <= RangeLimit  //keep turning until path is clear
      rTurn T
    wend
    rTurn T*(20+random(30))  //turn a little more in the same direction
  until false
end
//-------------------------------------------------
Initialization:
  RangeLimit = 30
```

```
    //draw some obstacle for the simulation
    erectanglewh 295,90,310,110,10,blue
    erectanglewh 700,400,100,140,10,blue
    erectanglewh 200,300,100,140,10,blue
    erectanglewh 600,230,100,40,10,blue
    rlocate 200,200
return
```

The **Initialization** subroutine creates some obstacles in the environment and defines a value for the ultrasound range to be considered as minimal distance to an obstacle.

We decide if there is something in front of the robot by using the sonar ranger (highlighted line). The reverse line is the way we decide to turn left or right. If the random number is bigger than 500 then the expression **(random(1000)>500)** results in 1 otherwise in 0. If we multiply that by 2 and subtract 1 the result is either -1 or 1, which determines if we turn left or right. Also notice that we turn until there is no obstacle as determined by the ranger and then also turn an additional random amount between 20 and 50.

With this simple and easily developed program we can try out our ideas on the RB simulator safely and conveniently and *on our own time*; we do not have to wait until there is a robot available to us. Notice the close analogy between the syntax of the program (**Main**) and the pseudo code of the algorithm. This alone is a major advantage.

> (i) Notice how the simulator enabled us to create an environment that may task the efficacy of the algorithm. With a real robot it may be inconvenient and expensive or untenable to create a good testing environment, let alone a *variety* of environments.

The Debugging Advantage

Upon running the program, straight away the robot crashes. It seems the Ranger is not working. So we add the following line just *after the repeat statement* to examine what the ranger is reading:

```
xystring 1,1, rRange(); spaces(20)
```

From this simple debugging ability we determined that the ranger is actually working but it may be that our limit for it is too small. So we increase the limit to 200, but that seems to not work either and besides the robot is keeping too far away from obstacles.

All this illustrates why the simulator is an indispensable tool. Imagine doing what we just did with a real robot and having to change its firmware. How could we even be able to read what its ranger is reporting? Even if we had an LCD on board what are we to do, follow it around trying to read the display? Maybe we can have it store its reading and then we can download and read them. Maybe we can have it send its readings to a PC wirelessly. If we are going to do this why even bother with programming the robot. Why not have the firmware as we have done in Chapter 8 and then we always know everything we want to know on the convenient PC screen and when we want to change programs we just change the RB program.

Can you now see how the system we have developed is a major advantage? Furthermore, combined with RB's simulator it is a "mega-major" advantage ☺.

Let's go back to the simulation. It seems we need to use the bumper sensor in addition to the sonar. Let's use the bumper to catch any sonar misses. So we change the line:

```
        while rRange() > RangeLimit
```
to
```
        while !(rBumper()&0%0100) && rRange() > RangeLimit
```

How we decide if there is something in front of the robot is now a combination of two things:
1. Bumpers
2. Ultrasound ranger

The reason we use a bumper is to make sure there is nothing that may have been missed by the ultrasound. Also notice how the bumper value is bitwise-ANDed (&) with 0%0100. This is because the simulator has four bumper sensors all reported in one byte where the third bit (bit 2) is the front bumper, so we mask out all the other bits from the value returned by the **rBumper()** function. When turning to move away from the obstacle we used just the ultrasound **rRange()** value.

> You now can see the advantages a simulator provides due to superior debugging tools during the algorithmic development stage.

> Remember on our hardware we only have one bumper sensor (simulated by the pushbutton on P5), and we are going to assume it represents the front bumper. So some *data mapping* is needed when we eventually move over to the real hardware (see later).

The Exhaustive Testing Advantage

Now run the new version. It seems to work, but will it eventually fail? Again, we have another illustration of the RB advantage. Even though the algorithm seems to be working now, we have only tried it for a short time and with only one environment. Can we try it out for a long time and with *various* random environments?

Imagine doing that with a real robot. How would you obtain various random environments for a real robot? How long do you have to stick around just watching it?

With the simulator we can do it so simply. Below is a new program that creates a random environment and lets the robot roam for a minute then tries out a new environment. We can run this program and leave it running for hours and that way we can try out many environments over many hours. If the robot never collides then we can be assured that the algorithm works. Change the value of **TimeLimit** to say 300 or 600 to let the robot try out each new environment for longer than just a minute (60).

> Note that the simulator provides options during the development stages that *cannot* be realized with a real robot.

Study how we create the random environment and note the use of the functions **vType()**, **Limit()** and **Random()**. Also the **KeyDown()** function is used to enable the detection of a spacebar press which a user can press to go to the next random environment instead of having to wait for the timeout. So if an environment is not to your liking then just press the space bar to go on to the next one.

> You do not need to stick around for the duration of the testing; you can go out to lunch. If the robot crashes it will halt the program and display a message. It will stay in that state until you come back. If when you come back from lunch the robot is still scurrying about then you know there was no failure. Your algorithm was tested with numerous environments and for a sufficiently long time on each. If no crash occurs then you can be reasonable assured the algorithm is a *robust* one.

Simulator_2.Bas

```
//Simulator_2.Bas
Main:
   GoSub Initialization
   while true
     if timer()-t > TimeLimit
        GoSub Initialization
        t = timer()
        waitnokey
     endif
     GoSub RoamAround
   wend
end
//-------------------------------------------------
RoamAround:
   while !(rBumper()&0%0100) && rRange() > RangeLimit  //while path is not
blocked
     if keydown(kc_Space) then t = 0 \ return
     rForward 1
   wend
   T = (random(1000)>500)*2 -1   //determine a random turn direction
   while rRange() <= RangeLimit  //keep turning until path is clear
     if keydown(kc_Space) then t = 0 \ return
     rTurn T
   wend
   rTurn T*(20+random(30))  //turn a little more in the same direction
Return
//-------------------------------------------------
Initialization:
   if !vType(FirstTime)
     t = 0 \ TimeLimit = 60000  //60 secs
     RangeLimit = 30
     LineWidth 10
     FirstTime = false
   endif
   clearscr
   //draw some obstacle for the simulation
   for i=0 to 3
     x = 50+ Random(700) \ y = 50+random(500)
     W = limit(random(400)+x,80,790)-x
     H = limit(random(300)+y,80,590)-y
     rectanglewh 50+random(750),50+random(550),W,H,blue
   next
   rlocate 30,30,135-random(45)
return
```

10.4.2 Implementation Onto the Real Robot

In addition to all the above advantages during the design stage, debugging stage, and the testing stage, we have one more advantage during the implementation stage. Implementation on a real robot is absolutely painless. There really is no actual implementation since there is no programming to be done on the robot. All the programming was already done when we created the firmware that implements the protocol.

To implement the algorithm on the real robot we just enable the communications link and start running the very same code on the real robot. There is no need to translate the code to another language. There is no need to plug the robot into a PC to program it; assuming, of course, that we have already accounted for *data remapping* in our program.

Sensory Data Mapping To RB's Requirements

When you move over from a simulation to a real environment there is an issue that has to be considered. Just as when you go from a scale-model to a real environment there has to be scaling of some static and dynamic properties to allow for the difference in areas and weights and so forth. Unless you have designed your simulation to the correct scale you will have to adjust parameters when switching over to the real control. This is just another application of *data mapping*.

Since the simulated RB robot works within the pixel limits of its screen environment, its scale reference is appropriately related to the dimensions of the screen. If the screen is 800x600 pixels and the robot has a diameter of 40 pixels, then the relationship of what a pixel is depends on the actual size of the real robot that will be simulated.

If our 40 pixels robot is simulating a robot with a 600 mm diameter then 1 pixel equals 15 mm (0.6 in). This means that the room the robot is in (screen) is 12 meters x 9 meters (39.4 ft x 29.5 ft). Anything that relates to distance in the real environment will have to be multiplied by this scaling factor to make it meaningful to the simulated robot and its environment.

The size of the simulated robot can be changed see the **rLocate** command.

We have already seen for example in the Ping))) case how we had to apply a formula to the reading returned by the firmware to make the reading have a meaning in distance. We also allowed for the formula to change if the temperature was different. We also saw how the reading of the pots had to be converted with a formula if we needed it to be Ohms.

With all the above conversions we could have applied them in the firmware before we transmitted the value. But we opted for the more versatile option of transmitting the *raw* data and applying the data mapping in RB because of its ability to do floating-point math. This way we won't lose accuracy and generality.

The exact same thing applies here with our *emulated* robot. We can go into the firmware and make it more apt as a robot and apply some conversion in the firmware itself. But that means we would lose generality and adaptability. We don't want to *fix* our firmware to be related *just* to the situation of the hardware being only a robot and only that particular combination and type of device.

For example, right now, as it is the PPDB has one pushbutton being read and returned in the Bumpers byte. If we do its conversion factors to make it the front bumper (see Section 10.3), the RB program would not need to do anything to the bumper reading. But if we opt to keep the firmware more general and just return the P5 button as normal, then RB has to perform some mapping. We opt to do the conversions in RB because:
1. We want to keep the firmware as general as possible and report raw data from the sensors without formatting.
2. We are using an emulated robot and not a real one, so sensors have to be reinterpreted.
3. We want to illustrate how we can achieve this since it is not always guaranteed that we can do remapping in the firmware.

Two items from our emulated robot have to be mapped as follows:
- Using **rRange()** on the hardware will report the Ping))) value in microseconds time round trip to and from the object. We need to apply the formula as discussed in Chapter 7.3 to convert it to an acceptable scale. We will convert it to millimeters, but we could also convert it to pixels in keeping with the scale of the screen and the robot in relation to the real robot's dimensions and so on. All you have to do to change the scaling is change the formula used as shown in Chapter 7.3.
- The hardware uses one pushbutton (P5) to emulate the front bumper. However the firmware is reporting the button in the first bit of the byte. In RB we have 4 bumpers and the front bumper is in the third bit of the byte. So we need to shift by two bits the value returned from the hardware using **rBumper()**to make it appear as the front bumper.

To achieve the required mapping and yet be able to run the same program with the simulator we will use if-statements to check the value of **Port**. If **Port** is set to 0 then the simulator will be active. If **Port** is other than 0 then the hardware is being controlled, and data mapping has to take effect.

Study Simualtor_3.Bas to see how all this is achieved with ease and effectiveness. Notice how it still works with the simulator if **Prot = 0** and with the real robot if **Port = N** where N is the port number for communicating with the hardware on your system. Notice how the factors are calculated for the real system and for the simulated system.

> Data mapping can be achieved either in the hardware, firmware or software. Implementing it in hardware is usually not an option. Implementing it in the firmware is a viable option but may lose resolution due to integer math, or may lose generality due to fixing the mapping in the firmware. The best option is to do it in software since now you have raw data and the software can reinterpret it as might be appropriate for the situation at hand. Being in software the mapping can be easily modified to be more suitable to a variety of situations and to be as accurate as desired.

Simulator_3.Bas

```
//Simulator_3.Bas
//works with Protocol_Firmware_Main_D.Spin
Port = 16 //change this per your system, if 0 then the simulator is active
Main:
   GoSub Initialization
   while true
     if timer()-t > TimeLimit
        GoSub Initialization
        t = timer()
        waitnokey
     endif
     GoSub RoamAround
   wend
end
//------------------------------------------------
RoamAround:
   //notice how Shift_Factor and R_Factor are used
   while !((rBumper()<<Shift_Factor)&0%0100) \
       && rRange()*R_Factor > RangeLimit  //while path is not blocked
     if KeyDown(kc_Space) then t=0 \return
     rForward 1
   wend
   T = (random(1000)>500)*2 -1   //determine a random turn direction
   while rRange()*R_Factor <= RangeLimit  //keep turning until path is clear
     if KeyDown(kc_Space) then t=0 \return
     rTurn T
   wend
   rTurn T*(20+random(30))  //turn a little more in the same direction
Return
//------------------------------------------------
Initialization:
   if !vType(FirstTime)
     t = 0 \ TimeLimit = 60000  //60 secs
     if Port                        //if not simulation
       rCommPort Port,br115200
       call mmDistance(,1,R_Factor)    //calculate Ping)) factor
       Shift_Factor = 2               //shift rBumper byte 2
       RangeLimit = 300               //ranger limit
     Else                            //if simulation
       R_Factor=1
       Shift_Factor = 0
```

```
      RangeLimit = 30
    endif
   LineWidth 10
   FirstTime = false
  endif
  clearscr
  //draw some obstacle for the simulation
  for i=0 to 3
    x = 50+ Random(700) \ y = 50+random(500)
    W = limit(random(400)+x,80,790)-x
    H = limit(random(300)+y,80,590)-y
    rectanglewh 50+random(750),50+random(550),W,H,blue
  next
  rlocate 30,30,135-random(45)
return
//-------------------------------------------------
sub mmDistance(Tc,t,&D)
   if !vType(Tc) then Tc = 22.2       //if no temp specified assume 22.2C
   D = 0.5*t*(331.5 + 0.6* Tc)/1000   //convert time to mm
Return D
```

10.4.3 An Exercise

As an exercise let's develop a program that turns a robot the smallest angle to a desired heading from the current heading and maintains it at that heading. Of course since our emulated-robot is not actually going to turn, you will have to turn it by hand to effect heading changes.

Please try this by yourself. Do not look below for the solution until you have given a good attempt at creating the programs. You may want to look up these commands in the RB help file: **rLocate**, **rCommport**, **rTurn**, **rCompass()**, **rCommand()**, and **abs()**.

Simulator_4.Bas

```
//Simulator_4.Bas
//works with Protocol_Main.Spin
Desired_Heading = 230
Port = 0  //0 means simulator other means firmware
rCommport Port,br115200
rLocate 100,100
//rCommand(242,40)  //uncommnet this line and the next to see
//rCommand(243,50)  //how the turns are now smoother - less jerky
while true
  Current_Heading = rCompass()
  dH = abs(Desired_Heading-Current_Heading)
  T = sign(Desired_Heading-Current_Heading)
  if dH > 180 then T = -T  //turn the shorter way
  rTurn T
  xyString 1,1, Current_Heading,spaces(10)
wend
```

A Comment About Feedback Control

The program Simulator_4.Bas implements a very simple feedback control. If the heading overshoots the desired heading the robot will turn the other direction and if it overshoots again in the other direction it will start turning in the opposite direction. This can cause an oscillatory motion, hunting for the desired heading.

This is a situation where PID control might be necessary. With our firmware being able to modify the turn speed we can have a PID algorithm that sets the turn speed and turn step size and vary them as needed using the PID algorithm depending on the amount of difference between the current heading and the desired heading.

10.5 A Simplistic Inertial Navigation System

An INS is used on airplanes, submarines, deep sea rovers, satellites, rockets, and a plethora of sophisticated vehicles that require accurate self-contained (i.e. not dependent on external devices) navigation. If an INS is small enough and accurate enough you can place one on the end-effecter of a robotic arm and you would be able to drive the manipulator to any position in the workspace of the arm and orient the end effecter to any required attitude in 3D space.

To implement a proper INS you need a tri-axis accelerometer unit as well as a tri-axis gyroscopic unit. Also you will need a computer capable of doing floating point math and some complex algorithms to perform filtering (e.g. Digital filters).

The principle is quite simple (unfortunately, the implementation is not). Using the gyroscopic unit you can obtain pitch, roll and yaw of the vehicle. Using the accelerometer unit you obtain acceleration readings in all three axes. Knowing the tilt angles from the gyroscopic unit you can calculate the amount of gravity acceleration in each of the axis. Then you can subtract the gravity components of the acceleration from the system's acceleration components along the axes, which result in the dynamic acceleration on each axis due to forces in three dimensions on the vehicle other than gravity.

Once you know the acceleration on each axis, you use numerical integration (e.g. trapezoidal) to calculate the velocity vectors along each axis and integrate that to obtain displacement vectors for each axis. With this data, and using vector algebra, you can calculate the vehicle's position in 3D. When combined with some great-circle navigation formulas (or rhumb-line – see RB's suite of navigation commands and function), you can calculate the latitude and longitude of the vehicle. The data can also give altitude (or depth).

Using an INS you can continuously track the vehicle's position on earth as well as its velocity and heading without using any external devices (e.g. GPS) and you do not even need a compass. You do however need a known starting reference point and heading. Also due to precession errors (if using mechanical gyroscopes) the system needs to be occasionally updated with a reference correction.

In our hardware we have half of the required hardware to achieve a proper INS. With the H48C you can measure accelerations on the three axes. You have seen how we used that to calculate roll and pitch. Of course, when we did, we assumed that there were no other forces on the board other than gravity. Therefore any acceleration in the axis direction would have been due to tilting of the axis, which results in a vector component of the vertical g-force along the axis. With this component vector we can calculate the tilt of the axis using trigonometry (e.g. **aTan2()** or **aCos()**).

Obviously while doing tilt calculation, accelerations due to forces other than gravity cause the calculated tilts to be erroneous due to the additional components of the other accelerations.

Conversely, the H48C can be used to calculate accelerations due to forces other than gravity on the device. The problem is that if the device is not perfectly level (i.e. there are tilts) then the component of gravity resolved along the axis would offset the total acceleration on the axis. However, if we know this component then we can easily calculate the acceleration due to dynamic forces. That is why a gyroscopic unit is needed.

10.5.1 The Experiment

On the Parallax web site there is a most excellent manuscript called <u>Smart Sensors And Applications</u>[64] and is part of the <u>Stamps In Class</u>[65] educational series. In Chapter 6 of the document there is an interesting experiment to calculate and graph the displacement of an RC car by using an accelerometer and the BS2 microcontroller.

The write-up of the activity has great details of the required processes and the principles behind them. The task of calculating all the integrations and the graphing was delegated to an Excel worksheet loaded with the data after having collected it during the experiment by logging it in the BS2's EEPROM.

This meant that the experiment had to be run and the data logged in the BS2's memory. Then when done you had to plug the BS2 to a computer and run another program on it to download the logged data. Then you had to copy the data and start the Excel program. Then you had to paste the data into the spreadsheet and write the appropriate formulas. And then you had to use the facilities of the spreadsheet to graph the data. To do another experiment you had to repeat this whole process.

One of the advantages of our protocol and the overall strategy of using a PC to interface to the hardware is that graphical displays and data collection as well as the floating-point math are easily achieved, and are an integral part of the system. So you won't have to resort to third-party software or go through the inconvenience of data formatting and so forth. Since RobotBASIC is a programming language you can use it to do all the data logging, calculations and graphing. In addition, all that can be repeated as often as you need without any plugging and unplugging, changing programs or any of the associated hassles.

To illustrate the power and efficacy of what we have achieved throughout this book we will use the simulator protocol to do a similar experiment as in the above educational document. We will move the PPDB by hand back and forth and then calculate its acceleration, velocity and displacement and log all that and graph it.

Rather than assume that the hardware is level and because we do not have a gyroscopic unit we will have to do an initial calibration before any dynamic forces are applied. We also have to assume that any initial tilts will not change. Using this setup we can then assume that the changes of accelerations along the axes from the original static reading are due to the dynamic forces. Knowing these accelerations, we can use digital integration to calculate velocities and displacements. The values will then be graphed.

Place the PPDB on a **steady and flat** surface that does not rock or shake and has no bumps. Then run the Simplistic_INS.Bas program. The program will run through the calibration then will sound a tone on the speaker. Once the tone stops start moving the PPDB on the surface.

A good experiment is to move the PPDB forward some distance then backwards past the starting point then back to the starting point. When you are done press the *Finish* button on the screen. The RB program will do all the calculations then display two graphs showing the acceleration, velocity and displacement in the x-axis against time and also in the y-axis. See Figure 10.4.

As you can see, the graph of the displacement shows that the PPDB was moved about 300 millimeters forward (positive) then backwards (negative) which was in fact the case.

10.5.2 The Results

There are shortcomings in the system. Despite the initial calibration being an attempt to eliminate any residual tilt, you can see that even when the system is static and there is no movement, the acceleration can be quite noisy. This noise can cause errors when integrating and even worse when integrating twice. Integration is a summing process and any systematic errors tend to accumulate. This is especially true if the sampling rate is not adequate for the dynamic frequencies in the system. See the next section for a brief discussion of this.

If you look at Figure 10.4 on the left side (x-Axis plot) and if you observe the right end of the graph you will notice that the velocity did not go back to 0 as it should. This of course is also causing the displacement to continue to increase. Notice the problem is even worse on the y-Axis. See Section 10.5.4 for a possible reason for this.

The system is simplistic and does not take into account any calibration errors in the H48C, temperature effects, tilt or noise. To improve the system we need a filtering algorithm to filter the noise out of the acceleration data. We also need a gyroscopic unit to eliminate any g-forces due to axial tilting. Another, shortcoming of the system is the sampling rate.

Too slow a sampling rate may cause problems for the integration process due to the aliasing aspect (Nyquist Criterion see Section 10.5.4).

Despite all the shortcomings, the system performed surprisingly well and the displacement was not far off the mark. Our aim was to demonstrate how our methodology enables:

➢ Easy and effective user interfacing.
➢ Floating point and other complex mathematical calculation to be an integral part of the system.
➢ Data logging and storage to be an integral part of the system.
➢ Data graphing and presentation to be an integral part of the system.

The experiment achieved the aim adequately.

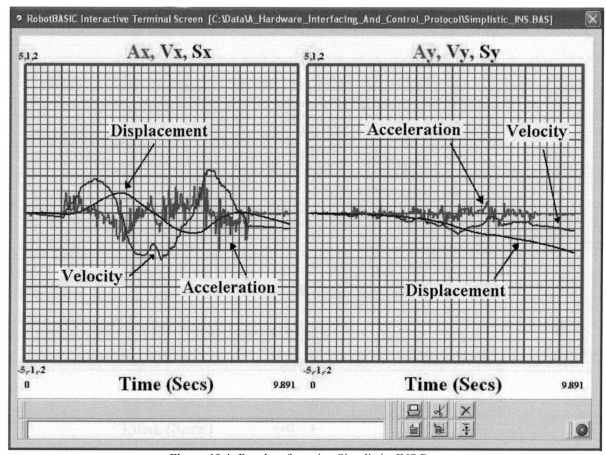

Figure 10.4: Results of running Simplistic_INS.Bas

10.5.3 The Program's Details

The program uses **rCommand()** of the simulator to send the H48C commands and uses the same calculations we did before to reconstitute the axes' accelerations. The calibration process averages 100 readings and that value is subtracted from all subsequent readings to eliminate any inherent tilt.

The formula used to calculate the velocity is
$$V_i = V_{i-1} + A_i * \Delta t_i$$

The formula used to calculate the displacement is
$$S_i = S_{i-1} + V_{i-1} * \Delta t_i + (A_i /2) * \Delta t_i^2$$

Rather than use a constant interval for the value of Δt_i we calculate the actual value. We use a timer to note the time each sample was taken. Thus we can obtain an accurate time interval between the samples.

To plot the graphs we use RB's graphics commands, which are quite versatile and convenient. Arrays are used extensively in the program to log the data and to make it easy to plot them.

The program will also save the results to a file called Simplistic_INS.CSV. This is a text file that can be viewed in the RB editor. However, it is also a file that follows a standard that can be viewed in Excel to display the data as a spreadsheet. So you can view the data if you need to in Excel. Study how simple it was to accomplish this in the **SaveToFile()** subroutine.

Notice the subroutine **Calculate2()** (with a 2). This is an alternative to the **Calculate()** subroutine. To use it change the highlighted line to say **Call Calculate2()**. This routine will perform some filtering on the acceleration data before it uses it in the integration to calculate the velocity and displacement. The filtering is accomplished using a *polynomial-curve-fitting* algorithm using the command **mPolyFit** in RB.

> ⓘ The program did not need to use the simulator protocol. It could have been written using normal serial communications commands as in previous chapters. We used the simulator protocol to illustrate the versatility of our whole system.

Simplistic_INS.Bas

```
//Simplistic_INS.Bas
//works with Protocol_Main.Spin
Port = 16 //change this as per your system
#include "..\Utilities&IncludeFiles\Instruments.Bas"
//-------------------------------------------
Main:
  rcommport Port,br115200
  rLocate 600,300
  gosub Calibrate            //calibrate
  Call CollectTheData()      //Collect the data
  Call Calculate()           //do calculations
  Call SaveToFile()          //save all the results to a disk file
  Call Plot()                //graph the data
End
//=================================
sub SendCommand(C,P,&s)
  m = ""
  s = rCommand(C,P) \ x = Length(s)
  if x < 5 then m= "Comms Error"
  xystring 500,20,spaces(30)
return (x == 5)
//=================================
Calibrate:
  print "Calibrating....please wait"
  Sgx = 0 \ Sgy=0 \ N = 100
  for i=0 to N-1
     call Read_H48C(0,,,,gX,gY)  //read N readings
     Sgx += gX \ Sgy += gY
  next
  data values;Sgx/N,Sgy/N  //initialize array with average
  clearscr
Return
```

```
//====================================
sub CollectTheData()
  clearscr
  print "When the tone stops start moving the Board"
  print "........Press Finish when done......"
  rCommand(73,70) \ delay 3000          //sound tone and wait 4 secs
  rCommand(73,0)                        //stop the tone
  addbutton "&Finish",300,300 \ FocusButton "&Finish"
  data values;timer()                   //starting time
  for i=0 to 5000                       //limit to 5000 readings (4 minutes)
    call Read_H48C(0,,,,gX,gY)          //read the accelerations
    data values;gX,gY,timer()           //insert in an array
    if lastbutton() != "" then break  //exit if button pushed
  next
  RemoveButton "&Finish"
Return
//====================================
sub Calculate()
  ClearScr \ Print "Calculating.... Please Wait"
  data T;0  \  data Ax;0  \  data Ay;0      //init arrays
  data Vx;0 \  data Vy;0  \  data Sx;0  \ data Sy;0
  for i=3 to maxdim(values)-1 step 3
    I = i/3 \ J=I-1
    data T;(values[i+2]-values[2])/1000    //timing array
    dt = (values[i+2]-values[i-1])/1000 \ dt2 = dt*dt/2
    data Ax;(values[i]-values[0])*9.81     //Acceleration
    data Ay;(values[i+1]-values[1])*9.81
    data Vx; Ax[I]*dt+Vx[J]                         //V[i]=A*dt+V[i-1]
    data Vy; Ay[I]*dt+Vy[J]
    data Sx; Ax[I]*dt2+Vx[J]*dt+Sx[J]         //S[i]=(A*dt^2)/2+V[i-1]*dt+S[i-1]
    data Sy; Ay[I]*dt2+Vy[J]*dt+Sy[J]
  next
return
//====================================
sub Calculate2()
  ClearScr\ Print "Calculating.... Please Wait"
  data T;0  \  data Ax;0  \  data Ay;0              //init arrays
  data Vx;0 \  data Vy;0  \  data Sx;0  \ data Sy;0
  n = Maxdim(values)/3
  dim AccX[2,n], AccY[2,n]
  mconstant AccX,0 \ mconstant AccY,0
  for i=3 to maxdim(values)-1 step 3
    I = i/3 \ J=I-1 \ t = (values[i+2]-values[2])/1000
    AccX[0,I] = t \ AccY[0,I] = t \ data T;t
    AccX[1,I] = (values[i]-values[0])*9.81
    AccY[1,I] = (values[i+1]-values[1])*9.81
  next
  m = 5 \ data CoefficientsX;m    //change m to 3 or 4 to see the effects
  data CoefficientsY;m
  mPolyFit AccX,CoefficientsX
  mPolyFit AccY,CoefficientsY
  for I=1 to n-1
    ax = 0 \ ay = 0 \ J = I-1
    for j=0 to m
      ax = ax+CoefficientsX[j]*T[I]^j
      ay = ay+CoefficientsY[j]*T[I]^j
```

```
      next
      dt = T[I]-T[J] \ dt2 = dt*dt/2
      data Ax;ax \ data Ay;ay
      data Vx; Ax[I]*dt+Vx[J]                         //V[i]=A*dt+V[i-1]
      data Vy; Ay[I]*dt+Vy[J]
      data Sx; Ax[I]*dt2+Vx[J]*dt+Sx[J]    //S[i]=(A*dt^2)/2+V[i-1]*dt+S[i-1]
      data Sy; Ay[I]*dt2+Vy[J]*dt+Sy[J]
   next
Return
//=================================
sub SaveToFile()
   s = "Time,Ax,Vx,Sx,Ay,Vy,Sy"+crlf()
   for i=0 to maxdim(T)-1
      s += ""+T[i]+","+Ax[i]+","+Vx[i]+","+Sx[i]
      s += ","+Ay[i]+","+Vy[i]+","+Sy[i]+crlf()
   next
   mFromString tA,s
   mTextFW tA,"Simplistic_INS.CSV"
return
//=================================
sub Plot()
   //plot the graphs
   Clearscr  \fnt = "Times New Roman"
   data GPx_Specs;10,100,380,400
   mGraphPaper GPx_Specs    //graph paper
   data GPy_Specs;405,100,380,400
   mGraphPaper GPy_Specs
   //label the graphs
   for i=0 to 1
      xyText 150+400*i,65,"A"+char(ascii("x")+i)+", ",fnt,20,fs_Bold,red
      xyText ,,"V"+char(ascii("x")+i)+", ",fnt,20,fs_Bold,blue
      xyText ,,"S"+char(ascii("x")+i),fnt,20,fs_Bold,black
      xyText 400*i,80,"5,",fnt,10,fs_Bold,red
      xyText ,,"1,",fnt,10,fs_Bold,blue
      xyText ,,"2",fnt,10,fs_Bold,black
      xyText 400*i,505,"-5,",fnt,10,fs_Bold,red
      xyText ,,"-1,",fnt,10,fs_Bold,blue
      xyText ,,"-2",fnt,10,fs_Bold,black
      xyText 140+i*400,515,"Time (Secs)",fnt,20,fs_Bold
   next
   mT = max(T)
   for i=0 to 1
      xyText 10+i*400,525,"0",fnt,10,fs_Bold
      xyText 350+i*400,525,Format(mT,"###0.0##"),fnt,10,fs_Bold
   next
   //plot Ax,Vx,Sx
   m=maxv(maxv(abs(Max(Ax)),abs(Min(Ax))),5)
   Data GxA_Specs;10,100,370,400,red,,,,-m,m     //graph specs..force limits
   mPlotXY GxA_Specs,T,Ax                         //plot acceleration against time
   m=maxv(maxv(abs(Max(Vx)),abs(Min(Vx))),1)
   Data GxV_Specs;10,100,370,400,,,,,-m,m        //graph specs..force limits
   mPlotXY GxV_Specs,T,Vx                         //plot the velocity against time
   m=maxv(maxv(abs(Max(Sx)),abs(Min(Sx))),2)
   Data GxS_Specs;10,100,370,400,Black,,,,-m,m   //graph specs..force limits
   mPlotXY GxS_Specs,T,Sx                         //plot displacement against time
   //plot Ay,Vy,Sy
```

```
m=maxv(maxv(abs(Max(Ay)),abs(Min(Ay))),5)
Data GyA_Specs;405,100,370,400,red,,,,-m,m      //graph specs..force limits
mPlotXY GyA_Specs,T,Ay                          //plot acceleration against time
m=maxv(maxv(abs(Max(Vy)),abs(Min(Vy))),1)
Data GyV_Specs;405,100,370,400,,,,,-m,m         //graph specs..force limits
mPlotXY GyV_Specs,T,Vy                          //plot the velocity against time
m=maxv(maxv(abs(Max(Sy)),abs(Min(Sy))),2)
Data GyS_Specs;405,100,370,400,Black,,,,-m,m //graph specs..force limits
mPlotXY GyS_Specs,T,Sy                          //plot displacement against time
Return
```

10.5.4 A Brief Note About Sampling Rates and the Nyquist Limit

When performing digital data processing we are not monitoring a system continuously. Rather, we are *sampling* the system at regular intervals. This is called the *sampling frequency*. The faster (i.e. more often) the sampling frequency the more accurate would be the digitization of a system.

Think of this as taking snapshots of an action. The more frames per second you can take the smoother the movie will be later when you play it back. That is why in old movies, people's movement looked weird. There was too much movement between each frame and moving objects looked like they were jumping from one point to another when the movie was watched later. The movie lacked those intermediate points of displacement and our brain is not used to that type of movements. If a person were to move his arm up and down between frames there would be no perceived movement of the arm at all.

In a dynamic system we need to sample the parameter we are monitoring (e.g. acceleration) at a rate that depends on the rate of change of the parameter. This rate of change is called the frequency of the system. A technical term that is used in Digital Signal Processing (DSP) is the Nyquist Limit. This states that the sampling frequency has to be at least double the highest frequency of the system. So if the parameter we trying to digitize varies at a maximum possible rate (including noise etc.) of F Hz then we cannot get an accurate information about the system unless we sample it at a rate of 2xF Hz or higher.

The reason is quite simple if regarded in a different way. The graph in Figure 10.5 below shows some acceleration over a period of time. The circles at regular intervals show when we sampled the system. By comparing the *perceived* and *actual* accelerations we can see that the sampling rate is obviously inadequate. The areas under the graphs are obviously different (remember integration is the area under the graph). Between the first and second sample there was some acceleration that was missed altogether. The deceleration between the 4th and 5th samples was also missed. Thus the calculated results later will conclude erroneously that the system has a higher velocity than it does. That is because the calculations on the sampled (digitized) data failed to catch the deceleration section, which would have resulted in bringing back the velocity some.

> ⓘ The difference between the actual and perceived graphs is the result of something called Aliasing.

This is in fact one of the reasons we had some problems in our experiment (among others limitations). Our system had a sampling rate of 31 ms (32 Hz) when using direct wire communication between the PC and the hardware. If we use the XBee the sampling rate slows down to 52 ms (19 Hz). These rates are in fact too slow for a dynamic system such as an INS. Moreover, the noise frequency will by itself upset the results due to aliasing of the noise frequencies.

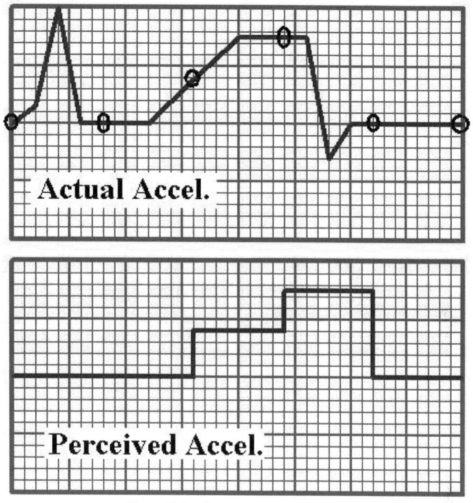

Figure10.5: Effect of too low sampling rate

10.6 Summary

In this chapter we:

❑ Looked at the RobotBASIC robot simulator and examined many of the advantages of using a robot simulator.

❑ Saw how the simulator's inbuilt protocol resembles the protocol we developed in the previous chapters.

❑ Saw how the hardware we developed could be used as a robot emulator and that if it is actually installed on the chassis of a robot it would in fact be functional as a robot controller.

❑ Saw that the RB simulator protocol can be used to control the hardware instead of using normal serial commands.

❑ Saw that with the change of one number (and some data remapping) we can have a simulated robot program start controlling a real robot.

❑ Converted many of the programs used to control the hardware in previous chapters to use with the simulator commands.

❑ Used the simulator protocol to develop a simplistic INS program to calculate displacements from acceleration data.

❑ Saw another application of the power, versatility and simplicity of using RobotBASIC as an integral part of a system to facilitate data presentation, data logging and data storage.

Chapter 11

Further Improvements

As impressive as our system is, it can still do with a lot more improvement. Nevertheless, it is not our aim to create the perfect system of any particular hardware devices or for any particular utility. The objective of this book is to show you a procedural strategy and some principles you can use to do your own systems. The details of the particular hardware arrangement you have and the nuances of using each individual device are of secondary importance, and so are the details of how the firmware implements the hardware. Even the details of the software that uses the hardware are incidental.

We hope to have convinced you that what is of direct importance and impact is the ***protocol***. A well-designed and versatile protocol makes it possible to use just about any combination of actuators (motors etc.) and transducers (sensors) and as long as the ***firmware layer*** makes them available through the protocol you can use them in any combination for different purposes using various ***software layers*** to accomplish your requirements.

11.1 Extending Our Protocol

The protocol is quite capable and versatile. However it is not the most powerful one possible. It is able to cope with a drop in communications but it is not able to detect if there are errors in the received data. A transmitted byte may drop bits or set bits due to a noisy transmission medium which causes its value to be altered. We have assumed that the wireless system being used has an ***error detection and correction layer***. With wired communications we assumed that short and shielded wires would be noise immune. Adding an error correction and detection layer can be easily included as an additional ***layer*** of firmware and software and therefore does not affect the principles of what we accomplished.

Our protocol also assumes that the control PC and the hardware have one-to-one communication. With a wired medium this is assured. With a wireless system this is not guaranteed unless the wireless hardware implements it. With the XBee and Bluetooth systems this is definitely the case.

It may become necessary that control should be carried out on multiple hardware systems simultaneously. If the control commands are the same for all the systems then our protocol suffices, however if different commands are to be sent to different systems then our protocol will again need an additional layer (software and firmware sides) to achieve this. One easy method to control multiple hardware without additional layers, is to use blocks of command codes. Say you have 5 devices you want to control simultaneously and from the same software. You can assign command codes 1 to 49 to be device 0, then 51 to 99 to the next and so forth. This way even though you would be broadcasting to all the devices only the device with ability to handle the code would actually respond to the command.

In fact, this is a simple addressing scheme. By adding $50*N$ to the command codes (1 to 49) where N is the device number (0 to 4) you have in fact addressed the device. A more sophisticated addressing mechanism requires header bytes added to the data bytes and to use packeting schemes. This is easily accomplished with the XBee and would require very minor changes to the software to make use of the facility.

Another layer of improvement that may become necessary is to have the protocol verify that the system it is connected to is indeed the intended one. This will require some identification procedure and is easily added to our protocol as additional commands. Again the XBee has this facility available and easily configurable with a few additional AT codes before sending the data. This would be similar to a preamble method of communication. At the beginning of every session some bytes are exchanged to verify and identify the link. Once the link is established the communication proceeds normally without any additional overhead of packeting for every chunk of data since the link is now a one-to-one.

Other improvements have to do with details such as the number of bytes to send and receive. Currently, we use a one byte command and one byte parameter. It may be necessary to increase the number of bytes for systems that need more commands and more resolution. Also the response bytes are currently just 5. This proved to be quite sufficient in most cases, but as we saw in the case of the accelerometer we could have benefited from more bytes.

An effective solution would be to increase the number of command bytes *when needed*. When the firmware receives certain commands that need additional bytes it goes to an area where additional bytes are received according to what the command requires. For instance in our firmware we had certain parameters we wanted to set that would have been better to set as a 4-byte integer (32 bits). In our protocol we had to finagle a little and do some data remapping to be able to send the 32-bit value as an 8-bit value. In the improved protocol these special case commands send the command byte as well as 4 bytes for the value. The firmware sees the command and knows that it is expected to receive 4 bytes next instead of the customary 1 byte.

Also on the RB side we can receive more than 5 bytes in certain cases. The software knows that it has just issued a command to the firmware that will send back N bytes not just the customary 5 bytes. The software would then expect these N bytes. So in our case where we had the accelerometer send the three axes data in the 5 bytes with some trickery to fit the values in the 5 bytes, we would just send 6 bytes or even 8 bytes where we can now also send the vRef value along with the axes.

Another, more general method is to have the protocol send a header byte that has in it the number of bytes to follow. The receiving side will then read this initial byte to know how many bytes to expect next and accordingly effects the receive procedure.

These improvements are very easily achieved and the firmware as well as the hardware would not have to be substantially modified. What is important to realize is that, again, the nuances and details are only secondary. You should be able to modify the protocol as you need to accommodate the details. What is of primary importance is the fact that the protocol should guarantee a reliable and resilient communication between the firmware and software.

> Our aim is that after having carried out all the projects in this book you will be able to design your own hardware and your own protocol and firmware to achieve control over it and your own software to interact with it. As long as you apply the principles and strategic *methodologies* in this book to the details of your requirements you should be able to integrate many hardware devices into one project all working in parallel and controlled by a firmware that implements the protocol to allow software applications to interact with the hardware to read it and actuate it as necessary.

11.1.1 Example of an Extended Protocol

As an example of how to implement some of the above suggestions, let's have a look at how we can extend our protocol as finalized in Chapter 8. We are only offering this as a template for you to follow if you need to do so. The firmware as implemented in Protocol_Main.Spin is in fact a little faster. The command turn-around in the extended firmware is about 1ms slower.

We will implement the following:

Command #71 (parameter does not matter)

Sends to RB the H48C three axes readings already adjusted from the reference voltage as 3 longs (12 bytes). Thus you will neither need to do all the byte and nibble trickery nor have to read the reference voltage, since it is already accounted for. All you have to do is read the value as a Little-Endian 32-bit integer from the received 12-byte buffer. To calculate the actual g-force you still need to multiply by 0.0022.

Command #254 (parameter either 0 or 1)

Will send all the system parameters (11 longs) back to RB in one go. In fact what is received are 12 longs with the first long being the count of longs to follow. This way the software does not have to know the number of parameters beforehand.

So the program receives a 4 bytes (little-endian 32-bit integer) and according to the value will expect to receive n*4 more bytes where n is the number of system parameters to be received. Again, the parameters are Little-Endian 32-bit integers in the buffer received.

If the command parameter is 0 then the parameter as stored in EEPROM are sent.

If the command parameter is other than 0 then the parameter as they in RAM are sent.

Commands 250, 251,252,253,211, 212 and 213 (parameter is the value)

To set the various system parameters; each of these commands uses a 4 byte parameter. The 4 bytes are a 32-bit long integer to set the system parameter to, again little-endian.

211: Set the blink duration of the LED on P22. The parameter is tick count for the on/off delay. It has to be a factor or multiple of 80_000_000. So if you need 1 second then it has to be 80_000_000, for half a second then it has to be 40_000_000 and so on.

212: Set the TimeOut1 time as a multiple of 80_000_000. Where 80e6 is 1 second.

213: Set the TimeOut2 time as a multiple of 80_000_000. Where 80e6 is 1 second.

250: Set the L_TimeOut time in multiples of milliseconds. This is the value for the latency time that keeps the motors on before a new command comes in (linear movement).

253: Set the T_TimeOut time in multiples of milliseconds. This is the value for the latency time that keeps the motors on before a new command comes in (turning movement).

251: Set the StepTime time in multiples of milliseconds. This is the value that keeps the motors on to go one step in linear travel.

251: Set the TurnTime time in multiples of milliseconds. This is the value that keeps the motors on to go one degree in turning travel.

As you can see from the list above we have implemented an example of:

➢ Sending a Long value to the firmware (commands to set the system parameters).
➢ Sending a fixed number of Longs to the software (command to read the H48C).
➢ Sending a variable number of Longs to the software (command to read all the system parameters in one go).

The Extended Firmware

The new firmware suite will be called Extended_Protocol_XXXX.Spin where XXXX is Main, Motors, Others, Reader. Reader is not changed. Below are listings of the changes in the other three objects. Only the changes are listed.

The main things of note are the methods **ReceiveRestOfLong** and **SendAllParameters()** in **Main**. Notice how **ReceiveRestOfLong** carries on receiving the remaining 3 bytes of the 4-byte long. Remember that the first byte was already received in the *normal* receive process. So if the command is one that needs to have a long parameter this method is used to *finish receiving* the long (three more byte).

Notice how **SendAllParameters()** uses the new **TertiaryBuffer** to fill with the longs of the 11 system parameters. However, see how the first long is filled with the number of longs to follow. See the discussion below about the software that receives the values to see why this is necessary (or above).

Also note how the new **H48C_AxisRef_Extended** method reads the reference voltage and the axes values and how it uses the **TertiaryBuffer** to send the values. Notice that it knows where the buffer is from the **Offset_3** constant which tells it how many bytes past the Command buffer is the tertiary buffer.

TertiaryBuffer serves the same purpose as **SecondaryBuffer** but for N Longs instead of 5 bytes, where N is as many as are needed for the command. Currently the buffer is set to be 18 longs; you will need to extend it in the source code if you need more than that.

Extended_Protocol_Main.Spin (Only Changes)

```
Var
   byte SendBufferOffset
   Long Buffer[BufferSize/4]    'read/write buffer for the EEPROM
   Long Extended_Value,NumBytesToSend
OBJ
   RB     : "FullDuplexSerial"
   D      : "SerialMirror"
   I2C    : "Basic_I2C_Driver"
   Others : "Extended_Protocol_Others"
   Reader : "Extended_Protocol_Reader"
   Motors : "Extended_Protocol_Motors"



Dat
   Command          Byte 0,0              'command and parameter from RB

   PrimaryBuffer    Byte 0,0,0,0,0        'primary 5 bytes to send to RB
   SecondaryBuffer  Byte 0,0,0,0,0        'secondary 5 bytes to send to RB
   TertiaryBuffer   Long 0,0,0,0,0,0 'tertiary buffer N Longs
                    Long 0,0,0,0,0,0 '18 longs for now...you can extend as needed
                    Long 0,0,0,0,0,0 'not all will be used
   Sems_Flags       byte 0,0,0           'semaphore1,flags,semaphore2
   Settings         Long F_P22_Blinker 'various settings buffer
                                         '[0] Reader blinker duration
                    Long F_P21_Blinker '[1] Others blinker freq
                    Long F_P23_Dimmer  '[2] Main dimmer level
   TimeOut1         Long F_TimeOut1     '[3] secs timeout to receive second byte
   TimeOut2         Long F_TimeOut2     '[4] secs timeout to allow sending data

Pri SendTheBuffer|x
   if Not Sems_Flags[1]        'if flags clear then send bytes
     'if SendBufferOffset == 0 'if using primary buffer wait for semaphore
     '                          'to ensure data congruity
     '   repeat until Not LockSet(Sems_Flags[0])
     '       'wait for semaphore forever, may need to do timeout but
     '       'uncomment these lines to assure data congruity
     '       'also the LockClr() below
     if SendBufferOffset < 10
       NumBytesToSend := 5
     repeat x from 0 to NumBytesToSend-1        'transmit the 5 bytes of data
       RB.TX(PrimaryBuffer[x+SendBufferOffset])
     'if SendBufferOffset == 0   'if data congruity with semaphore is used
     '    LockClr(Sems_Flags[0]) 'then also uncomment out these two line also

Pri ExecuteTheCommand|x ,a
   case Command[0]
       4: SendSystemParameter 'send requested parameter to RB
       5: StorePrintSystemParameters  'store params to EEPROM or print to PST

     255: Reboot 'reset the propeller
```

```
200:'set the Dimmer level on P23
     frqA := Command[1] *DimmerScale
     Settings[2] := Command[1]

201:'set blinker duration for Reader cog(P22)
     '256 levels between 0 to 2 secs (0=off)
   Settings[0] := Command[1]*(2_000/256)*(ClkFreq/1_000)

202: 'set the TimeOut1 for waiting for parameter byte (second command byte)
     'in seconds
     TimeOut1 := (clkfreq/1000)*Command[1]*500

203: 'set the TimeOut2 for waiting for a command to finish its actions
     'it should reflect and be related to the PC system's timeout (secs)
     TimeOut2 := (clkfreq/1000)*Command[1]*500

1,2,24:
   'commands in the Others cog that may fill the
   'the last two bytes in the primary send buffer
   Sems_Flags[1] |= OthersFlagMask    'set flag
   WaitForFlagResetWithTimeOut(OthersFlagMask)

66:'commands in the Others cog that fill the secondary send buffer
   SendBufferOffset := 5              'command uses the secondary buffer
   Sems_Flags[1] |= OthersFlagMask 'set flag to signal the cog
   WaitForFlagResetWithTimeOut(OthersFlagMask)

0,6,7,12,13,240,241,242,243,244,245,8,9,10,11:'commands in the Motors cog
   Sems_Flags[1] |= MotorsFlagMask    'set flag
   WaitForFlagResetWithTimeOut(MotorsFlagMask)

192,193: 'turret and ping commands in Motors and Others cogs
   Sems_Flags[1] |= MotorsFlagMask    'set flag for Motors
   WaitForFlagResetWithTimeOut(MotorsFlagMask)
   Command[0] := 192  'force the command code to 192, this way we do
                      'not need to change the Others object
   Sems_Flags[1] |= OthersFlagMask    'set flag for Others
   WaitForFlagResetWithTimeOut(OthersFlagMask)

70:'H48C if parameter is 1=>read vref, any other value => read the axes
   if Command[1] <> 1
     SendBufferOffset := 5                 'command uses the secondary buffer
   Sems_Flags[1] |= OthersFlagMask 'set flag to signal the cog
   WaitForFlagResetWithTimeOut(OthersFlagMask)

73: 'Speaker
   Reader.Play_Note(Command[1])

'-----Extended commands to receive/send additional bytes
71:  'read the H48C with extended send back of 3 Longs
     SendBufferOffset := 10        'command uses the tertiary buffer
     NumBytesToSend := 12          '3 Longs
     Sems_Flags[1] |= OthersFlagMask  'set flag to signal the cog
     WaitForFlagResetWithTimeOut(OthersFlagMask)
```

```
    211: 'set blinker duration for Reader cog(P22)
         'using full Long value
         if ReceiveRestOfLong
            Settings[0] := Extended_Value

    212: 'set the TimeOut1 for waiting for parameter byte (second command byte)
         'but using full Long value
         if ReceiveRestOfLong
            TimeOut1 := Extended_Value

    213: 'set the TimeOut2 for waiting for a command to finish its actions
         'it should reflect and be related to the PC system's time out
         'but using full Long value
         if ReceiveRestOfLong
            TimeOut2 := Extended_Value

    250,251,252,253:'commands to set parameters in Motors with received Long
         if ReceiveRestOfLong
            Motors.SetExtendedParameter(Command[0],Extended_Value)

    254:   'send all EEPROM/RAM system parameters all in one go as N Longs
         SendBufferOffset := 10        'command uses the tertiary buffer
         SendAllParameters(Command[1])
         NumBytesToSend := 4*TertiaryBuffer[0]+4

Pri ReceiveRestOfLong|t,n,y
   Extended_Value.byte[0] := Command[1]    '1st byte of long already received
   t := cnt
   repeat n from 1 to 3        'receive next 3 bytes but must be within timeout
     repeat                    'wait with timeout to receive parameter
        Process0               'call process that needs to be done always
        y := RB.RXcheck
        if cnt-t > TimeOut1
           quit
     until y <> -1
     if y == -1          'if no byte received exit function returning false
        Return false
     Extended_Value.Byte[n] := y
   Return true

Pri SendAllParameters(C)|x,n,a
   n := MotorsLongsToSave+MainLongsToSave
   TertiaryBuffer[0] := n
   if C == 0    'from eeprom
     ifnot i2c.ReadPage(i2c#BootPin,i2c#EEPROM,eepromAddress,@Buffer,BufferSize)
        repeat x from 0 to n-1
           TertiaryBuffer[x+1] := Buffer[x]
   else 'from RAM
     a := Motors.GetDataAddress
     repeat x from 0 to MainLongsToSave-1
        TertiaryBuffer[x+1] := Settings[x]
     repeat x from 0 to MotorsLongsToSave-1
        TertiaryBuffer[x+1+MainLongsToSave] := Long[a][x]
```

Extended_Protocol_Motors.Spin (Only Changes)

```
Pub SetExtendedParameter(C,P)
   case C
      250: L_TimeOut := P
      253: T_TimeOut := P
      251: StepTime  := P
      252: TurnTime  := P
```

Extended_Protocol_Others.Spin (Only Changes)

```
CON
  Blinker        = 21
  RCPin1         = 2
  RCPin2         = 3
  PingPin        = 4
  FlagMask       = %0000_0001    'mask for flag for this cog
  MotorsFlagMask = %0000_0010    'Mask For Motors Flag
  BlinkerScale   = 54            ' 2³²÷ 80_000_000 for NCO counter
  Offset_1       = 5    'offset for location of 2 byte data buffer
  Offset_2       = 7    'offset for location of 5 byte data buffer
  Offset_3       = 12   'offset for location of 12 byte buffer
  Compass_SDA    = 26
  Compass_SCL    = 27
  Compass_On     = 1    'if there is no compass make this 0
  Accel_CS       = 12
  Accel_DIO      = 13
  Accel_Clk      = 14
  Accel_Pause    = 200_000  '5 us

Pri Others
  Initialization
  repeat
    Process0
    if Not(byte[Sems_Flags][1] & FlagMask) 'if flag not set then no action
      Next                                  'required, just loop back
    case byte[Command][0]                   'execute the command
        1: Set_LEDS
        2: Set_BlinkRate
       24: 'compass commands
           case byte[Command][1]
              1: Is_Compass_Enabled 'return if compass is available or not
              2: Calibrate_Compass(0)
              3: Calibrate_Compass(1)
              other: Read_Compass
       66: Read_Pots
       70: if byte[Command][1] == 1
              H48C_vRef
           else
              H48C_AxisRef
       71: H48C_AxisRef_Extended
      192: Read_Ping
    OutputToPST                          'output some info to the PST
    byte[Sems_Flags][1] &= !FlagMask     'clear flag signal Main to proceed
```

```
Pri H48C_AxisRef_Extended|v,x,y,z
  v := ReadFromH48C(%11_011)
  x := ReadFromH48C(%11_000)
  y := ReadFromH48C(%11_001)
  z := ReadFromH48C(%11_010)
  Long[Command+Offset_3][0] := x-v
  Long[Command+Offset_3][1] := y-v
  Long[Command+Offset_3][2] := z-v
```

Software for Testing the Extended Firmware

All previous programs of course will work with this new extended protocol. In fact, the extended protocol is a superset of the normal final protocol. This means that it could be used as if it were the final protocol with no problems or any effects. The only thing that it does is provide new commands. So if you never use these commands it is for all intents and purposes just the normal final protocol.

To test the new commands we converted EEPROM_Tester_Extended.Bas and H48C_Plane_Extended.Bas. These new extended versions will use the new extended commands. The previous versions will still work too.

H48C_Plane_Extended.Bas is mostly the same as the normal one. You can read the full listing in the Zip file with all the source code in it. What is listed below is the subroutine **Read_H48C_E()** that performs the work of obtaining the readings from the firmware. Notice the difference between it and the normal subroutine. Notice how the data is obtained as 3 Longs and how the **BuffReadI()** function is used to extract them from the received buffer. Also notice that now there is no need to read the reference voltage and to subtract it from the axis readings since that is already performed in the firmware. However, there is still need to multiply it by 0.0022 to convert the value to a g-force.

EEPROM_Tester_Extended.Bas is also similar to the normal one. There are two subroutines to look at closely; **ReadAllParams()** and **SetParameter()**.

ReadAllParams() obtains all the 11 longs of the 11 parameters. However, before doing that it reads the first long as a separate action. This first long has in it the count of parameters to follow. Thus the subroutine does not have to know how many parameters there are. Rather the firmware *tells* it how many parameters are to be sent. This way the subroutine will know how many longs will follow next. If later you extend the system and add more parameters, the subroutine will still work since it does not assume the number of parameters.

SetParameters() sends to the firmware the Long value (4 bytes). Notice the use of the **BuffWrite()** function to create the 4-byte Little-Endian buffer to be sent.

Partial Listing Of H48C_Plane_Extended.Bas

```
sub Read_H48C_E(&x,&y,&z,&xG,&yG,&zG)
  x = 0 \ y = 0 \ z = 0
  xG =0 \ yG = 0 \ zG = 0
  m = ""
  clearserbuffer \ serialout 71,0
  serbytesin 12,s,x
  if x < 12 then m= "Comms Error" \ return false
  xystring 500,20,m,spaces(30)
  x = BuffReadI(s,0)
  y = BuffReadI(s,4)
  z = BuffReadI(s,8)
  xG = x*.0022   //convert to g-forces
  yG = y*.0022
  zG = z*.0022
return true
```

Partial Listing Of EEPROM_Tester_Extended.Bas

```
sub SetParameter(C,P)
   serialout C,BuffWrite("",0,P)
   serbytesin 5,s,x
   if x != 5 then return false
return (x==5)
//----------------------------------------------
sub ReadAllParams(which)
   serialout 254,which
   serbytesin 4,s,x
   if x < 4 then  return false
   n = BuffReadI(s,0)
   serbytesin n*4,s,x
   if x < n*4 then return false
   for i=0 to n-1
     print BuffReadI(s,i*4)
   next
   print
return true
```

Table of Extended Protocol Commands

See Table B.3 in Appendix B for a table of all the new extended protocol commands. These are of course in addition to all the commands in the final protocol (Table B.1).

11.1.2 Working the Extended Protocol Over the TCP Link

If you remember from Chapter 9 we converted many programs to work over the LAN. All of these will also work with the extended protocol over the LAN. Due to the design of TCP_Server.Bas the extended commands will also work just fine over the LAN.

To verify this we wrote EEPROM_Tester_Extended_TCP.Bas and H48C_Plane_Extended_TCP.Bas. These are the LAN versions of the programs given above. We will not list them here. You can read them from the Zip file. But before you do, please attempt the modifications yourself. The process is the same as we did in Chapter 9.2.7. Remember the subroutine **TCP_SendCommand**() that made it all easy. But the extended commands do not have the same counts of send and receive bytes, so you will have to do something about that.

11.2 Improvements For the Robotic Control Protocol

The hardware implemented by the firmware may be of any utility that you require. As long as the protocol provides the commands needed to manipulate the hardware using the software through the firmware then you have achieved the overall goal.

If what you need is to control a robot, then the hardware we developed could be used by just placing it on top of a robot chassis with the devices positioned appropriately. You may need an additional power source for the servomotors. This is very easily accommodated by changing the position of the Jumper next to the servomotors header on the PPDB to make it so that the external power supply would power the motors. You would then connect to the external power supply positive and ground to the provided adjacent screw terminal. As explained in Chapter 10 we still need to have more bumpers and also more and real infrared proximity sensors instead of the pushbuttons we have used to emulate them. But even without these additions, with a robot equipped with a compass, motors, ranger on a turret, line sensors, thermistors, photoresistors, and an accelerometer you should be able to design quite a variety of projects.

In our protocol we have provided methods to minimize jerkiness due to motors stopping and starting between consecutive commands. Another way we can maximize the smoothness of the movement of the robot is to provide *motor ramping*. Ramping can be easily added with the Servo32V7 object we used.

The system uses timing to assure one degree of turn. One way this can be improved is to use the compass module. However, this is not as simple as might appear. Overshooting and undershooting would require that we use a PID control system to eliminate oscillation and to assure optimal turn rates.

We are currently using timing to assure a step distance. We may need to use wheel encoders to measure an accurate distance. Another improvement is to allow for the fact that motors on the right and the left may not be exactly of the same speed which causes curved instead of straight forward/backward movement. We can provide parameters to vary the speeds of the motors separately so that we can tweak the straightness of the robot. This is described in one of our YouTube video tutorials[63] for the robot from the book *Enhancing the Pololu 3pi With RobotBASIC*[69] (Figure 11.1). The projects in the 3pi book implement the protocol and all the methodologies expounded in this book with a concrete robot to verify the versatility and portability of the principles and strategies propounded in this book.

Figure 11.1: Enhanced Pololu 3pi for working with the RobotBASIC Protocol

In our system here, additional hardware to implement the simulator's hardware would be desirable because things such as beacon detectors and color detectors provide an ability to create extremely useful robots with ease. The addition of a GPS would provide the robot with an effective navigation system, but GPS receivers only function outdoors and are of limited accuracy if you require fine control down to millimeters. One way to provide a GPS Augmentation System (GAS) that can also work indoors is through the use of an LPS (local positioning system) which can be implemented using beacons, as detailed in the Pololu 3pi book.

We can use the accelerometer and add a gyroscopic device[29] and some math to create an Inertial Navigation System (INS), which is one of the most powerful ways to navigate any vehicle. This combination is used on spaceships and space stations as well as submarines and deep sea rovers. With the math and great circle navigation functions in RobotBASIC you can do all the calculations necessary to implement an effective INS.

Some of the above improvements can be easily implemented while others are a little harder to make work properly. But we hope that with all the experience you have gained by reading and implementing the suggestions in this book you can now easily incorporate what you need when you need it.

11.3 A RobotBASIC Robotic Operating System (RROS)

When you buy your PC or laptop you do not expect that you are going to have to spend weeks or months creating an Operating System for it before you can start using the PC to do useful work. You expect that you can purchase an OS or one comes already installed. That way you can install software and start using the hardware effectively. If you use a programming language such as RB you can vastly extend the utility of your PC by creating your own proprietary software to accomplish tasks for which there are no readily available commercial applications.

An OS expects a certain type and combination of hardware but it also has allowances for additional or alternative devices. This way you do not have to use a different OS and Software for every new hardware arrangement. The Software says to the OS here is a file print it. The OS knows how to print it because it has the printer driver for your printer. An OS provides a *layer of isolation* between the Software and the Hardware and makes varied hardware available to the same software as a *category* of devices. But above all, the OS helps you as the user to not have to redesign how you use the PC every time you change or add hardware.

To that end we are currently working hard to make available a RobotBASIC Robotic Operating System. The RROS would be an operational *layer* that isolates the nuances of the hardware on the robot. This helps you in writing *standard* programs that would work on robots with varying types and quantities of devices.

Using the information and principles expounded in this book, and the strategic methodology outlined, you can create your own RROS and in fact you have already done so. Protocol_Main.Spin and Extended_Protocol_Main.Spin are in fact *rudimentary* RROSs. You can improve on them and impart them with more sophistication and robustness as you wish. Another solution would be to obtain our RROS and dispense with all the work and time investment necessary to create a professional ROS.

Our goal with the RROS is that you will be able to use the Propeller Robot Controller Board[71](PRCB Figure 11.2) and a variety of hardware to communicate with RB (or any other language) to create impressively capable robots that would be able to accomplish a variety of projects that make your robot an interesting and useful device.

But what is most important is that you can use the RobotBASIC simulator to create algorithms for robot control and then with the change of one number run the exact same algorithms on a real robot with the PRCB and the RROS as the firmware.

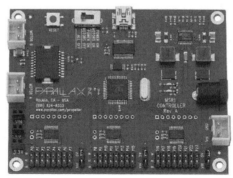

Figure 11.2: The Propeller Robot Control Board (PRCB)

The hardware is incidental and so is the language you use for the creation of the firmware. Neither is the language used to create the software of primary importance. What matters most is the protocol and the methodology as outlined in this book. The 3pi book mentioned above proves precisely this fact. The robot created in that book (Figure 11.1) is able to accomplish amazing projects and even some of the more advanced projects in our algorithms oriented book *Robot*

Programmer's Bonanza[70] where we first proposed the principles expounded throughout this text. In the Bonanza book we show how the ideas can be implemented on an enhanced Boe-Bot with the BS2 programmed in PBasic (Figure 11.3). In the 3pi book we show in concrete terms how to do it on a Pololu 3pi with an ATmega328 programmed in C (Figure 11.1). In this book we do not specifically build a robot nor did we want to. The principles are not confined to robots. In this book we show that *the principles are of wider utility and of more general applicability*.

We hope that you now have the tools to create your own RROS. If you feel that you need a more rigorous firmware, we hope that soon you will have an option with our RROS.

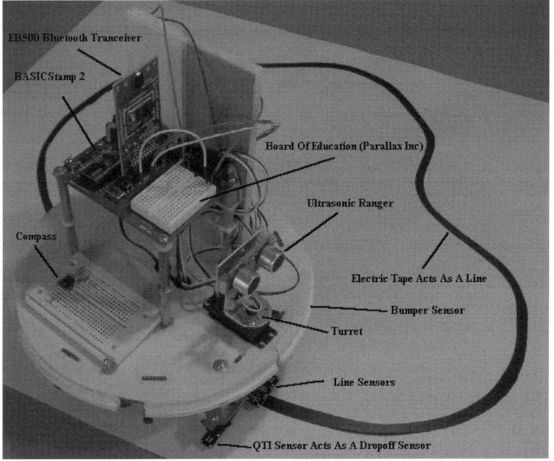

Figure 11.3: Enhanced Boe-Bot for working with the RobotBASIC Protocol

11.4 Summary

In this chapter we:
- ❑ Examined some ways we can improve the protocol.
- ❑ Implemented some of these suggested techniques and created a new extended protocol.
- ❑ Examined how even the extended protocol still might need some improvements to be a fully professional robot controller.
- ❑ Talked about how some of the techniques in this book have already been applied in concrete terms to robots with entirely different microcontrollers and firmware programming languages.
- ❑ Talked about how the RobotBASIC Robotic Operating System (RROS) could be a possible choice for a professional ROS.

Appendices

Appendix A
Web Links

1- Propeller Chip
www.parallax.com/propeller
2- RobotBASIC
http://www.RobotBASIC.Com
3- USBmicro
http://www.usbmicro.com/
4- A researcher at MIT
mit.edu/whall/www/heli/paper/node3.html#SECTION00030000000000000000
5- Propeller Demo Board (#32100 at www.parallax.com)
http://www.parallax.com/Store/Microcontrollers/PropellerDevelopmentBoards/tabid/514/CategoryID/73/List/0/SortField/0/Level/a/ProductID/340/Default.aspx
6- Propeller Professional Development (#32111 at www.parallax.com)
http://www.parallax.com/Store/Microcontrollers/PropellerDevelopmentBoards/tabid/514/CategoryID/73/List/0/SortField/0/Level/a/ProductID/515/Default.aspx
7- Propeller Plug (#32201 at www.parallax.com)
http://www.parallax.com/Store/Microcontrollers/PropellerTools/tabid/143/CategoryID/19/List/0/SortField/0/Level/a/ProductID/398/Default.aspx
8- Parallax USB2Ser Development Tool (#28024 at www.parallax.com)
http://www.parallax.com/Store/Accessories/CablesConverters/tabid/166/CategoryID/40/List/0/SortField/0/catpageindex/1/Level/a/ProductID/32/Default.aspx
9- Parallax USB to Serial (RS-232) Adapter (#28031 at www.parallax.com)
http://www.parallax.com/Store/Accessories/CablesConverters/tabid/166/CategoryID/40/List/0/SortField/0/catpageindex/1/Level/a/ProductID/379/Default.aspx
10- Ping))) Ultrasonic Sensor (#28015 at www.parallax.com)
http://www.parallax.com/Store/Sensors/AllSensors/tabid/760/CategoryID/46/List/0/SortField/0/catpageindex/3/Level/a/ProductID/92/Default.aspx
11- Parallax Continuous Rotation Servo Motors (#900-00008 at www.parallax.com)
http://www.parallax.com/Store/Robots/RoboticComponents/tabid/198/CategoryID/70/List/0/SortField/0/catpageindex/2/Level/a/ProductID/102/Default.aspx
12- Honeywell HMC6352 Compass Module (#29323 at www.parallax.com)
http://www.parallax.com/Store/Sensors/CompassGPS/tabid/173/CategoryID/48/List/0/SortField/0/Level/a/ProductID/596/Default.aspx
13- H48C Tri-Axis Accelerometer module (#28026 at www.parallax.com)
http://www.parallax.com/Store/Sensors/AccelerationTilt/tabid/172/CategoryID/47/List/0/SortField/0/Level/a/ProductID/97/Default.aspx

14- QTI Infrared Line Sensor (#555-27401 at www.parallax.com)
    http://www.parallax.com/Store/Sensors/ObjectDetection/tabid/176/CategoryID/51/List/0/SortField/0/Level/a/ProductID/100/Default.aspx
15- Propeller Object Exchange Library (ObEx)
    http://obex.parallax.com/
16- SerialMirror.Spin (SM)
    http://obex.parallax.com/objects/189/
17- SerialMirror.Spin (SM)
    http://obex.parallax.com/objects/189/
18- RobotBASIC_Serial_IO.pdf
    http://www.robotbasic.org/resources/RobotBASIC_Serial_IO.pdf
19- RobotBASIC_To_PropellerChip_Comms.pdf
    http://www.robotbasic.org/resources/RobotBASIC_To_PropellerChip_Comms.pdf
20- RobotBASIC_To_BS2_Comms.pdf
    http://www.robotbasic.org/resources/RobotBASIC_To_BS2_Comms.pdf
21- Motor controller module (HB-25 Motor Controller (#29144 at www.parallax.com))
    http://www.parallax.com/Store/Accessories/MotorServos/tabid/163/CategoryID/57/List/0/SortField/0/Level/a/ProductID/64/Default.aspx
22- RobotBASIC forum.
    http://tech.groups.yahoo.com/group/RobotBasic/
23- Parallax Propeller Forum.
    http://forums.parallax.com
24- Servo Pal (#28824 at www.parallax.com)
    http://www.parallax.com/Store/Accessories/MotorServos/tabid/163/CategoryID/57/List/0/SortField/0/catpageindex/2/Level/a/ProductID/481/Default.aspx
25- PWM Pal (#28020 at www.parallax.com)
    http://www.parallax.com/Store/Accessories/MotorServos/tabid/163/CategoryID/57/List/0/SortField/0/Level/a/ProductID/67/Default.aspx
26- Servo32V7.Spin
    http://obex.parallax.com/objects/51/
27- Piezoelectric Speaker (#900-00001 at www.parallax.com)
    http://www.parallax.com/Store/Accessories/Sound/tabid/164/CategoryID/38/List/0/SortField/0/Level/a/ProductID/106/Default.aspx
28- HMC6352.Spin
    http://www.parallax.com/Portals/0/Downloads/docs/prod/sens/HMC6352-Propeller-Examples-V1.0.zip
29- Gyroscopic Device (LISY300 Gyroscope Module #27922 at www.parallax.com)
    http://www.parallax.com/Store/Sensors/AccelerationTilt/tabid/172/CategoryID/47/List/0/SortField/0/Level/a/ProductID/588/Default.aspx
30- Bumper Switch
    http://www.pololu.com/catalog/product/1403
31- Infrared Proximity Sensors
    http://www.pololu.com/catalog/product/1134
32- PIR Movement Sensor (#555-28027 at www.parallax.com)
    http://www.parallax.com/Store/Microcontrollers/BASICStampModules/tabid/134/ProductID/83/List/1/Default.aspx?SortField=UnitCost,ProductName
33- Turret (Ping))) mounting Bracket Kit #570-28015 at www.parallax.com)
    http://www.parallax.com/Store/Robots/AllRobots/tabid/755/ProductID/248/List/0/Default.aspx?SortField=ProductName,ProductName
34- Accelerometer (Hitachi H48C Tri-Axis Accelerometer Module #28026 at www.parallax.com)
    http://www.parallax.com/Store/Sensors/AccelerationTilt/tabid/172/CategoryID/47/List/0/SortField/0/Level/a/ProductID/97/Default.aspx
35- GPS (Parallax GPS Receiver Module (#28146 at www.parallax.com)
    http://www.parallax.com/Store/Sensors/CompassGPS/tabid/173/CategoryID/48/List/0/SortField/0/Level/a/ProductID/396/Default.aspx
36- DC motors (HB-25 motor controller #29144 at www.parallax.com)

http://www.parallax.com/Store/Accessories/MotorServos/tabid/163/CategoryID/57/List/0/SortField/0/Level/a/ProductID/64/Default.aspx

37- Thermometer (Sensirion Temperature/Humidity Sensor #28018 at www.parallax.com)
http://www.parallax.com/Store/Sensors/TemperatureHumidity/tabid/174/CategoryID/49/List/0/SortField/0/Level/a/ProductID/94/Default.aspx

38- 2-Axis Joystick (#27800 at www.parallax.com)
http://www.parallax.com/Store/Accessories/HumanInterfaceDevices/tabid/822/CategoryID/90/List/0/SortField/0/Level/a/ProductID/581/Default.aspx

39- Sound Impact Sensor (#29132 at www.parallax.com)
http://www.parallax.com/Store/Accessories/Sound/tabid/164/CategoryID/38/List/0/SortField/0/Level/a/ProductID/614/Default.aspx

40- 5-Way button (#27801 at www.parallax.com)
http://www.parallax.com/Store/Accessories/HumanInterfaceDevices/tabid/822/CategoryID/90/List/0/SortField/0/Level/a/ProductID/615/Default.aspx

41- Quadrature System (Position Control Kit #27906 at www.parallax.com)
http://www.parallax.com/Store/Accessories/MotorServos/tabid/163/CategoryID/57/List/0/SortField/0/Level/a/ProductID/665/Default.aspx

42- Standard Servomotor (Parallax Futaba Standard Servo #900-00005 at www.parallax.com)
http://www.parallax.com/tabid/768/ProductID/101/Default.aspx

43- SD card reader (micro-SD card adapter #32312 at www.parallax.com)
http://www.parallax.com/Store/Microcontrollers/PropellerAccessories/tabid/786/CategoryID/85/List/0/SortField/0/Level/a/ProductID/597/Default.aspx

44- FSRW26
http://obex.parallax.com/objects/92/

45- H48C_Tri-Axis_Accelerometer.spin

46- Tutorial on how to use the QTI
http://forums.parallaxinc.com/forums/default.aspx?f=6&m=132921

47- XBee (#32405 at www.parallax.com)
http://www.parallax.com/go/XBee

48- XBee USB Adapter Board (#32400 at www.parallax.com)
www.parallax.com/go/XBee

49- XBee SPI Adapter Board (#32402 at www.parallax.com)
www.parallax.com/go/XBee

50- XBee X-CTU Software
www.parallax.com/go/XBee

51- Excellent tutorial on the XBee (#122-32450 at www.parallax.com)
www.parallax.com/go/XBee

52- Easy Bluetooth Module (#30085 at www.parallax.com)
http://www.parallax.com/Store/Accessories/CommunicationRF/tabid/161/CategoryID/36/List/0/SortField/0/Level/a/ProductID/550/Default.aspx

53- D-Link DBT-120 dongle
http://www.amazon.com/D-Link-DBT-120-Wireless-Bluetooth-Adapter/dp/B00006B7DB/ref=sr_1_1?ie=UTF8&qid=1289628417&sr=8-1

54- Parallax Easy Bluetooth documentation
http://www.parallax.com/Portals/0/Downloads/docs/prod/comm/30085-EasyBluetooth-v1.3.pdf

55- Tutorial on the EBT at the Parallax Forums
http://forums.parallax.com/showthread.php?112822

56- 433 MHz RF Transceiver (#27982 at www.parallax.com)
http://www.parallax.com/Store/Accessories/CommunicationRF/tabid/161/CategoryID/36/List/0/SortField/0/Level/a/ProductID/582/Default.aspx

57- RobotBASIC_Networking.Pdf
http://www.robotbasic.org/resources/RobotBASIC_Networking.pdf

58- Spinneret Web Server (#32203 at www.parallax.com)
http://www.parallax.com/Store/Microcontrollers/PropellerDevelopmentBoards/tabid/514/ProductID/710/List/0/Default.aspx?SortField=ProductName,ProductName

59- Boe-Bot (#28832 at www.parallax.com)
   http://www.parallax.com/Store/Robots/AllRobots/tabid/128/CategoryID/3/List/0/SortField/0/Level/a/ProductID/296/Default.aspx
60- Photo Resistor (#350-00009 at www.parallax.com)
   http://www.parallax.com/Store/Components/Optoelectronics/tabid/152/CategoryID/50/List/0/SortField/0/Level/a/ProductID/175/Default.aspx
61- Photo Diode (#350-00012 at www.parallax.com)
   http://www.parallax.com/Store/Components/Optoelectronics/tabid/152/CategoryID/50/List/0/SortField/0/Level/a/ProductID/176/Default.aspx
62- Four books that deal with the RB simulator
   http://www.amazon.com/s/ref=nb_sb_noss?url=search-alias%3Dstripbooks&field-keywords=robotbasic
63- Many YouTube video tutorials for RB
   http://www.youtube.com/profile?user=john30340#g/u
64- Smart Sensors And Applications
   http://www.parallax.com/Portals/0/Downloads/docs/prod/sic/3rdPrintSmartSensors-v1.0.pdf
65- Stamps In Class
   http://www.parallax.com/education
66- Extensive tutorial on the USBmicro devices
   http://www.robotbasic.org/resources/RobotBASIC_USBmicro_U4x1.pdf
67- USBToSerial (Pasrt#28030)
   http://www.parallax.com/Store/Accessories/CablesConverters/tabid/166/CategoryID/40/List/0/SortField/0/Level/a/ProductID/378/Default.aspx
68- Basic_I2C_Driver.Spin
   http://obex.parallax.com/objects/26/
69- Enhancing The Pololu 3pi With RobotBASIC
   http://www.amazon.com/Enhancing-Pololu-3pi-RobotBASIC-ebook/dp/B0044XUU5E/ref=sr_1_2?ie=UTF8&qid=1295347995&sr=8-2
70- Robot Programmer's Bonanza
   http://www.amazon.com/Robot-Programmers-Bonanza-ebook/dp/B001AW2QKE/ref=sr_1_2?ie=UTF8&m=AG56TWVU5XWC2&s=digital-text&qid=1295484609&sr=8-2
71- Propeller Robot Controller Board (#28230 at www.parallax.com)
   http://www.parallax.com/Store/Microcontrollers/PropellerDevelopmentBoards/tabid/514/CategoryID/73/List/0/SortField/0/Level/a/ProductID/584/Default.aspx
72- RobotBASIC_Subroutines.Pdf
   http://www.robotbasic.org/resources/RobotBASIC_Subroutines.pdf

Appendix B
Tables & Schematics

Final Protocol Objects Hierarchy Map

The entire system requires 2,565 Longs (11 Kbytes) and 7 cogs. Thus we have 1 spare cog.

Out of the 28 available pins (32 less 2 for programming and 2 are for EEPROM) we are using 26 pins. So we have 2 spare pins. We do use the 2 EEPROM pins to write/read from it

```
Parallax Propeller Chip Project Archive

 Project :  "Protocol_Main"
    Tool :  Propeller Tool version 1.2.7
            Protocol_Main.spin
                ├──FullDuplexSerial.spin
                ├──SerialMirror.spin
                ├──Basic_I2C_Driver.spin
                ├──Protocol_Others.spin
                │       ├──SerialMirror.spin
                │       ├──Pots_RCTime.spin
                │       └──HMC6352.spin
                ├──Protocol_Reader.spin
                │       └──SerialMirror.spin
                └──Protocol_Motors.spin
                        ├──SerialMirror.spin
                        └──Servo32v7.spin
                                └──Servo32_Ramp_v2.spin
```

Extended Protocol Objects Hierarchy Map

The entire system requires 2,700 Longs (11 Kbytes) and 7 cogs. Thus we have 1 spare cog.

Out of the 28 available pins (32 less 2 for programming and 2 are for EEPROM) we are using 26 pins. So we have 2 spare pins. We do use the 2 EEPROM pins to write/read from it

```
Parallax Propeller Chip Project Archive

 Project :   "Extended_Protocol_Main"
Archived :   Sunday, January 16, 2011 at 10:52:21 AM
    Tool :   Propeller Tool version 1.2.6

             Extended_Protocol_Main.spin
                  ├──FullDuplexSerial.spin
                  ├──SerialMirror.spin
                  ├──Basic_I2C_Driver.spin
                  ├──Extended_Protocol_Others.spin
                  │    ├──SerialMirror.spin
                  │    ├──Pots_RCTime.spin
                  │    └──HMC6352.spin
                  ├──Extended_Protocol_Reader.spin
                  │    └──SerialMirror.spin
                  └──Extended_Protocol_Motors.spin
                       ├──SerialMirror.spin
                       └──Servo32v7.spin
                            └──Servo32_Ramp_v2.spin
```

Figure B.1: System's Conceptual Schematic

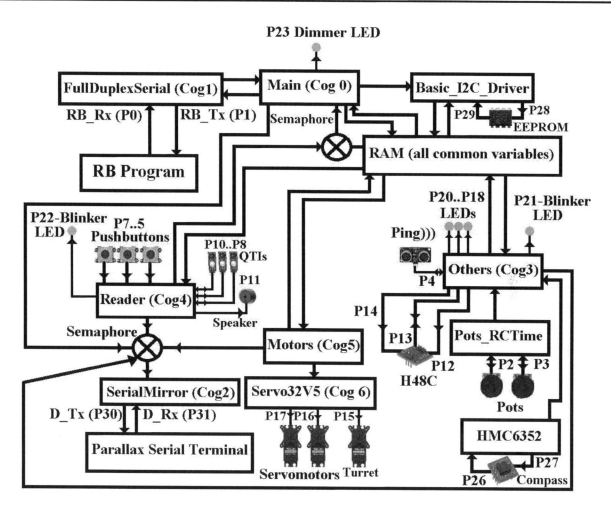

Cog numbers are only for reference.

Figure B.2: Propeller Pin Utilization

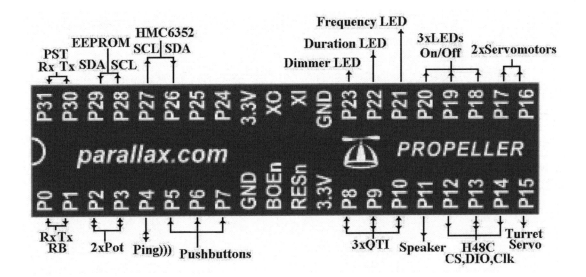

Figure B.3: Hardware Connection Schematics

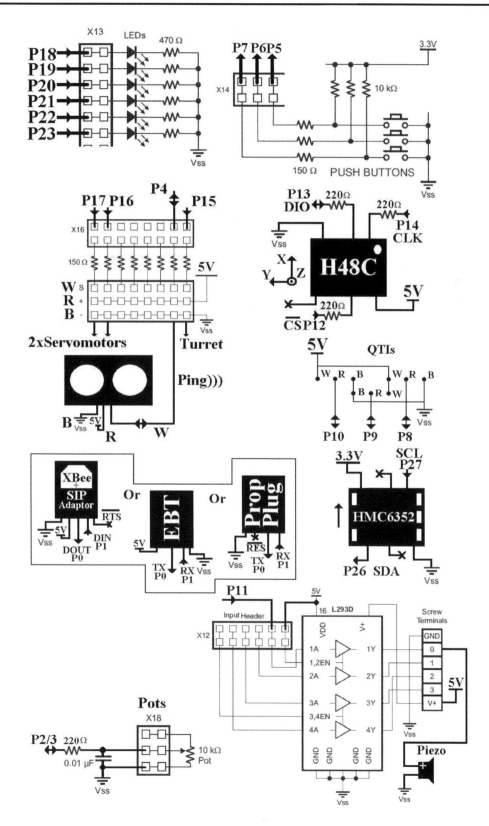

Figure B.4: Photograph of the Final PPDB Hardware Arrangement

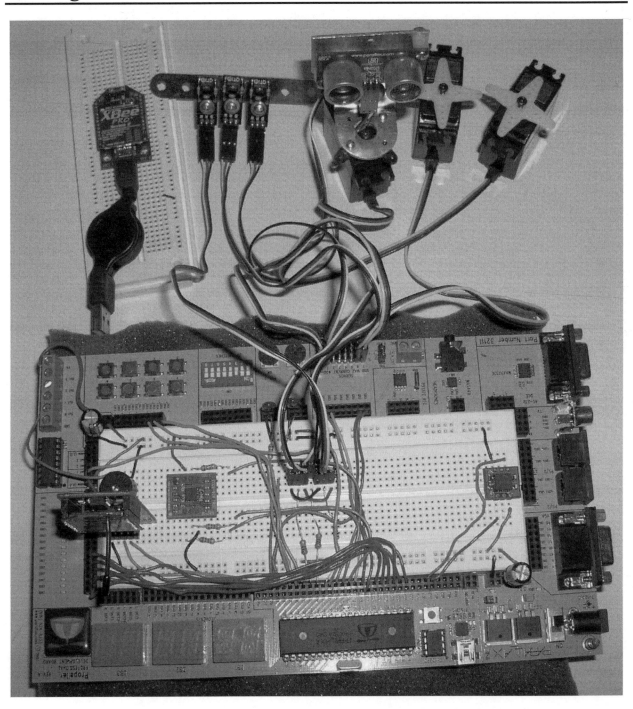

Table B.1: Final Firmware Protocol Command Codes

Command	Code	Parameter	Updates Three Critical Sensors	Data Returned
Stop Motors	0	0	Yes	None
Get System Parameter's value from RAM	4	Parameter# (See Table 8.6)	No	Value of Parameter Little-Endian in the first 4 bytes If success 5th bytes is 0 if failed then $FF
Save or Display System Parameters from RAM or EEPROM	5	0=Save 1=Restore Factory Settings 2=List EEPROM 3=List RAM	Yes	Only when saving. 5th byte is 1 if success or 0 if not
Motors On P17..P16 Forward Backward	6 7	Amount	Yes	None
Turn right motor on P16 forward Backward	8 9	Number Of Steps 0=off 255= all the time	Yes	None
Turn left motor on P17 forward Backward	10 11	Number Of Steps 0=off 255= all the time	Yes	None
Turn Motors on P17..P16 Right Left	12 13	Amount	Yes	None
Read the Compass On P27..P26	24	0	Yes	Last two bytes
Check if a compass is available	24	1	Yes	4th byte = 0, 5th byte =1 if available or 0 if not
Calibrate the Compass	24	2=Manual 3=Automatic	Yes No	None
Read the Pots On P3..P2	66	0	No	First 4 bytes
Read the H48C on P14..P12	70	0=Get Axis 1=Get vRef	Yes/No	vRef in 4th and 5th bytes Axis in 5 bytes
Play a note on the Speaker on P11	73	Note# (0-84)	Yes	None
Read the Ping))) on P4 and Move Turret on P15 Right and Left	192 193	Angle (0-90)	Yes	Last two bytes
Set P20..P18 LEDs	1	LED States	Yes	None
Set P21 Blink Frequency	2	Hz Value	Yes	None
Reset the Propeller	255	0	No	None
Set P23 LED brightness	200	Level	Yes	None
P22 LED Blink duration	201	Level	Yes	None
Set 2nd byte receive Timeout1	202	N x 10ms	Yes	None
Set operations Timeout2	203	N x 10ms	Yes	None
Set L_Speed	240	Speed	Yes	None
Set T_Speed	244	Speed	Yes	None
Set L_Timeout	241	N X 10 ms	Yes	None
Set T_Timeout	245	N X 10 ms	Yes	None
Set StepTime	242	N X 10 ms	Yes	None
Set TurnTime	243	N X 10 ms	Yes	None

Table B.2: System Parameters Mapping Formulas

When using the command to read back a system parameter the RB program will receive it from the Propeller as it is stored in the RAM, which is a 32-bit Integer. To convert the number into a value from 0 to 255 which is the value sent from an RB program to the Propeller, we will use a factor with which to multiply the value received from the Propeller. The table below shows these factors; F is the clock frequency of the Propeller, which should be 80 MHz for our purposes. In the top part are the values in the **Main** object and in the lower part are the ones in the **Motors** object.

Parameter Description	Command Number	Parameter Order	Multiply Factor
P22 blinker LED Duration	201	0	255/2/F
P21 blinker LED frequency	2	1	1
P23 dimmer LED brightness level	200	2	1
TimeOut1 for receiving second byte	202	3	2/F
TimeOut2 for a command to finish its working	203	4	2/F
L_Speed for speed of motors in linear movement	240	5	1
T_Speed for speed of motors in turning	244	6	1
Step_Time the time for keeping motors on to go one step linearly	242	7	0.1
TurnTime is the time to keep the motors to turn 1 degrees	243	8	0.1
L_TimeOut is the time to keep the motors on after finishing a step in linear movement	241	9	0.1
T_TimeOut is the time to keep the motors on after finishing a turn in turning movement.	245	10	0.1

Table B.3: Extended Firmware Command Codes (In addition to Table B.1)

Command	Code	Parameter	Updates Three Critical Sensors	Data Returned
Read the H48C 3-Axis values adjusted for the reference voltage.	71	0 (1-byte)	No	3xLongs (12 bytes). Each is a 4-byte Little-Endian Long.
Get All System Parameter's value from EEPROM or RAM	254	0 = EEPROM 1 = RAM (1-byte)	No	12xLongs, 1st long is count (11). The other 11 longs are the values of the 11 system parameters. Little-Endian 4-byte longs.
P22 LED Blink duration as a duration in Propeller ticks where 80_000_000 is 1 second.	211	Time duration 4-bytes Little-Endian Long	Yes	None
Set 2nd byte receive Timeout1 as a duration in Propeller ticks where 80_000_000 is 1 second	202	Time duration 4-bytes Little-Endian Long	Yes	None
Set operations Timeout2 as a duration in Propeller ticks where 80_000_000 is 1 second	203	Time duration 4-bytes Little-Endian Long	Yes	None
Set L_Timeout in milliseconds	250	Milliseconds 4-bytes Little-Endian Long	Yes	None
Set T_Timeout in milliseconds	253	Milliseconds 4-bytes Little-Endian Long	Yes	None
Set StepTime in milliseconds	251	Milliseconds 4-bytes Little-Endian Long	Yes	None
Set TurnTime in milliseconds	252	Milliseconds 4-bytes Little-Endian Long	Yes	None

Table B.4: RobotBASIC Inbuilt Protocol Command Codes

Command/Function	Code	Parameter	Updates Three Critical Sensors	Data Returned	Error
rLocate ne_X,ne_Y	3	ne_X	Yes	None	None
rForward +ne_Amount	6	ne_Amount	Yes	None	Halts program
-ne_Amount	7	ne_Amount	Yes	None	Halts program
rTurn +ne_Amount	12	ne_Amount	Yes	None	Halts program
-ne_Amount	13	ne_Amount	Yes	None	Halts program
rCompass()	24	0	Yes	Last two bytes	-1
rSpeed ne_Speed	36	ne_Speed	Yes	None	None
rLook({+ne_Angle})	48	ne_Angle	Yes	Last two bytes	-1
({-ne_Angle})	49	ne_Angle	Yes	Last two bytes	-1
rGPS vn_X,vn_Y	66	0	No	First 4 bytes	-1,-1
rBeacon(ne_Color)	96	ne_Color	Yes	Last Two bytes	-1
rChargeLevel()	108	0	Yes	Last two bytes	-1
rPen ne_State	129	ne_State	Yes	None	None
rRange({+ne_Angle})	192	ne_Angle	Yes	Last two bytes	-1
(-ne_Angle)	193	ne_Angle	Yes	Last two bytes	-1
rCommand(ne_Command,ne_Data)	ne_Command	ne_Data	No	String with 5 bytes	Empty buffer

Figure B.5: Protocol State Diagrams

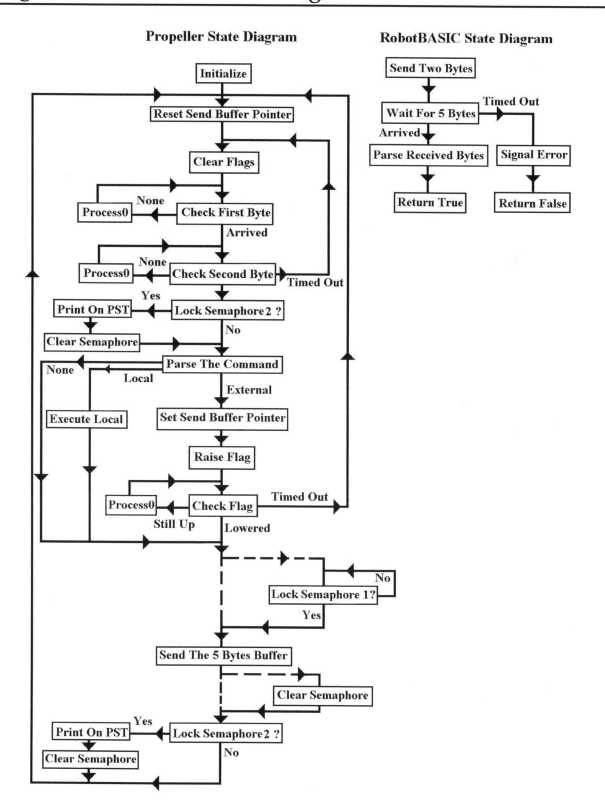

Index

10119384R00191

Made in the USA
San Bernardino, CA
05 April 2014